SPIKE MILLIGAN

D1151265

By the same author

The Angry Young Men
W.H. Auden: a biography
Benjamin Britten: a biography
The Brideshead Generation
The Envy of the World: fifty years of the BBC
Third Programme and Radio 3
The Inklings
Jesus (Past Masters series)
The Oxford Companion to Children's Literature
(with Mari Prichard)
Dennis Potter: a biography
A Serious Character: the life of Ezra Pound
Robert Runcie: the Reluctant Archbishop
Secret Gardens: the Golden Age of Children's Literature
That Was Satire That Was
J.R.R. Tolkien: a biography

Edited

The Letters of J.R.R. Tolkien
(with Christopher Tolkien)
The Puffin Book of Classic Children's Stories

For children

The Mr Majeika series
Shakespeare Without the Boring Bits
The Joshers
The Captain Hook Affair

Spike Milligan

The Biography

HUMPHREY CARPENTER

The International School of Amsterdam

coronet

CORONET BOOKS
Hodder & Stoughton

Copyright © 2004 by Humphrey Carpenter

First published in Great Britain in 2003 by Hodder & Stoughton
A division of Hodder Headline

This revised paperback edition, with text
and picture amendments, published in 2004

The right of Humphrey Carpenter to be identified as the author of this work has been
asserted by him in accordance with the Copyright, Designs and Patents Act 1988.

A Coronet paperback

11

All rights reserved. No part of this publication may be reproduced, stored in a
retrieval system, or transmitted, in any form or by any means without the prior
written permission of the publisher, nor be otherwise circulated in any form of
binding or cover other than that in which it is published and without a similar
condition being imposed on the subsequent purchaser

A CIP catalogue record for this title is available from the British Library

ISBN 0 34082612 6

Typeset in Sabon by Palimpsest Book Production Limited,
Polmont, Stirlingshire

Printed and bound by
Clays Ltd, St Ives plc

Hodder Headline's policy is to use papers that are natural, renewable
and recyclable products and made from wood grown in sustainable forests.
The logging and manufacturing processes are expected to conform
to the environmental regulations of the country of origin.

Hodder and Stoughton
A division of Hodder Headline
338 Euston Road
London NW1 3BH

Contents

List of Illustrations — vii

Preface — ix

PART ONE 1918–1946: *Terence*

1. The Rangoon Show — 3
2. Catford days, Harlem nights — 17
3. Gunnery or . . . Goonery — 32
4. WHOOSH-BANG! — 48
5. Khaki limbo — 58
6. Screaming, chattering and farting — 68

PART TWO 1946–1960: *Goon*

7. Grafton's — 77
8. I live in an attic — 90
9. Crazy People — 107
10. Exit Pureheart — 122
11. Life's work — 136
12. Fun Factory — 155
13. So certain of roars of laughter — 169

14. Gone for ever   184

PART THREE 1960–1971: *Spike*

15. The unfunniest person in the world   205
16. I do not do anything extraordinary   227
17. The funniest thing London
    has seen   245
18. What's the Q for?   265

PART FOUR 1972–2002:
The Last Goon of All

19. Partially sound mind   291
20. In the psychiatrist's chair   315
21. Just one of those things   344
22. I told you I was ill   365

Bibliography   380
Source Notes   387
Acknowledgements   406
Index   409

List of Illustrations

1a. 'All my life I've wanted to step on the BBC': horizontal producer Dennis Main Wilson endures vertical Goons (*left to right*) Bentine, Secombe, Sellers and Milligan.

1b. Beryl Vertue trying to stop her men from behaving badly: (*left to right*) Eric Sykes, Ray Galton, Spike and Alan Simpson at Associated London Scripts.

2a. 'She said to me, "Look, why don't we get engaged?"' Spike and first wife June.

2b. Spike attempts to ruin his 1962 wedding to Paddy Ridgeway with a false moustache. The bride is obviously more attracted to Harry Secombe.

3. The Dustbin Dance from *Son of Fred*, 1956: Milligan and Sellers with Tony and Douglas Gray of the Alberts.

4a. 'I leave Pakistan because there are too many wog': Spike (with Eric Sykes, *left*) blacked up for *Curry and Chips*, 1969.

4b. Spike depressed, from a 1970 TV documentary on his mental health problems.

5a. Milligan and Secombe with the Goons' most famous fan, 1973.

5b. Spike at Hatchards, with a bestseller on his hands.

6a. Spike (*right*) in *Milligan in Autumn*, BBC TV, 1972.

6b. 'I told him it might give him some idea of how a goose feels being force-fed': Spike (*right*) threatens the manager of Harrods food hall with twenty-eight pounds of spaghetti in 1986.

7a. 'He has bought her a ring, but they have not yet fixed a date for the wedding': Spike with Shelagh Sinclair in 1982.

7b. 'We should have burnt the house down and bought the view': Spike knocked flat by the sight of the English Channel from his last home.

8a. Revelations at breakfast time on 19 January 1991.

8b. 'Spike Milligan meets love child': James (*left*) and his mother Margaret shake hands with Shelagh as Spike approaches.

Preface

I was born in 1946. The Goons first appeared on the radio when I had just turned five. I don't know when I started listening to them, but, considering that I was allowed to have the family's big wooden-cased Pye mains wireless set switched on virtually all day long, it was probably fairly early in their nine-year run.

Pauline Scudamore, author of an earlier biography of Spike Milligan, began her book by stating that she was 'never a Goon fan' – rather an odd qualification for the job, one would have thought. Well, I *was* a Goon fan, and I still am; indeed I think that, at their best, the Goons are funnier than anything else in the history of comedy; and when I say 'the Goons' in this context, I'm really talking about Spike's scripts.

He fascinated me from the start of my Goon listening, because he seemed rather mysterious – the vaguely sinister one lurking at the back in the heavily posed *Radio Times* photos, peering over the shoulders of Harry Secombe and Peter Sellers (and, in the early days, Michael Bentine). The characters he played – Minnie Bannister, Moriarty, and of course Eccles – were especially strange. Sellers was so adept at voices, such a consummate professional at the microphone, that one's curiosity about the man behind the mask was never very great; and Secombe had an already Pickwickian joviality which didn't hint at profundity. But Spike – well, Spike was clearly a puzzle, a challenge.

When, in 2001, a friend suggested I write Spike Milligan's life (thank you, Emma), I couldn't think why I hadn't thought of the idea myself. I got to work at once, writing to Spike's agent-manager-minder Norma Farnes. But she was going to do her own book on Spike, and I didn't get her encouragement. I wrote to Spike himself (then eighty-three), and had no reply. I shelved the project.

And then the following February he was dead, and I knew at once that now the book had to be written. I also knew I was unlikely to get authorisation as the official biographer (indeed, I didn't – see the Acknowledgements at the back), but that didn't unduly worry me; too often an authorised biography is a censored one.

No one has censored this account of Spike's life. But how should it begin?

NOTE TO THE REVISED EDITION

In this printing, it has been necessary for legal reasons to remove certain quotations and photographs at the request of Spike Milligan Productions Ltd. The source notes have not been changed, to provide a record of what has been removed.

Part One 1918—1946

Terence

1

The Rangoon Show

ORCHESTRA: HIGHLAND LINK (GEORGE CHISHOLM
GETS OUT OF CONTROL ON BAGPIPE-STYLE TROM-
BONE)

MCGOONIGAL (for it is he): Oooooooooooo!
'Tis time to tell ye a tale that will thrill all good people but
is entirely without terror,
The story of the birth, marriages and death of Spike Milligna,
the well-known typing error.
Our hero was born—

GRAMS: JELLY SOCK HITS HIM FULL IN FACE

MCGOONIGAL: Ooooooooooooooooooooooooooo!

Yes, I think that we'd better deploy the famous sock filled
with jelly (the mere mention of which can still reduce our
future monarch to helpless giggles) to rid the stage of the
Poet and Tragedian. I had the idea that this cartoon Scotsman
could have opened the book by making Spike's ancestry and
family history a bit more palatable, with his inimitably awful
rhyming couplets. But you can only take so much McGonagall
before the joke wears thin.

Am I alone in finding the opening bits of biographies
almost always very, very boring? I fret to get on with the
real story, so I usually skip the genealogy. But I suspect that
Spike would have disagreed, since one of his last books,

The Family Album (1999), devoted many pages to his ancestors. And I admit that Spike's father, Leo, was a thoroughly interesting individual whose character gives us lots of insight into Spike. So let's get to Leo as quickly as possible.

*

Barry Cryer recalled how a man approached Spike at an *Oldie* literary lunch and said, 'May I shake the hand of the greatest living Englishman?' Spike replied, 'I'm Irish – fuck off!'

Another sure way to annoy him was to call him, as the press invariably did, an ex-Goon. 'The *Goon Show* was forty years ago,' he complained to a reporter in 1991, 'and yet people still insist on digging this fucking thing up. Ex-Goon, that's what the newspapers always call me, as though I'd never done anything else. I can see the obituaries already: "Spike Milligan wrote the *Goon Show* and died."'

He wouldn't have liked this book, because that's what I'm going to show: that the *Goon Show* was his 'life's work' (words he himself used of it in 1954), and he never equalled it, let alone surpassed it, in what came after. Which doesn't mean that the second half of his life was dull; there was actually a great deal more happening to him from 1960, when the Goons ended, until his death in 2002. This biography gets more and more exciting as it goes on, folks!

But the Irish thing is probably where we have to begin, because his ancestors tended to be Irish, and he believed that this explained quite a lot about him. 'I'm Irish and the Irish think sideways' was his racial explanation of Goon humour, and he also blamed his depressions on his Celtic blood: 'I'm an Irishman, and by decree we're a depressive people – we're never happy unless we're gloomy.' Which if taken literally suggests that he was 'happy' to be depressed, something else that we'll have to look into.

Strikingly, the Irish writer Sean O'Hagan, who interviewed Spike in 1995, rejected his claim to be significantly, distinctively Irish, and saw him as 'really much more English in character'. Certainly there are resemblances between Spike and another, very English depressive, who became the same sort of public monument, and took up many of the same conservationist causes. Was Spike, like John Betjeman, really an English eccentric?

'I was born of pure Irish stock on my father's side,' he insisted in an article, but he went on to admit that he was 'on the distaff side Kettleband (English) [and] Burnside (Scottish). Being born in India added a further dimension . . .' Ah yes, India.

One of his long-term girlfriends, Liz Cowley, whose company (and bed) solaced him during at least two of his three marriages, recalls that when they went for a midnight curry at an Indian restaurant in a remote corner of north Kensington, he would sometimes announce himself to the waiters with a flourish: 'The Man from Ahmadnagar.' It sounds like the title of a *Goon Show*.

And what on earth was he doing being born in a town rather more than a hundred miles from Bombay? The answer lies with Leo Milligan. Yes, we've managed to get to Leo already, suppressing the tedious ancestors who are bursting to get into the story.

*

'My father,' said Spike of Leo, 'had a profound influence on me, he was a lunatic.' This lunacy took the form of telling his son – who, by the way, wasn't called Spike in those days, but Terence – that 'we were descended from the kings of Ireland.' Well, any self-respecting Irishman likes to make such a claim.

'My father was like Baron Münchhausen,' said Terence on another occasion. 'He began to believe his own lies. He thought he'd ridden with Jesse James and robbed banks, when he wasn't shooting tigers in Bengal.' (Spike himself claimed that he once saw a tiger outside his bedroom window when the family was staying in a bungalow near Poona.)

Yet when Spike played his father in the feeble, sub-Ealing film of his book *Adolf Hitler: My Part in His Downfall*, he chose to make him seem slightly detached but perfectly sane; which is probably the truth, otherwise Leo could scarcely have been a successful soldier, combining this with a parallel career on the semi-professional stage.[1]

The Milligans were working-class Irish, and Terence Alan Milligan never pretended otherwise. 'Very Irish working-class family, very poor.' This is Spike talking about his forebears to Van Morrison, rock musician and fellow Irishman. ('Are you a Proddy, Van?' he suddenly explodes in jest, playing the Irish Catholic, which he was, up to a point. 'Don't come near me, I don't want to catch it.')

All right, the ancestors do have to make an appearance. But let's impose a strict limit. No more than ten facts:

1. The name Milligan – originally O'Mealagain – means 'small-tonsured one' (which might suit Bluebottle, with his Finchley scout troop pudding-basin haircut).

2. Spike told his first biographer, Pauline Scudamore, that the first of several Milligans to alleviate his poverty by joining the British army was his great-grandfather Michael, born in Donegal in 1816, who enlisted with the Royal Artillery. No Irish Catholic conscience there, eh? Still, the Queen's shilling sustained several generations of impecunious Milligans through the potato famine and all that. As Spike put it in an Australian radio interview in 1980: 'They were starved out of their own country, seduced into the British army so that they could get food, and then sent overseas so that they didn't cause trouble in Ireland.'

---

[1] Leo himself appeared on screen in an Australian TV feature on Spike at his parents' retirement home down under, and was indeed sane and detached. Moreover he spoke with an English middle-class accent.

3. He told his second biographer, Dominic Behan, that another member of the family had become an Irish Guardsman, despite being only five feet six inches tall: 'He lied about his height.' A joke, not a fact, but I can't resist it.

4. Spike's father used to say that an Uncle Willie Milligan had fought in the First World War and had lost a leg at Mons. He discovered that he could make the perfect replacement limb by stealing the leg of a grand piano and hollowing it out, so that in it he could smuggle grenades for the Republican cause. 'Jazes Christ, Leo,' he would say to Spike's father, 'but I could have blown me arse up most days of the year.' Spike, who included this story in his novel *Puckoon*, used to wonder what happened to the piano after it lost a leg.

5. Spike claimed that his father, who was born in Sligo in 1890, the son of an army wheelwright, would have been christened Percy Marmaduke but for the objections of the priest, who proposed Leo Alphonso, after the then Pope.

6. Leo caught the performing bug when his own soldier father, who had been posted to a London barracks, obtained part-time work as a stage-hand at the Queen's Music Hall in Poplar. Little Leo was soon appearing in various child walk-on roles, and when he was slightly older he worked with Fred Karno's Knockabout Kids, alongside an unknown boy a few months his senior called Charlie Chaplin.

7. Leo wanted to perform professionally but was made to join the army in his teens. He consoled himself by doing musical numbers in army entertainments (just as Spike was to do in the Second World War), and started calling

himself Leo Gann because it took up less space on the narrow variety posters.

8. Posted to India in 1911 at the age of twenty-one, Leo went on performing like mad, and when he met and married Spike's mother, an English girl called Florence Kettleband (daughter of a trumpeter-sergeant), he incorporated her talents as a singer and pianist into his act. They called themselves Gwen Gorden and Leo Gann, and the centrepiece of the act was a number called 'Fun Round the Sentry Box'.[2]

9. During the First World War, Leo fought in Mesopotamia and was promoted to sergeant. He also went bald early. Spike told Van Morrison: 'He was so incensed by it that he went to church and prayed for it to come back. I'm certain he went to a priest and confessed, "Dear Father forgive me, I have gone bald." "Go away, my son, buy three wigs and say one Hail Mary."'

10. In 1917 Leo was posted to Ahmadnagar – where Spike was born the following year, on 16 April – and was promoted to quartermaster sergeant. Consequently the Milligans began to enjoy comparative luxury. 'My old man lived the life of a gentleman on sergeant's pay,' Spike told Dominic Behan. 'Anything that wasn't nailed down was fair game. You know, he drank champagne because beer cost money!'

---

[2] In the Australian TV documentary mentioned above, Florence recalled that they went on performing this sketch after Spike was born: 'From a baby, he was practically on stage with us . . . And there was cannon going off, and shots being fired, and he'd lie there blissfully, not caring one iota what was going on.' Good practice for Eccles and Bluebottle putting up with a world of explosions?

*

India provided Spike with a paradise to be lost, a gift whose eventual removal may even have been the root cause of his manic depression. 'India was possibly the greatest experience of my life,' he said when he was nearly eighty. 'I grew up in bright sunshine. I grew up with tremendous space, I grew up with animals, I grew up with excitement . . . I was much happier then than I am now.'

No, wait a minute: that won't do. I've censored it. In my notes it reads as follows:

India was possibly the greatest experience of my life. I grew up in bright sunshine. I grew up with tremendous space, I grew up with animals, I grew up with excitement. I grew up believing that these people, white people, were superior to everyone else . . . I was much happier then than I am now.

Not so *simpatico* to your average liberal reader. The uncomfortable fact of Spike's racism – or at least his shamelessness at basing many of his jokes on what most of us have nowadays been drilled into calling racism – starts as early as this. Well, considering he was in the fag end of the British Raj, what would you expect?

But actually my boredom threshold for what you might call Childhood Experiences is almost as low as for Ancestry. Am I alone in finding biographies tedious until the subject becomes old enough to make choices, take decisions, do things?

It really doesn't interest me that Spike had hardly been born when his mother was advised to take him to England for six months for the sake of his health; let alone that, on the journey from India to London, he and his parents (for Leo came too) experienced a mild instance of shipwreck, and had to complete the journey partly overland. If you want to know about all this, and to see all the details of his childhood, you need to get hold of one of the last books he wrote, *The Family Album.*

Nor am I going to tell you about all the moves the family made after they had returned to India (Spike was nearly three by that time). There were addresses in Kirkee (near Poona), Poona itself, Belgaum and Hyderabad, and for a while they left India for Burma and lived in Rangoon. Life was much the same wherever they found themselves: Leo was well paid for remaining in the Indian army now that the First World War was over, and his steady promotion meant that the family's lifestyle became almost lavish. There were several servants in the Milligan household, including an ayah to look after Spike, and his mother was always free to join Leo for their song-and-dance act at some local entertainment.

It's probably significant that Spike grew up without being expected to do anything for himself; he said the rule was that you clapped your hands and a servant came and did it for you. On the other hand he wasn't totally Raj; the offi-cers' children weren't allowed to play with him (Leo, being working class, remained an NCO), so he picked up Hindustani, knocked about with native boys, and observed how the whites maltreated the Indians – he used to see his maternal grandfather hit his groom with a cane if the horse wasn't turned out properly.[3]

---

[3] Spike used to allege that Bloodnok in the Goon Show was 'based on all these Indian [army] Colonels I've seen who are all corrupt and screwing fellow officers' wives. Selling the regimental silver all the time, and knocking off Indian women in their tents when they were on manoeuvres.' I don't find this convincing. Bloodnok is the essence of scoundrel, but I suspect that he was invented by Sellers (who played him). The young Milligan wouldn't have had much chance to observe corruption, whereas Sellers, during his own war service, used to infil-trate officers' messes in a borrowed uniform and a disguised voice, and had some opportunity to see and hear what was going on behind the scenes.

Spike himself was quite often hit, too, by his mother; or at least he started to claim this quite late in life. Flo was still alive, and she denied it vigorously, but Spike insisted that his mother had been kindly but neurotic, and had a violent streak, which meant that she often hit him round the head. Worse, she alternated between smothering him with love, and yelling hatred at him. He said that these wildly contrasting aspects of his mother had left him dazed and confused, and ill-equipped to cope with the world.

This may all be untrue; Spike could have invented or at least exaggerated it while searching for the cause of his mood swings. On the other hand an unpredictable mother such as he described was at one time regarded as a factor in mental instability, especially when combined with a largely absent father – and Leo was often separated from the family and posted to other parts of India and Burma for lengthy periods. Spike blamed the fact that he was a childhood bed-wetter on these absences.

Until he was seven and a half he was an only child. Then another boy was born, and was christened Desmond Patrick. Spike ceased to be exclusively on the receiving end of his parents' attention. You can interpret the rest of his life as a protracted and often florid attempt to get that attention back again.

*

Richard Ingrams has suggested that Spike's originality of thinking was largely the result of his having had so little education. At the age of six he was sent to a convent school for girls in Poona (his mother's 'over-protective' choice, he said), and at first his school reports showed a haphazard performance. There was no educational back-up at home – allegedly not a book in the house, apart from *Robinson Crusoe* and *The Swiss Family Robinson*.

He seemed happy enough at school, but later in life the

recollection of a minor incident there would move him to disproportionate, shocking rage. He had disappeared from school one midday, and when he reappeared there was mud on his trousers, and the Mother Superior – understandably alarmed at the risk of pupils wandering off like this – hauled him up in front of the other children, and yelled at him, terrifyingly, shaming him in the eyes of all the school. The resentment of this incident still ate into him a lifetime later; he wished that some bloodthirsty terrorist had turned up out of the blue, to rape and murder the Mother Superior. Speaking as if she were still alive, he said: 'I hope somebody sets fire to the hairs on her fanny.'

Did he seriously wish such a fate had overtaken the poor nun? It would be nice to say no; but this was a characteristic Spike reaction to being put in the wrong: he was almost incapable of taking any blame, and would respond to criticism by lashing out (or retreating into depression). The spoilt former only child? Or a way of coping with the unpredictable attacks he alleged his mother used to make on him?

There's one piece of evidence that his mood instability was inherited. When he was eight a telegram came to say that his maternal grandmother, who lived in Poona, had threatened suicide because her younger daughter had been having an affair with an unsuitable man; indeed (according to one version told by Spike) she had actually staged a suicide attempt. Nothing more is known about the incident.

By this time his school-work was looking up – he came top of the class several terms running – and he also had a formative experience in a nativity play. 'Nuns are notoriously slow at scene changes,' he writes,

and to fill in the time they dressed me up in a clown's costume, blacked up my face, giving me big white lips, and pushed me out in front of the curtain to entertain. One of the few benefits of political correctness is that today's children will not be subjected to such an ordeal. All I could think of doing was to roll my eyes, open and close my thick white lips and jump up and down. That brought gales of laughter.

He was not supposed to appear in the last scene, when all the other children crowded round the Virgin and Child; but he thought this was unfair. 'So I went on and stood alongside the manger with the others. I thought the clown had a part in life.' He adds: 'I've been a clown ever since.'

What sort of career expectations did his parents have for him? Maybe none, for their artificially lavish Anglo-Indian lifestyle, masking their very low position in the British class hierarchy, perhaps confused their sense of what they and their elder son might expect from society. Terence seems to have had no real belief in himself and his potential: 'I didn't think I could do *anything on my own* – because I was working class.'

Leo, always a dreamer by nature, took refuge in a fantasy of himself and Terence as – of all things – cowboys. 'He [Leo] used to dress up in full Hollywood Western gear in Poona, and have his picture taken,' recalls Spike. 'Then he'd send it to me, signed "Happy Christmas, Dad!" For years I grew up in the belief that Father Christmas was a fucking cowboy.'

This wasn't entirely out of touch with reality: Leo had developed some skill in the saddle, and Spike recalls having to watch his father 'indulging his cowboy obsession with a display of horsemanship' at an annual sports day. Spike didn't share this enthusiasm. For his eleventh birthday in April 1929 his father gave him a cartridge belt with two holsters for revolvers, but the boy was uncomfortable at being 'forced to dress up as a cowboy'.

He had been through a phase, at the age of seven, of wanting to become a jockey. 'My hopes were dashed by our Australian horse trainer, Tod Hewitt. He was a friend of the family, whose swearing used to horrify my mother and Gran. "You'll be too bloody big for a jockey," he said.' Then came 'a thrilling occasion' which suggested another career: a Bristol fighter flew low over Poona and landed on the racecourse. 'We all ran to see it . . . It was so big and beautiful. The pilot let me sit in the cockpit – it was Heaven! From then on, I didn't want to be a jockey, I wanted to be a pilot.'

His parents may have expected him to become a soldier; certainly by the time he was twelve he had joined a cadet troop and was learning to shoot rifles and machine-guns. He says he was 'a pretty good shot', and there was a certain romantic appeal in the big military events that he often witnessed: for example, the Governor General's Annual Parade, which took place at the Polo Ground in Poona. 'Under the blazing Indian sun, regiments of infantry, lancers and gunners filed past in grand array . . . What I was experiencing was the end of the Empire.'

He discovered that he had some talent at music, taught himself the ukelele, and acquired his first jazz record, Fats Waller's 'I'll Be Glad When You're Dead You Rascal You'. During a spell in Burma, as his twelfth birthday approached, he was at last enrolled in a boys' school, St Paul's, Rangoon, run by Catholic lay brothers. But all the moving about between India and Burma had unsettled what little education he had acquired, and 'I sort of got lost and turned in on myself.'

*

In February 1931 Leo Milligan was granted one year's leave to take his family to England. Terence, nearly thirteen, loved the sea journey across half the world – 'We were second class passengers, but really had all the luxury of first class' – and was appalled by what he found on the other side.

'England . . . had weather,' he says, 'lots of it, and mostly bad . . . I spent twelve months longing for the clear sky of Rangoon . . .' They lived in rented rooms near Leo's sister, in the dreary south-east London suburb of Catford, and for the first time in her married life Flo Milligan had to cook for her family. Terence was sent to Brownhill Road School, where (as he recalled in a 1995 television programme) he encountered sex: 'It was the first time I'd seen chaps wanking – they used to go in the toilets and wank. My father caught me doing it once [*he dissolves into helpless laughter*], and he didn't know what to say. He said, "Stop that – do you want all your children to be thin?"'

Telling this story elsewhere, he added that he was so thin himself that his father 'must have spent all his spare time doing it'. He had inherited his father's fine bone structure, and had developed the same effortlessly handsome, almost delicate looks. Back in India and Burma, girls were already being attracted to him.

In February 1932 the Milligans returned from London to Burma: 'the end of our vacation couldn't come quickly enough for me and Desmond,' recalls Spike. Sadly, they had only been back a few weeks when an axe fell on Leo's army job. Since 1926 he had been at the top of the NCOs' tree, as regimental sergeant major, but now – as part of a ten per cent cut in British troops in India by the Ramsay MacDonald government – this post was abolished. Leo, who was still only in his early forties, faced an utterly uncertain future under the grey skies of Britain. 'He had no idea what kind of job he should look for on civvy street,' writes Spike. 'Something to do with horses, maybe? There aren't many openings for a retired cowboy.'

Leo had been given a year's notice by the army, and the time ran swiftly. All too soon it was April 1933 and they were sailing from Rangoon for London, with a brief stopover at Bombay to say goodbye to the relatives who were remaining in India. Spike was to become a much-travelled adult, but he never went back to the subcontinent ('I couldn't bear the sadness of it'). That day in 1933 as the ship began to carry him away from his birthplace, he cried bitterly, but would not let anybody see him. He had just turned fifteen.

2

Catford days, Harlem nights

After twenty years of knowing him, the psychiatrist Anthony Clare wrote:

Spike . . . is still a child. He never grew up; he stopped . . . when he came to England. It was so gloomy and disappointing to him that he wanted to remain the child he'd been in India. So, he kept his ability to think like a child, seeing the world in simplistic terms with [a] maddening innocence.

It's a persuasive piece of pop psychology, Spike as Peter Pan; and whether or not we agree with it, it's true that, following his unwanted, brutal transplantation from India to England just after his fifteenth birthday, he was never again at ease with his surroundings. There was always a dislocation, a discomfort, a feeling that wherever he belonged it certainly wasn't *here*. He was a foreigner on British soil.

In 1975 he played the part of an illegal immigrant to Britain in a BBC television series which he co-wrote himself. Realising rather late in the day that they had fallen foul of good taste, the BBC dropped *The Melting Pot* after one episode. Political correctness may have triumphed, but there was never any suggestion that Spike's own performance was anything other than sympathetic. He knew all too well what it was like to be stranded in a very foreign-seeming England, and to struggle for survival in a hostile environment.

Much of the *Goon Show* has the same motif: Neddie Seagoon, Bluebottle and Eccles are childlike innocents in a society that attempts to be corrupt (exemplified by the dastardly schemes of Grytpype-Thynne), and is not only deceitful but geriatric (typified by ancient Henry Crun and Minnie Bannister). This is Britain as perceived by a perennial outsider, a foreigner who – as we shall see – never acquired full British citizenship, and never wanted to.

The Milligans' ship docked at Tilbury on 26 May 1933, and the family travelled to London where they stayed for a few nights at the Union Jack Club in Waterloo, before finding part of a house to rent at 22 Gabriel Street in Honor Oak Park, on the edge of the nondescript south London suburb of Catford, where they had stayed before. The novelist Kingsley Amis had been brought up in just such a bleak setting, which he condemned with the memorable phrase 'Norbury, SW16 is not a place'.

Peter Sellers's famous sketch 'Balham, Gateway to the South' (on his LP *The Best of Sellers*) guys the pretensions of suburban London to nightlife and culture. Recently, a group of Catfordians attempted to advertise the district's delights in all seriousness on a website; but they had to admit that Catford's main arts and crafts were 'burglary and car theft', that the Catford Centre deserved a 'Demolish It Now' award, and that the district could boast just one distinguished resident in its history – Spike Milligan. The website concludes: 'Who'd want to live in Catford?'

In his whimsical rewrite of family history, *It Ends with Magic* (1990), Spike turns the Milligans' 1933 Catford address into a charming home for his parents:

Back in London the newly-weds rented a house at 22 Gabriel Street – a Victorian terraced house in Honor Oak Park, London, SE26. Florence . . . kept the little home lovely and clean: the doorstep was always white – the brass knocker and letterbox on the front door were polished every morning with Brasso – the fireplace was black-leaded with Zebo every day and the brass coal scuttle shone like the sun. The lace window curtains were washed once a week with Sunlight soap and rinsed in Recketts blue.

In reality, he reveals in his strictly factual book *The Family Album* (1999), 'the landlady was a 65-year-old harridan, Mrs Windust', and 22 Gabriel Street was a miserable, cramped little house, in which the Milligans were squeezed into a pair of rooms under the eaves. There was no bath, and the cooking-stove stood on the landing.[1] Once a week, the Milligans, armed with towels, would get the tram to Leo's sister and her husband, Kath and Alf Thurgar, who now lived in a modern semi-detached villa at 15 Newquay Road in the 'better' part of Catford, where Flo, Leo and the boys would all have baths.[2]

Mrs Windust had a front parlour which was nominally available to Terence and his family, but (like most owners of front parlours) she behaved as if the room were sacred: 'we were only admitted on Sunday'. The piano was covered with a cloth. 'Could my mother play it? "Yes, but I'll 'ave to unlock it first."'

On his previous visit to England, Terence had been too struck by the novelty of it all to make objective judgements. Now, it came home to him with a jolt. They had exchanged the blazing Indian sunshine, the cloudless blue of the sky, and the riot of marvellous colours, for entombment in south London, under a sky of lead. Moreover India had been quiet – or at least never noisy in the way that London was, an insistent, debilitating background noise, to accompany the

---

[1] Scudamore says Mrs Windust was their landlady during their 1931 visit to London, and gives their address on arrival in 1933 as 4 Riseldine Road, SE23, a few streets away from Gabriel Street. Documents reproduced in Spike's *Adolf Hitler: My Part in His Downfall* show that in 1940 they were living at 50 Riseldine Road.

[2] Behan, quoting Spike, gives the Thurgars' address as 15 Bargery Road.

perpetual coldness and greyness. A poem by Spike called 'Catford 1933' describes the yellow smog (fog caused by smoke from home and industrial chimneys) that was often waiting for them outside the front door.

Leo Milligan had been awarded an army pension of two pounds ten shillings a week, roughly half what a young semi-skilled worker might expect to earn; and at first this was all that the family had to live on. Leo began the dispiriting search for a job, equipping himself with a cheap suit from a chain-store tailor. To go with it, he splashed out on a black homburg hat and grey kid gloves. Thus attired, he took a silver-handled cane – maybe a prop from his stage act – and mounted the tram into the centre of Catford, where he would stroll up and down the main street. 'Must look good to get a job,' he told Terence. 'You never know who you'll meet.' He didn't meet anybody (said Spike) and came back dispiritedly on the tram.

Meanwhile Florence had to feed the family on the cheapest food she could find: 'pigs' trotters, tripe and onions, oxtail soup, cod's roe, sweetbreads and bread and butter pudding'. Another of Spike's poems about Catford life describes his mother spending her life bent over the sink, while he himself was unable to eat the unappetising food she dished up. Not surprisingly, Florence was often tense and angry. Trying to manage on next to no income, she had become a domestic tyrant, never considering that other members of the family had a point of view as well. She was tireless in her devotion to Spike and his brother and father, but she lacked a real grasp of their needs.

Spike recalls that the family's arrival in England spelled the end not just of his mother's performing career but his father's, too: 'She knew that Dad was hankering all the time to get back in front of the footlights. But she had decided that if she was not going to cavort about the stage, neither was he. God help him: I still have his dancing mat and make-up case.'

Terence and his little brother withdrew from parental tensions into elaborate games with toy soldiers, which they bought for next to nothing at Woolworth's, re-creating the imperial ceremonies they had watched in India. They called their imaginary country 'Lamania' (*mania*?), and Desmond, who was developing considerable skill at drawing, made pictures of its soldiers and airmen which Terence – whose own drawings were primitive by comparison – thought marvellous.

At fifteen, he had reached the school-leaving age, and his mother hoped he would qualify himself for a decent job. With this in mind, from June until Christmas 1933 he attended a local technical college, the Woolwich & Greenwich Day Continuation School, where he studied mathematics, technical drawing, geometry and workshop practice. 'He has a very good appearance,' reported one of his teachers, 'and is keen, energetic and reliable. He made steady progress in all subjects. I recommend him for employment with complete confidence.'

He still wanted to be a pilot, and somehow Leo found the money to provide him with some private maths lessons. 'I thought this would help me pass the entrance exam to become a pilot in the RAF,' recalls Spike. But it didn't. Sitting the exam in a building in Kingsway, he 'failed miserably'. More than fifty years later, he remained convinced that the air force had made a stupid mistake: he believed he would have made an ace fighter-pilot. He claimed that he had always had super-fast reactions, and could make decisions very fast. The strategic planning of warfare didn't interest him, but the idea of being up in the sky, alone on a crucial mission, appealed to the romantic side of his nature.

This failure meant that he had to contribute his share of support for the family by getting whatever job he could. In January 1934 he was taken on by a firm called Stones' Engineering: 'I was a clerk to a dying book-keeper. I was bloody hopeless.' Stones' was in Deptford, a few miles from

Gabriel Street, and to save money he left home very early each morning to catch a cheap-rate 'workman's tram'.

At work, it was his job to collect time-sheets and scraps of paper with seemingly meaningless figures on them, from all over the factory, and to bring them to the sick bookkeeper. For lunch, he ate banana sandwiches prepared by his mother – the cheapest form of nutrition. His first week's wages were thirteen shillings and fivepence, eleven shillings of which he gave to his mother. He was unable to understand how his life had suddenly become so grim.

It had gradually but painfully become clear to him that, whatever his status might have been as an Anglo-Indian, in Britain he was working class. 'Oh, what did class do to me?' Spike asks himself in one of his books, convinced that he had the brains to go to university.

Future generations of working-class children in Britain would find that university was accessible, thanks to the 1944 Butler Education Act, which greatly increased the provision of places for them. But for Terence Milligan, ten years before the Act was passed, university was virtually out of the question. Also, one wonders what he would have got out of it. His free-wheeling mind was unlikely to have taken easily to, or been enriched by, the intellectual disciplines of conventional academic studies.

Meanwhile, existence was not all early morning trams and senseless time-sheets. 'Around this time,' he writes, 'I also met my first girlfriend. Her name was Nina Hall. She had magnificent boobs. I would like to have screwed her, but I was too shy.' Nina worked alongside him at Stones'. He told Dominic Behan: 'I was in love with her, but then I've loved all the women I've ever liked', a confession of innate and rather naïve romanticism which is a more accurate self-portrait than the laddish talk of boobs and screwing.

The relationship with Nina proved to be important for Terence's interest in music: 'It was in her flat that I heard my first Bing Crosby record and I was hooked on him. I soon realised that I could imitate Bing very well.' He went off and did just that, winning a crooning contest at a local hall, and coming second in a talent contest at Lewisham Hippodrome. At first there was no money in it. 'I just did it for kicks . . . couldn't wait to put on my fifty-shilling tailor's suit, Brylcreem my hair and get on to the mike at Ladywell Baths to sing *Temptation*.'

Soon he was spotted and engaged by a local dance-band, the New Era Rhythm Boys, and he began to supplement his thin pay-packet from Stones' with a few bob from dance-band gigs. He doesn't say what Leo, who was still under Florence's performance ban, thought of his son suddenly displaying a stage talent. Probably he was entirely supportive.

Meanwhile at Stones', Terence was taken away from the ailing book-keeper and transferred to testing fuse boxes. This was dangerous work, and he kept giving himself accidental but powerful electric shocks, so they transferred him again, this time to a metal-cutting machine. Here, he soon managed to catch his hair in the machine, ripping out a clump, whereupon they sacked him, leaving him having to wear a protective cap until his scalp had healed.

Not surprisingly, Leo was pining for India. He had managed to get a poorly paid job in the Associated Press photo library, and in 1934 he was hoping to establish a branch office under Indian skies; he told his employers, hopefully, that his knowledge of the Indian languages and the different peoples of the subcontinent ideally qualified him for the task. But it was Spike who was making some sort of daydream start to come true: 'I was earning ten shillings a night doing gigs.'

*

He decided that it was not enough to be a vocalist. So 'I also learned to play the bass', and this brought him work with lots of bands.

To carry the bass to gigs, he had to ask the tram driver to let him squeeze it on board, and this usually meant someone cracking the joke which has irritated bass-players since the instrument was invented: 'How do you get it under your chin?' (The correct answer is: 'By keeping your big mouth shut.') Terence, keen to master the instrument, took it along to music classes at Goldsmiths College, where he learned to read notation. He also began to take an interest in the 'serious' branch of the art. 'I've listened to music right up to Schoenberg,' he told Van Morrison in 1989, 'but I'm baffled by him and this atonal music. I suppose it's technically very clever but it doesn't give me any emotion. I like Mahler.'

Playing the bass satisfies those who have a deep-seated feeling for pulse, and little interest in the limelight. Spike may have been a pulse man, but he was also an exhibitionist. 'I wanted an instrument to make a bigger noise. A trumpet, that's what I needed.'

He had to wait for it, since his next day-job paid very little. This was as a van boy, delivering confectionery to sweet shops. 'I had access to whatever [sweets] I wanted. I ate so many Bassett's Liquorice Allsorts that I had the shits for a week.'

Then, for a spell, he was a work-hand in the Chislehurst Laundry, a few miles from Catford, on the edge of London. It was a gruesome experience having to wash other people's grubby, sometimes faeces-smeared sheets. First, the load of dirty linen went into an enormous rotating drum; the sheets were pushed in, the doors were slammed shut, and Spike turned on the almost-boiling water and added the soap powder. When the actual washing was done, the sheets, heavy with water, had to be pulled out of the drum and thrown into a big wheeled basket, which Spike would push down to the 'hydro', a powerful spin-dryer in which centrifugal force would extract all the water from the load.

Then the sheets – now somewhat lighter – would have to be pulled out again, and dumped into another trolley, which he wheeled across to an area where a team of women were waiting to iron them.

The laundry employed just three men and himself along-side (he alleges) 'one hundred randy women. They would squeeze a wet pocket handkerchief into the shape of a man's willy and say to me, "Is yours like this?"' Fair-haired and blue-eyed, the sixteen-year-old Terry Milligan could have had his pick of them. 'Some of those laundry girls were luscious but I was too bloody shy to date any of them – oh the lost chances!' He left the laundry when his leaking wellington boots let in so much water that he developed a First World War ailment, trench foot.

He was still seeing Nina Hall, in whose flat he had first heard Bing Crosby, and he was also dipping into the turbulent waters of 1930s British politics. Deciding that the Labour Party was getting nowhere, he joined the local branch of the Young Communist League, and claimed that he was at the 1936 Cable Street riot in the East End, when the British Union of Fascists met the Communists head on: 'I was at the back, throwing rocks.'[3] Meanwhile another girl, Lily Dunford (Lily Gibbs according to Pauline Scudamore), took

---

[3] This, at any rate, is what he told Behan. However, Wolf Mankowitz used to claim that Spike had once admitted, on a TV talk show, that he had worn the Fascists' black shirt until it had stopped appealing to him. Graham Stark, too, is convinced that Spike was a Blackshirt in the thirties: 'I know someone who's in our profession who used to work in the CID, and he told me they have a file on Spike, because he was a Blackshirt.' There is no other evidence for this. What Spike does say, on page 89 of *The Family Album*, is: 'At the time of Mosley, [Nina] started wearing a black shirt. I wondered why Jews kept shouting "Fascist" at us in the street.' John Antrobus thinks Spike was trying to cover up the truth here, but adds: 'Even if he did join the Fascists, he made up for it later by fighting Hitler.'

the place of Nina, assisted him in losing his virginity, and – perhaps more importantly – generously paid for him to buy his first trumpet. 'It was four pounds ten shillings,' he writes, adding ungraciously: 'It was a piece of crap.'

Nevertheless he taught himself to play ('with a sock in the bell', to keep the noise down at home), and eventually 'I mastered it and started playing first trumpet with a weekend band.' He also taught himself the guitar – he says he loved the funky jazz chords the instrument was required to play in dance-bands – while as for a jazz guitarist role model, 'Eddie Lang was God'.

No recordings survive of Spike playing with the south London bands, such as Tommy Brettell's New Ritz Revels, in which (we know from a photograph) his trumpet was pitted against three saxophones and supported by a rhythm section of piano and drums (no bass or guitar – perhaps he supplied these now and then). The Revels, who played every Saturday night in one of the Catford dance-halls, look as smart as any top-line American band, spruced in their two-tone tuxedos behind their art deco music stands (both tuxedos and stands could be purchased through the *Melody Maker*); but Spike calls them 'a bunch of spotty musicians held together with hair oil'.

He had now developed the confidence to play ad-lib jazz solo choruses. Judging by his trumpet-playing in the later years of his life (when his lip had gone through lack of practice, but his musicianship remained unimpaired), he was probably rather good in his heyday in the thirties. He certainly came to believe that he had been. 'I was blowing that music real good, man,' he reminisced in somewhat self-conscious hep-talk to Van Morrison half a century later. 'One of the greatest feelings in the world is to play music, it's total freedom. When I was playing that trumpet I couldn't think about the rates, the rent. It was liberation, self-therapy. And you can induce that therapy in other people.'

Jazz found him, and brought him to life, long before he wandered into the field of comedy – except that the two are never very far apart. For some reason, jazz musicians have an especially highly developed sense of humour. Puns and wisecracks seem to go hand-in-hand with ad-lib musical solos, and there is a deep cynicism which never descends into sneering. The New Ritz Revels probably didn't rival the Marx Brothers as a bunch of humorists, any more than they equalled the Duke Ellington band as Harlem-style musicians; but we can be fairly certain that, on these Saturday gigs in Catford and other south-east London 'postal districts packed like squares of wheat' (Larkin – another jazz enthusiast), trumpeter Milligan began to experience something of the power of laughter and of making other people laugh.

*

The late nights on Saturdays made him reluctant to get up for mass on Sundays. This provoked a family disagreement big enough for him to move out and sleep at a friend's house, at least for a few weeks. His mother 'started [such] an unending attack . . . as to why I wouldn't go to Church . . . that eventually I left home and went to stay with Harold Fagg'.

This experience left his Catholicism somewhat dented, but not seriously damaged. 'I'm a lapsed Catholic and a practising Catholic,' he said towards the end of his life. 'I practise all the time. Then I lapse. Then I practise a bit more. It never stops.'

Back in the thirties, he continued to drift from one dead-end day-job to another, usually qualifying himself for the sack. He says he was dismissed from a stationer's at Blackfriars for failing to wear a black tie when George V died. Then he fetched up in Bond Street, as a stockroom assistant at Keith Prowse, the ticket agency and music shop. 'It was soul-destroying . . . All that kept my sanity in those days was playing evenings with the New Ritz Revels, and crooning:

"When it's June in January . . . "' This time he wasn't sacked, and his boss at Keith Prowse gave him a good reference: 'Terence Milligan was employed by this Company in our Wholesale Department from the 19th August, 1935, to the 29th February, 1936, during which period he discharged his duties to our entire satisfaction.' And these dates make nonsense of the black tie story: George V died on 20 January 1936. But his next job was definitely 'my downfall'.

It was in the stockroom of a tobacconist, Spiers & Ponds. 'All day,' he recalls,

I'd wrap up a selection of tobacco and cigarettes for shops in and around London . . . At the time, my £4 10/- trumpet was falling apart. How could I afford a new one? Simple, pack your overcoat pockets with fags and sell them . . . I flogged a few fags every day until I had enough money to pay for the horn. But somebody reported me and I was brought up before this old bastard of a manager . . . Had me arrested. My poor mother? My poor father, for God's sake? Poor father? Poor bloody me!

Looking back many years later, Spike expressed no remorse or even embarrassment over this incident. Typically, he seemed to blame the manager for it, rather than his own dishonesty or his greed for a better trumpet. He alleged that the boss had lounged back, with his feet splayed on his desk and his hands thrust deep in his pockets, scratching his genitals with an unpleasant rasping sound. Meanwhile he (Spike) felt quite calm. His employer was in a position of power over him, but the moral advantage was his, because the man was profiteering from the addictive power of tobacco, and from the starvation wages he was paying his staff. Spike felt that all he himself had done was compensate a little for that; he had only taken what was morally owing to him anyway.

To Dominic Behan, Spike said: 'I'll never forget that

terrible man as long as I live. Got my own back years afterwards. I wrote him into the Goons.' Indeed, Scudamore
notes that the very first *Goon Show* of all (the opening
edition of *Crazy People*) includes a courtroom scene in which
Harry Secombe is accused of the theft of 'two thousand
half-smoked cigarettes'; when questioned by the prosecuting
counsel, he can only cough. Did Spike feel he must get the
episode off his chest (no pun intended) and out into the
open before he began his career as a scriptwriter?

Spiers & Ponds dismissed him for the theft of the cigarettes, and he was summonsed to a local court. Leo Milligan
decided to be his son's defence counsel – a risky enterprise,
but fortunately his blarney was effective. According to Spike,
the line he took was 'Have pity on this boy because . . . he
could become a virtuoso!'

It seems that Terence was allowed to go unconditionally
free. Meanwhile with the cash for the stolen fags he had
bought the gold-plated trumpet on which his heart had been
set, and no one seems to have suggested that it should be
returned to the shop. Soon he was playing it in yet another
dance ensemble, as 'Terry Milligan, the Wild Man of the
Harlem Club Band'.

If his recollections are accurate, he took one more day-job
after the court case, as a semi-skilled labourer at Woolwich
Arsenal, making terminals for batteries. If he worked over-
time at this job he could earn as much as five pounds a
week, but he was still handing most of his weekly pay-
packet to his mother, whereas band gigs were now bringing
him almost as much cash over again, and he could keep this
band money.

Florence apparently failed to appreciate how working as
a freelance musician suited his temperament far more than
semi-skilled labouring, and she was probably also nervous
about the family's financial outlook if he gave himself totally
to music. At all events she continued to reproach him about

his lifestyle. Spike's brother Desmond recalled the battles: 'Mum was a great one at disapproving of everyone who didn't conform . . . "You'll ruin your health playing that trumpet!" . . . And I'd be in my bedroom, listening to Spike getting a hell of a roasting.'

*

'One day an envelope marked OHMS fell on the mat . . . In it was a cunningly worded invitation to participate in World War II . . .'

This is the joke that opens *Adolf Hitler: My Part in His Downfall*, and in every sense the arrival of his call-up papers marked the opening of a new chapter in Spike's life. The exuberance in the first pages of his war memoirs reflects what was obviously his huge sense of relief at being able to flee the family's cramped and dingy accommodation, the succession of day-jobs that he knew were beneath him, and his disapproving mother.

The timing of his call-up could scarcely have been better, given that he celebrated his twenty-first birthday in April 1939; he was old enough to be independent, and young enough to be inexperienced, the perfect balance for getting the best out of the war.

Yet it all started with a muddle, and at first he seemed reluctant to become a soldier. On 31 January 1940 Terence Milligan was given a medical examination at Eltham recruiting centre, and was passed Grade 1. But he wasn't called up at once, and during March he was an out-patient at Lewisham Hospital, suffering from back pains. Before the war, he had been a keep-fit enthusiast, exercising every morning at Ladywell Recreation Track, where he lifted barbells to the admiring glances of girls who worked at Catford Labour Exchange. Overloading the barbell in order to show off to these female admirers, he had experienced an agonising pain in his back.

His Lewisham Hospital out-patient card read '? Muscle Strain'. But he says he had a slipped disc. He allows that to get a 'bad back' at the same time as your call-up smacked a little of cowardice; nevertheless that was what happened – he did not join his regiment until June 1940. On the second day of that month, he reported to a military transport officer at Victoria Station in London, was given a travel warrant, and found himself on a train for the very unmilitary-sounding destination of Bexhill-on-Sea. Life was looking up again.

3

Gunnery or . . . Goonery

Terence Milligan's diary for 2 June 1940 reads: 'Joined the Regt. 56th R.A.[1] Dumbest crowd of blokes I've ever seen. Nearly all N. Country blokes.' This was the unpromising beginning to the most exciting – indeed, the happiest – part of his life, which eventually became the raw material for no fewer than seven volumes of memoirs, beginning with *Adolf Hitler: My Part in His Downfall.*

On the whole he sticks to the truth in the war memoirs, using not just his own diaries as source material, but consulting his old regimental comrades for their recollection of events. (He even revisited former battlefields in North Africa.) Consequently he was provoked to indignation when Clive James, reviewing one of the Milligan war books, called it 'an unreliable history of the war'.

Well [writes Spike], this makes him a thoroughly unreliable critic, because I spend [*sic*] more time on getting my dates and facts right than I did [*sic*] in actually writing. I admit the way I present it may seem as though my type of war was impossible and all a figment of a hyper-thyroid imagination, but that's the way I write.

But this is to jump ahead. If he didn't think much of his fellow soldiers that first day in uniform, their own reaction to him was no more enthusiastic. One recruit, Dennis Slogett, thought him shy, possibly even a little retarded mentally, while another, Ted Lawrence, felt from the outset that the

---

[1] That is, 56th Heavy Regiment Royal Artillery.

new Gunner was in some way different from the rest of the
recruits – if only because he was carrying a trumpet in its
own small case.

Milligan was lucky to have fallen among essentially kind-
hearted young men, who did not believe in submitting
newcomers to unpleasant initiation ceremonies. Dennis Slogett
makes it sound more like group therapy than the army when
he recalls that young Milligan progressed splendidly in a few
weeks – the others found they were able to coax him out of
his shell. Slogett also emphasises that they all faced the same
uncertainty: each was experiencing his first time away from
the comforts and security of home, and none of them had
much notion what the future held. And while some may have
been homesick, Milligan, at the age of twenty-two, felt
precisely the opposite: he was only too keen to get away
from the cramped Catford attic, the dreary day-jobs, and his
mother's protests at his late-night dance-band lifestyle: 'The
sergeant-major didn't stand at the top of the stairs and say,
"Terence, where have you been, you naughty gunner?" . . .
And there was nobody forcing me to go to chapel – if you
didn't go to church you peeled a potato . . . The sense of
emancipation! The feeling of freedom!'

He had no sooner arrived at barracks in Bexhill-on-Sea
than he had a belated chance to make up for his lack of
education. D Battery, to which he had been assigned, was
stationed in a former girls' school; the pupils had been evacuated, but remaining *in situ* was a well-stocked school library.
Milligan eyed it greedily. Then he approached an officer and
explained that he would like to tidy up the books, make
lists of them, and encourage the other men to borrow them.
He emphasised that the Battery was short of decent reading
matter. The officer's response was offhand – 'Oh, good idea,
Milligan' – but no objection was raised, and Spike began
to browse among the books, soon losing interest in being
a librarian, and simply beginning to soak himself in them.

He removed his bedding from the communal sleeping quarters and took it upstairs to the library, where for the first time in his life he was able to read a different book each night. Top of his list were Dickens (he particularly loved *Bleak House*) and George Eliot (*Silas Marner* and *The Mill on the Floss*). It was exhilarating. (He continued to read hungrily throughout the war. In Italy in January 1944, he was absorbed in Byron's *Childe Harold's Pilgrimage*, and in the summer of 1946 he was soaking up Francis Thompson's poetry and Mrs Gaskell's life of Charlotte Brontë.)

Bexhill enriched his life in another way. The Sussex fields and lanes surrounding the sea resort gave him his first experience of natural landscape since he had left India and Burma. The English countryside – as painted again and again by Constable – sang at him, and he learned to spot some of its less obvious features: a medlar tree, a dew-pond (made, it was said, in Saxon times), a wood carpeted with bluebells, a windmill where the grain was still being ground, and a Sussex thatcher who lived in a gypsy caravan and picked stinging-nettles to make a delicious and surprisingly mild soup from a recipe of Romany origin.

As he recalled it, he arrived at Bexhill on the day before the evacuation from Dunkirk – he claimed he had only been in uniform for a matter of hours when it happened. In fact the evacuation had begun on 26 May, a week before his arrival. He and his fellow Gunners could hear distant explosions from across the Channel. It was his first taste of the absurdity of war. Sitting in an Observation Point in the middle of the night, armed only with a rifle with just a few rounds of ammunition, made him feel utterly impotent in relation to what was going on over the water. Or, as he put it to Dominic Behan:

Here was me and Harry Edgington stationed [in a Martello Tower] to stop the entire Panzer divisions of Germany coming into

England – just me and Harry Edgington and one rusty gun! I just love the thought of it: the Germans were only going to land forty thousand men; all they needed to do was aim at us to blow us out of our Martello Tower.

D Battery was responsible for manning three Observation Points (OPs), of which the men's favourite was the tower on Pevensey Beach, because Pevensey girls (who could be lured there) were an easier lay than those of Bexhill, but you had to be fast about it because of the tide. At another OP, on Galley Hill, Milligan had a glimpse of one of the top Allied commanders, General Sir Alan Brooke, after-wards Lord Alanbrooke, who turned up one morning with a small group of officers and asked Milligan his name and what he did. Spike alleges that he answered that he 'did his best', and got the reply from Alanbrooke that (given Dunkirk, and the way the war was going) one's best might soon be not enough.

Alanbrooke's pessimism was not shared by Milligan and the rest of D Battery. The defeat at Dunkirk didn't spoil their summer. It was glorious 'shirts off' weather, recalls Spike. Really, there hardly seemed to be a war.

*

It was the trumpet that did the trick, transforming Gunner Milligan from an 'almost backward' recruit into a favourite eccentric. He took his trumpet to war, he says proudly in *Adolf Hitler*, and it seems that the officers (much credit to them), having already allowed him to appoint himself librarian, now let him become unofficial Battery bugler.

He would sound reveille in the early morning, having placed his mattress conveniently beneath a window, so that he could blow the wake-up call and then retire again between the sheets. Another member of D Battery, Reg Griffin, recalled that they used to see the trumpet sticking out of the window. An NCO used to wake Spike, who would blow the call to get everyone on the move, but he didn't get out of bed himself until it was absolutely unavoidable.

He spent a lot of his spare time lying on his bed, playing jazz phrases on his instrument, and somebody soon suggested that he should team up with a keen pianist in the Battery, a six-foot-two Gunner called Harry Edgington. This individual was self-taught, could not read music, and preferred playing on the black notes: F sharp and C sharp major, two of the hardest keys for a jazz musician like Spike. However, over the months that followed, Spike coaxed Edgington (at the NAAFI piano) away from the black notes, and taught him the names of crucial chords. They were soon playing in the usual jazz keys.

Milligan proposed that he and Edgington should get a band together, and maybe earn a bit of cash. By a stroke of luck, a driver named Alf Fildes was posted to the Battery, who turned out to play the guitar. Then, one evening, Edgington and Milligan were entertaining the lads when they noticed that a Gunner called Doug Kidgell was banging out the cross-rhythms on his mess-tin with his knife and fork. Milligan immediately enrolled him as their drummer.

Rumour reached them that an entire drum kit was 'lying fallow' under the stage of Bexhill's Old Town Hall, and they decided to 'requisition' it for Kidgell to play, using the excuse that they were preventing it falling into enemy hands – as Spike puts it, with Germany poised to invade, it was a matter of military urgency. They took the drums, and 'camouflaged' them by painting the Royal Artillery crest on the bass drum's front.

This habit of 'requisitioning' stayed with them throughout the war. A little later, they appropriated a string bass which had been left backstage in Bexhill's theatre, the De La Warr Pavilion, so that Alf Fildes could double on it. A wooden crate was made to its measurements, and the outside was stencilled 'MARK THREE BOFOR GUN SPARES'. In Africa during 1943 they somehow acquired a baritone saxophone, and a photo taken before they left Bexhill shows Milligan with an alto sax: yes, he admits, he played that too. (Did his sax-playing sound like Minnie Bannister's in the *Goon Show*, all slap-tonguing and crazy 1920s novelty phrasing? We shall never know.)

It was now that Terence Milligan acquired the nickname that would accompany him to fame. 'In those days,' he recalls,

we used to listen to Radio Luxembourg, and they were featuring one of the zaniest, noisiest bands anybody ever heard . . . Spike Jones and his City Slickers . . . I'd always wanted a public name – to hide behind, I suppose. The way my mother called me 'Terence' in a bid to make me respectable, and Dad said 'Terry', like I was some sort of chocolate. Soon the other guys began to call me Spike, and I loved it.

That's what Milligan told Dominic Behan. Scudamore has another version. According to her, Spike had discussed his jazz ambitions with Harry Edgington, and had said he wanted to play the trumpet as well as Spike Hughes. Edgington replied that in this case, they must all watch out for the debut of the famous trumpeter Spike Milligan.

But the music critic and bandleader Spike Hughes – more of a proselytiser for jazz than a notable performer – played the bass, not the trumpet, and in any case he seems an unlikely role model. A third version had it that Milligan took the soubriquet from the retractable 'spike' of his own double bass. However, that instrument failed to accompany him into the army. Meanwhile, whatever the explanation of 'Spike', he continued to sign his name 'Terry' when writing to his family.

Once applied to him, 'Spike' stuck firmly. A poster advertising a regimental dance calls the D Battery band 'Spike and the Boys'. Like all apprentice bands, they suffered at first from shortness of repertoire, and had to repeat numbers. Spike claimed they had bashed through *Honeysuckle Rose* no less than forty times. For a while, they allowed a civilian, a Mr Courtney who owned an antique shop, to announce the numbers, and to sing romantic ballads in a shaky baritone. But mostly the vocalist was Spike. Doug Kidgell recalled him rewriting lyrics as he performed them: 'Spike used to try and throw me – he'd sing: "Deep in my heart there is rupture, / But for that, I would have upped ya!" And so on – but I withstood it!'

The band's reputation spread beyond Bexhill. They were booked to entertain troops at remote military camps, and for private functions. One evening they were performing for an officers' dance at a requisitioned Sussex manor house when, according to Spike's memory, no less than Field Marshal Montgomery was present. Milligan did tend to run into the high-ups; it's one of the areas in which the war memoirs do feel a tiny bit unreliable, and he also claims to have glimpsed Gandhi in India and met George Orwell in Burma. He describes Monty 'during an interval coming to us and saying, in that high nasal voice, "Are you men being looked after?" I (as the leader of the band) said we could do with some more beer. And lo! within the moment, a dozen pints arrived . . .'

Gunners Edgington (piano) and Kidgell (drums), and Driver Fildes (guitar), didn't dispute Milligan's right to lead them. A trumpeter was the natural front man for any band, and Doug Kidgell comments that Spike had the advantage over the others of being able to read music. Alf Fildes could read chord symbols, but Edgington had never learned to interpret the 'dots', so Milligan had a major advantage over the others.

One evening, he came up with the subversive idea of adapting 'The Red Flag' as the last waltz. The tune was recognised by one of the sergeants: 'We'll have no more of that nonsense,' came the reprimand. '*And* in the presence of officers!' But generally the NCOs and officers refrained from giving orders to the band. Indeed, the four musicians were often the recipients of special treatment. 'We'd say that if they wanted us to play at dances then they'd have to give us the mornings off to rehearse,' recalls Spike. 'We used to lay in bed, get our breakfast late . . . It was wonderful.' Indeed, 'we were enjoying the war very, very much, I'm sorry to say – we didn't want it to stop. I thought of writing to Hitler and saying, "Look, keep this going for a while – just don't bomb my mother."'

*

Edgington and Milligan encouraged each other in verbal as well as musical invention. Spike recalls that they jointly wrote pieces 'very much in the vein of Beachcomber. It was pretty insane, but it was a start.' Beachcomber (the celebrated comic column by J.B. Morton in the *Daily Express*) was to be a perceptible influence on the *Goon Show*, but nothing survives of these copies of his style. All we have is a limerick by Spike about a fellow soldier called Arthur Eddser, who sometimes acted as MC for the band's performances:

> *There was a young bombardier called Eddser,*
> *Who, when wanted, was always in bed, sir.*
> *One morning at one*
> *They fired the gun,*
> *And Eddser, in bed, sir, was dead, sir.*

There may be a serious point behind it. Lying in bed, Milligan could see the glow of the fires on the nights when the Luftwaffe were making raids on London. 'The bombers were still going. Some must have been on their way back, as we heard cannon fire as [RAF] night-fighters got onto them. What a bloody mess. Men in bombers raining death on defenceless civilians.' He told Dominic Behan: 'For the love of me I couldn't get the feeling that I was part of this. Killing of civilians was an outrage I couldn't swallow on any basis, on any side. In the end there were no sides. Just living and dead.'

But this was said by the I-Will-Save-the-Planet-Singlehandedly version of Spike, who emerged in his later years: vegetarian, pro-animal rights, conservationist, and of course pacifist. And we need to remember that sharing a body with St Spike (as it's tempting to name this persona) was the Terence Alan Milligan who was charged in 1974 with deliberately shooting a teenage boy in the shoulder – admittedly only with an air-gun, but how many of us would even do that? Maybe the idea that D Battery in 1940 was harbouring an incipient pacifist doesn't need to be taken too seriously.

He was now writing enough humorous verse and prose to show to a sympathetic officer. Lieutenant Anthony Goldsmith, an Oxford graduate, had written a play with Terence Rattigan and translated Flaubert's *L'Education Sentimentale*. Spike makes him sound like Renaissance Man; but then Spike was only just beginning to discover the life of the mind. And it's a curious thing, but he never really developed what you might call an intellect. It was a superb collection of firecrackers, his brain, a world-class winner at the cognitive leap, but it didn't really do abstract thought. People who knew him well don't have a store of Spike's sayings to remember him by. They remember his *behaviour* (especially the depressions) but not the *ideas*. There weren't any. So it's interesting, during the war years, to watch him interfacing with a handful of real intellectuals.

Goldsmith commented on what Milligan showed him: 'This is mad. It's very like the Marx Brothers but it's very funny.' Slender encouragement, but Spike recalled with gratitude that his conversations with Goldsmith had given him the beginnings of an education. Goldsmith, he said, had liked him for being the untamed creature he half wanted to be himself. Goldsmith had a controlled mind, whereas Spike was like a wild horse, running unbroken and unsaddled.

Later, when part of the Battery was moved to Hailsham in East Sussex, Spike and Edgington would fill up time by drawing cartoons. These intrigued a young officer called John Counsell, who had worked in professional theatre before the war (and after it was over ran the Windsor Repertory Company). Again, Counsell's encouragement was slight, but important to Milligan. He had begun to realise that he needed more mental stimulus than he could get from most of his mates: 'I loved the lads, I really loved them, but I knew there was no mental food for me there.'

Besides Goldsmith and Counsell, there was a third encourager, Lieutenant Cecil Budden, a classical pianist who played Beethoven passionately. 'I learned so much from him,' Spike has said, 'he was so approachable. I was able to talk to him about all aspects of music.' But he doesn't reproduce any of their conversations.

Meanwhile Spike was beginning to do comedy spots with the band. The master of ceremonies would announce a number called 'The Invisible Trumpeter', the lights would come up to reveal a large sofa on the stage, and then the bell of Spike's trumpet would rise from behind it. Spike himself remained crouched or lying down out of sight, but a jaunty tune issued from the cushions. It had all been thrown together on minimal rehearsal.

All the encouragement of his officer friends, and the warm response of the band's audiences, led him to make a resolution in one of his letters from Bexhill to his parents. He announced that he was definitely going to have a career in show business, when the war was over. In her reply, his mother did not comment: was she horrified, or merely dubious about his ability to earn his living as a performer? At all events she restricted her letters to her concern for his safety and health, and his religious observances. He was to pray to St Anthony and St Francis every day, always say his catechism, and wear all his holy medals.

*

After weeks of training with the various types of gun used by D Battery, Milligan was picked out to be a signaller – an indication that he was regarded as above average mentally. He has said that this gave an enormous boost to his confidence. It meant being expected to use his brain a little. Learning Morse code was an exciting challenge; he found it much easier than school-work, which he had hated because of the demand (in maths) that he show how he had reached his answers. Morse was just there, as a given thing.

In *Adolf Hitler* he describes himself as a trainee Signaller who was severely incompetent with Morse code, semaphore flags and lamps. Yet it seems that he had not abandoned his childhood dream of being a pilot, since, after six months at Bexhill, he volunteered for the Air Force. He explains that fighter pilots were the heroes of the war – all the good-looking girls went out with them. It made the other servicemen green with envy. (So much for his alleged feeling that the war was an outrage in which he wanted no part.)

On 23 January 1941 Spike's father Leo – who had rejoined the army as an officer, and was in an administrative post – wrote to his son's commanding officer at Bexhill, asking that Spike should be allowed to transfer to the RAF. The major replied that he had no objection, but the decision lay with the Air Force. The next month, Spike was once again called for interview at Kingsway House. The result was a little better than last time: he was told they were happy to take him on as a rear gunner, but his eyesight was not up to the standard required for pilots. No, he answered, he didn't want to be at the back, he wanted to be in the driving seat. But it was all they could offer him, and he turned it down and set off dejectedly for Bexhill.

On his return to barracks, Harry Edgington told him there was some good news in the latest issue of the *Melody Maker*. Harry Parry, host of the BBC programme *Radio Rhythm Club*, was holding auditions to find the best unknown jazz musicians and the winners were to appear on the programme. They wrote off, and back came an invitation to attend the auditions. These were at the BBC's Maida Vale studios on 20 April 1941.

Spike says that the Bexhill band performed brilliantly, and that he himself was judged the best trumpet player of those present, recording several numbers on the spot with a winners' band that included the young pianist George Shearing. The day (he says) was a milestone for him – he felt he had been judged a real jazz musician of a high level, and before he left, Shearing said he hoped they would meet and play together again. It was the greatest praise Spike could imagine.

The BBC's files tell a rather different story. The list of the auditionees does not include Spike's name. However, there is a trio which had travelled up from Bexhill, and the auditioner's scribble against this ensemble appears to be: '6/10 [illegible] Guitar. P. Drums (2nd) G.P. Trumpet.' The instrumentation (guitar, piano, drums and trumpet) is right for Fildes, Edgington, Kidgell and Milligan, but what the initials mean is anyone's guess. George Shearing did appear on *Radio Rhythm Club*, but he was not present that day.

So Spike does not seem to have been a winner after all. But it appears that the experience of the audition was positive enough to give his increasingly show-business-minded ego another boost.

*

Spike provides us with a very precise account of the birth, at this stage of the war, of the very first version of the Goons, or at least of the concept 'Goon'.

D Battery signallers had been set an exercise of laying telephone lines at a disused rubbish tip at Mill Wood, two miles from barracks at Bexhill, and during it they lived in the wood, under canvas. Spike writes that it was during this period that 'the Goons in the Popeye cartoon appeared and tickled my sense of humour, and any soldier I thought was an idiot I called a Goon. This was taken up by those with a like sense of humour.'

In fact it was during the 1930s, not in wartime, that the Popeye newspaper strip (written and drawn by E.C. Segar) had introduced Alice the Goon, described by the strip's historian as 'a hairy, hulking monster who later became the family babysitter'. Spike says of this Popeye character: 'There was a creature called the Goon which had nothing in the face at all except hair. It had huge talk-bubbles with one little word in them like "Eeek!" It was very kind and gentle. I liked the word [Goon] . . .'

When the Popeye strip transferred from newspapers to movies, 'Goons' in the plural often made an appearance; for example in the short film *Goonland* (1938), where it is established that Goons live on their own island and do not like humans. Popeye and his father wage such a tough fight with them that the film itself seems to snap in two. These Goons have long noses and wear grass skirts, and look a little like Spike's future drawings of Eccles.

Then there is the question of the word 'goon' in the Second World War. Here, Spike denies a connection: 'Prisoners of war called their German guards goons but I got it from Popeye.' The *Oxford English Dictionary* (second edition, 1989) notes that in America 'goon' can mean a hired thug, but this seems to have come from Popeye. Possibly Popeye's creator was influenced by 'coon' (racist slang for a black person), or even by the Anglo-Indian word *goonda*, from Hindi *gunda*, meaning ruffian or gangster; but then Spike was in a better position than Mr Segar for picking this one up, and he never mentioned it. On the other hand, as a throwaway on one page of his war memoirs, he refers to 'Gunnery, or, as we used to call it, Goonery', which is quite another explanation of the word.

At first, in Mill Wood, 'Goons' were part of what sounds like a childish game of hitting each other over the head – or at least threatening to. Calling themselves the Clubbers, Spike and his pals built a rack outside the tent in which they were sleeping, and cut huge gnarled clubs from fallen branches. Each club had a name – 'Nurke's Nut Nourisher', 'Instant Lumps', and so on. The most spectacular, carved from the limb of a blasted oak, was five feet long, a club worthy of Hercules. They made it even more fearsome by hammering electrical earthing irons into its head, and gave it the understated name 'Ye Crust Modifier'.

The Clubbers assembled to a trumpet call by Spike, and would grab the clubs and run amok shouting, 'Death to the Goons.' One of the regular participants, Bob 'Dipper' Dye, recalled that these high jinks were almost beyond belief. Spike would strip down to some sort of loincloth, Tarzan-style, and tear through the woods brandishing a huge club, howling as he waved it. The others, said Dye, just accepted all this as typical Spike.

It did not last long. One summer night they were caught by the duty officer, naked and drunk, tearing through the woods, waving the clubs and yelling 'Viva Joe Stalin'. They were made to destroy the clubs; but by this time Spike had established himself as the Battery clown. He would give such performances as how to do rifle drill in Braille, how to sleep standing up while on guard, and how to march standing still.

Some of the clowning was done on paper, with the collaboration of Harry Edgington; in *Adolf Hitler*, Spike quotes a fragment from Edgington's writings at this time:

The door flew open and in crashed the master-spy himself . . . clad only in a huge fur coat of huge fur, a sou'wester, and two hand-painted barges strapped to his feet for a quick getaway . . . Curtain, to chord in various flats by orch. of military bugle, violin and Pianist who has one hand out to show he is going to turn right.

Spike comments that this was one of the first precursors of the *Goon Show*, and mentions that Edgington was sometimes known as 'Edge-Ying-Tong'. Those last two words eventually inspired a song.

*

Goon humour was everywhere in the army. One of D Battery's NCOs was removing a jammed shell from a gun when it went off. His severed hand was about to be interred where it had fallen, when the victim was asked if he would like to 'shake hands' before they buried it. On another occasion, part of the Battery was moved to a different area of Sussex, whence it was ordered to a secret destination – which proved to be Bexhill, where it had started.

At last, in December 1942, they were told to prepare for going overseas, though of course they had no idea in which part of the world they would be fighting. Spike travelled to Catford to say goodbye to his family – though most of his week's leave was spent 'sitting in' with local dance bands. Then, on 6 January 1943, he and the Battery set off by train from Bexhill for a destination that proved to be Liverpool docks. They boarded a black-painted ship that before the war had been the SS *Otranto*. So far it had all been a laugh, but now they were off to the real war. Without knowing why, Spike started to weep.

Left without its guard of Gunners, the De La Warr Pavilion at Bexhill-on-Sea was hit by an enemy bomb, which fortunately did not do much damage. Perhaps it was really a batter pudding.

4

WHOOSH-BANG!

It was soon evident that they were heading south – the climate was getting warmer – but there was still no news of where they were going. On 13 January 1943 they found themselves in a force nine gale. Men were vomiting everywhere, and with most people suffering from seasickness they all had to take turns on the anti-aircraft guns. The night Spike was on duty, one of the men was washed overboard. Next morning, they held a funeral service for him in the canteen. 'Poor bastard,' writes Spike. (*He's fallen in the water.*)

Then suddenly they were through the Straits of Gibraltar, and the gale was gone. The officers decided that some music would boost morale; whereupon Milligan, Edgington, Fildes and Kidgell confessed that they had disobeyed orders and smuggled their instruments on board, camouflaged among the stores. (Spike had his trumpet with him at all times – he thought it might come in handy should he ever be buried alive.) Now the four musicians went rummaging for the drum kit and Fildes's guitar among the guns in the hold, and that night they gave a barn-storming performance: 'We brought the roof down . . .'

At last they were told, over the ship's loudspeakers, the name of their destination. They were to land at Algiers, to be reinforcements for the First Army, and would be fighting alongside United States troops.

Disembarking at dawn, they marched through the palm-tree-lined, poverty-ridden streets of Algiers to a huge concrete stadium, where they spent a day and a night before setting off east along the coast road. Their destination was the mysteriously named Camp X, built to house German prisoners of war, which was to be their base until they were called into action.

Milligan and his friends were lucky to be allowed to drive there in lorries. Most of the men, softened by easy living on the sea voyage, had to march the twenty-six miles. One of them, Driver Reed, flaked out and tried to jump on a passing lorry, which was pulling a trailer, but he missed his footing and fell to his death between the two vehicles. (*Ye he he! Heuheuheuheuheu he! I've been deaded!*) Spike recalls that the only way to get his flattened remains off the roadway was by tugging at his straps.

At Camp X they practised route-marching, and were given a course in climbing tall obstructions, which became known as 'Leaping'. Milligan wrote a comic letter to his always sympathetic brother Desmond (on 29 January 1943) describing the 'Leaping' course, and suggesting that it could be introduced in civilian Britain to ensure physical fitness. For example 'Leaping Stones' could be installed in every doorway of the home. A 'Leapo-meter' would be fixed to all the family's ankles, measuring the number of leaps. Anyone not keen to leap would have an explosive charge fixed to the groin, which would detonate should they try climbing round the stone. And so on; embarrassing to read now, but he was beginning to forge some sort of humorous language.

He also started a comic newspaper at Camp X, carrying spoof war news, pinning it up outside his tent. It was called *Milli-News*, and he included a sample issue in his war memoirs. British Commandos (it alleged) had raided a mobile Italian laundry with their teeth blacked out. Chinese troops had been sighted with their eyes at the slope . . .

Again, spectacularly unfunny. And yet, in the laundry which advances like a fighting unit, there is a recognisable embryo of true Goon humour.

On 11 February orders were given for the move to the battlefront. They were heading for Tunis, to which Rommel had withdrawn following his defeat in October 1942 at the second Battle of El-Alamein. However, it is doubtful that many of Milligan's comrades could have come up with a summary of the tactical situation. Milligan quotes the puzzlement of a certain Gunner Woods: 'I don't understand, we're fighting *Germany* yet we're in *Africa* bloody miles from Germany.'

Milligan himself had a leisurely journey from Camp X to the battlefront, rolling (as he puts it) down to World War II at twenty-five miles an hour in a wireless truck. They were in country which revived his memory of boyhood readings of Rider Haggard. Overlooking them were the twin mountains of *King Solomon's Mines*, known (in Spike's phraseology) as 'Queen Sheba's Tits'.

There were now distant flashes of gunfire. Milligan felt strangely excited. It was teatime – the time at which, in civilian life, he would have been paralysed with boredom in his dead-end job at Woolwich Arsenal Dockyard. The foreman would be criticising the quality of his work, but he wouldn't care – his eyes would be glued to the clock, waiting for the hooter which would release the afternoon shift. Now, in North Africa, even if he got killed, it was better than that. (Though if he *did* get killed, he might change his mind about it.)

Reaching the outskirts of Tunis, they parked their wireless truck alongside the others in a *wadi* (dry river-bed). Living quarters were established, and, when evening fell, Milligan took out his trumpet and serenaded his comrades with 'Lili Marlene'. But it was not to be a peaceful night: the signallers had hardly gone to sleep than they were woken and sent to lay a telephone line, and Spike soon had his first taste of being under fire.

'WHOOSH-BANG!' is how he recalls the sound of the

shells. The first one caught him by surprise, with its flash of red-and-purple at the moment of explosion. He was so astonished that he walked over to where it had happened, to get a closer look – and suddenly, 'WHOOSH-BANG', another one landed right in front of him. He dropped the cable drum and made a one-person retreat.

His second day in battle, and, amazingly, he was still alive! Heavens, the enemy were bad shots!

Next to the *wadi* were living an Arab farmer and his family. Spike knew they were short of food, so he took them a tin or two of army rations, and amused the children by turning his handkerchief into a rabbit with wiggly ears. He was appalled by the damage inflicted by both the Germans and the Allies on the Arabs' homes and their livelihood. Many years later he told Dominic Behan: 'You couldn't believe that anybody could possibly survive such devastation; but young and old just stoically accepted that such desolation was an acceptable part of a poor person's life. They just buried another casualty and got on with it.' (This is a rare example of Spike empathising with other human beings – but then children always brought out the soft side of him.)

The signallers continued to lay and test lines, and were frequently shelled by the enemy. In a letter to his parents written on 18 March 1943, Spike claimed that he had been under more fire than anyone else in the Battery. Yet, despite the danger, he was enjoying himself. The life was good, especially if he stopped thinking about the future. After all, they were being paid, fed, clothed, and given plenty of travel – everything was being provided except women, and those they could dream about, free of charge.

He was promoted to Lance-Bombardier, and, towards the end of March, was among those billeted in an abandoned, bombed-out farmhouse with no roof. On what was left of the upper floor stood a piano. Harry Edgington and Spike, who as usual had his trumpet with him, headed for the instrument and performed a number together. They had scarcely finished when there came a horrendous sound – the tearing of the remaining floorboards, the crumbling of masonry, and then a vast crash, followed by voices swearing, and a musical twanging as the strings were struck by debris. It was a sound effect to die for.

On its sudden descent, the piano had only just missed one of the gunners, who had been shining his boots. It was the sort of thing that would happen to many a piano in the *Goon Show.* (Why *pianos*? Emblems of bourgeois stability, which become instruments of destruction – note the pun – in the world of Bloodnok and Bluebottle? There's material for a thesis here.)

The war, at least for Milligan, was settling into something of a familiar routine. However, one day the Battery Command Post suffered what seemed at first sight to be a direct hit from the enemy. In fact a shell from one of their own guns had exploded prematurely, with much loss of life. Then on 24 April 1943, a week after Spike's twenty-fifth birthday, he heard that Lieutenant Tony Goldsmith, who had encouraged him with his comedy writing, had been killed by a German mortar-bomb. Spike went back to the cave where he was sleeping, and wept, and called Goldsmith's name.

Goldsmith had died in the last serious fighting before Tunis fell to the Allies, who immediately gave chase to Rommel's retreating forces. Had this crowd of ragged British layabouts really beaten the mighty German army? They were given a heroes' welcome in Tunis.

While they were waiting for the next orders, Spike persuaded Fildes, Edgington and Kidgell to join him on a day trip to the ruins at Carthage, which he knew about from childhood reading of *Chambers' Encyclopaedia.* Another time, the four of them were booked by a local mayor to play for a *thé dansant*, at which what seemed like hundreds of gunners tried to dance with the only females – two girls and an elderly French matron. The band now had a bass-player, Gunner Douggan, a devout Catholic. 'Did you miss Mass?' he asked Milligan one Sunday, and received the reply: 'Not really.' (Repeat this carefully if you don't get the joke first time round.)

The band's reputation spread, and it was booked for an ambitious military variety show, to be called *Stand Easy*, which was recruiting performers from five regiments stationed between Tunis and Algiers. After the gunfire and the shelling, it was wonderful to be able to immerse them-selves once more in the music. By this time the band had achieved quite a professional standard. They were allocated several spots during the show, and Spike began to add some humour to their routine. He dressed up Doug Kidgell as a dwarf, and added a cello to the top of his own head, so that by comparison he looked gigantic. The two of them used to walk across the stage in the middle of someone else's act – it was (Spike emphasised) sheer lunacy, with no discernible reason behind it, absolutely meaningless, just like the war.

He remarks that, strangely, being under fire had released his inhibitions as a performer: 'It was as though everything that had been bottled up inside me suddenly started spilling over . . . It was all high-tension stuff, hysteria really, and ideas coming to me so fast and so many I could hardly contain them, or process them on the way out.'

*

Stand Easy ran for a week, then went on tour. It was such a success that rehearsals immediately began for a sequel, to be called *Stand Up*. Spike and the band were to get star billing. But news came of the Allied invasion of Sicily, and it was obvious that the Battery would soon find themselves on the Italian mainland. By mid-September 1943 they were on the move, sailing from Bizerte docks.

Arriving in 'sunny Salerno', they found the beach strewn with rubbish from a huge battle, and they could see hastily dug graves. Their task was establish gun positions in the mountainous country inland of Salerno, to which the enemy had withdrawn. But as they began to struggle up the narrow country lanes, they found themselves almost continuously under fire.

One moment Milligan was laughing. The next, he had collapsed and was vomiting. His head was spinning, and he was seeing stars – and, he claims, an upside down vision of the Virgin Mary. He was carted off to a doctor, who found that he had a temperature of 103.

An ambulance carried him to a military hospital, where he was told he had sand-fly fever. After a few days he was pronounced cured – or, as he puts it, ready to be killed again – but his Battery had moved on without him, and he found himself dumped in a field of tents called Corps Reinforcement Camp, which was largely populated by men suffering from shell-shock. One of them explained to him that it was a simple question of arithmetic. The longer you managed to remain alive in battle, the greater were the odds that you would be killed.

Life at this camp was very relaxed – Spike managed a sightseeing trip to Pompeii, which was only a few miles away – but he was told that there was no guarantee of his getting back to his own Battery, and this badly upset him. He wrote pleadingly to his commanding officer, Major Jenkins, and eventually a lorry arrived to fetch him.

Following a six-hour ride, he rejoined his comrades, in conditions very much like the First World War – trenches and mud (and mosquitoes) – and on many days they had to endure non-stop enemy fire. On 24 October 1943 Milligan wrote in his diary that he was feeling very nervous, couldn't eat a thing, and was thoroughly exhausted. What was wrong with him?

Absurdities abounded. A party of signallers, laboriously reeling in two miles of telephone line, eventually discovered that, at the other end, another battery was reeling it out. (In a 1955 *Goon Show*, 'The Sinking of Westminster Pier', Grytpype-Thynne and Moriarty are making a fortune from gullible Neddie Seagoon by pumping water out of the Thames – and are pouring it back into the river not far away.)

Meanwhile the mud was so awful that Major Jenkins ordered duckboards. They arrived, in pale wood, which would be an excellent marker for German planes looking for places to drop bombs; so orders were given for the men to cover them in mud. This was perhaps the best example they had yet experienced of the 'buggering about' which is so typical of war in all periods of history.

A Catholic priest made an appearance, offering Confession and Holy Communion. Milligan says that he nearly succumbed, but the war had begun to erode his belief in God. He found it impossible to square up all the killing by the Germans and the Allies with the fact that both of them claimed to be Christian civilisations.

By now, the Germans had retreated some distance, and the Battery was inching forward through the mud. Major Jenkins, unpopular with the men, turned out to have a clarinet. He played Schubert in his tent, and offered to teach Spike and the band some real tunes instead of 'that nigger music' (as he described jazz). The offer was not taken up.

The weather was so frightful that Alf Fildes complained that his guitar strings were going rusty, and Harry Edgington observed that the rain had been going on longer than Queen Victoria's. As they dug yet another trench, Edgington suggested that a fortune could be made by anyone who could invent and manufacture 'portable holes'. Spike seized on the idea and immediately turned it into a song, which suggested that such an invention would be useful to all soldiers, 'including the Poles' (who of course rhymed with 'holes').

He also invented a manic game to pass the time. Alf Fildes's diary described 'Milligan leading . . . his latest invention called "Drooling", a new game with effects on victims, who are pounced upon with verbal hoots and groans like gorillas. How mad we all are . . .' Spike writes of this that the cause of the game was sexual frustration. Players gave vent to a low groan, and pretended to grab huge imaginary erect phalluses, about five feet long, which they mimed banging repeatedly against the wall. Spike says that it was not unusual to come across entire gatherings of bored soldiers participating in this ritual.

What is one to make of the sexual element of this? It's both masturbatory and homo-erotic, yet at the same time also curiously sexless. There isn't really any sex in the *Goon Show*, apart from Bloodnok's implied goings-on, because the BBC was watching out for 'smut'; but if there had been, this is probably what it would have been like.

December 1943 found them still inching forward after the retreating Germans. Christmas Day was marked by a concert party compèred by Spike, and heavily featuring the band. He and the other performers were rewarded by four days' leave at the Rest Camp in Amalfi, on the coast near Salerno. In the town, Spike was able to find relief for his sexual frustration when they visited a brothel. He writes that he had never had sex with a prostitute, and being a Roman Catholic the thought of doing so horrified him. However, one of the girls took him into the next room and got to work. He liked it so much that he went back to her the following evening.

Early in January 1944, advancing towards Cassino, the Battery found themselves in a village in the foothills called Lauro, slightly inland from the coast to the north of Naples. By now, Spike had a terrible foreboding of his own death.

On 18 January there was a direct hit on their guns. The

ammunition blew up, setting light to the camouflage net covering the men, which fell on top of the trapped soldiers. Four died and six suffered serious burns. Spike was horrified by the sight of the incinerated corpses. For example, one little fellow, Gunner Musclewhite, had been killed while sitting up in bed. He was partially roasted, and his white teeth shone out of the black of his fleshless head.

Following hard upon this, Spike began to suffer from piles, a family ailment – both his father and his grandfather had been plagued by them. A medical officer put him down for forty-eight hours' bed-rest, but there was a serious shortage of men, and he stayed on duty in the Command Post, answering the telephone and looking after the wireless communications, for three nights without sleep. Then Major Jenkins told him to take four men with him to carry heavy batteries up a steep hill to an Observation Post.

As soon as they set out, the enemy began to shell them. *Crump, crump, crump!* went the mortars, and they threw themselves to the ground. The firing went on, and Spike decided to have a cigarette. He took out his packet of Woodbines, when suddenly there was a noise like thunder, right above his head, followed by a high-pitched whistle in his ears. He blacked out for a moment, and then quite literally saw red.

Deciding that if they stayed there they would all die, he started to scramble down the hill. Soon he was at the bottom: then he was speaking to Major Jenkins, who told him to get his wound dressed. Though he had not noticed it, he had been hit in his right leg.

That is how he describes it in the fourth volume of his war memoirs, *Mussolini: His Part in My Downfall*. Elsewhere, he recalls: 'The last thing I remember was counting my Woodbines . . . I thought, "Good place here. I'll have a lie down and a gasper", and the last thing I remember was thinking I'd five Woodbines when this tremendous noise came . . .'

5

Khaki Limbo

He was taken by ambulance to a dressing station where an orderly bandaged the wound – reassuring Milligan that it was only a small one – and gave him two small white pills and a bowl of hot, very sweet tea, which he couldn't hold for shaking. The pills made him drowsy.

He was helped back into an ambulance, and they drove off, soon passing through the British artillery lines as the guns were firing. Spike jumped at each bang, but – in a gesture he would always remember – a young soldier sitting next to him, who had one arm in a bloody sling, put the other around Spike's shoulder and tried to comfort him, telling him that everything would be all right.

They arrived at a camp, and Milligan was put to bed. He was brought more hot tea, and some more tablets, which swiftly knocked him unconscious. His career as an active soldier was over.

Waking in the early morning, he removed the dressing from his wound and examined it. It was no more than two inches long, and perhaps a quarter of an inch deep, rather like a razor slash. (In his later life, it would only be visible as a pale patch when he was sunburnt.) It wasn't doing him any harm, so why was he hospitalised?

The answer: he had been categorised as 'Battle Fatigue', and was to see a psychiatrist. He felt wretched, not least because he had been parted from his kit-bag, which contained his soap and towel. It was symbolic of his loss of personal identity – he had become just a number in the military hospital system. It's astonishing (he observes in his war memoirs) what simple things sustain our confidence in life.

The psychiatrist took a no-nonsense approach, telling him that 100,000 shells had to be fired before one soldier was killed. He concluded the session by barking at Milligan that he was *going to get better* – this was an order. No malingering.

A week later, Milligan rejoined the Battery. The first thing he noticed was the graves of those who had died in the fire. He felt deprived of all the energy and sense of fun that had carried him through the war so far – the main-spring that had driven him was broken. As soon as the Battery's own guns began to go off, he jumped. He tried to control himself, but gave up, and ran for shelter into his dug-out.

He found he was stammering. He knew Major Jenkins thought he was a coward. Perhaps he was; but if that was the case, why hadn't he tried to run away from the guns on his first day in North Africa? They put him on duty in the Command Post, although his medical discharge certificate said: 'This man must be rested behind the lines for a period to stabilise his condition.' He was also taking some more pills that they had given him. He guesses that they were early tranquillisers; all they did was make him into a zombie. (They were probably barbiturates, which also did duty as sleeping pills.)

Major Jenkins summoned him to his tent, for what felt like a court martial. Milligan was told he had been due for further promotion, but owing to his unreliable conduct he must now relinquish his Lance-Bombardier's stripe and revert to being plain Gunner. He guesses that in World War I, Jenkins would have had him shot.

By 10 February 1944 he was back in hospital, at Caserta, near Naples. All day long, he simply lay on his bed and read. There he saw another psychiatrist, and pleaded to be given something to do. In consequence he was posted to a rehabilitation centre north of Naples. This turned out to be a dreary muddy camp next to a small suburb which he says was called 'Afrigola'. It was actually Afragola; maybe Milligan made the error because he felt himself to be (as he puts it) 'frigging around in a sort of khaki limbo'.

Afragola camp was made up of 'loonies' and 'normals'. Following several medical boards, Spike was graded B2, which he says meant 'loony'. He was suffering from bleeding piles, and had developed a bad stammer. He and the other inmates were given sedatives, and that was all. Some of the medical officers believed that the patients merely needed to pull themselves together and get back to active service. Meanwhile they were virtually abandoned to their own devices.

Milligan was desperately glad to be away from the shelling. He worried constantly that he was behaving like a coward, but he knew that cowardice wasn't really the problem. True, though, other men were arriving at the camp in far worse conditions and with far worse experiences; some of them were crying or even screaming. Meanwhile, he writes, the food was helping the Allies to lose the war (he claims that the custard was transparent). Another inmate suggested that the cooks would be tried as war criminals.

A Sergeant Arnolds, who appeared to be running the camp, gave Milligan a job as reception clerk. He was told to sit in a tent at the entrance with a pile of blank army forms. As the 'PNs' (Psycho Neurotics) came in, he wrote down their details and put them in a file. He knew these forms would never even be looked at again, let alone serve any purpose.

At the end of February 1944 the Afragola inmates were moved *en bloc* (via a short stay in a Naples hospital) to Torre del Greco, a dusty village on the south side of Vesuvius. Some of the 'loonies' tried to climb the volcano. Spike wonders how many fell in.

Perhaps for this reason, within a few weeks they had been moved again, this time to a rehabilitation camp in the farming village of Baiano, north-east of Naples. Spike writes that he was now 'having recurring bouts of depression, just suddenly black, black gloom'.

In 1982, on BBC Radio 4's *In the Psychiatrist's Chair*, Anthony Clare discussed with Spike what appeared to be the beginnings of his manic depression, during these bleak weeks in the rehabilitation camps. Clare suggested that there were two versions of what had happened:

ANTHONY CLARE: At times, as I understand it, the story of you has a change in it – it's this bomb injury, the war injury, in Italy, where things are often described as having changed after it. But at other times it sounds as if you were always sensitive, always tense, always a rather anxious person?

MILLIGAN: Yes, to prove that I was a neurotic I just had to have that mechanism inside me tripped, and this mortar bomb blew me up and it did it.

This, Clare hinted, was a man who might have been unstable from the start. Milligan didn't deny it, but tied the two versions neatly together in an account of his mental history that somehow discouraged further investigation. (What about the suicidal grandmother? What about the child who lost his mother's sole attention with the birth of a sibling, when he was as much as seven years old?)

At Baiano, he was desperately missing his comrades in the Battery. He wrote Major Jenkins a sycophantic letter, asking to be given another chance in action. He begged Jenkins to let him get back to the regiment. He would do whatever Jenkins said, but please could he help him? Jenkins never replied, and Milligan noted that (during May 1944) he had three bad depressions.

Suddenly he heard that some of his mates from the Battery were on leave at Amalfi, just an hour away. He asked permission to go and see them, but the psychiatrist said that no patient was to leave the area of the camp. Depressed by this ruling, Spike went out and got drunk, came back and bolted the door of his hut, yelled abuse, and carried on drinking. Eventually he slashed his face with a razor blade, then fell asleep. He says it was done to draw attention to himself. The orderlies smashed down the door, and took him off to the sick bay. When he woke up, they gave him pills that sent him to sleep again.

Meanwhile he was still playing his trumpet. A Lance-Bombardier Reg Bennett, who had been in the North Africa stage show alongside Spike's band, and was sent to Baiano suffering from battle fatigue, wrote to Spike after the war, recalling how he was going insane with depression and boredom when one day he heard the sound of a trumpet coming from a tent. He recognised it as Spike, and sure enough, there was the fellow, lying on his bed, blowing for all he was worth.

Bennett recalled of his own psychological condition: 'I couldn't speak and I was twitching.' In comparison, Spike's mental state 'didn't seem as bad as me – he was still very sprightly and full of humour – but he was rather hysterical'.

*

In June 1944, five months after first being taken out of active service, Milligan was judged fit to be posted to an officers' rest camp at Portici, south of Naples, where he was to be receptionist and wine waiter in the Officers' Club, a Palladian villa in beautiful surroundings. He wrote to his mother that it was lovely and peaceful there.

He liked his job, and began to learn about wine, including the correct way to carry and serve a bottle (he would hold forth on this subject in later life). But he had scarcely settled in at Portici than he caught the attention of one of the club's members, Major Tony Clark, who invited him to be his personal driver, with his Lance-Bombardier's stripe restored. Clark was stationed at 'O2E' – short for 'GHQ Officers of the Second Echelon' – at Maddaloni, south of Naples, known familiarly as 'Mad and Lonely'. Milligan left Portici and was posted there, as a clerk-driver, on 8 August 1944.

Clark's interest in him was quickly explained. One evening, when Spike was driving him back to his billet, he put his hand up Spike's shorts. Spike briefly considered the possibility that this could mean promotion, but instead told Clark to 'fuck off, sir,' and received a hasty apology.

At first, Spike was miserable at O2E. But the place boasted a large dance-band, and he was soon enlisted by its leader, Sergeant Phil Phillips. He wrote to his mother on 30 August 1944 that he was now a member of this fifteen-piece ensemble. In his war memoirs he says that this gave a new meaning to life. The band played in all kinds of places, from smoky nightclubs to the splendid Palace of Caserta, the Allied Forces headquarters. They were even given their own rehearsal room, where they tried to learn the sophisticated dance-band arrangements they had bought from the Americans.

Around this time, Spike experienced chest pains, and was advised to give up the trumpet. Though he soon resumed it without ill effects, this may be why he took up the guitar again. He impressed the O2E bass-player, Lance-Bombardier Len Prosser, with his guitar-playing. Prosser wrote to Spike in 1975 that he remembered Spike's virtuoso single-string style, as he fooled around in the band-room – which was furnished with rugs and armchairs the men had stolen from places where they had been playing.

Spike was soon developing other talents besides music. He was enrolled in the painting of a huge mural (in a building that had been requisitioned as a bar), and when a drama group at O2E staged a play by Leon Gordon called *White Cargo*, Spike quickly put together a parody of it called *Black Baggage*. Similarly, when the drama group performed Mary Hayley Bell's *Men in Shadows*, Spike wrote a satire on it called *Men-in-Gitis*, staged a week later for a week's run. 'It was billed as "The Goons in Men-in-Gitis",' Len Prosser reminded him. 'That was my first contact with your "Goons" concept.'

Spike's own recollection was that he wrote *Men-in-Gitis* jointly with Prosser and Steve Lewis. (He believed it was the first such show, coming before *Black Baggage*.) The camp newspaper reviewed it, indicating that it was a sketch within an evening of music hall, rather than a full-length show. Describing it as the greatest success of the evening, the reviewer observed that some of the audience had hated it, but most had admired the achievements of '"Spike" Milligan' (as his name was given). The radio show *ITMA* was mentioned as an influence on the evening.

Spike himself described it as utter lunacy, with the play starting before the audience had arrived, the curtain ascending and descending throughout the performance, and the orchestra wandering around, demanding food, and tuning up at frequent intervals. Len Prosser made the acute observation that Spike's humour was closely linked with his aptitude at jazz. He (Prosser) had always been aware that dance-band and jazz musicians were endowed with an extraordinarily strong sense of humour – it was striking how many comedians, both British and American, had started life as musicians. The jazz saxophonist and club owner Ronnie Scott made this link too: 'Most musicians loved the *Goon Show* and they love Spike – he has their type of humour.'

The manic upswings which Spike seems to have been experiencing (as well as depressions) by the summer of 1944 probably played a part, too, in the creation of these shows at O2E. Ideas for them had begun to tumble out of him. It seemed that, until then, his imagination had been sleeping.

*

He remained at Maddaloni for most of 1945, becoming the star of the dance-band, which of course played on VE Night (8 May). They had never made such good music, claims Spike of that night. When their vocalist sang 'We're Gonna Get Lit Up When the Lights Go Up in London', it was like an anthem, with a great swell of voices coming from the dancers.

Spike realised that a surprising situation had come to pass: Hitler was dead, and he was alive. Moreover Britain now had a Labour government, though compared with Churchill the Labour prime minister Clement Attlee looked like an insurance clerk who suffered from constipation.

In October, Spike set off for three weeks' leave at home, travelling by train and Channel ferry. He spent much of it with Harry Edgington's parents in London, and took a pre-war girlfriend, 'Betty Cranley' (probably not her real name), to stay (as 'Mr and Mrs Cranley') at the Admiral Owen Inn in Sandwich.

He seemed to be reluctant to see his parents, not staying overnight with them until near the end of his leave. (Why? There hadn't been a rift. Maybe he feared that his mother would try to rein him in.) His brother Desmond was now in the 'Ox and Bucks' infantry regiment, and his father was back at Associated Press. With his parents, he talked about the future. Their line was that he should go back to the Woolwich Arsenal job, work hard, and wait for promotion. He pointed out that his workshop at Woolwich was now a bomb crater.

He writes that he now had a yearning for recognition. He didn't know what the recognition would be for, but he was certain that there was some goal in his life to be fulfilled.

It might possibly be as a painter – the experience of painting the mural had fired his interest in this direction – but on the whole it was as a musician, perhaps a composer.

Returning to Italy and uniform, as part of the Allied occupying forces, he was posted to the newly formed Central Pool of Artists (CPA) at Vomero near Naples. He alleges that the CPA had been recruited from soldiers who had been downgraded for health reasons. They were formed into concert parties and sent on tour to entertain the rest of the troops. In fact to be recruited to the CPA was a considerable compliment, a recognition of one's performing talents. The CPA was lavishly funded, with headquarters including rehearsal rooms, costume stores, a scenery dock and painting area, and a musical instrument store from which Spike helped himself to a guitar. He was mucking about with it, in the rehearsal room, when a tall cadaverous individual started to take an interest in what he was doing. This was Bill Hall.

Spike had suddenly met his match – or more – in terms of eccentricity and comic-musical talent. He describes Bill Hall as the double of Paganini, with identical dark and passionate eyes. Moreover, he played as well as Paganini – be it jazz or classical. But Hall was also a rebel, scruffily dressed, always unshaven, and already infected with the tuberculosis that would one day send him to his grave.

A surviving fragment of film of Hall playing the violin confirms everything that Spike has written about him. He was Irish, he ignored army discipline, and (according to Spike) he had been sent to the CPA with an apology note from his despairing regiment.

At his first encounter with Milligan, Hall took out his violin and began a crazy impersonation of a dreadfully bad musician trying to play 'Honeysuckle Rose', crossing his eyes, and putting on a fixed grin. Every note was superbly sharp or flat. To musicians, the joke was hysterical. Hall and Spike soon teamed up, with Spike on guitar, and they were joined by a Scottish bass-player named Johnny Mulgrew, who had played for Ambrose's dance-band before the war. The three of them sounded like the Hot Club de France. When they played, other musicians would stop and listen. They were soon booked for a show.

It was called *Over the Page*, and also in the cast was a soldier whom Spike described as 'someone from Mars, Gunner Secombe, H.'. The second Goon had arrived.

6

Screaming, chattering and farting

Milligan's first impression of the future Neddie Seagoon was of 'a little myopic blubber of fat from Wales', who 'spoke like a speeded-up record, no one understood him, he didn't even understand himself, in fact'.

Harry Donald Secombe, three years younger than Spike, had been born in a council house in Swansea in 1921. He was the third of four children of Fred Secombe, who had begun work in his uncle's barber shop when he was twelve, and later became a commercial traveller in a wholesale grocery firm. In his teens, Fred had shown considerable talent at drawing, and won a place at Swansea Art School, but he had to leave because his mother wanted him to earn a living and help support the family. Harry recalled him in later years entering cartoon competitions in one of the local papers.

There was plenty of music in the Secombe family. Harry's Uncle Cyril, an inspector on the Swansea buses, was an accomplished performer on the musical saw, while Harry's Aunt Margery played the piano in Woolworth's, demonstrating sheet music. Margery's husband George was a drummer and tap dancer, and Harry recalls how his paternal grandmother 'was the life and soul of many a social gathering when she put on my grandfather's working clothes and sang the old music hall songs'. With all these performers in the family, 'it seems pretty obvious how my theatrical ambitions began to take shape'. (Please note that I'm giving you almost more of Secombe's ancestry than Spike's. It's because I don't feel any obligation in the matter.)

Another influence was his time as a choirboy. 'From the

age of seven, when I first donned a cassock and surplice
. . . I was hooked on the church . . . I loved the hymns and
the ritual [but] wasn't so keen on the sermons.' When his
voice broke, he turned into a powerful tenor.

At school, he failed to distinguish himself either academ-
ically or at sport, and left in his mid-teens for a job as a
junior pay clerk in a colliery company. 'As time went by I
became the office clown. I was able to do impressions of
some of the staff . . .'

With the outbreak of war, he joined the Royal Artillery,
as it seemed less dangerous than the infantry, and was soon
given the chance to perform in an army variety show as an
impressionist, doing the comedians Stainless Stephen and
Sandy Powell, Stanley Holloway reciting 'Albert and the
Lion', and 'a falsetto rendering of a Deanna Durbin song
. . . I was always careful to blow a few raspberries in the
middle of it, just in case anyone got the wrong idea.'

Eventually, late in 1942, with the rank of lance-bombardier,
he found himself under fire in North Africa. One night –
or so the story goes – a big gun misbehaved, careering over
a cliff under which Secombe was sitting in a wireless truck:

The noise was quite terrifying and my first reaction was that if
the enemy had now taken to firing guns at us and not just shells,
it was about time we packed in the whole business . . . Suddenly
the canvas flap of the truck was swept aside and a dim face
appeared in the light of our paraffin lamp.

'Anybody seen a gun?' inquired the intruder.

'What colour?' we replied.

It was a certain Bombardier Milligan . . . At the time I had no
idea who he was, and it was only much later, when we were
discussing the North African campaign, that I realized it was he
who had lost the gun.

Rather more than a year later, Secombe was fighting in

Italy when he developed an inflammation of the bladder and kidneys. He spent five weeks in hospital, and was then posted to a convalescent depot where he began to perform in concert parties. He was still doing impersonations, but realised he needed new material. One morning:

I was shaving in a mirror . . . 'Come on, Secombe, hurry up,' [said one of the other men] 'I want to use that mirror.' I was slowly lathering my face [but then] began to shave at a maniacal speed, covering myself in lather as I did so. Bill Hall, a magnificent violinist, but as eccentric as they come and a notoriously bad audience, was lying on [his] bed . . . He burst into laughter at my antics, and I suddenly realized that I had the beginnings of an act.

Secombe's idea was quite simple, but nobody else seemed to have thought of it:

All I did was to demonstrate the way different people shaved. First was a small boy playing about with his father's shaving gear, then came a soldier doing his ablutions in a bucket of ice-cold water with a blunt blade . . . and I finished with an impression of a person who became embarrassed at being observed while shaving, which required me to drink the soapy water from the mug I'd been using . . . I closed with my version of Jeanette MacDonald and Nelson Eddy singing 'Sweethearts' as a duet – which included a fruity raspberry.

He began to use the raspberry as a kind of theme, blowing one every time he told a joke. 'It was really a desperate attempt to give myself the bird before the audience did.' In fact he was a great success, becoming the principal comedian in the Royal Artillery Training Depot show, which ensured he would not be sent back into action. When VE Day came, 'it was decided that because the show was so good, we ought to take it on tour . . . We were soon travelling around Italy . . .' By the time they reached Amalfi, Secombe had tentatively added some serious singing to his act: 'Previously I had sung only as a joke . . . but loosened by a few glasses of *vino rosso* I belted out a ballad or two, adding my raspberry.'

In the summer of 1945 recruiting began for the new Central Pool of Artists. Secombe and Bill Hall applied to join. 'We were both accepted.' So much for Spike's story that Bill Hall had been dumped on the CPA by a regiment that was desperate to get rid of him. Nor did Secombe describe the CPA as a bunch of battle-fatigued 'loonies': he rightly portrayed it as a troop of performers whose talents had been recognised by the military authorities.

Secombe claimed to have been present when the Bill Hall Trio formed itself: 'The effect was truly magical, and the rest of us . . . applauded in sheer delight as Bill Hall, Johnny Mulgrew and Spike Milligan began a musical partnership which was to last for a long time.' The trio and Secombe were assigned to a variety show to be called *Over the Page*, and Spike – who says he knew that just playing wouldn't be enough – worked out some comic patter to link the numbers.

Spike also persuaded the wardrobe to give the trio the most ragged costumes they could come up with. He had chosen to build on, rather than disguise, Bill Hall's scruffy, cadaverous appearance. It would make a very unusual comedy act: three ragged-looking tramps, but playing as sophisticatedly as the Hot Club de France. His own costume – a top hat worn over a shoulder-length wig, a black suit and a stand-up collar – made him look like a nineteenth-century undertaker with vampire tendencies.

A review of *Over the Page* in the forces' paper *Union Jack* on 12 December 1945 praised the show as 'something new in stage entertainment . . . Hit of the show in Naples so far has been Bill Hall's Trio . . . On Monday night they were called back for two encores, and exhibited an amazing ability for playing first-rate hot music in grand comedy style.' A later reviewer described the trio as 'an entire Spike Jones aggregation in miniature'. For example, when they played 'The Flight of the Bumblebee', a dummy bee appeared (on an invisible wire) and attacked Mulgrew, the bass-player. In another number, Hall and Mulgrew used their bows to play each other's instruments. The few moments of the trio that have been preserved on film show how accomplished and hilarious they were.

*

'I didn't know what to make of Spike at first,' writes Secombe, 'but when I discovered that it was he who had come looking for the 7.2 gun howitzer back in North Africa, we soon found that we had a lot in common.' Milligan was amazed by Secombe's shaving act. Secombe rushed onstage, chattering away, blowing raspberries, drenched with sweat as he lathered himself with shaving foam and started work at high speed with the razor. He would pause to give the audience only minimal guidance as to what it all meant. Then he launched into what Spike described as 'a screaming duet with himself', singing fortissimo in the manner of Nelson Eddy and Jeanette MacDonald. Finally he would give a cry of 'hup' and rush off-stage again.

Milligan noted that Secombe was just the same off-stage, a crazy powerhouse of nervous energy. He talked at an incomprehensibly high speed, interspersing his remarks with raspberries and fragments of songs. 'His record for staying in one place was three seconds.' When *Over the Page* moved to Rome, Secombe and Milligan shared a room. It was disastrous: Spike was tidy, Secombe was chaotic.

Secombe was now getting good notices too. The *Union Jack* reviewed *Over the Page* in Rome:

Rubber-panned, burlesquing Harry Secombe proved that he has a big and bright future ahead of him . . . He gave us his A.T.S.

officer, his voice-pill seller, his nervous man at a village concert and his western drummer in quick succession.

The hit of the night was Bill Hall's trio . . .

Life was good for all the CPA performers as they travelled around Italy: excellent hotels and food, free time all day, and the flattery of laughter and applause at night. But Bill Hall kept the other two members of the trio constantly on edge. Spike says that they never knew where he was or what he was doing. He would disappear immediately after the show, and not reappear until five minutes before the next one began. Sometimes Spike would have to go on stage without Hall even having arrived in the theatre. It was on these occasions that Spike began to tell jokes to the audience, just to keep things going.

*

The *Over the Page* tour continued, to Bologna, Florence, Bari, and the islands of Capri and Ischia. On the long journeys, Spike, Hall and Mulgrew sat at the back of the bus and discussed their future in England. They agreed to stick together and make their fortunes – considering how well they were going down with the audiences, how could they possibly fail? Spike also dreamed of opening a nightclub on the Thames.

Around June 1946, the Central Pool of Artists changed its name to Combined Services Entertainment. The trio were offered officer status and wages (£10 a week, plus food and accommodation) provided that – once they were demobbed from their regiment – they signed on to tour for another six months. They all said yes.

Secombe, who does not seem to have received such an offer, writes that he was demobbed in April 1946 and returned to Swansea. But Milligan's war memoirs describe him and Secombe meeting again in Rome, where Secombe said he would be released from the army in September, when he intended to audition for the Windmill Theatre in London.

Spike and the trio set off with a touring show called *Barbary Coast*, which included a petite, blue-eyed little dancer, scarcely larger than a doll. This was Marie Antoinette Pontani ('Fontana' in the war memoirs), known to everyone as Toni. She had been an understudy to the première ballerina at the Opera in Rome. 'She was so petite!' writes Spike. 'Five feet four inches.'

He began to woo her, jettisoning the persona of hormonally-driven Gunner Milligan, and turning into a nice boy called 'Terri'. When the show took them to Venice, they sat eating at an open-air table, and Spike looked across at Toni and said: 'I think I love you.' Toni shook her head – it wasn't good enough. 'When you are sure, you tell me again.'

Toni guarded her virtue carefully, and it was not until the tour of *Barbary Coast* reached Austria that she would allow the affair to be consummated. Years later, Spike wondered whether they should have got engaged. He guessed that if he had proposed to her, she would have accepted him. But at this stage of his life, he was still living from day to day, with no inclination to ruin things by planning further ahead.

In Vienna, he went to a party without Toni, and had sex with an Austrian woman. Toni immediately suspected something had happened. Since his Catholicism made him habituated to confession, Spike told her the whole story. She burst into tears and said she would never talk to him again. But she forgave him, and in Rome she introduced him to her mother and sister.

He took Toni on a week's holiday to Capri, then – with his commitment to the army fulfilled – said goodbye to her and sailed home from Naples to the UK on the SS *Dominion Monarch*. He was twenty-eight, and the war and its aftermath had taken up the years in which a career might have been forged. What on earth was in store for him now?

Part Two 1946—1960

Goon

7

Grafton's

The culture shock of his 1946 return from soldiering, and from being a star performer among his mates, was a little like the horrible 1933 arrival in England from India all over again. It meant saying farewell to the pleasurable companionship of the army, and to his assured position as a successful musician and comic. He had also fallen in love and experienced a passionate affair. Later, he felt, half seriously, that 1946 would have been the right time to die.

Meaning it to be a surprise homecoming, he arrived at his parents' latest cramped address, 3 Leathwell Road, Deptford – a terrace of workers' houses that backed on to a factory and a shunting yard – only to find that they were away. Eventually he persuaded the lodger, a Mrs Hicks, to let him in, and unpacked his things. His parents had a makeshift bedroom in the ground floor front room, and the only lavatory was in the garden.

After a night's sleep, he went in search of Bill Hall, who was living with his own parents in Highbury, and Johnny Mulgrew, who had found a room at 13 Linden Gardens, Notting Hill. The trio assembled for a cup of tea at the Lyon's Corner House in Coventry Street, and decided they must get an agent. They were seen and auditioned at Fosters, an agency in Piccadilly.

Meanwhile Harry Secombe was a step ahead of them, doing his shaving act at the tiny Windmill Theatre, a few yards from Piccadilly Circus, in one of the nude reviews that the Windmill had presented continuously during the war. 'He was the one with clothes on,' writes Spike. Secombe had been auditioned by the theatre's impresario, Vivian Van Damm, known throughout show business as 'VD', who (according to Secombe) had just turned down Norman Wisdom. Also appearing there was 'Professor' Jimmy Edwards, a former RAF pilot with a bushy air force-style handlebar moustache. Edwards had won a medal for great courage in the Battle of Arnhem, when he had piloted a troop transport plane through heavy enemy anti-aircraft fire, refusing to bale out and leave his men behind, and eventually crash-landing in flames. The moustache helped to hide the scars.

Edwards was a typical 1946 recruit to the variety stage. Harry Secombe writes:

The business was becoming swamped with returning ex-servicemen, who had had a taste of performing in army or RAF concert parties and were now, like myself, eager to try their luck in show business. People like Benny Hill, Tommy Cooper, Frankie Howerd, Max Bygraves, Norman Wisdom, Dick Emery, Eric Sykes . . .

Frankie Howerd could be seen at auditions, his long lugubrious face atop an ill-fitting 'demob suit' (supplied by the army to all personnel re-entering civilian life) as he introduced himself as 'Francis Howerd, spinster of this parish'. Much of his act consisted of innuendoes about his rather prim-looking accompanist: 'Poor thing, she can't help it! Well, I mean, all those hours sitting side-saddle on a piano stool . . .'

At the Windmill, Secombe found himself doing a gruelling six shows a day, six days a week, to an audience consisting of the proverbial men in dirty mackintoshes who were only there to see the nudes. Spike sat out front, in a free seat during a morning show, to see how the shaving act went down with these dingy voyeurs. He recalls that Secombe came on 'like a dynamo', carrying a table and his shaving kit, and was 'hypnotically funny – the energy could light a city.'

Without much hope, Spike himself auditioned for the Windmill; but Van Damm never gave him a chance to show what he could do. He had scarcely walked on stage and tried to raise a laugh by apologising for appearing fully dressed when Van Damm called: 'Thank you. Next please.'

Backstage, Secombe gave Spike a glimpse of the green room, where the bored girls lounged enticingly in their dressing-gowns. Between shows, Secombe would take Spike over to Allen's, a tiny first-floor bar in Windmill Street, where 'Poppa' Allen gave credit for drinks and meals, and the clientele included many of the ex-services comics and their writers. Secombe recalls drinking there with Alfred Marks, Norman Vaughan, the Australian actor Bill Kerr, Jimmy Edwards, the toweringly tall former RAF pair Frank Muir and Dennis Norden, and another Windmill comic, a young hopeful called Michael Bentine.

Secombe first set eyes on Bentine at a Windmill dress rehearsal. Bentine and a pianist named Tony Sherwood were doing a knockabout double act called 'Sherwood & Forrest'. Dressed a little like the Bill Hall Trio, in ancient frock coats and very tall and narrow black top hats, they recited an imaginary fairy story in 'cod' Russian, culminating in a wild boogie-woogie version of 'Black Eyes', with Bentine on the drums. 'My sides ached from laughing at their antics,' writes Secombe,

and I went backstage and introduced myself to them. Mike had already seen my shaving routine and congratulated me on my fresh approach to comedy. The two of us got on like wildfire and we were to spend many hysterical hours in Lyon's Corner House which, in those days, were open all night. We'd stay there till dawn talking about the things we'd like to do in the theatre.

A few months younger than Secombe, Michael Bentine was the son of an English mother and a Peruvian father, Adam Bentin, a pioneer of aerodynamics and aeronautics. Until Michael went on the stage professionally, he had spelled his surname the same way as his father. Michael had been educated at Eton, but the family was not wealthy; he claims that his school fees were paid out of his mother's winnings at bridge, and his father seems to have been more interested in holding spiritualist séances than supporting the family financially.

When war came, Michael joined the RAF, but a bungled inoculation left him unfit to be a pilot, and at twenty-one he became (so he claims) 'the youngest Intelligence officer in the Royal Air Force', attached to various Allied units. He had his share of comic wartime experiences, such as when the Germans complained that the Allies were violating the Geneva Convention by dropping metal cylinders containing foul-smelling chemicals. These were actually Elsan toilets, which the plane crews jettisoned when they became full, and after the German complaint an order went out banning 'this unorthodox secret weapon'.

Before the war, Bentine had sufficiently overcome a bad stammer to act in Robert Atkins's Shakespeare productions at the Regent's Park open-air theatre. Now, at the Windmill, Harry Secombe introduced him to a man Secombe had been raving about – Spike Milligan.

Bentine took to him at once. He recalls that Spike 'talked comedy like a recently released Trappist making up for six years' silence', and Bentine was captivated by this 'Irish streak of lightning'. Secombe speculated that Milligan was, for his part, slightly less enthusiastic about Bentine – this Old Etonian who had 'a whiff of the establishment' – but Bentine felt that any social differences were wiped out by a shared iconoclasm: 'The whole lot of us were deeply suspicious of authority and thoroughly sickened by what we had seen and been through [in the war], and we found our release in laughter.'

Having finished his Windmill engagement in the closing weeks of 1946, Secombe was without regular work, and signed on at the labour exchange. It was embarrassing meeting old army friends in the dole queue, but he began to pick up some nightclub jobs. Generously, he also helped the Bill Hall Trio to get some club work. The first date he found for them was at the Florida in Carnaby Street; Spike says it was about the size of six phone-boxes, and the band-stand was little bigger than a serving hatch.

Soon they were being booked by the Blue Lagoon, the Panama, and the Coconut Grove. On the strength of these earnings, Spike moved out of his parents' house and into 13 Linden Gardens, where Johnny Mulgrew was living. Spike writes that the previous occupant of his room had been Neville Heath, who had just been hanged for the sadistic killing of two women.

*

By May 1947 the Bill Hall Trio was beginning to get dates outside London. That month, they played Blackpool. On the seafront they were approached by an elderly man, who gave his name as Colonel Stanley Rowlands, ex-Indian Army. Spike was greatly taken with his rich voice – and a touch of the con man. 'This was the nearest I was ever to get to Major Bloodnok.' The colonel suggested a drink; then, in the pub: 'Forgotten me wallet.' They let him watch their act from the wings. He shouted: 'Bravo! Bravo! These boys were at Cassino', and they dragged him on to take a bow, which he happily did. Spike kept in touch with him until he died in 1958.

After Blackpool came bookings for the trio in Glasgow and Dublin – Spike's first visit to Ireland. He had never heard such wonderful conversation in all his life; loyally, he writes that they all talked like his father. He could have stayed for ever.

The trio's agent got them a booking on the BBC's rather low-key television service. The live broadcast, from Alexandra Palace in north London, was in black and white, but for some technical reason they had to wear green make-up. Few people in Britain had bought television sets as yet, and the trio's TV appearance did little to increase their reputation. At the Hackney Empire for a week, they mostly played to empty houses. Spike remembers the sound of a single pair of hands clapping. Desperately, he ad-libbed: 'Please sir, you're spoiling it for the other people.' This earned the only laugh of the night.

There was work available overseas: Harry Secombe went on a Combined Services Entertainment tour of Germany, while the trio performed in Zurich, and even went back briefly to Italy, where Spike met up with Toni; but her behaviour was distant, and she told him she felt his life had 'no *stabilità* – no stability'. This was not altogether fair – the trio was busy, and earning good money – but Spike admits he had become 'a mess of contradictions'. Before returning to Italy he had still thought of marrying Toni, but he was having affairs with girls he met on tour with the trio. He writes that he still wanted to play the trumpet, but he was a pre-war swing trumpeter in style, whereas these days jazz was being taken over by 'Bop'. He liked modern jazz, but he couldn't play it.

Also, the big bands in which he loved playing were disappearing. Indeed music itself was no longer a good place to earn a living. Talented people of all kinds were going into radio. Everyone was listening to the 'wireless', especially the comedy shows; yet most of these were old-fashioned and devoid of experiment.

Comedy historian Roger Wilmut notes that until the late 1930s the BBC's radio comedy performers had been drawn entirely from music hall and variety shows: 'Well-known comedians . . . did versions of their acts suitably modified for radio . . . in programmes constructed on the lines of a music hall bill.' A breakthrough had come in 1938 with *Band Wagon*, starring Arthur Askey and Richard Murdoch as a pair of friends who shared a flat on top of Broadcasting House. 'A large section of the public took this quite seriously,' writes Wilmut, 'and the fan-mail to this mythical address was enormous.'

Band Wagon was closely followed by *ITMA* (short for *It's That Man Again*), which began in July 1939 and ran throughout the war until its star Tommy Handley's death in January 1949, 'each show having a vague plot,' writes Wilmut, 'interrupted by two musical items' – which became the standard format for post-war BBC radio variety shows, including the Goons and *Take It From Here* (1948–58).[1] Moreover the humour in *ITMA* was (as Wilmut points out) derived from the same dramatic device that Milligan would later use. Like Neddie Seagoon, Tommy Handley tended to remain 'on-stage' throughout the plot, as the essentially sane central character around whom the eccentric goings-on revolved. Handley's 'normal' persona was contrasted with the string of various caricature-type individuals, who upon arrival always introduced themselves with their own catchphrases, the best-remembered being the charlady Mrs Mop's 'Can I do you now, sir?' and the saloon bar soldier Colonel Chinstrap's 'I don't mind if I do' when he believes he is being offered a drink. Jack Train, who played Chinstrap in *ITMA*, occasionally

---

[1] Written by Frank Muir and Dennis Norden, and starring Jimmy Edwards, Dick Bentley and Joy Nichols (later June Whitfield), this was the only radio comedy show of the period to rival the Goons in the sophistication of its humour (its mini-sitcom about the dysfunctional Glum family has never been surpassed).

appeared in the *Goon Show*, and always sounded perfectly at home there.

Nevertheless Milligan was contemptuous of what he regarded as the unsophisticated level of humour in *ITMA*. 'Heard *ITMA* on Radio this evening,' he wrote in his diary in January 1944. 'Corny bastards.' In his war memoirs he refers to it as '*ITMA* which, I am afraid, I didn't find funny (my humour was more Marx Brothers and W.C. Fields)'.

He praises what he calls the 'sideways' humour of the Marx Brothers, giving as an example a scene where Groucho is wooing Margaret Dumont, and there is a knock on the door:

And she says: 'Oh, that's my husband!' So Groucho says: 'What'll I do?' 'Duck behind the couch.' So he goes behind the couch, the husband comes in, Groucho stands up and says: 'There are no ducks behind this couch.' I thought that was a hysterical joke for that time, and that sort of humour drove me mad.

The BBC had developed its own radio comedy show in the Marx Brothers style. Called *Danger – Men at Work*, it ran for four series in 1939–40, with a post-war revival in 1946–7. Its regular characters included a Margaret Dumont figure called Mrs Ponsonby, who was the uncomprehending butt of Groucho-like insults, and there were musical interludes from a swing-style big band. Listened to today, the show sounds like a poor imitation of the Marx Brothers' films; but Spike identifies it as an important influence on him: '*Men at Work* was one that grabbed me. It's forgotten now, but it was what put the *Goon Show* on the road. *Men at Work* were [sic] ignoring logic and for me it worked, but nobody seemed to notice it.'

Two other humorists who influenced him worked on the printed page rather than in radio. For half a century J.B. Morton (1893–1979) contributed a humorous column called

'By the Way' to the *Daily Express*, under the pseudonym 'Beachcomber', creating such comic archetypes as the crazy inventor Dr Strabismus (Whom God Preserve) of Utrecht, the con-man Captain Foulenough, and pedantic Mr Justice Cocklecarrot, who is forever trying to restore order to a courtroom that has been taken over by a dozen red-bearded dwarfs. When Milligan was about to play Beachcomber on television in 1968, he emphasised: 'I'm a long-time fan of his. When I was a kid my brother and I used to clip Beachcomber cuttings from the paper, and act out the episodes . . . Bloodnok . . . was based on Captain Foulenough.'

Eric Sykes identifies another author whose work influenced the creation of the Goons: 'Spike used to enjoy reading books by a Canadian writer called Stephen Leacock. The way the books were written, they were almost like *Goon Shows* and I think he had a great influence on Spike.' The comedy writers Alan Simpson and Ray Galton agree:

ALAN SIMPSON: It was Spike who introduced us to Stephen Leacock, whom he loved. Leacock is one of the few authors who've made me laugh out loud when reading him.

RAY GALTON: What Spike got from Leacock was lines like 'He jumped on his horse and rode off in all directions.'

ALAN SIMPSON: And they were wonderful stories about people. 'The Rival Churches', for example.

Leacock (1869–1944) combined nonsense and satire. The story that Simpson mentions (from Leacock's *Arcadian Adventures with the Idle Rich*) is a wry comedy about two neighbouring churches in a big city, one wealthy, with a worldly minded rector, the other dingy and in the hands of a dreary preacher. There is little obvious affinity with Milligan; on the other hand Leacock's novel *Moonbeams from the Larger Lunacy* has a thoroughly Goonish opening paragraph:

Readers are requested to note that this novel has taken our special prize of a cheque for a thousand guineas. This alone guarantees for all intelligent readers a palpitating interest in every line of it. Among the thousands of MSS. which reached us – many of them coming in carts early in the morning, and moving in a dense phalanx, indistinguishable from the Covent Garden Market wagons; others pouring down our coal-chute during the working hours of the day; and others again being slipped surreptitiously into our letter-box by pale, timid girls, scarcely more than children, after nightfall (in fact many of them came in their night-gowns) – this manuscript alone was the sole one – in fact the only one – to receive the prize of a cheque of a thousand guineas.

*

While Milligan was listening to the radio, Secombe was managing to break into it and get some BBC work. He writes that, in June 1947:

I passed an audition for *Variety Bandbox* . . . the really big radio comedy show of the time, with people like Frankie Howerd and Derek Roy alternating as resident comedians . . . I can't remember exactly what I did for my first 'Bandbox', but I know that part of it was a rather wicked take-off of someone doing animal impersonations.

During the following twelve months, Secombe grew steadily more successful on the theatrical circuit, and began to be a popular choice for BBC radio comedy producers. The shaving act had finally been put to rest, but he still 'never considered singing seriously', and was in search of new material:

The most important item in my new itinerary for success was to find a good scriptwriter. Michael Bentine was very generous with ideas for some of the *Variety Bandbox* broadcasts I was [now] getting on a semi-regular basis, but he was busy making a career for himself. The problem was solved one lunch-time when Michael took me to a pub he knew in Victoria. It was known as Grafton's.

This pub – a tall, early nineteenth-century building in Strutton Ground just off Victoria Street – was officially the King's Arms, and is now called Finnegan's [*sic*] Wake. A few framed photos of the Goons, displayed in an alcove off the bar, commemorate their association with Jimmy Grafton, and the enormous part he was to play in launching them.

The hostelry had been kept by the Grafton family since 1848. Secombe notes that during the war Jimmy Grafton 'had been a Major in the Beds & Herts, [and] had played a vital part in the relief of Arnhem'. Michael Bentine supplies a little more detail: 'Demobbed at the same time as the rest of us, Major James Grafton, MC . . . "The Major" . . . as we called this urbane and clever man . . . had been one of the two brave men who had swum the Meuse River, to bring news of the rescue operation to the beleaguered paratroops at Arnhem.'

Grafton himself explains that, like so many people, he had first become involved with comedy during army days:

In 1946, newly demobilised from the army, with a wife and two small children to support, I had launched myself on the dual career of pub licensee and radio script-writer; the first to keep a roof over our heads, the second to fulfil an urge that had already impelled me to write shows for the entertainment of my unit while awaiting demob.

He was soon successful, being engaged by the BBC to write Derek Roy's material for *Variety Bandbox*. Then Harry Secombe hired him as his scriptwriter and manager.

Meanwhile Grafton – who also found time to be a Conservative city councillor for Westminster – and his wife Dorothy were generous with free meals for struggling performers. They were soon feeding Spike.

Grafton describes his first impression of Spike as 'a slim, good-looking young man, whose air of slight melancholy could suddenly erupt into manic glee, often ending in . . . tearful hysteria . . .'. Spike's mania was genuine, but Michael Bentine was developing an artificially manic personality as a comic. He had parted from Tony Sherwood, and after making a success with an act in which he broke a chair into strange shapes (which shows how desperate all these new comics were for original material), he had developed a successful stage persona as a mad professor, with a wild mop of hair and beard. This got him on to the bill at the Palladium.

'Bushy-haired and bearded,' Jimmy Grafton writes of Bentine, 'he . . . had the most lunatic appearance [of the four future Goons].' Meanwhile, after hours in the Grafton Arms, Spike would sit moodily at the pub's piano, ignoring everyone else, and letting them ignore him. Suddenly he would cheer up, abandon the piano, and join in the joking with Secombe and Bentine – with Grafton providing drinks; 'he was a shrewd man and he sensed we had something . . .'

Spike's jokes were often unconventional: 'I'd sit in Jimmy Grafton's bar and test my routines on the drinkers. They never laughed. Not once. That's when I knew I was out on a limb.' He adds: 'I think I was the first not to think in terms of punchlines or even jokes.'

When not on tour with the trio, he was usually to be found at Grafton's in the evenings, while in the daytime he would hang around with Bentine and Secombe, watching cartoons in the news cinemas, amusing them with his mad ideas. 'I was writing things on paper with no object in mind;

I'd joke a lot with Secombe.' Soon, as Bentine described it, they were joined by a fourth would-be comic, 'the youthful and then plump Peter Sellers'.

8

I live in an attic

Spike recalls that he first met Peter Sellers at Hackney Empire when Harry Secombe was appearing there. Michael Bentine introduced them in the bar; Sellers (writes Milligan) 'was "spraunced" up, felt trilby, gloves, Dick Barton collar-up mackintosh. As usual, Mike did most of the talking. That's all I remember of the occasion.'

Elsewhere he adds: 'Peter wanted to look like a male model – posh suit, posh collar and tie, mackintosh, gloves he carried in his left hand – oh, and a trilby hat. He was very softly spoken – I thought I was going deaf!'

Spike also alleges that Sellers 'didn't buy a bloody drink all night . . . Harry, on the other hand, spent his entire night's takings on alcohol for me and Peter.'

There are seven books by Milligan about his life in the 1940s alone; Secombe has left two volumes of memoirs, and Bentine wrote a self-portrait, *The Long Banana Skin*. Alone of the four original Goons, Sellers never indulged in an auto-biography. This was entirely in keeping with his apparent conviction that he had no concept of his own identity. 'I have no personality of my own,' he is quoted as saying, in the introduction to Roger Lewis's biography of him. 'I have no concrete image of myself . . . When I'm doing a role I feel it's the *role* doing the role, if you know what I mean . . . There used to be a me, but I had it surgically removed.'

Lewis, however, quotes this only to question its truth, and to suggest that Sellers's apparent conviction of his non-existence was actually a shrewd strategy which allowed him to duck out of personal responsibilities. Lewis accuses Sellers of being, in reality, a 'moral amnesiac' whose claim that he only existed when he was acting was 'a convenient and complicated fiction' that allowed him to 'detach himself from the consequences of his bad behaviour'.

Milligan never took sides in this argument, but when talking to Lewis about Sellers (long after Sellers's death) he did suggest that his fellow Goon had lacked a certain kind of humanity. 'Milligan thinks it indicative,' writes Lewis, 'that he never saw Sellers enjoy a hearth or home. He never put a kettle on and made a cup of tea; he'd never "sit round a fireplace – all those primitive tribal things that give each of us a sense of ordinariness and order. They seemed to be denied to him. He *had* no fireplace."'

Lewis's own opinion is that Sellers had little chance of normality, because he had begun life as a drastically spoilt only child, whose doting mother never reprimanded him. 'It doesn't take a nano-second for children to learn how much they can get away with,' writes Lewis, 'and Sellers was no exception.' This maybe explains the adult Sellers's astonishing self-confidence as a performer. 'Of the four of us,' writes Secombe, 'he was the most nerveless. I don't think that I ever saw him show any kind of nervousness about performing before an audience. He was always completely in command of himself and was never afraid to experiment.'

Jimmy Grafton, on the other hand, portrays the nastier side of Sellers's self-confidence, describing how one day (when Sellers had become a household name) they were walking together along Victoria Street and Sellers spotted a jacket and trousers of cavalry twill in the window of an outfitter. He immediately decided that he must have it, but on enquiring within was told that his size was not in stock.

Peter was annoyed. 'How dare you put something in the window that you can't supply?' he demanded. The manager apologized.

'We could get one for you from another branch, sir.' 'When?' 'By tomorrow, perhaps.'

By now Peter was well into an involuntary impression of an outraged customer. 'I don't want it tomorrow. I want it now.' 'Perhaps by this afternoon, sir?' 'No thank you. You've already wasted enough of my time. Good day.'

Elsewhere in this portrait of Sellers (in *The Goon Show Companion*) Grafton claims that he was 'the only member of the Goons with a show-business background', which is true only if one treats Leo and Flo Milligan as amateurs. But certainly Sellers had a 'born in a trunk' upbringing. His maternal grandmother, whose surname was Mendoza and whose Sephardic Jewish ancestors had been permitted to put down roots in London by Oliver Cromwell, owned a touring theatre company specialising in glamorous musical revues. She used the stage name 'Belle Ray', and her daughter Peg – Peter Sellers's doting mother – sang solo numbers and took part in sketches. The show featured a water-tank in which the chorus girls frolicked, dressed (or undressed) as mermaids, and Peter liked to claim that one night – 'at Huddersfield I think it was' – the tank had burst asunder, swamping the orchestra pit. He would mime the trombonists using their instruments as snorkels: 'Several were drowned. Seriously drowned.'

He was younger than the other Goons – born in 1925, seven years after Milligan – and only half-Jewish, because Peg had married a Yorkshire gentile musician called Bill Sellars (*sic*). In fact the couple had already produced a baby son, named Peter, but he had died in infancy. The second child was officially named Richard Henry, but his parents, still mourning, began to call him by the dead child's name. Meanwhile the surname, like Michael Bentine's, went through a change of spelling (probably accidentally, on a poster); so that 'Richard Henry Sellars' became 'Peter Sellers'.

He was educated at a Catholic boys' school in north

London – an odd choice; but then Milligan told Roger Lewis that Peg Sellers 'disregarded her religion – a lost Jewess – when she married Bill; and Peter was haunted by the uncertainty of his religion, and who he was, and he never found out.' Lewis observes that the Jewish characters whom Sellers played on the *Goon Show* were 'oy-vay caricatures, with names like Geraldo or Izzy', as if this were the only way he could approach his own Jewishness.

At school, he was just an average pupil in everything but his size. One of his teachers recalled that, although he was only ten when he joined the school, 'he looked more like fourteen'. And by the time he had reached fourteen, in September 1939, Peg had taken him out of school and evacuated the family to Ilfracombe on the north Devon coast, a Victorian seaside resort which Roger Lewis saw as 'Henry Crun's backdrop in the *Goon Show*'. Here, the teenage Sellers made ten shillings a week as odd-job man at the Victoria Pavilion, a theatre-cum-concert-hall, and developed a fixation with playing the drums. After some tuition from a local percussionist, he was hired by the local dance combo, the Goonish-sounding Waldini and His Gypsy Band.

Like Spike, he had a mother who fussed if his band gigs kept him out late. He recalls how, on one of his first dates with girls, he impressed the young lady by impersonating a film star – but then gave away how much he was still under the maternal thumb:

I remember I could say the word 'because' like Robert Donat – the only word I could say [in Donat's voice], so I fiddled the others so that 'because' came in the middle. I relied on the 'because' very strongly. She was very impressed, and she said, 'More!' and I said, '*Because!*' again! I remember I was kissing her goodnight. I said, 'Well, I have to go now, dear, *because –*' [*breaking into Bluebottle*], 'Because my mother says I have to go home.'

The Donat impersonation was just one from the gallery of voices that he was now developing. 'He would be in one room,' recalled a member of the Waldini band, 'and you'd be in the next, and you'd think the radio was on.' A London schoolfriend agreed: 'He was mad about the radio – he could do all the voices.' Roger Lewis suggests that one reason Sellers liked to slip into other identities was to escape from his own plain and stout physique.

Not until he had turned eighteen (in September 1943), and was called up into the RAF, did Sellers realise that doing impersonations might be more rewarding than gigging with dance-bands. He applied to take part in one of the Ralph Reader Gang Shows that the RAF Entertainment Division sent out, explaining that he played the drums and could 'do some bits of ITMA' – that is, impersonate the cast of the Tommy Handley show. Reader, who was taking the auditions himself, happened to overhear his own voice being mimicked so skilfully by Sellers that he gave him a ten-minute spot in the show, to do a one-man mini-*ITMA*, as well as having him play the drums in the show's band.

RAF Gang Show Unit Number 10 toured the Hebrides and the Orkneys before beginning its foreign travels. By the end of 1944 it was in Calcutta, and Sellers was mimicking his way into the officers' mess with the aid of uniforms from the show's costume basket:

Once I was a Sikh Officer. Once . . . I dressed up as an Air Commodore . . . I put a bit of grey on the sides of my hair, it must have been too obvious for words – but it was Christmas Eve, everybody was blind drunk, otherwise I should never have got away with it. I actually got talking to an Air Vice-Marshal . . . Even to me this seemed to be pushing my luck a bit far, for I was barely nineteen.

Sellers was demobbed in 1946 with a note from his wing

commander: 'The above-named is strongly recommended for any work with entertainment.' But at first he could only get drumming gigs; and when eventually he was booked as a comic for a week at Peterborough, he was booed off the stage and advised by the management to give up and go home.

In the circumstances it seemed like bravado to audition for the Windmill. Nevertheless Van Damm liked his act (which still included *ITMA* impersonations) and engaged him for six weeks, in March and April 1948. While there, he was spotted by a BBC radio comedy producer, Dennis Main Wilson, who gave him an audition which was reasonably successful. However, Sellers has claimed that he managed to queue-jump and get his first broadcast as soon as July 1948 by telephoning one of the producers and impersonating radio star Kenneth Horne, in whose voice he gave himself a superb testimonial: 'Listen, Roy, Dickie and I were at a cabaret the other night, saw an amazing young fellow called . . . what was his name? Sellers, Peter Sellers.'

Once he had proved his skills at the microphone, the BBC comedy producers were tumbling over each other to include him in such shows as *Workers' Playtime* and Ted Ray's *Ray's a Laugh*. Within eighteen months of his first broadcast he became one of the most ubiquitous performers in the BBC's variety output, not only impersonating the famous but also creating his own characters. However, as his BBC audition panel had noted, his material rarely equalled his talents; which was one reason why he was glad to join the gang that hung around Grafton's.

Not surprisingly, the precise where-and-when of Sellers being added to the Milligan-Secombe-Bentine group has become lost with the passing of time; but a crucial link was clearly a radio series called *Third Division*, recorded towards the end of 1948 and transmitted in January and February 1949. Describing itself as 'an experimental series of six humorous programmes produced by Pat Dixon',[1] it was broadcast on the usually deeply serious Third Programme, and was written by Frank Muir and Dennis Norden, who were already creating *Take It From Here* for the Light Programme. The cast included Secombe, Bentine and Sellers, and among the sketches was a solo for Sellers, 'Balham, Gateway to the South', which he later repeated on his LP *The Best of Sellers*.

Frank Muir said there was actually nothing experimental about *Third Division*: 'it was what we were doing all the time' (he meant sophisticated upper-middle-class wit rather than end-of-the-pier gags), and he added: 'There's no such thing as "experimental humour". You can try things, but you can't say, "I don't care whether people like it or not – I'm working up to something."' Yet this was exactly what Milligan was brewing at Grafton's pub;[2] and Sellers now became one of the ingredients.

*

'He could perform *wonders* with lines I wrote,' Milligan said of Sellers, forty years after their experimental sessions at Grafton's. Unfortunately no trace remains of what these lines may have been. It isn't even certain whether, at this stage, Milligan was doing the writing for the future Goons, or even if there was any writing to be done, as opposed to

---

[1] Dixon had already produced, in the summer of 1948, *Listen, My Children*, which ran for eight weeks on the BBC Home Service. The cast included Harry Secombe. Roger Wilmut writes of it: 'There were no regular characters, no catchphrases, and no studio audiences. The sketches were witty, often with a satirical edge . . .'

[2] Though Milligan recalls that he and Sellers first met backstage at the Hackney Empire, Secombe believed it was at Grafton's: 'I had a radio series with Pat Dixon . . . *Third Division* . . . Pat had gathered around him a team which [included] Michael Bentine and Peter Sellers . . . Naturally Mike and I took Peter along to Grafton's.'

mere ad-lib tomfoolery for the entertainment of whoever
was propping up the bar alongside them. The latter would
seem far more likely, were it not for a press cutting from
the *Evening News*, quoted by Alfred Draper in *The Story
of the Goons* (1976), who unfortunately omits to give the
date, though one would guess it to be *circa* 1949–50:

Four young men are planning to form a new 'crazy gang' when
they have made even bigger names for themselves as single acts.
Already they have formed themselves into what they call the Goon
Club and meet regularly at a pub in Victoria, with a strange ritual
and a handshake all their own. Soon they will have a club badge
– a humanized peanut.

The handshake and peanut sound more like Spike's faintly
homo-erotic army form of Goonery – clubbing each other
on the head and waving imaginary giant phalluses – than
the world of Bluebottle and Eccles; as does Harry Secombe's
recollection that Jimmy Grafton, acting as script editor for
the 'excesses' of their ideas, became nicknamed 'KOGVOS',
standing for 'Keeper Of Goons and Voice Of Sanity'.

If, as seems likely, Grafton was responsible for the *Evening
News* item (the pub isn't named, but its identification must
have spread, and can have done business no harm), it was
certainly he who pushed the incipient Goons up on to the
next rung of the showbiz ladder. Grafton writes that, by the
spring of 1949,

it seemed to me that we had the ammunition needed to fire our
ideas at the BBC . . . Peter Sellers, the most advanced in his radio
career, obviously had to be the figurehead. To accommodate the
zany characters of the others, Spike and I chose as a setting a
ramshackle castle owned by 'the twenty-second (FX: SHOT.
SCREAM), I beg your pardon, the twenty-*third* Lord Sellers'.

Grafton is talking about what we would today call a pilot; in 1949 the term was 'trial recording'. Evidently there was a script of some sort, very likely written jointly by Grafton and Milligan, with contributions from the others. There were parts for all – indeed, for more people than just the four core Goons (Bentine, Milligan, Secombe and Sellers). Alfred Marks was cast as an impresario with a singing protégé (Secombe), and Janet Brown, Peter Butterworth and Robert Moreton made appearances. Roger Lewis describes the totality of *Sellers' Castle*, as the recording was called, as 'a sort of Addams family – with Milligan's Eccles as the servant, Bentine as a mad inventor locked in the dungeons, Secombe as a wandering minstrel and Sellers as Crun-cum-Bloodnok, the reigning Lord of Misrule.'

Grafton confirmed that Spike's role was an early incarnation of Eccles, with at least one joke in what would become the classic Goon formula, mixing the absurd with a good old-fashioned pun: 'craziness and corn', as Grafton put it. 'Who are you?' someone asks, and the Eccles-like character responds, in his goofy voice: 'I'm a serf.' 'What's that man doing on your back?' 'Da – serf-riding.'

Rather than try to persuade the BBC to make the disc of *Sellers' Castle* (tape recorders were still rare, though prototypes had been looted from the Germans), Grafton hired a commercial recording studio, on 26 April 1949. To give the product a BBC flavour, he recruited a wartime colleague who was now one of the corporation's announcers, Andrew Timothy (known as 'Tim'), to read the links between scenes. Grafton sent the completed recording to one of his contacts in the BBC Variety Department, producer Roy Speer.

The results were initially exciting. Speer was sufficiently impressed to recommend to his colleagues that they commission a series. As a necessary preliminary, an in-house 'trial recording' now took place – maybe a re-make of *Sellers' Castle*, though this is speculation. Unfortunately the producer in charge of it was one of Variety's odder denizens, Jacques Brown, who had been a key figure in *Danger – Men at Work* (the mock-Marx Brothers series). According to Grafton, Brown 'had a bee in his bonnet . . . He insisted that it should not be necessary to use a studio audience.' (*Danger – Men at Work* had none.) But the Goons needed the cushion of audible laughter, and the audience-less 'trial' was rejected by the BBC planners as 'too crazy'. Andrew Timothy had not been impressed by it either: 'I didn't think it was the least bit funny.' (He was still saying this about the *Goon Show* more than twenty years later.)

*

So, for the time being, Spike and the others had to shelve the Goons. It must have been a difficult time, at least for Spike, easily the least successful of the four, who would have pinned considerable hopes on that trial recording.

He had now had enough of the Bill Hall Trio, and handed in his resignation. Hall could be venomous as well as funny. Furious at what he saw as desertion, he told Spike: 'I hope you never get another fucking job again!'

Once again it was Jimmy Grafton who helped, fixing Spike up with a place in the two-guitars-and-vocalist Ann Lenner Trio (she had been Carroll Gibbons's vocalist at the Savoy). This got him a certain amount of work, some of it abroad, but not for long. Grafton meanwhile encouraged him to get an audition as a comedian, at the Nuffield Services Club, a well-known jumping-off point for new acts, run by a severe lady called Mary Cook, who insisted that there should be no indecorous jokes. Spike passed the propriety test, so on the Friday night, wearing a velvet jacket he had borrowed from Army Welfare Services Wardrobe, he did an act which he describes as 'imitations of wallpaper', and ended up singing *Body and Soul*. 'I go down okay, but nothing to write home about.'

On 10 March 1949 his comedy act was watched at the Nuffield Centre by an anonymous person from BBC Television, who filled out a file card on him quite enthusiastically:

DESCRIPTION: Tall good looking young man of medium colouring.

PERFORMANCE: Patter, burlesque impressions, vocal finish etc.

REMARKS: Talent, good looks and a pleasant singing voice make him a very good subject for TV. But his material needs careful attention as he is inclined to overdo the 'crazy' parts.

Was he imitating wallpaper again?

Spike always dismissed his pre-*Goon Show* stage act: 'I had no confidence as a solo performer . . . If I hadn't written myself into the *Goon Show*, I'd never have been heard of.' But this is unjust. For a start, we have his own description of it:

Normally a comic comes on to a real fanfare of upbeat music. For me, there was nothing. Then, from the back of the stage, wearing a pair of zip-up slippers, I'd appear going 'Der-dum, der-doh – der-doh, der-dum' in an Eccles-type voice. Then I'd disappear again behind the back of the stage, 'Der-doh, der-doh, der-dum – der-dum, der-doh, dum, der dum.' It took a lot of nerve, this. Eventually, I'd make it to the microphone and say, 'I must be a big disappointment to you.' And I used to wonder why I never got any work!

But he did. The singer Teddy Johnson was on the bill with him one week, in a variety theatre, and went out front to watch his act, 'although really, nobody could call it an "act"!! I'd never seen anything like it; Spike was strolling around aimlessly on stage nowhere near the microphone, then he leaned against the side and played the trumpet, still not using the mike! . . . The audience reaction was negligible.'

At the Croydon Empire, where he was also booked, Spike performed to an audience including the young Roy Hudd, who recalls him as a 'pencil-thin scarecrow with wild hair, crossed eyes and a peculiar voice', who 'picked up a trumpet and played it pretty well – at least he had a finish'.

The 'peculiar voice' was presumably Eccles, though not yet under that name. Roger Lewis called Eccles 'a relative of Disney's gormless Goofy', but Harry Secombe, Alan Simpson and Ray Galton all trace Spike's Eccles voice to the dummy Mortimer Snerd, in ventriloquist Edgar Bergen's radio show in the USA. Secombe wrote that this 'quintessential "idiot" voice was adopted by Spike in a slightly different form'.

Spike himself has said that Eccles 'represent[s] the permanency of man, his ability to go through anything and survive', albeit through stupidity. For example (as recalled in Spike's *Guardian* obituary), the Goons are trying to get off a ship on the Amazon and lower a boat: 'When they get to the shore Eccles is already there. "How did you get ashore?" "Ho hum, I came across on that log." "Log? That's an alligator!" "Ooh. I wondered why I kept getting shorter."'

Jimmy Grafton writes: 'Eccles, I have always maintained, is the real Milligan; his id or alter ego; a simple, happy soul, content for the world to regard him as an idiot, provided that it does not make too many demands upon him.' But, as Pauline Scudamore comments, Spike was far from simple and rarely happy. Dominic Behan claimed that Spike put it slightly differently from Grafton, telling him: 'Eccles was really the innocent creature that I was – the one that didn't want to cause any offence and loved simplicity, which I still do. Yes, Eccles was the essential me.'

*

On 3 June 1949 he gave another performance at the Nuffield Services Club. This time we know it went well, because it was reviewed in an RAF newspaper, the *Raven*. The critic described Spike – whose real name, he revealed, was Terry – as a British version of Danny Kaye (a compliment later paid, with more accuracy, to Jonathan Miller). His burlesque antics had caused hysterics in the Nuffield audience, and, the article went on, he had joined forces with three other up-and-coming comedians and formed the Goon's (*sic*) Club. Its object was to get better (and cleaner) comics on the air again. The review concluded by exhorting readers to scan the *Radio Times* for the name of Spike Milligan, who promised to be the best thing since Charlie Chaplin. (Give that anonymous critic the Good Guesswork on Small Evidence award.)

In the autumn of 1949 the BBC decided that his performing was good enough to book him for the cast of a new radio show, *Hip Hip Hoo Roy*, starring Derek Roy. We may assume that the suggestion of using Spike came from Jimmy Grafton, since he was writing the show (under the *nom de plume* James Douglas). Spike's character in it was pure Eccles – except that he was called 'Spike'. Derek Roy would ask him, 'Well, Spike – what brings you here?' and get the answer: 'Da – der fifty-three bus.' Spike then read out a telegram, but didn't seem to understand it:

DEREK: You read what he said, didn't you?
SPIKE: Da – yeah, but I wasn't listening.
DEREK: Stop acting like an idiot, Spike.
SPIKE: (indignant) Da – I ain't acting.

Not only was he appearing in *Hip Hip Hoo Roy*; Grafton invited him to help write the show, giving him equal billing for the script and of course a share of the fee. In later life,

Milligan complained that Grafton's patronage hadn't been altogether unselfish: 'He was using me . . . I was obviously writing superior comedy to him.' The script of the first episode of *Hip Hip Hoo Roy* shows how untrue this is. Reproducing the whole of it in *Peace Work*, the last volume of his war (and post-war) memoirs, Spike has underlined what he recalls as his own contributions. These are few in number, and not particularly funny (certainly not funnier than Grafton's gags). Grafton emphasises how much his collaborator still had to learn: 'His mind was full of ideas, some of them brilliantly inventive and comic, but his ability to express them on paper was limited . . . His early attempts at written work were an incredible mixture of funny lines, nonsensical padding and non-existent punctuation . . .'

Nevertheless Grafton soon had him writing material for other people besides Derek Roy: Spike lists Secombe, Bill Kerr, Alfred Marks, Graham Stark and Dick Emery. Some of it was commissioned, some 'on spec' for unknown comics like Dick Emery, who would pay if he used it.

Soon, Spike was virtually living at the pub. Grafton could only find time to write in the gaps between running the pub. By the time he and Spike had finished work, it was too late for Spike to catch a train back to his parents' house, where he was again based, so he slept on a mattress in the pub attic, using a pile of overcoats to keep warm. At busy times, he sometimes helped behind the bar.

There were two Grafton children, James (seven) and Sally (six), and Spike began to discover that he had a Pied Piper touch. He told them stories, and left them notes and tiny parcels of sweets which allegedly came from the Hobbley-Gobbley Men (who were nice) or threats from Alfie From the Boneyard (who wasn't). Meanwhile Spike himself was being entertained by Jacko, the family's rhesus monkey, who at night was locked into the attic next to him. One evening, writes Spike, 'out of curiosity I wondered what he was doing and I looked through the keyhole only to see his eye looking at me'.

The attics could only be reached by a ladder, so, recalls Harry Secombe, 'we all christened [Spike] "The Prisoner of Zenda"'. In *Peace Work*, Spike makes it sound idyllic, but a note he wrote late one night, in the early days of his friendship with the Grafton family, caught him in the middle of a depression, when everything seemed hopeless. He was already thirty-one (he complained); he had always tried to love the good, and never to harm the weak – but where had it got him in life? An attic, came the answer, a bare garret where he could only keep warm by sleeping under borrowed overcoats. He was reminded of the misery endured by Mozart, who ended up in a pauper's grave. Really, it would be best for everyone if he went to sleep and never woke up again. Jimmy Grafton probably never saw this note, but he accurately describes 'Spike's highs and lows . . . swinging from a state of euphoria in which he was happy, out-going and spontaneously funny, to the complete opposite . . .'

*

Grafton had acquired one of the newly available tape recorders, which he described as 'a rather massive affair in a wooden cabinet', and the Goons started to record funny voices. Spike recalls that they discovered how to make speeded-up recordings – 'hilarious' – and Roger Lewis lists some of the characters created by them on tape: 'Arnold and Mrs Fringe, Ernie Splutmuscle, Phillip String, Harold Vest, Sir Harold Porridge (seeker of the East Pole), and Yoghurt Muleboot, "a displaced Siberian haddock-stretcher"'.

Sometimes Peter Sellers would invite Spike to stay the night; he too was living with his parents, in a block of flats off Finchley Road. Bill, Peter's father, was almost invisible – Spike fantasised that he was kept in the airing cupboard – while Peg, Peter's mother, was her son's slave. Waking in the morning, the recumbent Sellers would wail pitifully: 'Pe-eggy – Pe-eggy.' 'What is it, darling?' 'Tea, Mum.' And of course she brought it.

Spike soon realised that Sellers was overweight because Peg overfed him. He was also amused by Sellers's insatiable appetite for cars: 'Always changing his cars, Peter. I used to call it Metal Underwear because he used to change them so regularly.' (Milligan satirised this in a 1958 *Goon Show*. Sellers arrives making Mr Toad noises ('Parp! Parp!') and says he's on his way to buy a new car. Seagoon objects that he's only just bought one. Sellers replies that it's facing in the wrong direction. The joke persisted to the very end of the entire saga; in the final *Goon Show* of the last series (1960) a stupendously long car draws up, every inch of it covered in priceless mink – it could only belong to Sellers.

During the early part of 1950, Spike toured American army and air force bases in East Anglia, appearing as a solo comic with the Frank Weir Orchestra. He spent every spare moment making up jokes, scribbling them down on scraps of paper and the backs of cigarette packets. Jimmy Grafton recalls: 'Spike was still searching for the right formula, in between bouts of depression and withdrawal.'

The following year (1951) he was booked for a few weeks as a comic supporting the Joe Loss band. When the tour reached Nottingham he was reviewed in a local paper, which praised his new type of 'grotesque knockabout', and reported that he went down well with the audience.

Using Grafton's tape recorder, Spike and Sellers made a tape of Goonish dialogues, and sent it to BBC producer Pat Dixon, who had produced Sellers in *Third Division*. Michael Bentine calls Dixon 'scholarly and intelligently humorous . . . a bit older and more show-wise than any of us, and as radical in his approach to comedy as we were'. Frank Muir said Dixon was 'a terrific chap, and a rebel – he used to attend producers' meetings carrying the Confederate flag, which was propped up in his office. He was knocking on a bit, not young, but he started all sorts of ideas and shows.'

Dixon was sufficiently impressed by the tape to persuade his colleagues that the Goons should be given another chance, and on 4 February 1951 they assembled in a BBC studio for another trial recording. This time the BBC hierarchy liked it.

9

Crazy People

At the whim of the BBC, the second pilot was recorded under the title *The Junior Crazy Gang* – greatly to the irritation of Grafton: 'This implicit comparison with the very popular Palladium Crazy Gang[1] was both unapt and inept. "Why not *The Goon Show*?" I demanded. They brushed this aside as being meaningless.'

Pat Dixon, who had championed the cause of the Goons at the BBC, did not produce the second pilot, but passed it on to a rising young man in the Variety Department, Dennis Main Wilson. He was to be the Goons' first producer, and his energy and faith in them were a big factor in the show's success. 'Dennis's . . . great asset was his enthusiasm,' writes Jimmy Grafton.

Born into a working-class family in Dulwich in 1924, Wilson had become fluent in German at grammar school, and at the age of only seventeen had been taken on by the BBC European Service to write satirical anti-Nazi propaganda for broadcast to occupied Europe. He then joined the army, and was among the first British troops ashore on D-Day. In Normandy, half his regiment were wiped out within forty-eight hours. This was a man who would fully understand that the explosion-ridden landscape of the *Goon Show* was, in part, a reflection of the lunacies of war.

Rejoining the BBC when peace came, Wilson was put in

---

[1] Bud Flanagan and the rest of the Crazy Gang, whose speciality was slapstick, appeared frequently at the London Palladium, before making their home at the Victoria Palace.

charge of Variety auditioning, where his many discoveries included Bob Monkhouse and Peter Sellers. By the time he was chosen to produce the Goons, he was a regular at Grafton's.

With the second pilot completed to everyone's satisfaction, Wilson commissioned Spike to start writing a Goon series, to begin transmission in just under four months, at the end of May 1951. 'Material compiled by Spike Milligan' was how Wilson worded the writing credit in the *Radio Times*, probably meaning that the ideas in the show had been contributed by all four Goons, and Spike had rounded them up.

Wilson had much else to do besides supervising the Goons, and it was apparently not until a few days before their first programme was due to be recorded that he became aware that Spike's scripts needed a lot of work done to them. On 24 May he wrote rather anxiously to the Assistant Head of Variety:

The Milligan scripts, whilst they are extremely good in their basic form (those I have seen for the first four shows have been most promising), require considerable editing from the point of view of continuity and overall construction. This I have done for the first show, but for the rest of the series . . . I shall not be able to devote enough time to re-hashing the script . . . In addition to this, I feel that one man alone cannot write a half-hour comedy show – Milligan agrees with this, and wishes to work with Larry Stephens (whom I thoroughly recommend) . . . The script having been written, he then proposes to let James Grafton edit it from the point of view of continuity – and then finally pass it on to me. I feel that this is a sound suggestion . . .

Larry Stephens had first come to Grafton's in the company of Tony Hancock, for whom he was writing, and Jimmy Grafton felt he was the ideal person to give Spike some discreet support. Born in Birmingham in 1923, the son of an electricity board official, Stephens had joined the Commandos just after his twentieth birthday, and had been involved in heavy fighting against the Japanese in Burma. Before the war, he had played jazz piano in a local band, and he was also a talented cartoonist. After being demobbed he decided to try his hand at comedy scriptwriting. He came to London and, at the Nuffield Services Centre, met an agent who introduced him to Hancock, with whom he 'clicked' at once. Later he also wrote TV material for Bernard Braden and Dickie Valentine. In 1951 he and Hancock both got married to models who were friends with each other; Hancock was Stephens's best man.

'Larry Stephens was a lovely man,' says Eric Sykes, 'a brilliant jazz pianist, but he was a very quiet man. I don't think I ever heard him say more than about two words at one time and if you said something to him he would just blush.'[2]

The billing for the third programme in the first Goon series shows Wilson's proposal being implemented: 'Script by Spike Milligan, Additional material by Larry Stevens [sic] and Jimmy Grafton'. Later still, with the start of the second

---

[2] Spike and Stephens collaborated on another radio series, *Bumblethorpe*. Jeff Walden of BBC Written Archives writes: '*Bumblethorpe* was an eight-parter broadcast (on London Home Service only) from 12 November 1951. Written by Spike Milligan, Larry Stephens and Peter Ling and produced by Peter Eton, it was a vehicle for Robert Moreton. The plot concerned the search for the elusive character Bumblethorpe, supposedly the writer of a diary that had fallen into the hands of blackmailers. There was a different Bumblethorpe each week, respectively Leon Cortez, Alfred Marks, Jack Train, Bernard Miles, Bonar Colleano, Eric Barker, Cortez again and Tony Hancock. The other regulars were Avril Angers, Valentine Dyall, Kenneth Connor and Graham Stark, with Spike himself playing the odd character. One of these, incidentally, was an old dear called Miss Bannister.'

series, this became: 'Script written by Spike Milligan and Larry Stephens, Edited by Jimmy Grafton'.

Spike never showed any public gratitude to Stephens for easing the burden of scriptwriting. 'Larry Stephens was small beer,' he once said. 'He was never really a writer . . . Larry would occasionally think of an idea, but by then the show was over.' One of the Goons' producers, Peter Eton, believed the opposite to be true, and has testified to Stephens's importance: 'Spike used to have the marvellous lively extrovert ideas, and Larry used to bring them down to earth.' Indeed, addressing a meeting of the Goon Show Preservation Society, Eton (possibly after a drink or two) belittled Milligan as a writer in comparison with Stephens: 'Larry was the strong man. Spike used to have these paradoxical ideas and wrote them down in the form of one line gags. Most of it was rubbish, utter rubbish. It was Larry who used to pull it into shape and make sketches out of it.'

Studying the *Goon Show* scripts soberly, Roger Wilmut deduces: 'Stephens's plots tend to have a beginning, a middle, and an end; whereas Milligan's tend to have a middle.' Certainly it is striking how often the best programmes turn out to be Milligan–Stephens collaborations; for example, they are both credited with writing the 1957 script which includes the famous Bluebottle–Eccles scene beginning 'What time is it, Eccles?' – arguably the funniest set-piece in the entire history of the show.[3]

John Antrobus, a later writing partner of Spike's, emphasised how tactful a collaborator had to be: '[Spike] has to be one hundred per cent right, there's no disagreement. If you say, "No, Spike", you run the risk of him shutting down

[3] The scene (from 'The Mysterious Punch-up-the-Conker', 7 February 1957), in which Eccles explains that he has had the time written down for him on a piece of paper, may be found in Roger Wilmut's *The Goon Show Companion*, pp. 85–6.

the whole enterprise.' Pressed by Pauline Scudamore to acknowledge the contributions of his co-writers (of whom there were many over the years), Milligan became deliberately vague; he said he wondered how much help they had really been to him. Also (and this was devastatingly unkind) he questioned what any one of them had achieved on their own. Only Eric Sykes (recruited much later in the show's history) was treated as an equal.

Writing twenty-five years after the event, Jimmy Grafton recalled that Michael Bentine, too, definitely contributed to the scripts: 'Mike would throw in ideas.' Grafton added that Bentine's eagerness to contribute 'sometimes led to argument, which Dennis [Main Wilson] found not always easy to control'. The *Radio Times* included a short article to mark the debut of the Goons, and this gave the impression that (even before Grafton and Stephens had joined the team) the script was a collaborative effort: 'This series is based upon a crazy type of fun evolved by four of our younger laughter-makers.' (It also stated, wrongly, that the four had 'met during the wartime perambulations of the "Stars in Battledress"'.)

As to the matter of the show's title, Grafton says that, after the pilot had been made, and a series was commissioned, 'we compromised with the title *Crazy People*'.

*

'CRAZY PEOPLE, featuring Radio's own Crazy Gang – "The Goons"' was how the *Radio Times* billed it, indicating that the BBC was still uncomfortable about 'Goons'; but an article by the radio and TV critic of the *News Chronicle*, published on 17 May 1951, eleven days before the broadcast of the first programme, did not duck it:

GOONS TAKE THE AIR

J. P. Thomas discourses upon a strange phenomenon in radio
What is a Goon? Ask Messrs Pat Dixon, Ian Messiter, Jacques

Brown and Dennis Main Wilson, BBC producers all, and you will get an answer which could only appear as asterisks. Now, in order to prepare you for the shock due on 28 May, I will explain . . . A Goon is someone with a one-cell brain. Anything that is not basically simple puzzles a Goon. His language is inarticulate; he thinks in the fourth dimension. Goonism is described (by the Goons) as 'Bringing any situation to its illogical conclusion.'

The Goons are a mad quartette . . . who met on Service during the war, invented their own system of Goonism (borrowing the name from Popeye), and have battered at the BBC's door for three years . . . Now that Mr Main Wilson has agreed to produce the Goons (the other three having given it up in succession for one reason or another), my only ambition is to sit with the BBC governors and tune into the Home Service on 28 May . . . At least the Goon Show will be different.

The first programme was recorded in one of the studios at Aeolian Hall in New Bond Street, the headquarters of BBC Variety, on Sunday, 27 May 1951, and transmitted at 6.45 the next evening on the Home Service (at first in the London Region only). Sunday was a favourite day for making Variety programmes, since stage and film performers tended to be unavailable during the week. Recording only a day before transmission was standard BBC practice, even for a show like this which was an almost unknown quantity – just one step away from doing it live. Indeed, it might as well have been live, since the disc-recording system then in use did not permit editing. Many other Variety programmes at this period did actually go out live, but nobody ever dared risk this with the Goons, thanks to their complex sound effects and a general air of irresponsibility. Nowadays the entire first series of an experimental comedy show would probably be recorded well before transmission began, which might have made Spike's life more bearable; on the other hand, without the weekly deadline he might not have written the show at all.

Besides the four Goons and Andrew Timothy, the performers billed for the first programme were harmonica-player Max Geldray, the Ray Ellington Quartet, the Stargazers close harmony vocal group, the BBC Dance Orchestra conducted by Stanley Black – and Margaret Lindsay. Spike must have been referring to her when he wrote, long afterwards: 'Not many people know that my girlfriend, Margaret McMillan, was in the first show.' He also reminisced about this to Norma Farnes: 'Do you know there were only three women who appeared in the *Goon Show*? The first was Margaret McMillan, a classy girl. I was going out with her at the time.'[4] Nothing else is known about her, and in fact she did not take part after all. There are no lines for a female performer in the script, and the closing announcement says: 'We regret that Margaret Lindsay, who was billed in the *Radio Times*, was unable to appear.'

Jimmy Grafton explains that the shape of early *Goon Shows* was different from the single-storyline programmes of later years: 'They consisted of four or five unconnected sketches, separated by musical items . . .' Peter Eton calculated that in those days the music took up half the programme, leaving Spike and his co-writers with no more than fifteen minutes for the script. 'This was all right for sketches, but wasn't long enough for a storyline to be developed.'

---

[4] As to the other two, he recalled Charlotte Greenwood, who played Maid Marian in a Robin Hood spoof at Christmas 1954 – he alleged that Sellers was dating her – but could not name the third, 'a little girl . . . who was hopelessly in love with Peter'. In fact there were several more. They included Lizbeth Webb and Carole Carr, who appeared in Goon pantomime editions at Christmas 1951 and 1952 respectively; Ellis Powell, star of the hugely popular BBC radio soap, *Mrs Dale's Diary*, who made a brief appearance in a *Goon Show* broadcast on 30 December 1952; and Cécile Chevreau, who has a brief romantic interlude with Bloodnok in 'African Incident' (30 December 1957).

Spike recalls that 'Ray [Ellington] and Max [Geldray] were both recruited by Pat Dixon, who was a jazz buff.' Geldray was born Max van Gelder in Amsterdam, and as a young man became a star on Dutch radio, then moved to Paris and worked with the Ray Ventura band. Being Jewish, he fled to England when the Nazis occupied France, joined the Dutch army in exile, and was wounded during the Normandy landings. Ray Ellington's real name was Henry Brown; he had a black American father (comedian Harry Brown) and a Russian Jewish mother. Ray worked as a drummer and vocalist on the British dance-band scene from the mid-thirties, was an RAF gym instructor during the war, and by 1950 had formed his own quartet. This included pianist Dick Katz, who wrote the neat little arrangements for Ray's *Goon Show* numbers.

Jimmy Grafton explained that it was he who had suggested to J.P. Thomas of the *News Chronicle* that Goon humour operated by bringing 'any situation to its illogical conclusion'. Roger Wilmut points out that there is nothing illogical about it: 'In fact, much of Goon humour depends on the *misuse* of logic.' Regrettably, Spike never discussed this. Other than acknowledging the influence of Beachcomber and the Marx Brothers, he seems to have regarded his attitude to logic as essentially Irish: 'I started writing the *Goon Show* and . . . most certainly, my Irish father's fantasies had their effect on me.'

The opening of the first *Crazy People* – the first *Goon Show* of all[5] – promises 'zany' (eccentric) humour:

---

[5] The script of this first programme is reproduced in *The Essential Spike Milligan*, edited by Alexander Games, Fourth Estate, 2002. A number of later *Goon Show* scripts may be found in published collections – see Bibliography. The entire run of scripts can be seen on microfilm at the BBC Written Archives.

ANNOUNCER: This is the BBC Home Service. (fanfare) What
is the zaniest comedy show on the air today?

SPIKE: Er – *Today in Parliament?*

ANNOUNCER: No, it's those 'Crazy People', the Goons.

However, each of the four sketches that make up the
programme is characterised not by zaniness but by 'misused
logic'. 'My name is Jones,' says Secombe, in the role of the
supposed scriptwriter of the show. 'I wrote this programme
strictly for radio – but they said as a radio show, it was ahead
of its time.' 'When was that?' asks Sellers, and Secombe replies:
'1852.'

A sketch about motor-racing has Bentine, as 'Captain
Pureheart', ordering his technical adviser, Ernie Splutmuscle,
to 'go to Italy and bring back the finest motoring brains
that money could buy', and Splutmuscle duly returns with
the brains – in a jar.

Incidentally it is clear that the manic inventor Pureheart
and his sidekick Splutmuscle had both been developed as
Goon characters before *Crazy People* began. Splutmuscle,
played by Sellers, is an early version of Bluebottle; he has
an odd verbal mannerism (the apparently meaningless word
'n'at', which he scatters through his sentences), and he
addresses Pureheart as 'Captain' – hence Bluebottle addressing
Neddie Seagoon as 'my Capatain' (*sic*) in later series.

'Misused logic' is frequently applied to the human body;
for example, in a *Dick Barton* parody in the first programme:

PETER: Good heavens! Snowy's fainted, quick Jock you take
his legs.

SPIKE: I can't, they're joined to his body . . . Here, Mr Barton,
you better have my gun.

PETER: No thanks Jock, I've got my two fists.

HARRY: Yes, pity they're both on the same arm.

At times, the humour is derivative. A gag in an Ancient Egypt sketch in the first programme could have come straight from the Marx Brothers:

PETER: My name is Porridge, Sir Harold Porridge. For months my expedition had been digging for the lost tomb of the greatest of the Pharaohs . . . Finally, we received a cable from the Egyptian Government. It said simply:
HARRY: 'Stop digging Hackney Marshes – try Egypt!!'

Another line in this sketch could be the work of Lewis Carroll:

SPIKE: It was a hot night in June. Unable to sleep, I took out a sleeping pill. I then woke it up, and swallowed it.

Milligan often wrote in the Carroll style; for example, in a 1954 *Goon Show*, Neddie Seagoon observes, 'Gad, it's hot', and Bloodnok responds, 'Yes, it must be the heat.' The Tutankhamen sketch in the first edition of *Crazy People* – which has the sort of storyline that the Goons eventually used for entire programmes (and which is far better than the very pedestrian Festival of Britain sketch that ends this first programme) – has an ending of triumphantly original absurdity:

MICHAEL: I can see him!!
SPIKE: Look – King Tutankhamen!
PETER: Stop!!
MICHAEL: What is it?
PETER: We're too late!
MICHAEL: You mean – ?
PETER: (*dramatically*) Yes. He's dead!!

*

J.P. Thomas, who had previewed *Crazy People*, reviewed the first show enthusiastically in the *News Chronicle*:

The Goons got away to a fine start on Monday with a slick and original 30-minutes which now need the polish that experience will bring. But who wants to listen to this kind of specialised humour at 6.45 in the evening? And how many crazy gang fans are likely to find it, tucked away in the sober Home Service? . . . If the Goons are to have a fair chance, the Light is the place. And not before 9 pm, please.

After the second programme, the Home Service moved *Crazy People* to 7.45 p.m., and the Light Programme eventually began to run repeats; but the show's relationship with the Light was always on-off, and Spike eventually discovered that its assistant controller was influenced by his wife, who couldn't stand it.

In the second *Crazy People*, Sir Harold Porridge went in search of the East Pole (a good example of the Goons going in for pure nonsense of the Edward Lear-Lewis Carroll variety – though there is also an echo of Winnie the Pooh's 'Expotition' to the North Pole in the A. A. Milne stories). This episode has Ray Ellington singing a number supposedly written by 'Yogi Carmichael', and there is the birth of a classic Goon joke (probably descended from 1930s variety) about playing the Palladium – you never heard it played better! (Later variations on this include: 'I must ask you to accompany me on a safari.' 'But I've never played one.')

The third *Crazy People* also included a snatch of dialogue in which Eccles (not yet given his name – and why 'Eccles', one wonders, though it is fruitless to ask) gives away more about himself than is usually the case. 'Spike', as the future Eccles is called here, reveals to Secombe that he has jumped up in the air, but has found himself falling to earth again. Why on earth should that be, wonders Secombe. Comes the answer: because Eccles *lives* here.

The fourth programme concluded, for the first time, with a sketch that was as funny as the best of future *Goon Shows*, 'The Conquest of Everest'. The expedition, led by Sir Harold Porridge, sets off with a memorable list of baggage – unlikely, incongruous and unrelated objects ranging from a full-sized drill hall made of rubber to a toothbrush, accompanied by a tooth.

This is the comedy of surrealism, in which nothing makes sense except the absence of sense itself. Edward Lear had been there:

> On the coast of Coromandel
> Where the early pumpkins blow,
> In the middle of the woods,
> Lived the Yonghy-Bonghy-Bo.
> Two old chairs, and half a candle; –
> One old jug without a handle, –
> These were all his worldly goods.

And it came from a tradition much older than Lear:

Last Sunday morning at six o'clock in the evening as I was sailing over the tops of the mountains in my little boat, I met two men on horseback riding on one mare; so I asked them, could they tell me whether the little old woman was dead yet who was hanged last Saturday week for drowning herself in a shower of feathers? They said they could not positively inform me, but if I went to Sir Gammer Vans he could tell me all about it. 'But how am I to know the house?' said I. 'Ho, 'that is easy enough,' said they, 'for 'tis a brick house, built entirely of flint, standing alone by itself in the middle of sixty or seventy others just like it.'

That's at least a couple of centuries older than the Goons.

Spike recalls that he was not performing much at the beginning. 'I used to say "Yes" and "Shut that window" and do odd voices. I didn't think I could compete with Harry and Peter.' Quite long stretches of *Crazy People* do indeed go by without a line for him. He says that, in those days, he never thought he had any major performing talent; he believed the others were the performers, and he was the writer, just saying the odd line now and then.

While he had the huge responsibility of leading the writing team, he was at least based in London, where the show was recorded; whereas Bentine, Secombe and Sellers had to get themselves to the capital each Sunday morning, however far away they might have been working the previous night – it might even be Glasgow. 'My first port of call when I got to London was Grafton's,' recalls Secombe, 'where Jimmy and Dorothy would provide coffee and bacon and eggs.' Arriving at Aeolian Hall, 'we spent the first half-hour swapping gags and generally behaving like kids in school at playtime. Then Dennis Main Wilson would try to get some semblance of discipline into the proceedings . . .'

Secombe describes a major feature of the programme: 'There was always a "spot-effects" man behind a screen with a miniature door with a knocker on it, half coconut shells for horses' hooves, a swanee whistle, a rattle as used by football fans, and anything else that Spike or Mike had decreed.'

Pre-recorded sound effects (many of them created especially for the programme) were 'played in' by another studio manager, working in the control cubicle with a bank of 78 rpm turntables and a Chinagraph pencil to mark the exact groove required. (As yet, tape recording had scarcely penetrated the BBC, and each half-hour programme was being recorded on a sixteen-inch coarse-groove $33^{1}/_{3}$ rpm disc.) 'Spike would perhaps want the sound of Big Ben mixed with a chicken cackling,' continues Secombe, 'so the engineer would need two turntables going at the same time. Sometimes four or five machines would all be going together with the poor fellow going berserk to keep up with all the effects.'

Andrew Timothy describes the proceedings each Sunday:

We'd start at 9.30, when the script, if there was a complete script, was delivered, and the Goons pored over it, criticized the jokes . . . and thought of something much funnier themselves – and this went on steadily without a break until 7 o'clock [the opening time of pubs on Sundays], when there was a mass exodus . . . to a little Edwardian pub called the Grosvenor, just round the corner.

Meanwhile the audience would take their seats. Secombe judged that much of *Crazy People* 'mystified more than entertained' them, and Milligan agreed: 'The audience didn't understand a word of it. God bless the band; they saved it. They were all muzos and they really dug the jokes.' (As observed already, it was a jazz musician's humour.) However, the radio audience at home seemed to like *Crazy People*; the original booking for six shows was extended by the BBC planners to a further six, and then five more, making a total of seventeen – pretty good for a newcomer. Meanwhile the various Regional Home Services[6] began to broadcast it too. The listening figures, starting out at only 370,000 for the early shows, had risen to 1.8 million by the end of the *Crazy People* series on 29 September 1951. And although there

---

[6] The BBC Home Service, predecessor of Radio 4, operated for certain programmes as a single national network, but for much of the day the Regions (Scotland, Wales, Northern Ireland, the North, Midland and West of England) separated from the London output and broadcast programmes of regional interest.

were no letters of praise in *Radio Times*, neither were there any complaints.

'I didn't know that the first show would be the first of two hundred shows,' writes Spike. 'I didn't know that I had that much in me.'[7]

[7] Others give a higher figure, e.g. Mike Brown in the *Goon Show Preservation Society Newsletter*, June 2002, who says there were '224 main *Goon Shows*'.

10

Exit Pureheart

'Round this time,' writes Spike,

Peter [Sellers] had the hots for a girl called Anne Howe. He was
going to meet her and a friend at the Edgwarebury Club. First
we had to pick up her friend, June. We knocked on the door and
something that knocked me off my feet appeared in the doorway,
wrapped in the briefest of towels. She was Italian, huge dark eyes,
black hair, huge boobs. Yes, she was for me! We were soon going
steady.

In another version of how he met this north London
'sex-bomb' who was to be his first wife, Spike says he
covered up his nervousness on the blind date by pretend-
ing to be a foreigner with very little English. He soon
relaxed with June, and began seeing her regularly, but he
admits that he was still fairly immature for a man of
thirty-three.

June Marlow eventually disappeared from Spike's life as
abruptly as she had entered it, and little has been recorded
about her background. According to Spike, her father was
a successful tailor of Italian origin, who had a rather grand
mansion. June's Italianate looks may have reminded Spike
of his adored Toni.

He had scarcely met June when his parents, having decided
to emigrate, sailed for a new life in Australia, in hopes of
a sunnier and more comfortable retirement than the austerity
of fifties Britain could offer. With them went Spike's brother
Desmond and his recently wedded wife. Indeed June Marlow's

family were about to move to Australia too,[1] and a ticket was already booked for June herself. 'We went to a little restaurant near Leicester Square,' recalls Spike,

and she said to me, 'Look, why don't we get engaged before I go.' So I was stunned. I said, 'Oh! All right.' I never asked her to marry me. I just wanted to please everybody, so I said, 'All right then.' So we got engaged, then she said, 'Look, why don't we get married before I go away.' So I said, 'Well, all right, but you're going away?' And she said, 'Well, my father insists that I go to Australia with him first and then I can come back.' So we got married . . .

Terence Milligan and June Marlow were married at Caxton Hall in Victoria on 26 January 1952; among the friends at the ceremony was Peter Sellers, wearing his Dick Barton mackintosh. The couple had two nights' honeymoon at a Bayswater hotel, and then June was off to Australia.

Four days before the wedding, the BBC began to broadcast the second series of Goon programmes. It was launched in the *Radio Times* with a photo of Milligan looking at a script, flanked by Dennis Main Wilson, Jimmy Grafton and Larry Stephens, while Secombe, Bentine and Sellers clowned in the background. The BBC agreed to call it 'THE GOON SHOW, with those crazy people . . .' Jimmy Grafton alleged that 'one puzzled planner was heard to ask, "What is this *Go On Show* people are talking about?"'

Initially, the BBC booked six shows, then a further six, then another fourteen (adding up to twenty-six, the standard run for an established show, though in the event one was cancelled because of the death of King George VI). During the series, the ratings reached as many as 3 million

---

[1] Which seems unlikely if her father ran a successful tailoring business.

for some programmes, which in those days – before TV had eaten into radio listening – was quite good.

After the first six shows the Stargazers departed, and for a while Secombe sang a straight vocal number. In the last of the *Crazy People* series, Sellers had a pun about these tenor set pieces and operatic arias – to the effect that Harry Secombe was demonstrating the *strains* of the human voice.

Gradually, Secombe was moving towards the role of the show's straight man, though 'Neddie Seagoon' had not yet arrived. Spike described Secombe to Joe McGrath as 'that sheet-metal voice, coming through with perfect timing, and saying exactly what I wrote – you never had to correct him . . . He was the greatest straight man in comedy.'

As yet, the narrative drive tended to come not from the naïvety of Neddie, but from the schemes of the madcap inventor Osric Pureheart, played by Bentine, who in the second series built his own versions of the Suez Canal, the Trans-Siberian Express, the Crystal Palace, the Atlantic Cable and the Channel Tunnel, as well as a Time Machine. Meanwhile two familiar names made their first appearance: Minnie Bannister (initially Pureheart's aunt), and Henry Crun, first introduced as a lawyer from the firm of Wacklow & Crun. Milligan told Dominic Behan that Crun was suggested by 'a solicitor we knew', adding: 'The conversation between Henry and Minnie was really based on my father and mother who used to talk to each other and not listen – from separate rooms: they never listened to each other.'

By now, the scripts were more confident in their surrealism and use of the absurd. The Earl of Secombe wants to know why his very goofy manservant is wandering around with a garden rake. Answer: he's making the beds (obvious, isn't it?). And best of all, Major Bloodnok (played by Sellers) begins to make his entrances with what can only be described as a long verbal shudder. With this enormously extended set of vowels (no, Major, I said *vowels*) Bloodnok was able to hint at outrageous sexual adventures without upsetting the genteel listener. A touch of larceny, too, with Spike surely remembering his own father pocketing the regimental knick-knacks before ambling home from the officers' mess.

Eccles was now well developed, his apparent stupidity often concealing cunning, which in turn concealed further stupidity, and so on. Appearing in the role of Pureheart's servant, he explains that his master is displeased with him: this morning he was cleaning up and he left a bucket of dirty water in Pureheart's bedroom – balanced on top of the door. And, conjectures Bloodnok, it fell on Pureheart? No, it fell on Eccles himself – who was wearing Pureheart's best suit at the time.

Sound effects were playing a more crucial role than before. Sailing to Africa in the SS *Goonitania*, Pureheart is warned by Bloodnok to take care of passing trains. He scoffs at this – how can there be trains in the middle of the ocean? At which point the sound effects produce a fast-approaching express, followed by a crash.

This comes from the eighth show in the second series (18 March 1952), which breaks new ground by having a single plot right through. It opens with Andrew Timothy telling the audience: 'Recently the Goons have been reading Rider Haggard's famous novel – *She*.' 'And so tonight,' says Bentine, 'we present in four dramatic scenes . . .' The programme, called 'Her', tells the story of the search for She whose beauty is constantly renewed in the flame of everlasting youth – until the man from the Gas Board comes to disconnect it.

'Her' was a one-off; after it, the *Goon Show* returned, for the time being, to the miscellaneous sketch format, which gave comparatively little opportunity for the development of the characters. Discontent began to be expressed by two people who were watching the progress of the Goons. 'The present state of radio humour leaves something to be desired,' wrote the radio critic of the *Sunday Times*, Maurice Wiggin. He complained of a 'dreadful sameness', saying that he had had 'some hope that the Goons might . . . be diverting, for they are avowedly as mad as hatters. But in fact their show is quite conventional in pattern, and for wit they substitute mere noise, and some smuttiness. No personality emerges.'

An even harsher verdict was passed in-house, by the BBC's Head of Variety, Michael Standing, in a memo to Dennis Main Wilson, on 29 May 1952:

I think that the Goons are in danger of being submerged by the very qualities that have helped them to success, namely their own gusto and extreme eccentricity. The former all too often develops into a noise from which speech, effects or music do not emerge at all clearly, and the latter seems to tempt the authors to rely too much on crazy, inconsequential sequences without giving enough thought to the shape of the show and to effective curtain lines for the sketches . . . If these tendencies are not arrested very quickly the show may well collapse like a pricked balloon.

*

Even before June Marlow – now June Milligan – had completed her voyage to Australia with her parents, she guessed that she was pregnant. When it was confirmed, and Spike received the news, he was both excited and alarmed. Aged thirty-four, he would at last have to make a home.

Peter Sellers's mother was related to the house agent Mendoza, who would soon be letting some small flats at Shepherd's Hill in Highgate. Sellers had married Anne Howe in September 1951, and would be renting one; so Spike followed suit and signed the lease of Flat 4, Highview, moving there with June – back from Australia and heavily pregnant – in August 1952.

The second series of the *Goon Show* had ended in July, and despite Michael Standing's criticisms a third series, of twenty-six programmes,[2] simply billed as the *Goon Show*, was to begin on 11 November. Each week's edition was – for the time being – to be repeated on the Light Programme, and the *Radio Times* gave the show the accolade of a full-length article, written by Milligan and Larry Stephens. They claimed they had tried to persuade the cast to resign, so that the show could be

turned into a sort of half-hour interval when the listeners could go out for a sandwich. The plan was abandoned when it was discovered that when the *Goon Show* was on, 99.9 per cent of the listeners went out anyway. (The odd .1 per cent is a Mrs Langton, who stays in for the express purpose and pleasure of switching off.)

The musical content of the show had been pruned once more; Secombe's song was cut, and there were to be only three sketches, with a number each from Max Geldray and Ray Ellington. The BBC Dance Orchestra and Stanley Black were taken off the show because of another commitment, and the young composer and arranger Wally Stott, who had been writing for the Goons since *Crazy People*, was contracted to pick a band of freelance players and conduct it himself.

Initially, Stott's band (like its predecessor) included a string section, and it did not begin to sound special until this was scrapped to save money. Then a first-rate big band emerged, and did justice to Stott's brilliant jazz arrangements. The players included multi-instrumentalist E.O. Pogson (who, besides doubling on saxophone and clarinet, could oblige

---

[2] Again, one was cancelled because of a royal death, in this case Queen Mary.

with a plaintive violin when the script required it), and virtuoso Scots trombonist and clown George Chisholm, who (like Max Geldray and Ray Ellington) was sometimes given brief speaking parts.

Dennis Main Wilson now moved on (he was later to produce the first series of *Hancock's Half Hour*), and the Goons acquired a new producer, Peter Eton, who by comparison with Wilson was a disciplinarian. He had come to radio via commercial art and films, served in the Royal Navy, and was invalided out and joined the BBC in 1941. Eton insisted on proper rehearsal and a high standard of performance. Spike also recalls that, in the history of the *Goon Show*, 'Peter Eton was the one guy that used to beat the shit out of the sound-effects boys to get the right atmosphere.' Moreover Eton defended the Goons against attacks from senior BBC officials. Eton himself says of this:

I was nearly sacked because of a joke about OBEs. Peter said to Harry 'Have an OBE' or something like that. For that I was hauled up before a board with these old boys sitting round a table and saying we mustn't say this and that. It happened altogether about eighteen times and once it was an official reprimand which got entered in my BBC records. John Snagge, who was Head of Announcers and therefore a powerful figure in the BBC, was in favour of the *Goon Show* and Milligan's right to creative freedom,[3] [and he] would always take me aside afterwards and say, 'It's all right, Peter, just go away for a while and forget about it.'

All these changes were important, but far more crucial was the fact that the cast no longer included Michael Bentine.

---

[3] Snagge, best known for his commentary on the Oxford & Cambridge Boat Race, appeared in several *Goon Shows* as a kind of *deus ex machina*.

Nine days before the start of the third series, he wrote to Peter Eton: 'I honestly do feel that the "Goons" have a much better balance with three comics and a straight man [Andrew Timothy the announcer] . . . and that the foregoing series did show a decided overbalancing of comedy . . .' In his autobiography Bentine writes of his decision to leave the *Goon Show*:

I knew, intuitively, that the Goons would really get off the ground in a big way if there were only three of them . . . The Ritz Brothers, the Three Stooges, and the Marx Brothers . . . were made up of three people . . . As I, with the exception of Spike, was the only self-contained writer-performer unit, I felt the choice of the one to leave must be me . . . I told Harry what I felt, to get his reaction. He was very upset, but he did see my point . . . Peter and Spike were very sad about the break-up . . . The PRO at the BBC must have talked to the press, because they . . . proceeded to blow the whole simple business up into some personal feud between the four of us.

There were indeed rumours of a major row, and Bentine went on to say that a few months later he returned for a guest appearance on the *Goon Show*, 'so that we could prove that the quarrel was a load of bunk'. (This was on Boxing Day 1953, in a show called 'The Giant Bombardon'.) Yet Bentine admitted that, at the time, his departure was 'a sad business'.

Andrew Timothy recalls 'a permanent sparring match between Bentine and Sellers', and interprets it as a class war: 'Any funny suggestion of Bentine's was immediately destroyed by Sellers – because he thought that Bentine looked down on him. Bentine was Eton; he was more or less East End.'

Roger Lewis was told by Secombe that there had been jealousy between Bentine and Milligan as to who was responsible for the best ideas. 'We would turn up for a session,' Secombe recalls,

Spike and Mike would spark each other off, and at the end of the session both of them would go away thinking that most of the ideas were theirs. So there was a little bit of friction in that respect. Each one accusing the other of plagiarism, though not seriously. But that disappeared when Mike decided he wanted Sundays for the family [he was married with children]. Which was fair enough, and he left.

No recordings survive of Bentine as a Goon, but the four of them appeared in a mediocre 1952 B-movie called *Down Among the Z-Men*, which is available on video. Bentine plays Pureheart throughout, and his mad-professor voice and bandy walk clearly come from a different comic stable than the others.[4] His style is first and foremost visual: Pureheart's appearance (wild black hair and beard) is a big part of the joke. In contrast, such characters as Bloodnok, Minnie and Henry had evolved in a radio context, and were better imagined than seen.

With the passing of the years, Spike tended to be harsh about Bentine. To Dominic Behan he said: 'He was full of ideas that became boring very quickly. Student humour.' He told an interviewer in 1990, when Bentine was still alive: 'I don't think he basically likes me. During the Goons, it hurt me deeply when he told Peter Sellers that I wasn't talented and shouldn't be in the show.' Spike repeated this allegation to Joe McGrath, who says that Harry Secombe recalled it too.

---

[4] The Goons appeared in several other short British film comedies during their early days together, probably thanks to Jimmy Grafton, who wrote the screenplays for a couple of them. See Roger Wilmut's *The Goon Show Companion* for details.

Spike did sometimes express admiration for what Bentine had contributed to the show; he told Dominic Behan: 'He [Bentine] wasn't the most sociable person in the world and he never mixed like the rest of us, but he was a very funny man.' And when Spike first saw the Goon Show Preservation Society headed paper, he wrote to them to say that Bentine's name should be on it, along with the other three: 'He was one of the Goons, wasn't he? And he was marvellous as Dr Osric Pureheart; he was so funny we used to cry.'

Whatever he may have said earlier, by the end of his life Spike had turned against Bentine (who died in 1996): 'I went to his memorial service, and they all eulogized this bastard – whereas he only bluffed his way.' Max Geldray even detected hostility by Spike to the other two Goons. Geldray recalls that, when he was chauffeuring Spike to a theatre ('since Spike had not then learned to drive'), he 'would talk about the other two Goons as "Secombe" and "Sellers" . . . in a way that was so antagonistic that a stranger might feel that he could hardly wait to get back at the bastards.'

*

The first show of the third series (11 November 1952) consisted of a sketch about Peter Eton's amorous feelings for his secretary, Miss Flangebox (played by Spike in his Minnie Bannister voice);[5] a spoof of a boys' adventure story, 'Fred of the Islands', in which a nautical expedition turns out to have been sailing down Oxford Street; and a parody of a radio magazine programme. This programme was picked for the Goons' first surviving BBC audience research report. 'The *Goon Show*,' it began,

---

[5] The wobble in it was achieved by grasping the flesh of his neck with one hand and causing his larynx to shake.

might well be described as illustrative of the saying 'One Man's Meat is Another Man's Poison'. Listeners' comments gave strikingly little evidence of a neutral attitude towards the programme as a whole . . . According to most of the 'Anti-Goon' section of the audience, this show had nothing to recommend it – it was silly, childish, noisy, infantile rubbish. The 'Goon' enthusiasts were, however, not entirely uncritical. Many thought this edition was 'thin' and patchy and decidedly less amusingly slick than any of the previous series. At the same time most in this group seemed confident that the show would improve when it had settled down – a Gasworks Foreman, for instance, wrote: 'A little bit rusty in parts but the material is there. Give them time.'

Shortly afterwards came another report, on the edition of 9 December 1952, in which a woman listener – the wife of a tax official –wrote: 'I find the high spirits of these awful people very infectious. I have to listen because my schoolboy son insists on turning on the radio against my wishes, but many times I do chuckle into my knitting – to my own undoing.'

The next surviving report, on the edition of 9 October 1953, showed how the Goons were becoming part of British life: 'A Fitter remarked: "The pure fantasy of this show is the perfect answer to the blues." . . . A housewife . . . wrote: "This show has influenced my husband and myself to act a little crazier when we meet our friends and we find we enjoy life all the more!"' (Did they give dinner parties in the roles of Henry and Minnie?)

*

Spike and June's first child, a daughter, was born on 2 November 1952, and was named after what Spike called 'that wonderful theme song' from the George Sanders film *Laura*. Shortly after June had returned home from hospital with baby Laura, she became ill with puerperal fever. Full-time nursing had to be provided, and paid for, and Spike – who was sleeping on the sofa – had to stand in for the nurse when she was having time off, mixing the baby's feeds and changing nappies.

He had never known this sort of responsibility in his life; there had always been his mother, or the army, to step in and take charge. Moreover there were no grandparents to supply help and advice; both his own parents and June's had disappeared to Australia. He was at a loss, and meanwhile the pressures of the *Goon Show* were growing, and he had to earn to keep his family (and the nurse).

He was being paid extremely well for writing the *Goon Show*: 60 guineas per script (though this had to be shared with Stephens and Grafton), and there was also a fee for performing. When the show was on the air, he was earning 'big money . . . Bloody marvellous money'. But Sellers and Secombe (being better known) commanded higher fees as performers, which he resented, and he was only being paid for the six months of the year when the show was being broadcast. Money was therefore a considerable worry once Laura was born.

He was giving himself a stressful time at the BBC, complaining about their failure to create the complicated sound effects he demanded, and grumbling at their attempts to censor the scripts. Harry Secombe remembers that half the things Spike devised would be rejected as technically impossible. Spike himself writes: 'Sound effects used to be a knock on the door and a trudge on gravel. I tried to transform that and I had to fight like mad and people didn't like me for it. I had to rage and bang and crash. In the end it paid off but it drove me mad in the process . . .'

In return, he was receiving complaints from members of the BBC hierarchy:

Dear Mr Milligan,

It has been reported to me by Mr Peter Eton that despite his constant requests for early delivery, your scripts . . . continue to arrive late, in some cases not until the morning of the pre-recording . . .

To which he responded that he would hand in the scripts seven days in advance if they could guarantee that the sound effects would be prepared during that period, and not keep everyone waiting for them at the rehearsal on Sunday.

Looking back at the *Goon Show* in later years, Spike portrayed his job as sheer martyrdom: 'I had to write a new show every week for six months. If Hitler had done that to someone it would be called torture.' Yet this was standard practice for comedy writing at that period, as Alan Simpson and Ray Galton emphasise:

> RAY GALTON: Anyone who was writing a series had that pressure – as opposed to these days, when (if you get a commission) you write the whole series in advance.
>
> ALAN SIMPSON: That's right, and nowadays you'd probably only do a short series, half a dozen programmes each year; whereas in the 1950s we were writing forty shows each year.
>
> GALTON: Nobody told us that you can't do that, so we did it! If we had advance notice of a series, we might start two or three months ahead, but by the time we got to the third or fourth script, time would catch up with us, and we were on a deadline.

As the third series of the *Goon Show* made its inexorable demands on his imagination, Spike began to be gripped by insomnia. 'I was seen by a stupid doctor who kept giving me sleeping pills – you name 'em, I've taken 'em.' Meanwhile Sellers was little practical help as a neighbour. He would arrive in the Milligans' flat late at night, to play Spike some new record or chat about the *Goon Show*, keeping Spike awake when there was a chance that he might have been sleeping. 'In December [1952],' recalls Spike, 'I was writing the third series of *Goon Shows* when I finally broke down.'

He described it as quite a slow process:

The madness built up gradually. I found I was disliking more and more people. Then I got to hating them. Even my wife and baby. And then there were the noises. Ordinary noises were magnified in my brain until they sounded a hundred times as loud as they were, screaming and roaring in my head . . . [Finally] I thought, 'Nobody is on my side. They are letting me go insane. I must do something desperate so they will put me in hospital and cure me. I know what I'll do. I will kill Peter Sellers.'

11

Life's work

His head felt full of pain, and he was terrified by the feeling that his brain was going to burst. His mind buzzed with strange hallucinations as he snatched a potato knife from the kitchen and ran across the hallway into Peter Sellers's flat. He was so mad he thought he would have to kill Sellers before everything would come right.

That's how he described his December 1952 breakdown to Pauline Scudamore, thirty years after the event. And then there is this: 'Milligan walked straight through Sellers' glass front door and cut himself. He was in a trance . . . covered in blood from the glass.' This is the *Sun* and the *News of the World* describing Spike's re-enactment of the breakdown in a 1970 TV documentary, *The Other Spike*. Evidently he was happy to re-stage it for the camera, which suggests that nothing so very terrible had actually happened.

'I'm certain I walked through the plate-glass front door,' he told the *News of the World* in 1970. 'I remember shouting, "I have come to kill Peter Sellers." If I had meant it, I would have said, "I have come to kill you, Peter."' *If I had meant it*. So what *did* he mean?

He presumably hoped to be released from what had become the intolerable pressures of professional and domestic life. Later, he would usually experience depression rather than mania as his means of opting out. The December 1952 incident was a rare excursion into potentially violent behaviour; though actually the only real violence was directed against himself (the cuts from the glass door). Whatever his deep-level feelings about Sellers – and one remembers Max

Geldray's story about his usually hidden anger towards his fellow Goons – it seems highly unlikely that there was any intention to do him harm. It is not even clear whether he thought Sellers was at home.

In short, it is impossible to escape the suspicion that this 'breakdown' could have been at least partly play-acting. However, June Milligan took it seriously, and summoned a doctor, who decided to send him to the nearest psychiatric hospital, St Luke's, in Woodside Avenue, Highgate. Meanwhile, Spike's behaviour seems to have calmed down for the time being. 'As I got out of the ambulance,' he writes, 'there was a cat sitting on the doorstep. I stroked it.'

He told Pauline Scudamore that he was put in a strait-jacket and restrained in an isolation ward. We do not have access to his medical notes to verify this. All we have, besides his own very subjective memories, is a brief paragraph in the *Daily Mail* on New Year's Eve 1952: 'Terence A. ("Spike") Milligan . . . is ill and will be out of the show for a month.'

His hospitalisation caused *Goon Show* producer Peter Eton remarkably little bother. The scripts for the next two programmes were already written – which suggests that Spike, Stephens and Grafton were more comfortably ahead of the deadline than Spike later claimed – and these programmes were recorded with Sellers acting Spike's parts as well as his own ('No one seemed to notice,' recalls Secombe). Thereafter Stephens and Grafton provided the scripts, while Dick Emery and Graham Stark alternated in the cast, week by week. Also, Valentine Dyall, whose camply sepulchral voice had featured for many years in the radio series *Appointment with Fear*, began his occasional appearances as an extra Goon.

Meanwhile Spike reports that, at St Luke's, 'they put me in a room next to a noisy bloody kitchen. I screamed "Get me out of here!" A doctor gave me a jab of something and in ten seconds I was unconscious.' He says he remained in a drugged sleep for fourteen days, though he was woken occasionally to drink some liquid food. 'I grew a dark brown beard and I remember one nurse saying, "He looks like Our Lord."'

June came to visit him. 'She looked terrible with worrying about the breadwinner having come to a sudden halt.' So says Spike, and certainly he received no money for shows not written or performed by him. But he fails to mention that Harry Secombe generously took care of the unpaid domestic bills.

Spike also writes that, when half asleep, he began to have hallucinations: a lion crouching on a cupboard, coat hangers dangling from the ceiling, a woman with silver hair down to her shoulders. John Goldschmidt, who directed the 1970 TV documentary about the breakdown, says Spike also imagined that a figure from some painting had joined him in bed. In another hallucination, he believed himself to be an onlooker at the Crucifixion. ('One good thing,' he adds, 'I was a heavy smoker and being unconscious for two weeks had abated the craving . . . I've never really smoked since.') The hallucinations could have been caused by the drugs he was being given. It is likely, though, that they were of more significance.

His behaviour to June varied greatly. Sometimes he was delighted to see her, but at other times he would refuse to have her by his bedside. He later told Goon historian Alfred Draper: 'In the end I imagined even my wife was against me. I would shrink from her, screaming in terror, refusing to let her touch me.'

If this is true, it sounds to the layman uncomfortably like paranoia, which in its full-blown form is a symptom or manifestation of schizophrenia. Plenty of comedians and clowns have been manic-depressive, but paranoid schizophrenia does not sit comfortably with laughter.[1] In his later years, Spike

---

[1] A rare exception is the school butler who inspired Peter Cook to invent the character E.L. Wisty. It began with Cook impersonating the man, who believed he had seen stones move. Jonathan Miller (hearing about it from Cook) believed the butler was schizophrenic.

certainly displayed the paranoid schizophrenic's conviction that everyone else is to blame when things go wrong, as opposed to the depressive's underlying belief that he or she is worthless and undeserving (something that Spike, for all his bouts of depression, never seems to have felt about himself).

The build-up to his 1952 breakdown (if there really was a breakdown, and it was more than play-acting) certainly sounds very like the emotions and delusions of the paranoid schizophrenic – becoming suspicious of other people, and hearing noises. On the other hand, clearly he was not a full-blown schizophrenic; we are talking, at the most, about an underlying tendency towards mildly paranoid delusions. Moreover, paranoid symptoms are found in at least fifteen per cent of manic-depressive patients who are at their most ill. They frequently blame others, and seldom themselves, when things go wrong.

So the potato knife episode reveals him as both more and less sane than he himself thought: more sane in that he was not really a violent maniac (potato knives are usually blunt); less sane in that there may have lurked within his personality the seeds of persecution fantasies. Later episodes of instability will show us more about this.

*

He missed a total of twelve shows as a performer, but soon resumed writing scripts. 'By February [1953] I was well enough to leave hospital, but still very shaky. I went back to the slog of writing . . .'

Peter Sellers liked to joke that the scripts that Spike turned out during this and later breakdowns were even better than usual. Sellers was contemptuous of his colleague's psychological fragility – 'Spike used to get suicidal because someone would shout at him' – and had no sympathy for the stress Spike went through to create each script: 'I don't know why he did it for so long in that case.'

A thoroughly tetchy memo from Peter Eton to Michael Standing in BBC Variety on 8 January 1953, while Spike was still at St Luke's, reveals some of the background to the potato knife episode. Eton reported that, before Spike was carried off to hospital, the 'two so-called "collaborators" on the script', Spike and Larry Stephens, had been

working apart without discussing their ideas with me or each other as they were not on speaking terms. At the commencement of this [third] series Spike was already showing signs of mental strain and Larry was proudly boasting that he [Larry] was drinking more than four bottles of rum a week, so you can see that my main concern . . . was to try and make a regular 'noise' on the air that bore even a slight resemblance to the old *Goon Shows* . . . I have recently seen Spike Milligan and succeeded in patching up his quarrel with Larry Stephens . . .

Oddly, this memo makes no reference to Spike's breakdown and hospitalisation, which raises the faintest suspicion that it may never have happened, and that the illness which for twelve weeks kept him away from performing, but not from writing, was not psychological at all; not that there is the slightest evidence of what else it might have been.

Looking back in 1988, Spike recalled this as a tricky period in the Goons' history. As he saw it, he was beginning to outrun his collaborators. He remarks that Stephens and Grafton 'didn't have the sane oblique insane comedy attitude that I had; I was starting to outdo them and they were becoming an encumbrance to me.'

He returned to the *Goon Show* as a performer on 3 March 1953, a few weeks before the nation was gripped by Coronation fever. In the twenty-fourth show of the third series (28 April 1953) the Goons again tackled Everest, just as Hillary and Tenzing were about to in reality. This time the Goon attempt was a solo effort by Lord Hairy Seagoon, who is lured by the offer of £10 million to the first man to sing 'Rule Britannia' on the summit – with piano accompaniment. Unfortunately the piano becomes out of tune, and, while Seagoon waits for a replacement to be sent from England, he writes in his diary that the monsoon has begun at the most inconvenient time imaginable – right in the middle of the rainy season.

This joke particularly pleased the young Tom Stoppard – he recalls it in his autobiography, with total accuracy. One wonders if British theatre would have been the same had Harold Pinter been a Goon fan too. As it is, the Goons certainly had an influence on the British segment of that rather short-lived mid-twentieth-century movement known as the Theatre of the Absurd – and did Samuel Beckett study their work before deciding that what we were waiting for was Godot?

Since Bentine departed, the Goons had mended their noisy, chaotic ways, and the BBC now trusted them to the extent of commissioning a Coronation special on the evening of the great day itself (3 June 1953). This forty-minute programme (ten minutes longer than usual) parodied the radio and television commentaries on the procession to and from Westminster, with Secombe, as 'Richard Dimblegoon', trying to describe the scene from the top of Nelson's Column, while being dive-bombed by pigeons. The other commentators (supposedly 638 in total) included Graham Stark as John Snagge and Spike as 'Peter Dimwit' (Peter Dimmock), and the programme consisted largely of aborted handovers: the sort of joke about broadcasting that we associate more with *Monty Python's Flying Circus* than with the *Goon Show* (though as we shall see, Spike was really the father of the Pythons, more by virtue of his television programmes than by his radio work).

*

The fourth series began on 2 October 1953, and ran for a mammoth thirty programmes – further evidence that the BBC now had considerable faith in the Goons. This series saw yet another round of important changes. For the first time (as Roger Wilmut points out) the principal characters were indicated in the scripts by their own names rather than those of the performers; for example, 'Bloodnok' rather than 'Peter', a mark of the extent to which the characters were taking on a life of their own. Jimmy Grafton was no longer script-editing (feeling it to be unnecessary now), and by the end of the series Larry Stephens had dropped out, leaving Spike – for the time being – as sole writer. On the technical side, magnetic tape replaced gramophone records as the medium on which the sound effects and the show itself were recorded. The cast were consequently able to indulge in ad libs without ruining the programme's timing, since editing was now possible.

'We created some marvellous sound effects,' recalls Spike of the switch-over to tape, 'like the Wurlitzer organ crossing the Sahara desert, changing key each time they change gear.' This was in 'The Mighty Wurlitzer' in the sixth series (3 January 1956), in which Neddie Seagoon makes an attempt on the world land speed record while seated at the organ. These are the instructions in the script:

GRAMS:[2] ORGAN STARTS UP – THEN FALLS TO PIECES. SOUND OF GREAT HOLLOW ORGAN PIPES HITTING THE CONCRETE PAVEMENTS.

Spike's own favourite sound effect, often called for, once he had discovered it, was Fred the Oyster, which first appeared in 'The Sinking of Westminster Pier' (15 February 1955). Henry

---

[2] Retained as a technical term for pre-recorded sound effects after the introduction of tape.

and Minnie are oyster sexers ('We can tell the difference,' says Min), and they persuade a sceptical Seagoon to address a few words to an oyster named Fred, which opens its shell and responds with a strange sound. This was a recording, which the BBC happened to have, of a group of donkeys or mules hee-hawing and then apparently farting, though Spike says they were blowing raspberries with their lips (like Secombe).

Soon after the beginning of the fourth series, Andrew Timothy left, to read the news on television as well as continue with radio duties. John Snagge made a clever choice of successor as the *Goon Show* announcer, telling Peter Eton that in his opinion 'Greenslade would be the man'.

Wallace Greenslade (addressed as 'Wal' by Neddie Seagoon, but known to his friends as 'Bill', and designated thus in the scripts) was a highly experienced microphone performer, one of the few announcers who were allowed to read the fifteen-minute Home Service news bulletins. Peter Eton was dismissive about his intellect: 'Greenslade . . . was an amiable bum. He was a lovely man – he was a great, fat, sozzled announcer – a sweet boy – but he had nothing up here at all, bless his heart.' This was unfair. Andrew Timothy had put a sardonic edge on his *Goon Show* performances, but Greenslade read his announcements utterly straight – which required a considerable sense of comedy. As time passed, Spike made him adopt foreign accents, sing, and undergo various indignities. On one occasion during a recording, Peter Sellers suddenly said: 'Stop the show, it's time to auction Bill Greenslade's bum.' Spike remembers: 'In no time, bids were coming in, even from the audience. It was all lost in the editing.'

By the second half of the fourth series, each show at last had a continuous plot. Three new principal characters now arrived: as Roger Wilmut puts it, 'a young idiot called Bluebottle, an old idiot called Willium "Mate", and a smooth George Sanders-type character who was to develop into the Hercules Grytpype-Thynne of the fifth series'.

Bluebottle introduces himself (in the opening show of the fourth series) as 'Compton Bluebottle'. In the tenth programme (4 December 1953) he is 'Ernest Bluebottle', and gives a recitation in what became his characteristic fashion, describing his own movements as if they were stage directions, and – after a gun goes off – announcing that he has been shotten.

The story is often told that the voice of Bluebottle – which could be described as that of a boy scout for whom puberty has been indefinitely delayed – was based on an eccentric individual named Ruxton Hayward, who originally approached the Goons (bearded, and wearing shorts) to ask them to open a scout troop fête. But Spike names another model:

Bluebottle was a character that Peter Sellers had known at school – an awful 'spotty Herbert' (as he used to call him) that used to hang around him with a little high, semi-castrato voice. When anybody brought a toy to school, this kid would always say, 'Can I be the one that sees nobody touches it for you?'

Roger Lewis reports that Sellers felt that Bluebottle represented a certain side of himself: '"I am only a little thing," he'd wheedle to Lynne Frederick [his last wife] in the aftermath of some outrage, "I am really Bluebottle and nothing else. All this acting is brown paper and string."'

'William "Mate" Cobblers', to give him his full name, was what has come to be known as a jobsworth. 'Now uniformed doorman at Aeolian Hall, wears full war medals at all times,' noted Spike in some mini-biographies of the Goon characters. 'Informs all visitors to the BBC, "It's nothing to do with me, mate."' To which Sellers added: 'All the Goon characters are real, you know . . . William Mate, he's got a furniture shop near Spike's office. You go in and say, "What sort of wood is this?" And he says, "Solid wood, that is."'

Grytpype-Thynne is one of the hard-faced men who did well out of the war, a racketeer or black-marketer who hides behind an impeccable public school accent, and operates in eccentric partnership with Count Moriarty, ruined scion of some great European clan (his name of course echoes that of Sherlock Holmes's great enemy). Spike says of Grytpype-Thynne and Bloodnok: 'The Goons gave me a chance to knock people who my father, and I as a boy, had to call "Sir". Colonels, chaps like Grytpype-Thynne with educated voices who were really bloody scoundrels. They'd con and marry old ladies; they were cowards charging around with guns.' Bloodnok is referred to in one *Goon Show* as 'Major Denis Bloodnok, coward and bar'.

Peter Eton says much the same: 'The Goons were a strong reaction against the pomposity we all shared during the war . . . Spike and Larry tried to cut through this . . . and there were lots of BBC Execs (retired generals, all sorts) who said "bad taste", especially about anything against the Forces.'

Dennis Main Wilson writes: 'For years we'd been sold the idea that the British Army never loses. Now, in the figure of Bloodnok, you had a Major who would take any bribe, tell any lie, to save his skin.'

It is a pity that Spike never wrote Bloodnok's autobiography – or at least never went further than the note in *The Goon Show Scripts*, which mentions that he joined the Army under an assumed height (that old Milligan family joke again), and on one occasion was found by military police wearing false testicles in a freak show. He also served in the ATS (women only!) and was only unmasked when he reported a sailor for molesting him in an air raid shelter. Needless to say he was a Freemason.

Roger Lewis argues that not merely Bloodnok but the entire *Goon Show* was 'a surreal response to the violence and behaviour [*sic*] of the war'. Milligan, however, seems to have regarded it as having a wider frame of reference than the Second World War. In a 1957 interview with Philip Oakes, for the magazine *Books & Art*, he said: 'Essentially, it is critical comedy. It is against bureaucracy, and on the side of human beings. Its starting point is one man shouting gibberish in the face of authority, and proving by fabricated insanity that nothing could be as mad as what passes for ordinary living.'

A number of different and not very clearly worked-out ideas seem to be jostling together here. 'Gibberish' and 'fabricated insanity' (*fabricated insanity*? Is there an echo here of the supposed attempt to knife Sellers?) seem to be odd terms to use of the *Goon Show*, and the last idea ('nothing could be as mad as what passes for ordinary living') does not appear to relate to the show at all. There is much more clarity in a claim Milligan made in an interview in 1995: 'Myself and Sellers,' he said, 'always thought of ourselves as comic Bolsheviks. We wanted to destroy all that went before in order to create something totally new. We were actually very serious about that.' More specifically, he told Pauline Scudamore that they had wanted to perform political satire. With Sellers able to impersonate the voice of any politician in the land – the Queen included – the Goons were potentially lethal. The BBC was too nervous, otherwise the *Goon Show* (he said) could have anticipated *Beyond the Fringe*[3] by ten years. He felt badly frustrated.[4]

In one of his own books, he adds: 'Peter [Sellers] could do anything from a dustman to the Queen, but the BBC

---

[3] The ground-breaking satirical review *Beyond the Fringe* opened in the West End in May 1961.

[4] Peter Eton said much the same to a 1978 meeting of the Goon Show Preservation Society: 'We weren't trying to undermine the BBC. We were trying to undermine the "standing order". We were anti-Commonwealth, anti-Empire, anti-bureaucrat, anti-armed forces.'

didn't like us doing voices like General Montgomery, Churchill or the Queen.'

Forced underground by this repression, the Goons took on some of the characteristics of samizdat art under Stalin, in which the state and the authorities were not directly challenged, but the total result was highly subversive.

John Cleese compares the *Goon Show* scripts to the writings of a group of authors who were expressing a degree of rebellion against 1950s British society – the Angry Young Men: 'It was a time when people were getting fed up with the stuffiness of England . . . Writers like John Osborne and John Braine dealt with it all through fury . . . The Goons challenged the stuffiness with joy. They created a sense of liberation which went beyond laughter . . .'

It is arguable that the Angry Young Men did not really exist as a group of writers with shared ideas, but were an invention of the media.[5] But if there was such a creature as an 'AYM', then – as Cleese argues – Spike Milligan had a powerful claim to be regarded as one:

He was the very bright working-class boy who went into the Army, saw it all from the inside – and knew exactly what a load of old cobblers it all was. The *Goon Show* was comedy but it was also a challenge to the whole social order. It was the very clever NCOs making jokes about the officers that the officers wouldn't quite have understood.

Spike's membership of the working class should not be overlooked in any analysis of the Goons. With *Beyond the Fringe* in 1961, the torch of British comedy passed into the hands of Oxbridge graduates. It stayed there for the next twenty years or so; a critic on Radio 4's *Front Row* has described *Monty Python's Flying Circus* (of which John

---

[5] See the present writer's *The Angry Young Men* (2002).

Cleese was, of course, a member) as 'nice cosy middle-class boys aping the stupid proletariat'. The Goons, by contrast, were the proletariat impersonating and mocking their social superiors.

Cleese, who was born in 1939, emphasises that the Goons tended to arouse hostility in his parents' generation; he says his own father 'thought the Goons were rubbish'. Cleese's fellow Monty Pythonite, Michael Palin, four years younger, reports a similar reaction on the home front: 'My parents didn't know what was going on when they heard Henry and Minnie Crun [*sic*], Eccles and all those strange voices. I think my father thought the wireless was broken.' Palin adds that, until then, radio comedy had been something he could share with his mother and father; they would listen *en famille* to the witty but unthreatening *Take It From Here*, and to the cosy sitcom *Much-Binding-in-the-Marsh*.

The Labour politician Michael Foot got to know Spike when they both took part in the anti-nuclear Aldermaston Marches, from 1958. (John Antrobus alleges that Spike only marched from Kensington to Trafalgar Square, on the grounds that he had avoided all the marches he could in the war, and wasn't going to start now.) 'The *Goon Show* was the proper antidote to what was happening in this country then,' writes Foot. 'Spike found comic answers . . . He came out on the side of the ordinary person . . . He was a rebel from the start . . .' But Peter Eton suggests that it is a mistake to treat the Goons as political or social satire: 'The *Goon Show* was less a criticism of any social system than a bold and melodramatic rearrangement of all life. It was obliged to create a nightmare landscape of its own and people it with men, beasts and machines terribly at variance with the observable universe.'

So what purpose does this rearrangement serve? Eton's phraseology makes one think of *Gulliver's Travels*, rich in the reinvention of people and their ideas; but Swift's purpose is never in doubt – his invented lands and their inhabitants are caricatures of the follies of the real world. The problem with treating the Goons as Swiftian satire is that we feel affection for the characters, which does not happen when we read Swift. More than that, we want to *be* Bluebottle, Eccles and Henry Crun.[6]

Roger Wilmut lists as influences on Milligan's scripts 'the satire of Aristophanes, the anarchy of the Marx Brothers, the violence of the Hollywood cartoon, and the broad comedy of the English Music Halls'. One of Spike's achievements was to revive and revitalise the music-hall joke, which had become anaemic with the transformation of the working-class music halls into the more decorous middle-class variety theatres. BBC rules forbade jokes about sex, which had played a big part in music hall, but Spike was a master of that other stalwart, the pun: 'I'm not a spy, I'm a shepherd' – 'Ah, shepherd-spy!' (This needs to be said aloud.)

Maybe Spike had read Aristophanes, as Wilmut suggests, but generally he was in haste to reject the suggestion that the *Goon Show* had literary influences, such as Kafka or

---

[6] We do this, of course, by impersonating their voices; but one must not forget the catchphrases, the meaningless repetition of which qualifies one as a Goon. The principal ones include 'Ying-tong-iddle-i-po', 'There's more where that came from', 'I'm der famous Eccles', Bluebottle's 'You rotten swine' and 'You've deaded me', Henry Crun's 'You can't get the wood, you know', Bloodnok's 'Gad, it must be hell in there', Little Jim's 'He's fallen in the water', Grytpype-Thynne's 'You silly twisted boy, you', and a couple dancing to the ballroom music of Victor Sylvester: 'Do you come here often?' 'Only during the mating season.' Roger Wilmut notes that in a sketch in *Crazy People*, 'Milligan had propounded the theme that a catchphrase was simply a meaningless remark repeated until the audience was brainwashed into laughing at it.'

Ionesco. He says he didn't need to go to books for 'influences' – they were all around him, in daily life. Oddly, nobody seems to have asked him if he felt he was influenced by Edward Lear and Lewis Carroll, which obviously he was. Carroll supplied models of logic run wild, while as for Lear, an anonymous contributor to the *Goon Show Preservation Society Newsletter* (January 1975) rightly observed: 'A destructive and brutal streak can be traced in Lear, in whose work countless characters are smashed, burned, devoured or otherwise annihilated, and this violent image can be seen dramatised in the Goons.' The film director Richard Lester, who often worked with Spike, sums up: 'he is a traditionalist, his roots are in Lear and Carroll . . .'

There remains one point, perhaps the most important. Pat Dixon, the BBC producer who had 'discovered' the Goons, and later took charge of the show, wrote to Spike on 10 November 1954: 'It is the only show that is real radio.' Spike himself writes of 'radio, where the pictures are better because they happen on the other side of your eyes', and he once described radio as 'the great mind medium'. The *Goon Show* is the cleverest use anyone has ever made of radio; nothing else has ever come near its effortless depiction of the impossible (such as transporting pianos up Everest). Spike's instinctive understanding of the possibilities of the medium hugely enlarged the show's comic range. Where else could a distinguished broadcaster be found attempting to give a commentary on the coronation from his bath? Where else could Minnie Bannister descend an almost endless set of staircases to answer the front door, although she and Henry live in a bungalow? Where else could Bluebottle enjoy immortality – 'deaded' in one show, he rises again on the seventh day, to be blown up once more? Where else could a man turn out to be a shepherd's pie?

*

Much of the *Goon Show* audience was listening overseas. The BBC General Overseas Service (now the World Service) had broadcast many of the earlier shows, and from the fifth series (starting in November 1954) BBC Transcription Service recordings were made available to radio stations all over the world. As many as 4½ million people listened in Commonwealth countries and the USA. It was this that made the BBC keep the tapes of the shows from the fifth series onwards; previously the recordings had been destroyed as a matter of routine.

One wonders what listeners in the Indian subcontinent made of the scenes involving the characters Lalkaka and Banerjee, in which Sellers and Milligan vie to see who can produce the funniest Indian accents; or whether Caribbean and African listeners felt entirely comfortable with the frequent jokes about the colour of Ray Ellington's skin – such as Eccles saying to him, 'I didn't see you in the dark', and Ellington replying, 'Hardly surprisin'.' The scripts also frequently called on Sellers to caricature Jews.

Pauline Scudamore tried to get Spike to talk about this. She argued in his defence that he was born into a racist society (Anglo-India), and that he had not been able to shed its indoctrination, making racist jokes that weren't funny. He would try to justify the use of 'wog' or 'nigger' on the curious premise that if these words were said often enough they would become meaningless. But, concluded Scudamore, he was not happy to talk about racism; it made him anxious, defensive, perplexed but also arrogant.

His refusal to accept that attitudes to race had changed since his Indian childhood was to cause problems many years later. Meanwhile in November 1953, almost a year after he had been hospitalised, Peter Eton described his state of mind as a 'very finely balanced present mood of comparative sanity'.

The following March, Eton reported to the Head of

Variety that he and Spike had just run into John Snagge, who had congratulated Spike on the *Goon Show* and told him that the Home Service was very pleased with it. Spike, who regularly complained that the BBC high-ups never told him what they thought of the show, was so pleased by this that he told Snagge that he had two great wishes. One was to write and record an experimental *Goon Show* without an audience. The other was to be commissioned well in advance to write the next series, so that (reported Eton) he could

devote the whole of the summer to preparing for the return of his 'life's work'. Snagge, realising that Milligan lives only for the *Goon Show*, said he felt sure this could be arranged and Spike went away from the meeting 'really thrilled' . . . As a result of this little social, Milligan has turned in two of the best scripts he has ever written and is now writing like a man inspired.

This is the only recorded occasion on which Spike declared how much the *Goon Show* mattered to him: it was no less than his 'life's work'. Snagge, impressed by Spike's commitment, made both wishes come true. Eton wrote to Spike three months later, on 10 June 1954: 'The position is that from now onwards, any script or part of a script which you would like to write for the new series will be paid for immediately you send it in.' As to Spike's other request, an audience-less (and music-less) show called *The Starlings* was recorded by the Goons in a BBC studio in Newcastle and broadcast on 31 August 1954, during the summer break between the fourth and fifth series.

It tells how the starlings who have become a nuisance in Trafalgar Square are removed by means of explodable bird-lime. Unfortunately the explosion blows up the church of St Martin-in-the-Fields. A Member of Parliament declares that if the starling nuisance persists, the government will have no hesitation in blowing it up once again – and again, and again.

The recording – one of the first to have survived – lacks the exuberance of the normal *Goon Shows*, and the plot is rather plodding. Nevertheless at least two of the radio critics loved it, according to unidentified cuttings in the BBC files. One wrote: '*The Starlings* was so funny that it makes me despair of the future of TV comedy . . . When you think of the limitations of a TV studio, you can understand why the Goons stick to radio.' The other compared *The Starlings* to Kafka, S.J. Perelman, or 'Hieronymus Bosch with explanatory footnotes by Groucho Marx . . . I found this programme hilarious and slightly terrifying.'[7]

The Starlings increased Spike's confidence as a writer, though senior BBC officials objected strongly to Sellers's performance in it as the Duchess Boil de Spudswell, which was in the Queen's voice. 'Peter imitated the Queen,' writes Eton, 'and I was hauled up again . . . I believe that it was only John Snagge's continued defence of the programme . . . which saved us.' Later *Goon Shows* occasionally had Sellers impersonating Churchill, but finally, to Milligan's fury, this was banned too. (He did however slip in a Harold Macmillan impersonation – 'You've never had it so good' – during a 1958 *Goon Show*, three years before Peter Cook's take-off of Supermac in *Beyond the Fringe*.)

By the start of the fifth series, it was fashionable in highbrow circles to declare yourself a Goon fan. The Home Service's austere arts review programme *The Critics* discussed the Goons, and one of the contributors, the visual artist Michael Ayrton, described the show as 'the wittiest, most irrational of those weekly diversions which derive from the

---

[7] Three years after *The Starlings*, the Goons recorded another audienceless show, *The Reason Why*, broadcast on 22 August 1957. The plot concerned the bringing of Cleopatra's Needle to England.

golden age of *ITMA* . . . It has a tremendous pace and flaw-less timing . . .'

Peter Eton told the *Radio Times* that the Goons now received 'hundreds of letters a week from . . . generals, bus-drivers, padres and charladics . . . "One of the appeals of the *Goon Show*," said Eton, "is that its humour is class-less." . . . It also sometimes carries a very sane message to a very mad world.'

12

Fun Factory

As Spike's first child, Laura, started to run around the family's cramped flat in Highgate, she distracted him so much from writing the weekly *Goon Show* script that he accepted an invitation from Eric Sykes to come and share his office, at 130 Uxbridge Road, Shepherd's Bush, over a greengrocer's shop. In doing so, Spike acquired a collaborator who played a key part in making the Goons even better.

Sykes, a Yorkshireman who had left school at fourteen and had learned how to write and perform comedy during wartime service as a signaller, had been listening to the Goons since *Crazy People*, when he had sent Spike a fan letter. He himself was now writing for the hugely popular BBC radio show *Educating Archie* (starring Peter Brough and his ventriloquist's dummy Archie Andrews), in which Harry Secombe was appearing. Sykes says that, when he first met Spike,

I thought he was a bit hyperactive and trying desperately hard to make sure that everything he said was funny instead of just relaxing. I remember thinking that he would learn, when he became more accepted as a writer, to enjoy his leisure hours instead of going round with a placard on him saying 'I am a funny man'.

Sykes claims that 'in *Educating Archie*, I think I was one of the first people to try to create mental pictures on radio using lots of sound effects. Spike took this idea . . . and raised it to another level altogether.'

Spike recalls that, at Uxbridge Road, Sykes (wearing an overcoat to keep warm) was sharing the premises with an agent called Stanley 'Scruffy' Dale; but there were two floors of empty offices. Looking around him at the unused space, Spike came up with the idea of forming something that he believed was badly needed in Britain: a writers' commune or co-operative.

The plan went ahead – an example of Spike the organiser and even businessman, a side of his personality that tends to be forgotten in comparison with the creativity and the mood swings. The first writers to be invited to join Associated London Scripts (as it was called) were Alan Simpson and Ray Galton, then in their early twenties and starting to make a name in BBC radio comedy.

ALAN SIMPSON: I can remember vividly our first contact with Spike. Ray and I had only just started in the business – we were working on a show called *Happy Go Lucky*, with Derek Roy. It was around 1953. We were working at my mother's house, and there was a phone call, and it was Spike. It was the first time I'd spoken to him, though we were already great fans of the *Goon Show*, which had started about two years before – we were besotted by it. So it was like being phoned by Jesus Christ!

RAY GALTON: There were only a few shows that we admired – *Take It From Here* we thought was wonderful.

ALAN SIMPSON: And the *Goon Show*, and that was it!

RAY GALTON: And [Bernard] Braden.

ALAN SIMPSON: Braden, yes. Anyway, Spike said, 'Have you got an agent yet?' I said no we hadn't. He said, 'Eric Sykes and I, we haven't got an agent either.' And he said, 'You don't want to sign with an agent – they take ten per cent for doing nothing. Why don't you come and meet us and have a chat?' So we got a bus, and went over to Shepherd's Bush, and basically what Spike was suggesting was that we form a group, a non-profit-making co-operative, and be our own agents.

RAY GALTON: It was above a greengrocer's shop in Shepherd's Bush. Spike was working there –

ALAN SIMPSON: Spike and Eric were working there.

RAY GALTON: Frankie Howerd and his agent Scruffy Dale –

ALAN SIMPSON: Who was also Eric's agent.

RAY GALTON: Yes, they were going to use Scruffy, and Frank was going to be one of the founders.

CARPENTER: It sounds to me like an expensive way to do it – more expensive than paying ten per cent to an agent.

ALAN SIMPSON: No, no, not at all – financially it was the best thing we ever did. In all the years that we were working there, we never once paid for a telephone call or a sheet of paper, or a secretary.

CARPENTER: And it was all being paid for out of the ten per cent?

ALAN SIMPSON: Yes, deducted from the cheque – though Ray and I earned nothing compared to the rest of them.

Needing a secretary-cum-office-manager, they engaged a girl of twenty-one, who had been at school with Simpson. Her name was Beryl Vertue, and these days she is one of the most successful independent TV producers in the country (her credits include *Men Behaving Badly*). 'I didn't really want the job,' she says,

but at the interview Spike was charming, and asked me very unusual questions like, 'What sort of tea do you make?', and I asked for ten pounds a week, which in those days was a lot, and Spike said that would be fine – he didn't seem to be consulting Alan, Ray or Eric – so I found myself in the job, or rather jobs, because I was typist, tea-maker, and also their agent!

Simpson and Galton recall that, for a while, Tony Hancock

was a member of Associated London Scripts (ALS); but not for long.

ALAN SIMPSON: Hancock eventually pulled out because he felt he had no right to be there – he wasn't a writer. That was an honourable position in a way. Whereas Frankie Howerd didn't care. He stayed in because he thought he'd get free material.

RAY GALTON: We acquired a lot more writers: Johnny Speight, John Antrobus, Terry Nation.

Beryl Vertue says Speight had been selling insurance, and Nation (future creator of *Dr Who* and the Daleks) had done a spell as a furniture salesman in Wales. Nation himself recalls that he had failed as a stand-up comic, and got an introduction to Spike. 'I was starving to death. He instantly wrote a cheque for ten pounds, and that was a lot of money in those days. He said, "Go away and write a *Goon Show*, and if it's any good, we'll represent you."' Nation passed the test, though his Goon script does not seem to have been used.

ALAN SIMPSON: We had about thirty writers at one time, and eventually quite a large staff – ten or twelve people.

RAY GALTON: We had a meeting, and one of the newcomers said: 'If this is a non-profit-making co-operative, how come all the directors have free offices?' And Spike just got up and walked out, went back to his office and locked the door, and started playing the trumpet.

From the summer of 1954, Spike's address for correspondence was Associated London Scripts, 130 Uxbridge Road, W12 (the headed paper lists him, Sykes, Galton and Simpson as the members), and Beryl Vertue had taken over his business affairs. For example, on 14 June 1954 she wrote to the BBC to ask for his 'performing fee' for the *Goon Show* to be raised to 20 guineas. They agreed at once. (Sellers and Secombe were being paid twice as much.)

Later letterheads show that by October 1956, Hancock and Howerd had joined Associated London Scripts, Alan Simpson had become chairman, and Stanley Dale was managing director. By May 1957 the company had outgrown Uxbridge Road and moved to 2 Cumberland House, Kensington High Street. Beryl Vertue says this was altogether grander, but less matey: 'By that time the press had nicknamed us the Fun Factory, but in Kensington we all had offices on the ground floor, and it didn't have the same cheerfully dishevelled feeling.'

Simpson and Galton recall the Shepherd's Bush days, when they were writing alongside Spike:

ALAN SIMPSON: We would come to work every day.

CARPENTER: So you saw quite a lot of Spike?

ALAN SIMPSON: Every day.

CARPENTER: What was that like?

RAY GALTON: Good – on occasions. Some days quite normal, and then sometimes he would get the black dog, and you'd watch his eyes glaze over. He'd be all right one minute, and then he'd get some bad news – it could be quite trivial, maybe something to do with his house, the taps not working or something like that, and his eyes would glaze over, and he'd walk back to his office, turn the key, and we wouldn't see him for a week. Well, it would seem like a week.

ALAN SIMPSON: Certainly days at a time. All the others used to worry about it, all the secretaries – he used to get very bad-tempered with the secretaries and shout a lot, and quite frighten them.

RAY GALTON: Leave them notes.

ALAN SIMPSON: Leave notes. And he'd send telegrams to his

secretary downstairs! He used to do it as jokes as well, send telegrams to us. They were gags. But on good days he'd come out of his office as if nothing had happened, be all bright and breezy and giggling.

RAY GALTON: Another thing – Spike wrote by himself, Eric [Sykes] wrote by himself, and we worked together. They would both come in and ask us to listen to what they'd been writing. Not all the time, but quite often: 'What do you think of this?' Whereas we never asked them, because we'd got each other. Though sometimes we'd come in and find Eric sitting at our desk, reading the Hancock script we were doing.

ALAN SIMPSON: Spike used to do everything straight on to the typewriter. He used to hammer it out, and he couldn't bear to stop for five minutes, to think. So he'd type away, and get through twenty pages, and that would be a *Goon Show*. And then he'd start from scratch again. He'd do five or six drafts of each show, and when, for instance, he couldn't think of anything for Eccles to say, he'd just put 'Fuck off!' or 'Bollocks', and then he'd go back later and fill that in. And you used to hear his typewriter clacking away – he never stopped, whereas someone could go past our office, and wonder if there was anyone in there. If you opened the door, you might see Ray with his pipe and me on the floor, both of us thinking of the next line. And sometimes it could be hours before we'd type one line.

CARPENTER: You say that Spike wrote alone, but he did in fact use a lot of collaborators.

ALAN SIMPSON: In the beginning, yes.

RAY GALTON: Larry Stephens and Spike started together. Larry was a lovely man, charming man.

ALAN SIMPSON: Spike was less than generous, in subsequent years, about Larry's contribution. As far as we knew, Larry had contributed as much to those scripts as Spike. Certainly

Larry used to do the typing, and he had a very bright mind. But he was a grasshopper – he couldn't finish anything.

RAY GALTON: Spike used to say that Larry was the highest-paid typist in the business. Which was less than fair.

Beryl Vertue recalls a strange aspect of Larry Stephens: 'Larry was a very nice man, but very fastidious and very scared of dirt, always going round with white gloves on.' She confirms Spike's eccentric use of telegrams:

If he was working at home, he would phone me to send a telegram to his wife, who was downstairs, saying 'Where's my bloody dinner?'

If he had a really bad depression, he would shut himself up in his office. Once, he'd been in there for two or three days, and it was a really sunny day, and I felt so sorry for him. I knocked on the door, and a feeble little voice said, 'Yes?' 'It's really lovely out,' I said, 'it's spring, and I've bought you something.' Eventually he opened the door, and I'd bought him a bunch of primroses. He had all the blinds down, and some joss-sticks burning, but he was really touched by the primroses, and he went to the window, and lifted up a corner of the blind – just enough for the primroses to get the sunshine, and no more. It was sad, but then all of a sudden he'd buck up.

Beryl used to type the fair copy of each week's *Goon Show* script, and she confirms Galton and Simpson's description of his working method: 'He used to type loads of drafts himself, putting down every bit of stream-of-consciousness that occurred to him – and then all of a sudden it had to be the final version because it was time to send it in.'

She also used to help him to answer the *Goon Show* fan mail – 'It was coming in by the shoal, and most of them were trying to be funny!' – and to take dictation for his other correspondence: 'He used to say, "If you've got a problem, go straight to the people at the top – don't start low down." And I remember the day his milk hadn't been delivered at home, and he said: "Get me the chairman of United Dairies." Which I did – and it worked!'

*

Spike himself recalls that, with the office established, 'I worked a long day, leaving home at nine in the morning and working until ten or eleven at night. I had to work long hours to make the scripts as good as I could.' June, who now saw very little of him, would leave food out for him to warm up when he got home. Beryl Vertue met June quite often, and recalls her as 'quite an uncomplicated person. Spike was always passionately fond of his children, but – you know, it was a case of "whichever wife, whichever year".'

In September 1954 the Milligans' second child was born, a boy, whom they named Sean; he was baptised with his sister Laura, who had not previously been christened, at a Catholic church in Hendon. Two other additions to the family were a puppy and an elderly car – a 1929 Austin soft-top which Spike, who could now drive, bought from Peter Sellers for £300. It was named 'Little Min', after Minnie Bannister.

Two weeks after Sean's birth, the fifth series of the *Goon Show* began. Spike wrote the first six scripts by himself, and several of these were among the best there would ever be: 'The Whistling Spy Enigma', 'The Affair of the Lone Banana', and – particularly – 'The Dreaded Batter Pudding Hurler of Bexhill-on-Sea', Spike's tribute to his war years there. But the effort of turning out these half-dozen shows seems to have exhausted him, since for the remaining twenty of the series he co-opted Eric Sykes to write them with him, despite the fact that, as Sykes himself says, 'I really had enough of my own work to do'.

Sykes, whose even-tempered personality made him an ideal Milligan writing partner, recalls that the two of them 'wrote together for a few shows and then eventually I wrote one week and he wrote the next week'. Both Sykes's and Milligan's names appear on all the scripts written during this period of collaboration, so it is impossible to tell which are the work of Sykes alone.[1] 'As far as I was concerned,' he says, 'writing *Goon Shows* was an absolute gift. All the characters were there and all I had to do was to give them their ration of air time.'

Roger Wilmut judges that the Milligan–Sykes collaborations created scripts that were 'more consistently high [in quality] than at any other time. Nearly every show is first class.' They include 'The Mystery of the Marie Celeste (Solved)', 'Nineteen Eighty-five', inspired by the TV dramatisation of Orwell's *1984*, and 'China Story', which was chosen for another dissection of the Goons by *The Critics* (23 January 1955). The discussion was led off by the humorist Stephen Potter. He observed that 'the *Goon Show* . . . began rather thinly, as far as I remember, in 1951, and it's been improving ever since.' The chairman, John Summerson, suggested that the show could only be appreciated fully by regular, initiated listeners – 'I must say the whole thing went too fast for me' – and T.C. Worsley (who was also on the panel) described it appreciatively as 'surrealism in sound'.

Although Spike's writing load had diminished greatly with the co-opting of Sykes, the fifth Goon series seems to have taken its toll, since on 15 May 1955 Dr William Townsley of 399 Hendon Way, London NW4 signed a chit to state to the BBC that 'Mr T. Milligan' was 'suffering from nervous

---

[1] However, they appear in different order, Sykes's name first some weeks, Milligan's first other weeks, which may indicate which was the author. Moreover the Marie Celeste script (16 November 1954) is credited to Sykes alone, though in the BBC microfilmed copy Milligan's name has been added by hand in the closing announcement.

debility and is unable to follow his occupation'. Pauline Scudamore says this was a major depression, and notes that he spent several weeks in a private nursing home. But he could be high-spirited too. Thanking someone at the BBC for a party in March 1955, he added that since the party he had seen no sign of Eric Sykes – he hoped that the cleaners would keep an eye out for him.

He was now undertaking occasional variety theatre dates. In June and July 1954 he went with Harry Secombe and Max Geldray on a tour of Moss Empires theatres, and there was also a legendary week in which all three Goons appeared at the Coventry Hippodrome. It was very far from being a triumph. 'I was to do my usual performance,' writes Secombe,

a mixture of gags and straight songs; Spike was at that time still working on his act; and Peter, who was completely without nerves, was experimenting with all kinds of comic ideas because he hated doing the same act night after night. The only piece of material we did together was a skit on Morris dancers (called the East Acton Stick Dancers) which Eric Sykes had written for one of my television shows . . . One night Spike had a particularly bad reception from a bewildered audience and, after delivering the immortal line 'I hope you all get bombed again',[2] he walked off to his dressing room and locked the door . . . We knew that Spike was going through a bad time with his manic depression, though I was beginning to think I might catch it off him.

Spike had recently purchased a hangman's noose, with a label saying 'only used once', and Sellers and Secombe now feared the worst. According to Alfred Draper's *The Story of the Goons*, 'When the door finally gave way to

---

[2] Coventry Cathedral and much of the city had been destroyed in wartime air-raids.

their combined weights, they saw Milligan standing on a chair with the noose around his neck, and trying to hook it round an overhead pipe.' But he told Pauline Scudamore that this was nonsense: 'What, hang myself for Coventry?' He said it was never meant to be anything more than a joke.

Scudamore's version of the Coventry incident is that he screamed at the hostile audience, telling them he knew they hated him. Then he stamped on his trumpet, stormed off the stage, and locked himself in his dressing-room for hours.

*

Late in 1955 or early in 1956, the Milligans left their Highgate flat and bought, on a mortgage, a semi-detached house, 127 Holden Road, Finchley, which had a large garden with a stream at the bottom.

Finchley now became to the Goons what Neasden is to *Private Eye*, symbol of all things drably suburban – and home of Bluebottle. Bloodnok refers to 'the steaming hell of Finchley', and Bluebottle's girlfriend is 'Miriam Reene of 33 Croft Street, East Finchley'.

In fact Spike seems to have loved it there. Certainly the garden at Holden Road inspired a new pastime. He began writing miniature letters to his children, supposedly from the fairies, and placing these for Laura and Sean to find among the plants and rocks. Each letter was in miniature calligraphy – penmanship was one of his accomplishments.

Asked if he ever met June Milligan, Alan Simpson says:

Yes, frequently. She was Mother Earth – she used to run a good old Italian-style household, you know, spaghetti Bolognese. We used to go to their house quite a lot – I remember going there for dinner, and she was in the kitchen, cooking away. Real sort of stoutish Italian mum. She wasn't Italian, but she was very

Mediterranean-looking. And totally, completely, utterly un-show-business. As different from Spike as you could imagine.

Laura Milligan has said of her parents, at this stage in their marriage: 'She was a lovely simple woman and he was a difficult man who was just becoming famous and was under a lot of pressure.' Spike let June take the children for their 1955 summer holiday without him: 'I couldn't go,' he writes, 'as I was still working hard to deliver a complete *Goon Show* script once a week.' But the show was off the air in the summer. He was both developing an intense relationship with his children, and (for reasons that aren't really clear) detaching himself from June.

On 2 April 1955, at the beginning of the Goons' summer break, he appeared on BBC Television's *Variety Parade*, doing a solo act. The 'script' he supplied to the producer indicates that after some clowning around he would demonstrate his skill at boxing, and would then perform a trumpet solo with the orchestra. This skimpy running order for his act shows how much he depended on the inspiration of the moment.

The pressure was certainly on him again when the sixth Goon series began on 20 September 1955, with Sykes only collaborating on a few scripts. Towards the end of the series, Peter Eton left (for television) and was replaced by Pat Dixon, who had played a crucial part years earlier in getting the show on the air, and now gave the Goons a rather looser rein than Eton. Meanwhile a key relationship was now showing some strain.

On 18 January 1956 the BBC's Variety Booking Manager reported:

The agent of Master Peter Sellers informs me that this artist now doesn't wish to be associated with the *Goon Show* ever again.

This, I believe, we take with a pinch of salt for it seems it stems from an upheaval between Sellers and Spike Milligan, something which I believe happens at fairly regular intervals.

This particular row was indeed resolved, but Sellers was becoming restless; he was beginning to get decent film roles – *The Ladykillers* (1955) was his breakthrough – and was starting to chafe at his *Goon Show* commitment. On the other hand, almost by chance, the Goons gave him an excursion into the pop record charts.

In February 1956 the Musicians' Union called a strike, and Spike found himself without Geldray, Ellington or the band. In the *Goon Show* broadcast on 21 February ('The Great Tuscan Salami Scandal'), Spike himself sang all the musical links in the nasal tones of 'Adolphus Spriggs'. He also performed a song he had composed while going home one night on the Tube, 'I'm Walking Backwards for Christmas'. Sellers accompanied him on the piano, and the song went down so well with listeners that several record companies competed to record it. Decca won the bidding, and issued it, coupled with a solo for Sellers, 'The Bluebottle Blues', as a 78 rpm single in the summer of 1956. It peaked at number four in the charts.

Spike was encouraged by this to try an experiment: 'With the pop scene as it was, I thought, I bet I can write a hit record, I'll write the worst song in the world, with three chords and no words. And I did it.' (He means nonsense words.) The result was 'The Ying Tong Song', which was coupled with another Sellers solo, 'Bloodnok's Rock'n'Roll Call', and reached number three.

Spike himself played the guitar on 'The Ying Tong Song': 'My total record as a musician! . . . I sent it to my mother, and wrote, "By the way, that's me playing guitar in the middle." So she invited all her cronies in, "Listen to this now." And she'd marked it with a chalk, where the guitar started and where it finished. "Oh he's a powerful good player!"'

Meanwhile he was beginning to find ways of transferring his brand of comedy to television.

13

So certain of roars of laughter

In 1955 a twenty-three-year-old American psychology graduate arrived in England, hoping to find a backer for a musical he had written. He was unsuccessful at this, but was already an experienced TV director, and was hired by Associated Rediffusion, which was providing ITV programmes for the London region. His name was Richard Lester, and at Christmas 1955 he was allowed to fill a hole in the schedules with an ad-libbed comedy show. He says it was an 'absolute total disaster', but it picked up quite a big audience, including Peter Sellers.

He was impressed, and phoned Lester, and they talked about whether a TV version of the Goons was possible. Then they went to see Spike. 'He was lying on the floor,' recalls Lester. 'He didn't get up and the first thing he said to me was, "You can't do comedy on TV – there's no point in talking about it." That was that.'

Nevertheless Lester and Sellers decided to go ahead. As Lester recalls it, the first in a series called *The Idiot Weekly Price 2d.* was assembled and broadcast by Associated Rediffusion without Milligan, who phoned promptly the following morning, full of ideas for the next programme, and, says Lester, 'completely took over' the remaining six programmes in the series.

In fact there were only two *Idiot Weekly* shows, and Spike was in both of them. The *TV Times* billing for the first, on 24 February 1956, read: 'Scripts provided by Associated London Scripts, edited by Eric Sykes with contributions by Spike Milligan'. Spike also appeared in it, as did Graham

Stark, Valentine Dyall and Kenneth Connor, with Sellers playing the *Idiot Weekly* editor. This programme was reviewed in the *Evening Standard* by guest critic Wolf Mankowitz:

this satirical saga of irritation with the fatuous and the pretentious broke every convention of respectable comedy . . . By the time pretty Patti Lewis finished her song, to be rewarded by a custard pie full in her smile and a typically idiotic interview as the custard dripped on to her beautiful gown, I knew that Peter Sellers, Eric Sykes, Spike Milligan and their producer, Dick Lester, had saved the larger, less pretty and normally inane face of Channel Nine[1] comedy.

A second *Idiot Weekly* was broadcast – live, like the first – on 6 April 1956. No recordings survive, and it is impossible to reconstruct the programmes, but Graham Stark remembers a sketch by Spike in which 'we played out-of-work actors making a living by deputizing for animals at the zoo, which entailed Ken Connor going in a cage with monkeys, Valentine Dyall joining a vulture in its cage, and myself swimming . . . in the sea lion pit'.

Dick Lester says that from the outset he was hugely impressed by Spike:

In terms of naked comedy I've been very fortunate to have worked with Buster Keaton, Groucho Marx. But . . . Spike was the most constantly inventive. An absolute nightmare to work with, especially during live television, but extraordinarily clever creative brilliant mind. Quite unique.

Associated Rediffusion now gave Lester the green light for a series of five programmes by the same team, which

---

[1] The channel on which Associated Rediffusion broadcast.

went out in May 1956 as *A Show Called Fred*. The designers included a young Scot called Joe McGrath, later to play an important part in Spike's life. 'I wasn't aware of it at the time,' he says, 'but that series was almost Dali or Buñuel. It's amazing that we were allowed to do it.' Again, Graham Stark describes a typical sketch:

One camera suddenly took a wide shot of the studio, showing all the rest of the cameras . . . Then the studio doors swung open and three other cameras burst in. The cameramen on those cameras were wearing plumed hats and announced they were the . . . Light Cavalry cameras, come to steal a free show. Our cameramen immediately drew wooden swords and battle commenced. It was glorious anarchy.

Happily, a recording does survive of this sketch. The rogue cameras which burst into the ITV studio are labelled 'BBC'.

Julian Symons (also guesting on the *Standard*) reacted as enthusiastically to *A Show Called Fred* as Mankowitz had to its predecessor:

A man plays noughts and crosses on his forehead while reading a letter. A would-be bird man fails to rise an inch from the ground. When an interviewer comes to Belvedere Towers, home of the Pimms family, Lord Pimms . . . wears no trousers. Put down in print this may sound silly . . . But *A Show Called Fred* really has the stuff of television in it.

Neither *Idiot Weekly* nor *A Show Called Fred* was shown nationally. However, a third series, *Son of Fred*, which ran for eight programmes from mid-September to mid-November 1956, did have national networking, and was billed in the *TV Times* as 'PETER SELLERS in SON OF FRED by SPIKE MILLIGAN'.

Participants in *Son of Fred* included the eccentric musical group the Alberts ('These artists appear by arrangement with money'), who provided the accompaniment as Spike and Peter Sellers, dressed in long white nightgowns, jumped about in dustbins, singing:

> *When you're feeling lonely*
> *And you can't find romance*
> *Jump into a dustbin – and dance.*
>
> *When you've got no trousers*
> *And ragged underpants*
> *Jump into a dustbin – and dance.*

In just a few months, Spike had mastered the possibilities of television; indeed, he was already challenging and extending them. His scripts called for outlandish special effects, some of which had to be invented, and his achievement was recognised when the *Fred* shows were awarded Best TV Show of the Year – although he remarked ruefully that 'there were only about 350 TV sets in England at the time, so nobody really noticed'.

He was also puzzled that no further shows were commissioned by Associated Rediffusion. However, there was another opportunity during 1956 to experiment with visual humour, when he and Sellers (and Dick Emery, but not Secombe) took part in a half-hour film featuring some of the Goon characters, and giving Sellers a role as a stupid detective which anticipates his Pink Panther films.

The Case of the Mukkinese Battlehorn is widely assumed to have been written by Milligan and directed by Dick Lester, but in fact Larry Stephens and two others get the screenplay credit, and the director was one Joseph Sterling. This little film, very conventional compared to the *Fred* TV programmes, occasionally surfaces in cinemas, for example in 1975, when it accompanied the first release of *Monty Python and the Holy Grail.*

*

This television and film work, coming on top of the continuing demands of the Goons, made 1956 a year of extra pressure for Spike. He missed the *Goon Show* on 25 October because of illness (maybe depression), and had to give that week's performing fee back to the BBC, which still paid him show by show, rather than providing the security of a longer-term contract.

His insomnia was now chronic. Despairing of doctors who prescribed pills of all kinds and gave useless advice, such as a complete rest, or a change of job, he decided to try hypnotherapy, and became a patient of Dr Joseph Robson. He moaned to Robson about having to write a script every single week to make a lot of idiotic people laugh; how could they laugh when he was in such agony? Robson did his best, and they became friends, though Robson, who was Jewish, squirmed at Spike's racist and anti-Semitic jokes.

Spike was getting on badly with Pat Dixon. Choosing not to reveal the reasons, he wrote to the Variety Department asking to have Peter Eton back again. He was told that this was 'quite out of the question'. Consequently he refused to write any more scripts, though the seventh series was about to start (on 4 October 1956). Eton did produce the first two shows of the seventh series, but Dixon then returned.

Spike tried to get Pat Hillyard, now Head of Variety, to lunch with him. In all his dealings with the BBC, he emphasised how much busier he was than the staff producers and managers – not the way to ingratiate himself with them, though in fact they were patient.

With Spike writing most of the seventh series solo, and

Dixon being an indulgent producer, the plots became much untidier, with long scenes, often between Bluebottle and Eccles, which provided hilarious moments but tended to bring the storyline to a halt. Secombe was often reduced to genuine hysterics by Sellers and Milligan ad libbing. But, as Roger Wilmut writes, 'there was the danger of the cast having more fun than the audience'.

For the first time, the scripts were vetted before recording. The edition for Christmas Eve 1956 was to be made 'with the Trans Antarctic Expedition in mind': it was being carried by the BBC's General Overseas Service. Spike seems to have done his best to toe the line, but the head of the service asked for several alterations: 'The remark about NAAFI profits should be cut . . . *Land of Hope and Glory* over-done . . . There is no British Embassy in Calcutta. This was a weak ending.'

The *Goon Show* files also include an undated and unsigned memo, written at the time of Suez and the Soviet invasion of Hungary; the writer had obviously been asked to vet the script:

This script is perfectly innocuous until p. 8. We then have the first hint of a military operation. This continues off and on (mainly off) for the next eight pages but, since it is carried out by means of a zeppelin, which as a method of attack is as outmoded as the crossbow, I felt on a first reading that it could be passed. There is no reference, oblique or direct, to Middle East or Hungarian matters. But if it is felt that any reference to a military opera-tion, however remote from current matters, is dangerous, then perhaps we should think again.

Pat Dixon was under pressure to keep anything political out of the show. 'Of course we have cut the reference to Harold Macmillan as you instructed,' he told the Assistant Head of Variety on 24 January 1957.

My only point in putting this on paper . . . is to make an official protest against a policy that debars a reference to a Cabinet Minister in a comedy show . . . Churchill was constantly mentioned in the *Goon Show* during his ten years of office and even impersonated on many occasions. I think it is very dangerous to have these subtle encroachments on free speech.

When there was yet another attempt at censorship, Dixon responded even more toughly: 'We really must grow up and stop shivering in our shoes every time someone thinks that there might possibly be an angry phone call from some moronic listener.'

Spike complained to the press about the censorship: 'Their censor might be the doorman one week and the liftman the next.' He went on: 'The BBC doesn't tell me anything. I haven't even heard what my ratings are for two years . . . I'm experimental and the BBC is not. I want to improve the show but they do not'. Pat Newman of the Variety Department referred to such outbursts as 'his now rather tedious "chip on the shoulder" cracks at the BBC'.

Another of his reactions to the censorship was to make the producer's life harder by slipping in dubious jokes which he hoped would not be spotted. Roy Speer noted that in one programme there was 'a reference to Grant Road, Bombay, which, as anyone like myself who has served in India knows, is the notorious brothel quarter'. (Bloodnok is reminiscing about his adventures in Grant Road, though as usual he only alludes.)

With the general public, meanwhile, the *Goon Show* was more popular than ever. Spike reported to his parents in Australia that it was being broadcast in the USA by NBC, and, as for Britain, the *News Chronicle* had carried a Gallup Poll in which it had been voted top comedy show. It had been a hard slog, but hugely worth while, and he felt confident of being employed for at least the next five years.

Much later in his life, he looked back at the popularity of the *Goon Show* and said:

I couldn't believe it was such a success. It was like I was in some twilight world. I had never been anything but a trumpet player . . . I was doing this show, I got paid for it and I went back to writing it every Monday. I was so certain of roars of laughter that I never doubted my ability to do it.

*

Around now, the Goons acquired their most famous fan. 'It has always been one of my profound regrets,' writes HRH Charles, Prince of Wales,

that I was not born ten years earlier than 1948, since I would then have had the pure, unbounded joy of listening avidly to the Goons each week. Instead, I only discovered that the Goon-type humour appealed to me with an hysterical totality just as the shows were drawing to a close. Then I discovered the *Ying Tong Song* in record form and almost at once I knew it by heart. I plagued everybody with it . . . to such an extent that when my small brothers heard a recording of the Goons for the first time they thought it was their elder brother!

Prince Charles is uncertain when he began to listen. According to one press report, he did so 'on his transistor radio under the bedclothes at Gordonstoun'. But he did not attend Gordonstoun school until 1962, after the *Goon Show* had finished. Elsewhere he has said: 'My father was listening to the Goons on his wireless – that's when I first heard them . . . I suppose it must have been the late 1950s.'

Prince Philip seems to have been a fan, since in the spring of 1958 he chose the Goons to be his Royal Champions for a charity tiddlywinks match against the Cambridge University Tiddlywinks Club ('Goons versus Gowns'). The Goon team was Sellers, Milligan and Secombe, Wallace Greenslade, Graham Stark, Max Geldray and Alan Simpson and Ray Galton. John Snagge was the umpire. The match, at the Guildhall, Cambridge on 1 March 1958, was filmed and broadcast on the Light Programme.

Simpson and Galton say they were the only team members who actually practised before the match. Consequently, Cambridge won by 120½ points to 55½. According to the *Sunday Dispatch*, Secombe and Milligan were 'dragged away protesting'.

For somebody who called himself a 'comic Bolshevik', Milligan cared a remarkable amount about royal interest in his work. In December 1957 the Duchess of Kent attended a *Goon Show* recording, and Milligan wrote to the BBC Light Entertainment Department (as Variety had been renamed) complaining that nobody had told him she was coming. He was inappropriately dressed for the occasion, already had an engagement to eat out that evening, and had to hurry off immediately after the recording. He regretted the discourtesy.

The duchess was lucky to get a seat. Attending the *Goon Show* recordings, which were now at the Camden Theatre, north of Regent's Park, had become a Sunday evening cult for Londoners. 'People used to fight to get in there,' says Harry Secombe, and Alan Simpson agrees: 'Yes, among the radio shows it was the hottest ticket in town.'

The procedure for rehearsal and recording remained much the same as it had been for *Crazy People*, except that Secombe and Sellers no longer reported for duty on Sunday morning, but after lunch.[2] 'On a typical *Goon Show* recording

---

[2] On 22 September 1955 Spike wrote to the Variety Department objecting to a *Goon Show* recording being moved temporarily to mid-afternoon: it was (he said) like having to perform *Rigoletto* in the middle of Bond Street.

day,' writes Secombe, 'I would arrive at the Camden Theatre at around 2.30, musing on which car Peter had rolled up in.' Wally Stott, the show's arranger and conductor, was equally entertained by this: 'Outside the Camden Theatre on a Sunday evening there'd always be Peter's latest car – a different one every week.'

There would be a read-through – 'We never saw the script in advance,' emphasises Secombe – and Spike would watch the others anxiously to check that the laughs were coming in the right places. Then, as the audience arrived, there was a warm-up ritual. Secombe would deliver a fruity rendition of the waltz-song 'Falling in Love with Love', accompanied by Ray Ellington's pianist, Dick Katz. Sellers would join in on the drum-kit or the timpani, and Spike might blow a chorus or two on his trumpet. At some point, Sellers would remove Secombe's braces but (an old music-hall trick) it was Milligan's or Sellers's trousers that fell down.

Secombe recalls that, behind all this rather forced jollity, there could be tension between Milligan and Sellers: 'Peter [might have] a touch of the sulks, and perhaps Spike would . . . adopt the foetal position.' The producer would ask Secombe to break the ice: 'I'd think of some Army joke I'd heard and within a few minutes we'd all break out and all be laughing. And, of course, the brandy helped. By God, the brandy helped.'

They were now in the habit of bringing in a bottle of brandy, to share during the musical numbers, mixed with a pint of milk to disguise it from BBC officialdom. Hence the cries of 'Brandy!' or 'Round the back for the old brandy', followed by the sound of stampeding feet, as the music begins. John Browell, the Goons' last producer, says he 'noticed from time to time that the bottles of brandy were getting larger and larger'.

As the recording time approached, Wallace Greenslade, the plump announcer, would introduce any distinguished guests who might be in the audience, and the studio manager in charge of recorded sound effects would blast them with a round of machine-gun fire. Greenslade would then call up to the balcony: 'Are you all right on the shelf up there? Good, because you can't get out, the doors are locked.' Consequently the audience was already laughing when the red light came on, and Greenslade said: 'This is the BBC Home Service . . .'

*

On 26 September 1957 Spike wrote to Roy Speer, who was to produce much of the next Goon series (the eighth) and had asked for scripts in advance. He thanked Speer for an inspiring letter, and emphasised that he needed inspiration; he could not develop any ideas at the present moment because he felt totally uninspired.

His attacks of depression were becoming public knowledge. Just before Christmas 1957 – about halfway through the eighth series – the *Sunday Graphic* reported:

For three days last week arch-Goon Spike Milligan lay in a darkened room at his home . . . telephone unplugged, door locked, incommunicado . . . His wife, June, shrugged a philosophic shoulder and told me: 'I expect he'll ring down for something to eat . . .' His doctor said: 'Overwork. Overwork. Complete rest now, or something worse later.'

Larry Stephens had been contributing substantially again since the seventh series,[3] easing Spike's writing load (Sykes seems not to have been available), but was suffering from

---

[3] Spike wrote to Pat Dixon on 11 October 1956 that he would take responsibility for paying Stephens when they wrote any *Goon Shows* in collaboration. In fact all the programmes but two in this, the seventh series, were written jointly by Milligan and Stephens.

high blood pressure and was under a doctor's warning. For two shows towards the end of the eighth series, Spike co-opted a young writer called John Antrobus as his collaborator.

Antrobus, who was twenty-one, seemed at first glance a younger version of Spike. His father was a regimental sergeant major in the Royal Artillery, who had served in India. In his teens, John became an officer cadet at Sandhurst, but then chucked it all in to write gags for Frankie Howerd, and became a junior member of Associated London Scripts.

Antrobus and Spike hit it off from the outset. On days when Spike had retreated to his office and locked the door under a cloud of depression, Antrobus was one of the very few people for whom he would unlock it, and soon they would be laughing aloud, fortified by the jam doughnuts (three each) which were Spike's favourite food when he was climbing out of depression.

On other days, when there was no 'GO AWAY' notice on Spike's door, Antrobus, arriving for work, might hear music echoing across Shepherd's Bush Green. Looking up, he would see Spike standing at the open window of his office, blowing one of his favourite numbers on his trumpet, stopping to wave to the passing shoppers.

Like Galton and Simpson, Antrobus was amazed by Spike's method of writing when he was in manic mood:

The typewriter clicking manically. The waste paper basket over-spilling and balls of screwed-up paper littered round his feet. Totally absorbed. The balls of paper rise. The room fills with cast-off pages. Work. The typewriter clicks and rattles. Faster and faster as Spike submerges under the tide of revisions . . . Until he emerges out of his office, clutching the finished script, paper balls rolling on to the landing, and shouts: 'It's done! I'm going home!'

Antrobus recalls how, on many days at Associated London Scripts, everything stopped for lunch, which took place lengthily and boozily, often at the Shepherd's Bush branch of Bertorelli's Italian restaurant. On an exceptional day, all three Goons might be present, vying with each other for the last laugh:

PETER: (*as Sanders of the River*) Hello. Sorry I'm late. No, I'm not sorry. I'm glad, do you hear me? I'm glad all over. Very very glad it's taken me so long to get here. Yes – you see, I bought a new car this morning.

SPIKE: Did the old one fall off the number plate?

PETER: Yes, you're right, it wasn't securely fastened. I was parking my number plate last night and I noticed that the car had vanished. That and Ying Tong Iddle I Po.

SPIKE: With nerdles, I trust?

PETER: Exactly, Spike. With nerdles. It played havoc with my suspension.

SPIKE: I didn't know you'd been suspended.

PETER: Yes, ever since that business with a guardsman.

SPIKE: Really? They're not available in my district yet.

PETER: Then you'll have to move if you want that sort of thing, won't you?

HARRY: Agreed.

SPIKE: You filthy swine!

HARRY: I didn't know you cared.

PETER: And what are you doing these days, young Johnny?

ANTROBUS: I'm listening.

SPIKE: He's a listener! Don't let him get away.

PETER: We must get him to a radio set immediately!

HARRY: I knew a man who could listen to the radio and watch television at the same time in his bath while playing the mandolin and eating porridge through a straw.

SPIKE: Was he versatile?

HARRY: No, Jewish.

Spike Milligan

PETER: Some of my best mothers are Jewish.

HARRY: In that case, take that! (*he blows a raspberry*)

PETER: (*blows a raspberry too*) God, it's catching! (*as Major Bloodnok*) The screens, nurse, quickly!

However, Antrobus also recalls the tension between Milligan and Sellers during the rehearsal for 'The Spon Plague' (3 March 1958), one of the two Antrobus–Milligan *Goon Shows*: 'We have a read-through. It goes well. Everyone laughs a lot. Then Peter says, "Is it funny?" and Spike says, "I bloody well hope so." And nobody talks to each other for half an hour. Then we have a run-through on stage and the band is laughing so everyone gets their confidence back.'

Perhaps the most extraordinary incident in the Milligan–Antrobus partnership was the day when Spike noticed that a goldfish in a bowl in Antrobus's office was looking poorly. Antrobus explained that there had been three of them, which he was looking after for a friend, but two had died. Spike went off looking thoughtful, and when Antrobus came back from a lunchtime session at the pub with Johnny Speight, the fish and its bowl had gone. 'Then Beryl Vertue told me: "Spike has taken your goldfish in a taxi to London Zoo, John." I knew he was busy writing a *Goon Show* and that this represented a major disruption to his day.' Eventually, he came back without the fish. Antrobus asked what had happened to it. '"They had to put it to sleep," said Spike. Resignedly he went to his room and shut the door behind him. He knew he had done his best.'[4]

Antrobus recorded that, when Spike had a particularly

---

[4] Some years later, Spike wrote to Sir Charles Curran, Director General of the BBC from 1969 to 1977, objecting that an earthworm had remained pinned to a display board after an Open University lecture. Couldn't it be taken from the heat of the TV lights and put in some damp earth?

bad attack of depression, he would check into a north London nursing home and sleep a drugged sleep for several days – usually complaining, on his return, that the silly bastards had once again put him in a room next to the establishment's clanging dustbins. When he was at home, he was now on heavy medication to ward off depression and help him to sleep: according to his own testimony, 'eight Tryptizol a day, three Seconal at night'. These sedatives 'did sedate me; sometimes they turned me into a zombie'. Eventually, 'I decided that the psychiatrist was a middleman for Roche. All the pills I took never cured the illness, they just clouded it.' He said in 1990 that he had never experienced psychoanalysis, though 'counselling' does feature in his description of treatments to an interviewer in 1993.

The *Sunday Graphic* report on his state of mind included a rather bitter observation from Peter Sellers: 'He has changed a great deal. Now everything he does is part of his war against the human race.' Meanwhile, in an interview with Philip Oakes at the end of 1957, Spike indicated that he was considering winding up the *Goon Show*: 'The point is that it must continue to be experimental. And the support for the kind of experiments that I want to make simply isn't there.'

14

Gone for ever

Pat Dixon had to pull out of producing the eighth Goon series (which began on 30 September 1957) because of illness. He was replaced first by Charles Chilton, whose field was science fiction rather than comedy (he was the creator of the hugely popular *Journey into Space*), then by Roy Speer, then by Tom Ronald, who did not like the *Goon Show*, and infuriated Spike by censoring scripts. Spike protested to Jim Davidson, Assistant Head of Light Entertainment, about one of Ronald's requests for a cut. He could not believe that objections had been raised to Secombe, on being told that there was a house waiting outside to see him, asking what sex it was. (Willium replies that he cannot tell whether it is male or female, because the blinds are drawn.) This whole sequence was cut from the tape. Spike observed that anyone who found this joke objectionable was unsuited to produce the show.

Davidson's reply does not survive. Spike soon wrote to him again: 'Pat Dixon is the only producer . . . who knows what the *Goon Show* is all about. He was instrumental in putting it on the air, he thinks the same type of humour, and he has a touch of the rebel, all of which create the ideal climate.' But Dixon – with whom Spike had actually been getting on badly in the recent past – had cancer, and was dead within the year.

Not surprisingly in these circumstances, the shows in the eighth series were very uneven in quality, with the performers often splitting their sides at in-jokes, but the listener left out in the cold. There was a particularly undisciplined guest appearance in the penultimate show by the veteran actor A.E. Matthews, who had been in the news because he objected to his local council erecting a concrete lamppost outside his house. He appeared unannounced in the closing minutes of 'The Evils of Bushey Spon' (17 March 1958). 'He cocked it up completely,' recalls Spike. 'It wasn't funny and I remember the embarrassed laughter of the rest of the cast.' But it was scarcely Matthews's fault – he had not been allocated any lines in the script.

One programme in the eighth series, 'The Thing on the Mountain' (6 January 1958), was written by Larry Stephens and Maurice Wiltshire, without Spike, perhaps because the Milligans' third child had just been born. They named her Silé (pronounced 'See-lay'), an Irish version of Sheila.

By now, Spike was being very highly paid for the *Goon Show*: 115 guineas per script and 70 guineas for performing (Sellers and Secombe had reached 80 guineas). Nevertheless he wrote to the Director General, Sir Ian Jacob, complaining about the low fees he received for non-Goon BBC work. He also got Beryl Vertue at Associated London Scripts to send a complaint about Wally Stott: 'Mr Milligan would be glad if the Corporation would try to see that the musicians in the show perform new numbers rather than the old ones which crop up time and time again. This also refers to the musical links, as here too the same links have been used for an extremely long time.'

He heard that someone in Light Entertainment had been describing him as 'awkward'; and this too resulted in an aggressive letter, to Pat Newman in Light Entertainment. Spike issued a mock-apology for being difficult, but was clearly proud of it, and intended to remain so, whatever the BBC thought about him. It was a snappy letter.

He liked to conclude such letters with a sharp pay-off; for example, to another member of the BBC staff: 'I don't get paid for writing these letters but you do.' Alan Simpson comments: 'Spike's moments of antagonism could be totally unreasonable. And he couldn't take criticism. If he asked you to look at something he'd written, and cajoled you into being a bit critical, he'd go totally berserk.'

When the ninth series of the Goons began to loom, he proposed to the BBC that the first eight scripts (November and December 1958) should be written by other people – 'Larry Stephens (with Maurice Wiltshire), John Antrobus and Dave Freeman' – because he himself would be too busy. He guaranteed that he would 'edit their scripts before they are sent in to the producer', and after Christmas he would be able to take on the remainder of the series himself. The BBC refused to accept this proposal.

In March 1958, in an interview in the *Daily Mail*, he laid angrily into the BBC:

In his Kensington script-factory, behind a door on which are scrawled again and again the words LEAVE ME ALONE, Milligan gave free rein to his anger . . . 'I don't care what I say about the BBC,' he said, glowering behind the huge dog-basket he uses as an out-tray. 'I'm always on the verge of getting the sack, anyway. But somehow we have to rid ourselves of these torpor-ridden people . . . I'm the most progressive comedy writer in the country . . . But they don't want ideas . . .

'I resent being called a Goon . . . I find it increasingly difficult to write funny stuff. I look at my children and I ask myself: "What is their future?" . . . Why should they live with this brooding horror [nuclear weapons] hanging over them?'

The following month, he, June and the children sailed to Australia.

*

The trip was in order that they could see his and June's families, and for Spike to make an Australian version of

Idiot Weekly for ABC television. He recalls how, on the voyage, there were terrible arguments between himself and June. He alleges that she had embarrassed him by visiting the ship's bars in the evening, drinking by herself, and he would have to search for her, and plead with her to come back and look after the children. Sean was particularly distressed by all the shouting, and would jam his fingers in his ears, sobbing that he didn't want his parents to quarrel. Spike says that this particularly tormented him, so much did he love his children.

On arrival, he gave an Australian interviewer a taste of what *Idiot Weekly* might be about: 'the Great Barrier Reef, and how to grind it up for toothpaste; how to make a pair of boots out of Sydney Harbour Bridge; how to grow carbon paper in Central Australia . . .'

Idiot Weekly ran from June till August 1958, and was not a great success; the critics were bewildered by it. Nevertheless a second series was commissioned for 1959.

While making the programmes, Spike rented a house in an outer suburb of Sydney, for June and the children, but himself spent most of the time in a hotel close to the television studios. His parents Leo and Flo had now settled in the town of Woy Woy, on the coast about an hour from Sydney ('Woy it is called Woy Woy oy'll never know,' writes Spike). His parents were enchanted with their grandchildren, but they could see that Spike and June's marriage was in difficulties. Flo made it perfectly clear to June that she put the blame entirely on her. June later observed that absolutely no wife would have been up to Flo's demands for her beloved Terry. June was also under pressure from her own parents to make the marriage work, whatever sacrifices that required of her. She has said that her father's attitude was that a girl simply had to put up with her husband, however he turned out.

Spike recalls that they hired a car, which June drove. 'She

came home late one evening. I discovered her knickers in the glove compartment. I didn't know what to think.'

He was back in London by the beginning of October 1958, when he told the *News Chronicle* that he might move permanently to Australia:

It's a fabulous place with a wonderful sense of urgency . . . AND it's the one place where I can get away from writing these wretched *Goon Shows* . . . I've tried to write other stuff but no one will take it over here . . . But in Australia there's a chance. I'm going back there again next April, by myself, for a while and maybe after that I'll go back for good with my wife and kids.

*

The ninth series of *The Goon Show* began in November 1958 with a new producer. Spike had demanded that Bobby Jaye, who had been the studio manager on the mixing panel for the last three series, and with whom he had got on excellently, should produce; but Jaye was not yet regarded as qualified, and Spike's second choice was a young producer called John Browell, who had been the panel studio manager for three series under Peter Eton. 'At first,' writes Roger Wilmut, 'this suggestion was rejected on the grounds that Browell was too junior, but in the end he was appointed, and was an excellent choice . . . able to combine an understanding of Goon humour with the tight control that the show now badly needed.'

The listening figures for the ninth series had declined to around 1 million for the first Home Service transmission of each programme; the show had perhaps become too esoteric for many people, and the growth of TV was a factor too. In the event, Spike wrote all the ninth series on his own, except for 'The Seagoon Memoirs' (15 December 1958), which was the work of Larry Stephens and Maurice Wiltshire. The edition of 12 January 1959, 'Who is Pink Oboe?', was remarkable in that Sellers had a throat infection, and it took four actors to replace him: Valentine Dyall, Kenneth Connor, Graham Stark and Jack Train. Equally remarkably, this was the only programme that Sellers missed in the entire run from 1951 to 1960.

Shortly before the series began, the BBC tried to drop Max Geldray, to save money. Sellers immediately said that if Geldray went, he would leave the show himself. Meanwhile Spike was restless. 'I get bored very quickly,' he told Dominic Behan, who described him, at this juncture in his life, as 'a prisoner of the Goons'.

On 13 January 1959 John Browell noted that Spike's office had told him that it was 'doubtful' whether Spike could take part in the show to be recorded the following Sunday, and he would be unable to write the one after that. 'She said that Spike was ill and that the doctor had informed her that "he was suffering from anxiety neurosis caused by strain".' He refused to go into hospital, although he allowed the doctors to prescribe sedatives. June found it impossible to manage him, as his moods swung to and fro, from furious ranting to despair-laden silence, and he spurned all offers of food and drink.

Nevertheless he managed to write the remainder of the series without help, and to appear in the show as usual; and his scripts were of an exceptionally high standard; they are almost all to be found in the 1973 collection *More Goon Show Scripts*. They include 'The Tay Bridge Disaster', in which Sellers plays the Scots poet William McGoonigal (*sic*), and 'The Scarlet Capsule', a brilliant parody of Nigel Kneale's recently shown TV thriller series *Quatermass and the Pit*, which has possibly the best dénouement in the entire run of *Goon Shows*.

A month before the ninth series ended, at one of the

Sunday recordings, John Browell canvassed the reactions of the Goons to the prospect of a tenth series. Spike told him: 'I suppose I could write another six but not thirteen or twenty-six.' Sellers said: 'I think we should leave it now before the standard goes down – we aren't adding anything new and the original drive and enthusiasm has gone.' Secombe told Browell: 'It's more or less up to the others – I don't mind coming here for a lark on Sundays – the programme still has a following and they'll be disappointed.' (Browell commented that Secombe 'is getting less and less enamoured of being a buffer between Milligan and Sellers and generally helping to keep the peace'.)

On the day that Browell wrote this, 25 January 1959, Spike was going out to dinner with Larry Stephens and his wife Diana. In the car, Stephens had a brain haemorrhage. He was rushed to hospital, never regained consciousness and died later that night, aged thirty-five. It seems he had not been heavily rewarded by Spike for his years of work on the *Goon Show*, since his estate was valued at only just over £1,000.

Spike recalled rather inaccurately, near the end of his own life: 'Larry Stephens . . . died in my arms in a restaurant.' One hopes that what he said to a meeting of the Goon Show Preservation Society in 1988 was never seen by Stephens's widow, who was still alive then: 'Larry Stephens died conveniently, it was very nice of him, and I went on to write them on my own.'

In reality, Stephens's death probably increased his desire to be rid of the whole thing. He gave an interview to Paul Tanfield of the *Daily Mail* in which he spoke as if there would be no more *Goon Shows*: 'I don't know what I shall do now. With my three children I could draw £6 a week from the Finchley Labour Exchange. That'll be enough for us to live on, if I can persuade my wife to give up her luxurious tastes – such things as soap.' More seriously, he said:

'The show was starting to degenerate. It had to come to an end.'

*

Peter Sellers's extravagances went beyond cars. In the spring of 1959 he had recently treated himself to a professional 16mm cine camera, and it was with this that *The Running, Jumping and Standing Still Film* was made.

Spike claimed to have proposed the project, written and directed it:

I said to Peter [Sellers], 'Look, films are being made for millions – I think we can make one (not very long) for – what's the cost of the cameraman?' He said, 'Seventy-five pounds.' So we paid that, and the sound engineer was fifty.

We had about twenty ragged characters in a van and we just drove up the Great North Road until we saw a suitable field . . . We just went to the hill, and I wrote the script out, what I wanted roughly, and we had just to improvise how to do it.

Similarly, to Pauline Scudamore he spoke as if he were the film's *auteur*, saying that it had been the only project in which he had had total freedom. He claimed to have directed it, though he did acknowledge that Lester had given excellent advice, and had helped with the editing.

To the Goon Show Preservation Society he said: 'I . . . directed [it] but Dick Lester came along and edited it and took it over.' But Joe McGrath, who had been a designer on the *Fred* TV shows and appears in *The Running, Jumping and Standing Still Film*, says that Lester directed from the outset, and that Spike was only there for one of the two days' filming.

In view of its rarity, it is worth giving a synopsis:[1]

---

[1] My thanks to Joe McGrath for identifying people.

Jazz drums on the soundtrack, then music from a modern jazz combo. The opening titles appear against a background of stubbly human skin (the film is in sepia):

THE RUNNING, JUMPING & STANDING STILL FILM
>   Thoughts by Spike Milligan
>   Peter Sellers
>   Mario Fabrizi[2]
>   Dick Lester

(A finger appears and scratches the stubble.)
>   Devised by Peter Sellers
>   Directed by Dick Lester

The camera pulls back: the stubbly face is that of the actor Leo McKern,[3] a tubby figure not unlike Secombe (who doesn't appear in the film). He wears a top hat, and peers through a telescope. It shows him a field in which a Victorian charlady (Graham Stark) is on her knees, scrubbing the grass with a brush and bucket. She gets up and waddles off, and Spike, in an antique-looking anorak, arrives carrying a doormat and a tent. He wipes his feet on the mat, and puts up the tent, wiping his feet again before going into the tent.

He is being watched by a moustachioed man (Fabrizi) with an antique tripod camera, who fires a pistol in the air to lure Spike out of the tent, and then takes his photograph. He offers Spike his business card, but Spike tears it up in disgust.

A change of scene, to a woodland stream; the photographer arrives, pulls the film from his camera and starts to develop it in

---

[2] An actor friend of Peter Sellers, whose family owned an Italian restaurant in Finchley Road.

[3] Then a little-known immigrant from Australia, where Spike had discovered him. According to Graham Stark, McKern was driving past the field and stopped to ask what they were filming. 'We told him to get out of the car and come and be in it!'

the stream. Sellers, his face now covered with a snorkel mask, arrives and peers at it. They are distracted by the sound of a violin, and we see on a hilltop a violinist (Sellers again) whose music stand is a long distance away – to the extent that he needs a telescope to see it, and has to go by bicycle to turn the page. [Spike described this as 'my favourite joke of all time'.]

The violinist is distracted by the arrival of Graham Stark and a gaggle of supporters (who include Joe McGrath), carrying a large kite made of the Union Jack. A long rope is tied to it, and Stark evidently intends to get airborne. But when the supporters run off, pulling the kite's string in the hope of launching it, it merely collapses around Stark.

A man with a beard (David Lodge)[4] is doing press-ups, when a painter (Dick Lester) and a girl (unknown performer) arrive. He is painting her portrait, and she uses the bearded man (still pressing-up) as a chaise-longue. Sellers arrives carrying a hunting rifle, but is sent away by the painter. He finds a dreamy man (Bruce Lacey, who sometimes performed music with the Alberts) who possesses a gramophone stylus-head (78 rpm style); he puts a record on a tree-stump and manages to make it play by running around the stump while holding the needle on the disc. [This is easily the most inventive idea in the film.]

The bearded man is now swinging a weight on the end of a rope. It comes off, flies in the air, and is shot down by Sellers. He and the bearded man have an argument, and Lacey proposes that they settle it with a duel. He acts as umpire, but is accidentally shot by Sellers.

A beckoning hand, emerging from behind the camera, persuades Graham Stark to come down the hill. Stark (still tangled in the Union Jack) reaches the camera – and is knocked out by a fist. The camera pulls back to show that the fist belongs to McKern. He enters the doorway of a house, takes off his jacket, puts a

---

[4] The actor, not the novelist. Later he appeared in many of Spike's TV shows.

boxing glove on one fist, yawns, lies on a bed, and turns out the light.

A closing caption says simply; 'FXIT.'

Spike once explained the final joke: 'There was a wanker [in the army], and his bed was touching mine, and my bed would shake like this! And he went on for hours . . . So next day I went to the sports store and got this right-handed boxing glove and put it on his bed! [*Convulsed with laughter.*] Oh dear, oh dear!'

Joe McGrath remarks that the style of *The Running, Jumping and Standing Still Film* is influenced by Buster Keaton, whom Dick Lester hugely admired; the characters all have Keaton's deadpan expressions. There is no resemblance to the *Goon Show*.

Lester began to edit the footage. Meanwhile ABC in Australia had booked Spike to make another *Idiot Weekly* TV series. This time he and June agreed that he would travel to Australia alone. He left for Sydney by ship at the end of April 1959, sailing under the alias of Alan Mills, for the *Goon Show* had made him a celebrity.

He had just written his first book. Two years earlier, the publisher Dennis Dobson, who specialised in humour (his successes included a series of little books of the musical cartoons of Gerard Hoffnung), had approached him to ask if he had ever thought of writing a book. Dobson believed his humour would work well in print. Spike's first suggestion was a book of *Goon Show* scripts, but Dobson did not think it would sell. Meanwhile, Spike was making up rhymes to amuse his two older children, Laura and Sean, and he showed them to Dobson.

By the time he reached Australia, the proofs of *Silly Verse for Kids*, a collection of these verses, were waiting to be read. The book had a strong personal importance for him; he told Pauline Scudamore that he had been determined to do something for his children to show them how much he loved them. His marriage was collapsing, he might be separated from them, and if he were to die now, what would they remember of him? So he wrote the book of poems for them.

He had total confidence in his empathy with the young. 'I think I grew down to my children, rather than them growing up to me.' This could tip over into Wordsworthian child-worship. 'Children,' he sighed to an interviewer, 'ah, their innocence . . . Children are the most perfect thing a person will ever be given.' And in 1982, on the Radio 4 programme *In the Psychiatrist's Chair*, he told Anthony Clare: 'I think I have stayed a child all my life – that's why I get on much easier with children. As soon as I get a child in my house, I get on with it, more than anybody else. It's great fun – it's like having your own captive fairy, all that gurgling laughter that comes out if you do the right things.'

A father with such beliefs and attitudes could be a suffo-cating parent, but the Milligan children have never made that criticism of him – or any other, at least in public. 'My earliest recollections,' says his daughter Silé, 'are of a father who used to come home very late at night, and I used to get up and wait on the stairs, and he used to take me up to his bedroom, and open the windows, to look at the stars together. That was really nice, and then he'd put me to bed.'

Sean Milligan, who was five when *Silly Verse for Kids* was published, saw his father in Spike's own terms: 'He was reliving the innocence of his childhood, because he couldn't bear the world. And he's told us, quite categorically, that he would have killed himself if it wasn't for us.'

Spike told Pauline Scudamore that he did not consider writing poetry (as opposed to prose) to be real work. It came directly from his imagination, without the intrusion of intellect, and he had to get it right first time; he wouldn't polish or edit it.

Dennis Dobson brought out *Silly Verse for Kids* for Christmas 1959. (Sales were excellent and it was immediately reprinted.) It begins 'This book is dedicated to my bank balance', and is lavishly illustrated with line drawings by Spike, one of which, the general who threw away his gun, is clearly Major Bloodnok from the Goons.

There is a one-paragraph foreword: 'Most of these poems were written to amuse my children; some were written as a result of things they said in the home. No matter what you say, my kids think I'm brilliant.' And the brilliance of the poems is that they either reflect the kind of things children really do say ('Those bees *are* silly things, / But *how* I *wish* I *had* their *wings*!'), or look at the world as the child-like Eccles might see it: 'Today I saw a little worm/ Wriggling on his belly. / Perhaps he'd like to come inside / And see what's on the Telly.'

Some poems show the influence of Edward Lear (particularly 'On the Ning Nang Nong / Where the Cows go Bong!' and 'In the Land of the Bumbley Boo'); but on the whole the book marks the debut of the most original voice in children's poetry since A.A. Milne.

*

Spike was in Australia for four months in the summer of 1959. *Idiot Weekly* went well, and possible future projects were discussed. But shortly before he embarked for England, he received a letter from June, saying that she regarded the marriage as over. She had left home, taking the children with her.

Spike was plunged into mental agony. He had been living for the sake of his children (he told Pauline Scudamore). They were the only stable, truly worthwhile thing in his emotionally chaotic life. Now, half a world away from them, mentally very volatile, he thought he was going to lose them.

On the voyage home, he was receiving telegrams from

friends, telling him that June and the children had left the house, had moved away, and June was filing for divorce. He wrote to her, pleading for a fresh start, another try at the marriage, but she refused (Spike guessed that she had already begun a relationship with another man).

During the voyage, he took an overdose, a big handful of barbiturate sleeping pills. But it slipped his mind that he had invited the ship's doctor to come for a drink in his cabin. The next thing he knew was a stomach pump, and the doctor asking how many he had taken.

That was what he told Pauline Scudamore. In a 1970 *Observer* interview he added: 'I remember I wanted to be clean. I had a hot bath and put on some clean pyjamas . . . And I took a handful of sleeping pills.' In *The Family Album* he calls it 'a token suicide attempt . . . really a cry for help'.

When he eventually reached London and the family house in Finchley, there was nobody there. June had begun divorce proceedings, and had taken the children to an address in Richmond (14 Maze Road). She told Spike that she had met someone who wanted to marry her. Nearly forty years on, Spike described June's lover as 'some heavy she met at Hammersmith Palais'. On 20 October 1959 the *Daily Mail* carried this headline: '"MY WIFE HAS GONE," SAYS A GOON, "AND I JUST CAN'T BEAR TO THINK ABOUT IT."' Beneath it, Paul Tanfield interviewed Spike:

He is living in the office these days. For he and his wife have parted, and she has taken the three children with her. The grey-stone house in Finchley is locked. There is a collection of milk bottles on the doorstep. And Spike . . . is hurt, bewildered, lost . . . 'Fortunately [he said], I do still see the children. Otherwise life just wouldn't be worth living at all. This is all the more horrific because I am a Catholic who has tried to live a high moral life.'

The next series of the *Goon Show* would normally have

started by this time. Rumours had got around as early as February that the ninth series was likely to be the last, and a group of students from Regent Street Polytechnic had laid siege to Broadcasting House, with banners reading 'Mind What You Do With Our Goons'. At the end of the recording session for the final programme in the ninth series, a group of protesters had filled the foyer of the Camden Theatre, calling for Spike, and handing in a petition signed by well over a thousand listeners: 'We, the undersigned, implore you . . . not to leave England for Australia, but to remain here and continue to write, produce and perform the *Goon Show* for ever and ever.'

During the autumn of 1959 the popularity of the show took an upward hike when, for the first time, recordings of some of the programmes began to be issued commercially on LPs. In the end, the BBC decided to commission a rather belated and very short tenth series – a mere six shows – starting on Christmas Eve, with John Browell producing, and Spike writing solo.

The series kicked off to a good start with the Goons' version of *A Christmas Carol*, followed by 'The Tale of Men's Shirts'. But the remaining shows lacked structure, and showed signs of the emotional strain that Spike was enduring.

'I was allowed to visit [the children] on Silé's [second] birthday, 2 December 1959,' he writes in *The Family Album*. 'I took her a teddy bear and a birthday cake. She was totally aware of the break-up of our marriage.' He also took the children to spend part of Christmas in Surrey with Eric Sykes and his family. Meanwhile his feelings swung between pain and rage.

He described June's new man (to Pauline Scudamore) as a Covent Garden porter, claiming that he was violent and abusive, and that June had taken to wearing long gloves to hide bruises on her arms. He could not contemplate his children living in such a household; he noticed that they had already begun to swear. He became determined to contest the divorce and win custody of the children.

Yet as well as anger there was guilt. He had to blame himself for the collapse of the marriage, he said to Scudamore about twenty years after the event. He couldn't claim it was all June's fault. Poor girl, he remarked, she couldn't cope with him, and who could blame her?

He continued to live mostly in his office. Meanwhile his fellow CND supporter Michael Foot sent his stepdaughter Judy round, in the hope that she could help. Spike recalls that she was a ministering angel. He grew very fond of her, and they even became engaged, but both knew it wouldn't really work.

The six-part *Goon Show* series came to an end on 28 January 1960 with 'The Last Smoking Seagoon'. The plot of this final programme is very thin, the jokes are perfunctory, and at one point Willium observes that Spike is running out of ideas. Neddie Seagoon urges on his weary colleagues with the encouraging news that they've already reached page 13. At the end, Greenslade bids the audience the most casual of farewells. So the curtain came inconspicuously down.

After recording this final show, Sellers and Secombe accompanied Spike to a Czech restaurant in the Edgware Road, where presumably they drank to Spike's new Goon-free life. However, a few months later, the BBC – which up to now had shown little concern about the passing of the Goons – began to stir into some sort of attempt to save the show.

On 21 June 1960 Jim Davidson of Light Entertainment told the Contracts Department that 'we would like a new series of six "Goons" programmes', and asked them to 'negotiate with the artists'. Contracts replied that they had had 'a favourable reaction from Secombe'.

Spike was not enthusiastic. He told the BBC that he had been offered film work which was far better paid. (As we shall see, the offer came from MGM). He suggested that they gave the Goons two repeats so as to increase his fees both as writer and performer. The Corporation replied that they could not guarantee repeats. Milligan wrote back to them that this made the continuation of the show unfeasible – although he was interested he simply could not take it on under the limitations that the BBC wished to impose on him financially.

Nevertheless, during these negotiations, he began to write more Goon scripts – six in all. They have never been performed, but Spike allowed David Nathan to see them for his book *The Laughtermakers*. Nathan described them as 'macabre and doom-laden'. In the final, uncompleted one, Moriarty is starving and he and Grytpype-Thynne are looking for a variety booking in Blackpool for the summer season. They get one on the same bill as Neddie Seagoon, and have to acquire themselves a piano. They find the Luminous Plastic Piano with Built-in Oven – and at this point the script stops abruptly, with a note in Spike's hand: 'Here ended incompleted [*sic*] and unperformed – the last Goon Show, No. 227.'

On 9 August 1960 he wrote to the BBC that there was a faint possibility of a new series, because the two MGM films to which he had been signed up had been postponed. This would make it possible for him to write the show at the usual financial rates. In response he was told that the BBC must have his decision by 1 October.

Exactly a month after that deadline had come and gone, the *Daily Herald* carried the headline '"GOONS" HAVE GONE FOR EVER. MILLIGAN IS BLAMED (UNOFFICIALLY) FOR CONTRACT HITCH'. The paper quoted the BBC's Pat Hillyard of Light Entertainment: 'We understand Peter Sellers will be unavailable because of film commitments.' The report continued:

Unofficially . . . the BBC is secretly blaming Milligan for taking too long to sign a contract. Milligan last night denied the charge. He said there was no undue delay, and it was not his fault . . . Secombe and Sellers [have] signed their contracts. A contract was sent to Milligan. Beryl Vertue . . . told me: 'Mr Milligan signed his contract a few days ago . . .'

On 4 November Spike wrote protestingly to Pat Hillyard. He had promised that he was going to write the show and he had only taken twelve days between receiving the contract and signing it. Nobody at the BBC had given him the slightest indication that it was urgent. He had always been regarded as a reliable artist who had delivered his scripts on time – but suddenly they were treating him as unreliable. But the letter ended amicably, with Christmas wishes to its recipient.

Hillyard replied that he hoped that 'sometime during the coming year we will be able to get rolling'. But they didn't.

'I don't think I could be a success again at that same level because I just couldn't go through all the tantrums,' Spike writes of the *Goon Show* in *The Family Album*. 'It had made me famous, made me ill, destroyed my first marriage . . . It is still hell to think about it.'

He never expressed regret that he had stopped writing the show – quite the opposite – but for the remainder of his life he grumbled that the BBC had not given the Goons the repeats they deserved: 'Most of those [*Goon Show*] tapes lie gathering dust in the BBC. You'd think they would have the *nous* to broadcast a series for a whole new generation of kids to hear it. Is anybody listening?'

Part Three 1960—1971

Spike

15

The unfunniest person in the world

'When the Goons finally finished,' Spike recalls, 'I was out of work. I didn't know that you could disappear from the scene.' He didn't disappear, and he wasn't out of work, but the whole pattern of his professional life changed beyond recognition.

More than a year before the *Goon Show* ended, he had been looking for other employment. On 2 December 1959 Beryl Vertue had written to the BBC to suggest that he should have a turn at presenting *Housewives' Choice*, the hugely popular daily 9 a.m. record show on the Light Programme. The reply was that 'no new names' were being recruited for the time being. Vertue then proposed him for the comedy radio panel game *Does the Team Think?*, but was told that it had a regular team and there were no vacancies at present.

These barefaced approaches to possible sources of work sometimes paid off. In January 1961 (a year after the end of the Goons) he wrote to Eamonn Andrews, who presented the famous and long-running TV show *What's My Line?*. Spike, claiming to be 'partially skint', offered himself as a Guest Celebrity on the programme. The idea was taken up. And while the door to *Housewives' Choice* remained shut, he was booked to present the radio programme which occupied the 9 a.m. slot on the Light each Saturday, *Children's Favourites*, for November and December 1961. It went very well.

He began to be regarded as a useful comedy all-rounder, ideal for such little jobs as impersonating Father Christmas on the Home Service's *Radio Newsreel*. He made occasional appearances doing comic turns on the *Today* programme, which in those days entertained as well as informed. Spike lunched with *Today's* jovial presenter, Jack de Manio, to discuss appearing as 'Paprikon de Villion (Ace Detective)' – apparently an anticipation of Inspector Clouseau. On 22 February 1961, de Manio had a letter from Spike thanking him for the meal, which he said had primed him to continue drinking throughout the day. He had finally landed up at the flat of one of his mistresses, where she introduced him to her future husband. This encounter may be reflected in a poem published a few months later in *A Dustbin of Milligan*: 'So fair is she! / So fair her face / So fair her pulsing figure / Not so fair / The maniacal stare / Of a husband who's much bigger.'

Joe McGrath, who had worked on the *Fred* TV programmes, says: 'All the time I knew Spike he was having affairs – BBC PAs, producers and so on.' There is no evidence that he had been unfaithful to June (and no evidence that he hadn't), but it is clear that being left by her set him off on a fairly high-octane pursuit of women.

Despite the letter to de Manio, which sits brazenly in the BBC files, he was usually discreet about his relationships. We would know next to nothing about his involvement with Elizabeth Cowley had she not chosen to write about it (while he was still alive). Born nine years after Spike, she had emigrated from her native Canada and made a successful London career as a journalist and TV producer; for some while she worked for the BBC's innovative early evening programme *Tonight*. Radiantly attractive, she made a habit of 'seducing famous men', as she puts it in her autobiography *A Tender Contempt* (1998); but her relationship with Spike was different:

Spike Milligan was somehow always there – in-between his wives – for a late-night Indian meal and the gentlest of sex, usually to a background of jazz or music by his newly discovered favourite, Ravel . . . He was . . . a unique presence, with his tortured phone calls at three in the morning and his strange withdrawals into depression and what seemed a total loathing for the human race. Because it was love rather than lust, this diffident relationship has lingered on, well past the *Tonight* days.

Talking about Spike today, seated in a corner of one of his favourite London restaurants, Liz Cowley recalls that she first met him when she was sent to write a piece on the *Goon Show* for the forces' newspaper *Reveille*. She was young (about twenty-six) and inexperienced at journalism; Harry Secombe was exquisitely kind to her, Peter Sellers ignored her, and Spike was 'gawky'. But it was he who telephoned her and asked if she would accompany him to a party. 'I learnt later that his main reason for asking me out was that I'd said I had a university degree, and Spike was painfully aware of being what he called "embarassingly inadequite educationally". (This was in a letter – he never could spell.)'

She went on: 'Physically I thought he was very attractive, but at that date I was still a total virgin, and at first all that was way out of bounds.' They used to meet roughly every two weeks for a cheap meal. Spike, says Cowley, was 'usually between marriages and/or nervous breakdowns. He loved talking about life, death, the universe and politics – but rarely about showbiz and almost never about personal relationships. There were no invitations to each other's weddings [she was married for a while], no discussions about our respective divorces. His was a compartmentalised life.'

Asked when the relationship became sexual, Cowley says: 'It must have been well into the sixties. One evening I said: "To hell with all this. Let's go to bed." From then onwards, the sex just gently slotted in with the rest.' They went to bed either in her Earl's Court flat or in the 'lovely darkened bedroom' he had made out of his office. 'He may have been promiscuous,' she went on, 'but I don't think his sex-drive was that great. He was very unsophisticated in bed. Foreplay? Forget it! There were no climaxes – well, I think he had the odd climax, but I was left all wound up.'

It seems that Spike's feelings for her were stronger than she realised. 'There was a woman named Liz, a television producer,' he said in a 1998 interview. 'I had an affair with her for quite a while and I was very, very much in love with her.' This surprised Cowley, but Joe McGrath confirmed it: 'I have quite a few letters from Spike about Liz Cowley, saying how much he felt for her. And I liked her a lot.'

*

The lunch with Jack de Manio led to Spike doing several short comic pieces for *Today*, at a mere 5 guineas a time (one thirty-seventh of what he had finally been earning per *Goon Show*). This in turn led to more lunches with de Manio. Spike wrote to de Manio after one of them, in November 1961, thanking him for good food and talk but warning him to keep his eyes off Spike's current lady. He had to be careful about being seen with girlfriends, since he was accusing June of being the guilty party in their divorce case, which was now under way.

During 1960 he had hired a private detective to watch the house in Richmond where June and the children were living, to gain evidence of her adultery. Her lover was staying with her at night, and leaving very early in the morning, in the hope of remaining undiscovered. 'I had the detective with me as a witness when I caught him leaving,' writes Spike. 'I petitioned for divorce naming him as co-respondent.'

Although his amount of broadcasting work had dimin- ished drastically, his office accommodation had become much grander. A property dealer had bought Associated London Scripts (ALS) out of their High Street Kensington premises, and they were able to purchase even more lavish accommodation at 9 Orme Court, Bayswater Road, a highly desirable address adjacent to Hyde Park.

Soon afterwards, there was a split in the company. Spike felt that he had earned so much for ALS from the *Goon Show* that he deserved his own secretary/personal assistant. The other directors disagreed, and Spike threatened to resign. Meanwhile the showbiz entrepreneur Robert Stigwood appeared on the scene and made an offer for the company. Simpson and Galton take up the story:

ALAN SIMPSON: Ray and I thought that having Stigwood was a good idea, because he was going into film production, but Spike and Eric Sykes didn't want to get involved with an entrepreneur. So we had a board meeting, and Ray and I voted to go with Stigwood, and Spike and Eric voted against it. Beryl Vertue and the other staff all wanted to go to the new premises Stigwood was providing in Brook Street.

RAY GALTON: Then the question of the Orme Court building came up, and we sold our share in it to Eric and Spike.

ALAN SIMPSON: Its value doubled between 1961 and 1968. And I hesitate to say what it's worth now! Subsequently we heard that Spike had sold his half-share to Eric, who now owns the whole freehold.

Beryl Vertue says of the winding-up of ALS:

I wanted to produce more, to make more use of our writers' work ourselves, rather than waiting for someone to come and hire them. And we were introduced to Robert Stigwood, and he bought a controlling interest in ALS. But Spike and Eric weren't keen on that, so they stayed at Orme Court, and the rest of us went to

Brook Street in Mayfair – lovely! – and I became deputy chairman of the Robert Stigwood Group; not bad for someone who'd started as a secretary.

Spike, however, felt disappointed by what he saw as the defection of his friends. He told Pauline Scudamore that he felt badly treated, especially since he had started the company, and that Sykes was the only one who had behaved honourably. Hence Spike had 'cut him in' on 9 Orme Court.

The new premises became a second home for Spike, who picked an upstairs room with a balcony, and had it furnished with a bed as well as bookshelves and a desk. Norma Farnes, who joined the Orme Court set-up a little later, describes (in her edition of Spike's letters) a major feature of his life there:

No matter what the situation is at the office . . . the birds must be fed . . . Spike has a small balcony at the back of his office, and every day he feeds the birds, and he has names for them all. I can understand that the pigeons are quite tame, but he has tamed the sparrows that come there, and they literally eat out of his hands . . . On the balcony Spike has window boxes, and . . . last year . . . he kept two wasps alive for weeks, by putting a spoonful of jam inside a jar, turned on its side, so they could get to it.

Two *wasps*? Why? Were they ill? Couldn't they provide for themselves? It seems even more eccentric than whisking John Antrobus's dying goldfish off to Accident & Emergency at the Zoo. This is behaviour designed to provoke; a facet of the increasingly aggressive Spike who had been steadily emerging over the Goon years – but at the same time it's extremely funny (whether or not it's intended to be); and to some extent this puts up a smokescreen, so that we find ourselves ignoring the aggression, because he can still make us laugh.

*

Though Spike's BBC work was sparse in the period immediately following the demise of the *Goon Show*, two major
jobs did turn up – as a result of what had seemed a thoroughly uncommercial project.

When Dick Lester had edited *The Running, Jumping and
Standing Still Film*, it ran for a mere eleven minutes, but it
was widely agreed to be superb. Michael Palin describes it
as 'way ahead of its time and [it] encouraged a lot of us
who wanted to make films in that surreal vein'. Spike was
very proud of it: 'I made that with my ideas. That was me.
And it was perfect. It was very funny.' (But the ideas were
other people's too.)

It was shown at the Edinburgh Festival, where it won a
prize, and was spotted by the organiser of the San Francisco
Film Festival. It won there too, and was even shortlisted for
an Academy Award. 'And so,' says Lester, laughing, 'this
£70 film was suddenly nominated for an Oscar!'

The *Daily Express* for 3 February 1960 puts a date on
this unlikely event: '[It] has been nominated for a Hollywood
Oscar.' Though it didn't get one, its success was a factor in
the choice of Lester to direct the Beatles in *A Hard Day's
Night* in 1964.

Meanwhile, two months after the Oscar nomination, in
April 1960, came a press report that 'Hollywood has discovered Spike Milligan . . . He has signed a contract for at
least seven years and for "a sizeable sum" to make films
for Metro-Goldwyn-Mayer. A spokesman [for MGM] said:
"Spike is a great personality, and we hope to make full use
of his talents as a comic, actor, writer and ideas man."'

He was soon cast in two MGM films made in Britain,
Invasion Quartet and *Postman's Knock*. The latter (released
during 1962) is a sub-Norman Wisdom comedy about a rural
postman (Spike) who is reassigned to the big city, where he

is pursued by a gang of would-be mail robbers (including Warren Mitchell, Lance Percival and Arthur Mullard, looking like cast-offs from *The Ladykillers*). Spike's character – who is almost silent throughout – displays sub-Eccles intelligence without being funny, thanks to a childish plot by Jack Trevor Story and the plodding direction of Robert Lynn.

'I'd very much like to have done comedy in films,' Spike said ten years after *Postman's Knock*. '. . . And I wonder how people who are less funny than I am have got into it.' The answer was that they picked better scripts. And he admitted that *Invasion Quartet*, released by MGM in 1961, was 'desperately unfunny'.

It stars Bill Travers as the leader of some hospitalised servicemen who scheme to get to France in order to put a giant German gun out of action. Spike plays a shell-shocked explosives expert who can't stand noise (a touch of autobiography here), and the screenplay (by Jack Trevor Story again) is neck-and-neck with *Postman's Knock* for predictability.

However, Spike writes that 'the one thing that came out of it was that I saw a very pretty, shapely girl extra. I asked her out to dinner. Her name was Patricia (Paddy) Ridgeway.'

Paddy – as Spike liked to call her, maybe because it sounded Irish – was twenty-five and came from Yorkshire, though she spoke with a 'posh' accent. She had trained as an actress in a regional drama school, then come to London to study opera. 'We got on very well,' writes Spike. 'The short of it was, we fell in love.'

Spike wooed her flamboyantly, taking her hand and telling her across the dinner table that – though she might not believe him – in a year's time they would be married. She was then appearing as a nun in the London stage production of *The Sound of Music*. Spike went to see it. 'My God, she had a wonderful voice.' (She made a few recordings, and Spike is right – well, it's certainly rich.)

Meanwhile the success of *Silly Verse for Kids* had led to

Spike's first venture into 'grown-up' humorous books (though there wasn't much difference). *A Dustbin of Milligan*, a collection of his prose and verse, illustrated with his own drawings, was brought out by Dennis Dobson in time for Christmas 1961. It includes five short stories, several of which read like *Goon Shows*, and feature some authorial intrusions: 'How dare he! That's the last time he's in a story of mine – Signed Spike Milligan.' But the most memorable thing in it is a four-line poem: 'There are holes in the sky / Where the rain gets in, / But they're ever so small / That's why rain is thin.'

John Lennon was once asked which writers had influenced his own song lyrics: James Joyce, Edward Lear, Lewis Carroll or Spike Milligan? He answered: 'Spymill. Do I know the others?'

A section of *A Dustbin of Milligan* is headed 'Politics and Other Nonsense'. Here, Spike turns his hand to satire, which had suddenly become fashionable: this was the year that *Beyond the Fringe* opened in London, and *Private Eye* came into existence. In a telephone conversation about the Aldermaston March, the prime minister declares: 'I, Harold Macmillan . . . hope to turn the tide by marching in the exact opposite direction! I will march all the way by Rolls Royce . . . Following me will be the "Atom Bombs for Peace" group with the banner – *Strontium 90 is Good For You* . . . Small miniature flower-clad A-bombs will be exploded *en route* to give festive gaiety to the occasion.' Selwyn Lloyd (one of Macmillan's ministers) asks if this will be safe, and Macmillan answers: 'I'm not sure. Anyhow, we can afford a few Tories, the woods are full of 'em.'

The *TLS* gave a respectful review to *A Dustbin of Milligan*, particularly praising the satire: 'There is little to console those who lament the departed Goons, though the letters . . . have that old lunatic cheeriness in adversity . . . But . . . these jokes are too angry to be "rubbish" . . .' Meanwhile Spike was writing and rewriting his first novel.

*

During 1961 he told his mother that one of the chief reasons for his coming to Australia the next year would be to give him the peace he needed to finish his novel, which he had started to write almost two years earlier at Woy Woy.

He told Dominic Behan he had written *Puckoon* 'to prove that I was Irish and to prove to my father that I was a writer. That was a great pride to me – that I was actually an author. It was an Irish book, and I thought: Can I write without ever having been there? . . . When it was published, everybody thought I'd been to Ireland.'

Actually he had been there, in 1947, but only to Dublin, whereas *Puckoon* has a rural setting. Its principal source, which helped him to 'become a real Irish writer', was 'stories my father had told me'. His second visit to Ireland didn't happen until 1967, some while after the publication of *Puckoon*, when he took Paddy for few days to Dublin. 'It was wonderful being in my own country.'

Puckoon was originally 'a much longer work – but parts of it were too sad, so I asked my father to burn them, which he did, very reluctantly, in Woy Woy. I wish I'd listened to him now.' Writing the book 'nearly drove me mad and I vowed I'd never write another novel'. (In the event he wrote two more, both Irish in setting.)

One could describe *Puckoon* as an Irish *Under Milk Wood* with explosions. The plot – inasmuch as there is one – concerns the Boundary Commissioners' decision to move the border between Ulster and the Irish Republic so that it runs slap through the middle of Puckoon village, with various farcical consequences (many of them based on his father's anecdotes about rural Ireland). But for most of the book, Milligan pays almost no heed to the plot, and lets a wonderful gallery of Puckoonians sidetrack him liberally with their peculiarities.

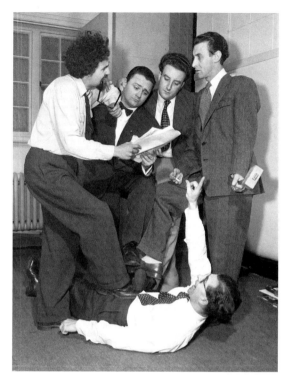

1. 'All my life I've wanted to step on the BBC': horizontal producer Dennis Main Wilson endures vertical Goons (*left to right*) Bentine, Secombe, Sellers and Milligan.

2. Beryl Vertue trying to stop her men from behaving badly: (*left to right*) Eric Sykes, Ray Galton, Spike and Alan Simpson at Associated London Scripts.

3. 'She said to me, "Look, why don't we get engaged?"'
Spike and first wife June.

4. Spike attempts to ruin his 1962 wedding to Paddy Ridgeway with a
false moustache. The bride is obviously more attracted to Harry Secombe.

5. The Dustbin Dance from *Son of Fred*, 1956: Milligan and Sellers with Tony and Douglas Gray of the Alberts.

6. 'I leave Pakistan because there are too many wog': Spike (with Eric Sykes, *left*) blacked up for *Curry and Chips*, 1969.

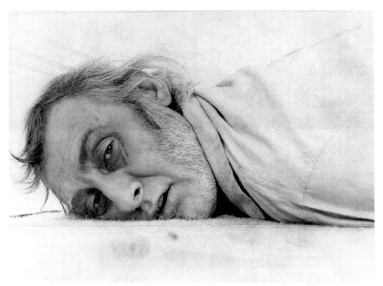

7. Spike depressed, from a 1970 TV documentary on his mental health problems.

8. Milligan and Secombe with the Goons'
most famous fan, 1973.

9. Spike at Hatchards, with a bestseller on his hands.

10. Spike (*right*) in *Milligan in Autumn*, BBC TV, 1972.

11. 'I told him it might give him some idea of how a goose feels being force-fed': Spike (*right*) threatens the manager of Harrods food hall with 28lbs of spaghetti in 1986.

12. 'He has bought her a ring, but they have not yet fixed a date for the wedding': Spike with Shelagh Sinclair in 1982.

13. 'We should have burnt the house down and bought the view': Spike knocked flat by the sight of the English Channel from his last home.

14. Revelations at breakfast time on 19 January 1991.

15. 'Spike Milligan meets love child': James (*left*) and his mother Margaret shake hands with Shelagh as Spike approaches.

First to appear is 'The Milligan', a somewhat Eccles-like figure whom we meet dozing on a grass verge and quarrelling with the Author about the spindly legs he has been given: 'Did you write these legs? . . . Well, I don't like dem at all . . .' ('I must be the first one who ever wrote a book in which the author spoke to his characters,' Spike claimed.)

The Milligan shares his creator's background ('born in India, the son of a Sergeant-Major in the Indian Army'), though it is not him but another character, Farmer O'Mara, who is given a Gothic version of the author's own marital experiences:

O'Mara had married a raving beauty, Silé Kearns. When he started courting her every man in the village had been through her . . . The marriage bore three children, Sean, Laura and Sarah. It seemed that at last Silé had left her old ways behind her. Then O'Mara had caught her red-handed, the lover had fled across the countryside without his trousers which were shown as evidence. O'Mara was awarded custody of the kids. That seemed the end of it, things settled down, all but Silé, who was slowly going out of her mind.

Losing the kids had done it. One night Silé got into their bedroom and cut their throats. She would have had O'Mara too but for the fact that he couldn't sleep for the toothache. She was taken away and put in Gedstow Asylum . . . From a man who laughed and loved life, O'Mara was cut down to a walking dead.

This is almost the only 'sad' passage allowed to remain in *Puckoon*. Most of the book reads like an Irish-flavoured *Goon Show*, packed with superb jokes.[1] Spike was clearly

---

[1] To pick a sample trio, from the early pages of the book: 'He was a tall handsome man touching fifty, but didn't appear to be speeding.' 'Money! The Lord will provide, but to date he was behind with his payments.' 'There was a short pause, then a longer one, but so close were they together, you couldn't tell the difference.'

revelling in the freedom to invent as many outlandish comic characters as he wanted – and to put in a lot of comic sex, unrestrained by the BBC. And though he scarcely bothered with the plot for the first two-thirds of the book, he managed to resolve everything at the end, in a *tour de force* of a farcical finale.

*

In March 1961, when *Puckoon* was still far from finished, 'the divorce was finalized [writes Spike] and I was given custody of the children. Of course, June was seen as the guilty party, having committed adultery. They didn't say anything about me being fucking mad, insane, unstable, suicidal. That was okay. You could have three kids and look after them when you were like that.'

On 1 March the *Daily Telegraph* reported that Milligan 'was granted a decree nisi in the Divorce Court yesterday because of adultery by his wife, Mrs June Angela Milligan . . . at Maze Road, Kew . . . The suit was undefended . . . Judge Blagden said he was satisfied with arrangements for the three children, who are with Mr Milligan, and granted him custody.'

Laura, Sean and Silé were handed over to their father, who took them back with him to Holden Road, 'fully realizing that I had parted them from a very good mother. To this day that haunts me, but her lover was a rough, crude man and the children would have grown up the same.'

According to Spike, 'June never visited the children. Her excuse was that I never gave her money for petrol. All news to me.' Elsewhere, he supplied a more plausible reason for June's behaviour: 'The man my first wife married didn't want her to see the children. I couldn't force her. But it marked them for life.'

On the radio programme *In the Psychiatrist's Chair*, twenty-one years after the divorce, he told Anthony Clare:

When my first marriage broke up . . . I watched the haunted faces of my children, who had lost their mother, and I never quite got over that, I just can't get over it, it's left a scar on me, I know it left a scar on them. I can't keep up with trying to love them enough to make up for all the shortcomings.

It was the one area of his life in which he admitted to feelings of guilt – perhaps because it was bound to elicit the response 'It wasn't your fault.' And one can't help noticing the melodramatic language.[2]

In reality, once he had the children to himself, he seems to have run a happy household. 'We lived in jeans, jumpers and Wellingtons,' recalls Laura, the eldest, who was eight at the time of the divorce.

He used to take us out to really nice restaurants like that. He didn't like to see children all dressed up . . . His psychology was brilliant. He said we could stay up late for ever and ever. By the second night we were so tired and ill we pleaded to go back to early bedtimes!

When Dad was ill it was awful, but I decided when I was very young that it was no use me getting depressed as well: I couldn't help him. He'd go off and suffer by himself, just withdraw from the world. My schoolfriends found it a bit weird to come round at two in the afternoon and have to tiptoe around 'because my father was asleep upstairs' for the third day running.

When he was on a high it was fantastic. We travelled, saw all sorts of things. He made us appreciate beauty, and look at things which were right under our noses.

He would try endlessly to entertain us. When I was nine I really believed there were fairies at the bottom of the garden and we

---

[2] If he did feel guilt, could it be because his treatment of June had been – subconsciously or consciously – designed to drive her out of the family while the children were still of an age to be bewitched by his humour and storytelling? They were, after all, his perfect audience.

would all write them notes. In the morning we would find tiny letters that Dad must have spent half the night painstakingly writing in minute script.

In the same 1988 interview, Spike forgot the histrionics about haunted faces and admitted to having had the time of his life: 'Bringing up three children practically alone is an experience more magnificent, I would venture, than being the first man on the moon.'

He was less slapdash about clothes than Laura suggested:

At one stage I was obsessed with Victoriana and I thought they'd look marvellous in little flannelette nightgowns with frilly white collars and cuffs. They all had their own colours – Laura's was red, Silé's yellow and Sean's green – which went for all their towels and things so everyone knew which was which.

Though he liked neatness and order about the house, he was a gentle disciplinarian: 'I've never hit any of my children, I think that's very wrong.'

He didn't try to run the home single-handedly. Not long after the divorce, when his MGM films were footing the bills, he told his mother he now had three servants: a housekeeper, a maid and a Maltese nanny. Later the three staff were reduced to two: a housekeeper (Mrs Ferguson) and an Irish nanny (Miss O'Brien).

And then – though she didn't yet share the home with them – there was Paddy, whom he wanted to marry. He introduced her to the children, and she took him up to Yorkshire to meet her mother and father, who was a director of Monsanto, the huge chemical company (this was before it became synonymous with genetically modified crops, which would surely have put Spike off marrying into it).

'They seemed to accept me as a "nice boy",' he said of his future in-laws. He was now forty-three.

He took Paddy and the children to the Sussex cottage of former *Goon Show* producer Peter Eton and his wife Squirrel, who had been a sympathetic friend to him for several years. After the visit, Spike questioned the Etons closely as to whether they thought Paddy would make a good wife and stepmother.

For her part, Paddy hadn't immediately accepted Spike's marriage proposal, but had asked for a month to think it over – and he wasn't to see her or have any contact during that period. 'It nearly drove me mad,' he told the *Daily Mail* (he wasn't someone who was used to being kept waiting for anything). He passed the time by feverishly rewriting *Puckoon*. 'I wrote from morning till night to get Paddy out of my mind. At the end of a fortnight I had finished it. Thirty thousand words! The odd thing is that though I wrote it in torment, I reckon it is one of the funniest books in years.' Modest as usual – but he was right.

After Paddy had said yes, and the engagement was announced, she admonished the *Daily Express*: 'Don't call me a dancer or a showgirl. I am a classical singer. I've been mixed up with straight drama and opera, not *that* side of entertainment.' And presumably the Goons came from *that* side, so did she know exactly what she was marrying?

Possibly not. The first time she saw Spike, in uniform on the *Invasion Quartet* film set:

he reminded me of a picture of my grandfather in the 1914 war . . . I find Spike very funny, though my own humour is a slightly quieter type . . . I come from a conventional family and I'm conventional . . . [Spike] is a quiet, serious man, with a great sense of responsibility, and he's not casual or wild . . . What we both want is a quiet, happy family life . . . Writing is his main love and he will be concentrating on it.

And what was Spike after, marrying someone who thought he was a quiet, serious novelist? Deep down, he told Pauline

Scudamore, he supposed he wanted a decent-minded mother for his children, who didn't smoke or drink or sleep around. Moreover, when they first met, Paddy was in showbiz. However, she was soon out of it, as Alan Simpson recalls: 'Paddy was different from June, an artist in her own right. She was a very good singer, but she gave up her career entirely when she married Spike.'

*

During the summer of 1960 he had a show on ITV – *The Men's Performing Show*, which has vanished utterly – but for all his cursing of the BBC, he admitted to preferring them. 'I've been trying to get on the BBC,' he told the *Daily Mail*, 'but I'm not going to grovel.'

He succeeded, albeit not on a large scale. *Spike Milligan Offers A Series of Unrelated Incidents at Current Market Value* was a one-off, shown on BBC television on 5 September 1961. The cast included Graham Stark, Bill Kerr and the Alberts, and the producer was G.B. Lupino. The programme included Spike promoting 'noise clothes' – garments from which issue appropriate sound effects (a honeymoon nightie makes a ripping sound) – and Stark as an end-of-the-pier entertainer who uses Portable British Laughing Audiences to improve the response to his act; also a hat fitted with a personal Early Warning System, which allowed you to receive notice of the start of World War III in the privacy of the home.

The *Radio Times* sent a reporter to watch a rehearsal, who noted, promisingly, that the crew were 'convulsed' over the pictures on their monitor screens:

(1) Pair of legs, female. (2) Citizen receiving custard pie in left eye. (3) Valentine Dyall hiding under an enormous gramophone horn. (4) A Portable British Laughing Audience. (5) Small man in bowler hat and shroud, carrying his own bus-stop.

Corner Spike and ask how he would describe the show. Answers crisply: 'Chaotic!'

Around the time this one-off was transmitted, Spike was invited to make his stage acting debut. A letter arrived from Bernard Miles at the Mermaid Theatre in the City of London, asking if he would play the part of Ben Gunn in *Treasure Island* at Christmas 1961. The salary would be £15 a week. 'I told him, "I'm not an actor",' recalls Spike, 'but he said: "I think you are."' Miles would soon be proved right, and in consequence Spike would embark upon a new phase of his life.

The Mermaid had opened in 1959, on the site of a blitzed warehouse, and *Treasure Island* had been staged there the first Christmas, with Miles himself as Long John Silver, Sean Kenny designing and Peter Coe directing. The 1961 production was the first of many revivals.

Bernard Miles explained his casting of Spike by declaring that he saw him as a prophet or seer standing out there alone, cut off from the usual human relationships simply because he was so different. In other words, he was marooned – just like Ben Gunn.

Spike was delighted when one of the critics called it 'inspired casting'; it was the first time someone had trusted him to do some character acting. Milton Shulman wrote in the *Evening Standard*: 'Spike Milligan, crouched and bouncing like a chimpanzee on a trampoline, certainly brought a new dimension of insanity to old Ben Gunn. It seems on this evidence that being shipwrecked alone on a desert island for three years is perfect preparation for a part in the next *Goon Show*.'

A more conventional compliment was paid by Eric Keown in *Punch*: 'The most original performance . . . comes from Spike Milligan, whose zany Ben Gunn, twittering and leaping and dreaming of toasted cheese, is a joy.' Bernard Miles called him 'the best Ben Gunn that ever was or will be', and Barry Humphries, who was in another Mermaid revival of *Treasure Island* with Spike a few Christmases later, writes:

Spike stole the show every night in a make-up which took at least an hour to apply . . . [He] soon left the text far behind as he went off into a riff of sublime absurdity. In what was meant to be a climactic confrontation, Spike's Ben Gunn drew his pistol and fired it vehemently at the marauding pirates. There was a loud bang and his pistol extruded a limp daisy. When the cheers and laughter from the audience had subsided, Spike cast a conspiratorial glance at the stalls and said, 'See, flower-power.'

The 1961 *Treasure Island* ran for two months, twice daily. During the pause between shows, Spike began talking to Bernard Miles about an idea he was kicking around with John Antrobus: a play about life after the nuclear holocaust. Back in 1959, Miles had asked Spike for a play for the brand-new Mermaid, but Spike had been too busy, and had proposed 'one of our lads' (Antrobus, a junior member of Associated London Scripts) to write it. Antrobus agreed, and accepted an advance from the Mermaid; but nothing happened until *Treasure Island*.

Word of the upcoming Milligan–Antrobus play reached a newly formed touring educational theatre company called Tomorrow's Audience, one of whose members was Richard Ingrams (who had not yet taken the helm at *Private Eye*). They wanted the play to be ready almost instantly. Bernard Miles recalls that Antrobus and Spike began work in Spike's dressing-room at the Mermaid, 'with the door locked and a typewriter going like mad . . . and shouting at each other, and Spike was banging the table'. It was tried out by Tomorrow's Audience at the Marlowe Theatre Canterbury in February 1962, and had an excellent review in the *Observer* from the country's leading theatrical arbiter, Kenneth Tynan:

Mr Milligan and his partner have imagined England as it might be three years after the next war, which is referred to as 'the nuclear misunderstanding'. It is suggested that the Russians started it, but no one quite knows who won it . . . The protagonist, a plump horn-rimmed doctor hilariously played by William Rushton,[3] runs a 'surplus army and psychiatry store', whither people fervently traipse in search of second-hand boots, instant psycho-analysis and prescriptions for food. They are bothered by genetic mutations; indeed, the play draws its title from a peer of the realm who undergoes an inadvertent metamorphosis into a Paddington bedsitter ('No coloureds', he sternly insists). Stethoscope to the wall, the doctor examines him for dry rot.

We are deep in Goon country, where the fifth and basic freedom is that of free association . . . Yet it is capable of finesse, at least as practised by Messrs Antrobus and Milligan . . . It would be well worth a trial at the Royal Court.

In fact the Mermaid was to be its next port of call, with Ingrams and his Tomorrow's Audience co-founder Jack Duncan left seriously out of pocket, and feeling thoroughly misled by Spike and Associated London Scripts, who had apparently let them believe that they would have a major financial interest in the play's future; though since the Canterbury production used up Ingrams's capital and caused him to abandon the theatre for *Private Eye*, we may be grateful to Spike for depriving us of an actor but providing the country with one of its great editors.

*

A week after *The Bedsitting Room* had opened at Canterbury, on 23 February 1962, Charles Chilton at the BBC noted

---

[3] Who had been at school with Ingrams and was another of the gang who created *Private Eye*.

that he had just had 'a long talk' with Spike about his writing a new radio comedy series:

He is very willing, in fact keen, to do this. He assures me that he would give us new material with entirely new artists and . . . the series would have an Australian background . . . Spike is off to Australia at the end of May or early June and returns at the end of the year. Do you think it would be a good idea to make a sample programme before he goes?

Jim Davidson, the next person up in the hierarchy, did not: 'we do not think it wise to rush a Milligan script.'

The senior managers in the Light Entertainment Department, so often castigated by Spike when the Goons were still running, were evidently in no hurry to recommence a working relationship with him. And Spike's aggression was the theme that emerged from an interview he gave in his Orme Court office to Herbert Kretzmer of the *Daily Express*, published on 13 March 1962. Kretzmer (future lyricist of the English-language version of *Les Misérables*) had provided the words for the song played behind the opening credits in *Postman's Knock*. He seems to have been the first writer to be aware of, and want to explore, the side of Spike that might be called Angry Young Milligan.

'Terence Alan ("Spike") Milligan enters . . . in a chunky green jersey and a foul temper,' Kretzmer's interview began.

He is against everything and everybody. Yesterday's stubble peppers his chin . . . [He] announces: 'I hate the human race.' . . . Then he sits down . . . to start the day's work. There is not, it appears, much work. 'I am unemployed,' says Mr Milligan. 'Nobody wants me. The Television [*sic*] doesn't want me. The BBC doesn't want me. I have become little more than a nuisance to the cowards and idiots who run the BBC. The hell with them.'

Milligan's detestation of the BBC has become fused into his maverick personality. It is just one of the destructive elements that devour the man . . . There are many more. Milligan sees himself as a man persistently harassed and harried by mammoth unseen bureaucracies . . . Everywhere there are faceless men persecuting him. Even a burning electric light bulb symbolises to Milligan these invisible curbs on his liberty. 'Somewhere some idiot in a bowler hat is totting up the amps. It's costing us money to bloody well sit here and breathe.'

Mr Milligan is widely recognized and venerated as a comic genius. But he insists: 'I am basically the unfunniest person in the world.' He sees himself as a compassionate Roman Catholic, but his capacity for hate is practically unlimited. The basis of his humour has always been ridicule, essentially mirthless. Once he thought of becoming a priest.[4] Today he follows the bare footsteps of Gandhi. 'I would not detest the human race did I not love them so much,' he told me. Despite such mysticism, the hate remains, warping his days.

He worries himself sick about Russian dogs shot into space and emaciated piccaninnies[5] starving in African famines . . . 'When they crucified that dog in space I couldn't sleep for nights,' he says . . . [6]

But such conscious martyrdom has no real basis in fact. In any other terms than his own Spike Milligan is a success . . . Last year . . . he starred in two MGM films, *Invasion Quartet* and *Postman's Knock*. He brought out a long-playing record called *Milligan Preserved*, and a book, *A Dustbin of Milligan*, which became one of the country's bestsellers. His tenure as radio compère of *Children's Choice* [sic] was a runaway triumph.

Milligan appeared in the Mermaid Theatre production of

---

[4] If he did, this is the only time he said so.
[5] Astonishing that this could be said as late as 1962.
[6] The dog Laika, the first living creature to orbit the Earth, was sent up in a Russian Sputnik in November 1957, and died while in orbit.

Treasure Island. He also found time to . . . write a novel [*Puckoon*] . . . and a play [*The Bedsitting Room*]. Yet . . . Milligan insists on seeing 1961 as a disastrous year which saw him tottering on the edge of bankruptcy. 'I don't work any more. I am living on the cash I've saved . . .'

He picked up the telephone and issued curt instructions to his housekeeper: 'Mrs Beveridge, I want you to measure the children . . . I never know what size to order. Measure their arms, feet, chest, legs, everything.' Milligan put the phone down without any farewell salutations . . .

He called the electricity board and became stiff and white with anger over some real or imaginary mistake the electricians had made in his home. [He] looked at me, breathing hard. 'I'd like to drop a bomb on the whole world.' . . . Thus Spike Milligan's morning sped on . . . He sees the future as an uncertain and arid nightmare . . . 'I'm the last man alive who speaks the truth.'

16

I do not do anything extraordinary

Terence Milligan and Patricia Ridgeway were married in a Catholic church in Yorkshire on 28 April 1962. Harry Secombe was in the congregation, but apparently no one asked him to sing a solo, and the best man was not the former Goon but the record producer George Martin, soon to mastermind the Beatles' recording career. Spike had met him through Peter Sellers, whose *Best of Sellers* comedy LP Martin had produced. Martin and Milligan collaborated during 1962 on *The Bridge on the River Wye*, a Parlophone disc spoofing Alec Guinness's River Kwai film (the cast included Sellers, Jonathan Miller and Peter Cook, but not Secombe). Martin also produced Spike's solo LP *Milligan Preserved*. 'We became firm friends,' says Martin, 'and he used to pour his heart out to me about his unhappy [first] marriage. Mind you, I think it would have had to take a saint to live with such a genius every day.'

Spike was taken aback by the splendour of Paddy's father's plans for the wedding. He and June had got married speedily in front of a registrar. He now felt powerless, and attempted to hijack his father-in-law's control: 'As Paddy and I stood at the altar, I put on a big, black handlebar moustache and turned to the congregation. It did get a laugh, but Paddy's father took me aside at the reception and said, "What a terrible thing to do at my daughter's wedding!" *Her* wedding? I was there, too!'

A somewhat exaggerated version, this. The *News of the World* has what is probably a more accurate report:

On the way to the reception . . . he pulled out a huge ginger moustache, fixed it to his nose and waved at passers-by . . . doffing his topper. The bride couldn't stop laughing. Spike kept popping on the moustache during the reception . . . 'I was tempted to wear it in church. I'm still a rebel but today I decided I must be on my best behaviour.'

Spike and Paddy had a brief honeymoon in Cornwall, then sailed for Australia, where Spike had been booked by ABC for more radio and television work. Before he set off, he began a contretemps with the Foreign Office which spluttered on for the rest of his life.

It started when they wrote to him refusing to renew his passport, which was about to expire, because recent changes in the law meant he was no longer a British citizen. Thanks to his having been born in India, his classification was now 'British subject without citizenship' – in effect stateless. He could reapply, but would have to swear the oath of allegiance to the Queen. This he absolutely refused to do, on the grounds that he had served the British monarchy loyally during the war, and it was insulting to be asked for further proof of his patriotism.

Enquiring what were the alternatives, he was told he could 'become a Hindu', which would mean writing to the Indian authorities. But he had a scheme of his own. 'He went down to the Irish Embassy,' writes Dominic Behan, 'and asked if he could join the Republic. They told him, "God, yes, Spike – we're awful short of our own people." They gave him a jar of Jameson's and a passport, and Spike Milligan has never been happier with himself.'

The Australia trip was the longest he had yet made, from May to December 1962, and during it Spike's children were left boarding at Laura's convent school. Pauline Scudamore reports that he didn't tell them how long he would be away, which she considers 'curious' considering the intensity of his love for them. Perhaps, she suggests, he simply wanted to avoid seeing them distressed. If this is true, it seems both cowardly and selfish, especially given that he had been worried about Laura since she had burst into tears at the wedding.

In Australia, he made another series of *Idiot Weekly* – Paddy appeared in it as 'featured vocalist', so she hadn't quite given up her career – and also wrote and appeared in a one-off, *The Spike Milligan Show*. The latter attempted to make a serious point, with Spike declaring that it was a wonderful world against a background of film of nuclear explosions and global violence; but the Australian *TV Times* covered the programme as if it were the usual Milligan comic mixture: 'TOP PROFESSIONAL IDIOT SPIKE MILLIGAN ON VIEW AGAIN'.

He spent some time with his parents at Woy Woy – he had financed an extension to their house, in which Leo could show off his large collection of guns – but his new marriage was already showing signs of strain. 'Paddy nearly drove me mad with constant bickering,' he writes in *The Family Album*. 'One night I ran out of the house and slept in a bus shelter.'

*

He and Paddy returned to England in just enough time for Spike to rehearse *The Bedsitting Room*, which was to open at the Mermaid on 31 January 1963. Spike and Antrobus were to have directed it jointly, but since he was acting in it and Antrobus wasn't, he left Antrobus to call the shots – a task made difficult by Spike's decision to improvise (or to put it another way, the fact that he couldn't be bothered to learn his lines). 'With his best improvising,' recalls Antrobus,

he would be wonderful. But he'd say something crass the next minute, and you'd tell him, 'Spike, we can't use that.' And he'd say: 'Oh, all right, I'll say nothing.' Either the tap was on, and you got the lot, or it would be [*speaks in a Dalek voice*] 'Tell-me-what-to-do-and-I-will-do-it. Minds-greater-than-mine-obviously-know-better.'

The Bedsitting Room takes place on 'the first anniversary of the Nuclear Misunderstanding which led to World War Three . . . the shortest World War on record, two minutes twenty-eight seconds precisely, including the signing of the Peace Treaty . . . The Great Task of burying our forty-eight million dead was carried out with cheerfulness and goodwill.'

Among the survivors is Lord Fortnum of Alamein (played at the Mermaid by Valentine Dyall). He calls on psychiatrist Pontius Kak (Graham Stark) and tells him: 'Ever since they dropped this bomb, I've had the morbid fear I might turn into a Bedsitting Room . . . Oh dear, what should I do?' Kak advises him to charge tenants at least thirty shillings a week: 'at a push you might get two quid'. At this juncture, Mate, a traffic warden (recognisably Willium from the *Goon Show*, played at the Mermaid by Milligan himself), interrupts to say that Lord Fortnum's horse-drawn Rolls-Royce is illegally parked. When another character tries to sing the national anthem, he is told: 'No, no, we don't sing that any more, we now sing "God Save Mrs Gladys Scroake". She is the nearest in line to the throne.' (The Queen and her corgis have run off to Canada.)

In Act Two, Lord Fortnum's worst fear has come to pass, and he has become a room at 29a Cul-de-Sac Place, Paddington: 'No coloureds and no children and definitely no coloured children.' The prime minister has turned into a parrot, which is cooked and eaten, and at the end God announces that, owing to extreme nuclear radiation at celestial altitudes, heaven is being moved to the Paddington bedsitter.

The Bedsitting Room is a typical *Goon Show* (without the usual Goon characters), and not a very coherent one at that; but in 1963 the Goon-starved critics were almost unanimously enthusiastic. Milton Shulman wrote in the *Evening Standard*: 'Occasionally the jokes miss because of bad timing, but when this production gets into a settled, mad tempo, *The Bedsitting Room* should become one of the delights of London. Spike Milligan himself leers, fulminates, cackles and races through the evening like some one-man Marx Brothers.'

A few critics dissented. John Russell Taylor in *Plays and Players*, who said he was bored, noted that the play had

> started as a one-acter last year at Canterbury . . . with the dubious advantage of a preliminary rave from Kenneth Tynan . . . Bits have been added here and there, the Temperance Seven have been brought in to play two or three numbers at the beginning of each half and provide an interlude in the second act, and – what does most of the damage – the whole thing has been spun further out by the simple expedient of playing it very slowly . . .

But most of the reviews were raves. 'It is both outrageous and cosy, savage and whimsical, ingratiating and alienated, school-boyish and educational,' Alan Brien wrote in the *Sunday Telegraph*. 'The jokes are very good,' said Harold Hobson in the *Sunday Times*, while the *Guardian*'s Philip Hope-Wallace was 'contorted with laughter'.

The Bedsitting Room ran at the Mermaid for a month, and then (in March 1963) moved to the Duke of York's Theatre, where it stayed until the beginning of 1964. John Antrobus writes that when the production reached the West End the cast was lacking Graham Stark, who had been 'brilliantly funny' but 'had not got along with Spike'. Antrobus continues:

His leaving the play was dramatic. Towards the end of the run at the Mermaid, Spike phoned his home and spoke to Audrey Stark . . . He said: 'Tell your husband that if he comes to the theatre tonight I will shoot him.' . . . [Then] the [Starks'] bell rang and Patricia Milligan, Spike's wife, fell through the door in tears . . . She begged Graham not go to the theatre that night, saying she was convinced Spike had a gun and meant what he said.

According to Antrobus, for the remainder of the run at the Mermaid, Stark's understudy took the part. 'One hundred per cent professional that he is,' adds Antrobus, 'Graham did not leak the story nor take action against anyone.' But Antrobus supplies no explanation of the incident. Instead, he gives another frightening example of Spike's behaviour during *The Bedsitting Room*:

One night [in the West End], Spike was off ill. But he phoned from his Highgate home to ask to speak to [Barry] Humphries [who had taken over Graham Stark's part]. 'He's on stage,' said the stage doorman. 'I know exactly when he's on stage,' said Spike. 'Put me through.' The stage doorman hung up.

Spike summoned a taxi to the West End, told the driver to wait, and limping with a walking stick went to the theatre's stage door. He aimed a blow at the doorman . . . 'Don't tell me when Barry Humphries is on stage!' shouted Spike, who did not enjoy being contradicted, and returned to his taxi.

Graham Stark confirms Antrobus's account of the gun incident, with the exception that he says he did transfer to the West End, where the incident took place, rather than at the Mermaid. He believes Spike had become uncontrollably jealous of the plaudits he had received for his performance; Stanley Kubrick was among those who came backstage to praise him. He says that, following Spike's telephone threat, his agent sent the police to the theatre, where Spike reassured them that no harm was meant, and produced a dummy gun. However, says Stark, he also had a real one, which he had concealed.

Stark emphasises that, though he was genuinely terrified by the gun incident, he and Spike eventually made it up. Spike would send him conciliatory Christmas cards, and Stark invited him to appear in a film he was making, *The Magnificent Seven Deadly Sins* (1971), in which Spike played Sloth. Stark continued to find Spike uncomfortable in certain ways: he hated his harping on about Jews, and is among those who believed that Spike belonged to Mosley's Blackshirts in the 1930s. Yet his final verdict is approving and affectionate: 'He was very naughty in lots of ways, but he was the most brilliant bugger I ever knew.'

Anthony Clare once asked Spike whether he had experienced impulses to violence. 'I wanted to be violent,' Spike admitted, 'but somehow I felt inhibited . . . I felt like killing people [but] I thought that would be the last straw if I turned violent . . . I had terrible tantrums [during the *Goon Show*] . . . I smashed a room at Broadcasting House once, all the furniture, because Dennis Main Wilson said something to me.'

Barry Humphries says that, in his early days as a comic actor in Australia, so many people told him how funny Spike Milligan was that he built up a resistance to him. '"You mean you haven't heard the *Goon Show*?" my friends would cry in chorus. "It's right up your street!"' Then, one evening when he was performing in Sydney, he was told that Milligan was in the audience. 'I was . . . petrified, and when he came backstage afterwards I was surprised to meet an affable, sane and astonishingly youthful man.' Humphries needn't have worried; Spike later described him as 'absolutely magnificent . . . not just a drag artist'.

Soon afterwards, Humphries was in London, trying out

'Mrs Edna Everage' (as she then was) at Peter Cook's Establishment Club, and playing the undertaker in *Oliver!* 'A telegram arrived . . . from Spike Milligan inviting me to join the cast of *The Bedsitting Room*.' He noted that Spike, though only in his mid-forties, was 'already somewhat grizzled. He had grown a beard for his role but he never allowed it to fully develop, so that one might say he was a pioneer of designer stubble.'

Humphries found that acting alongside Spike was one of the oddest and most exhilarating experiences of his career. 'One could never be sure what would happen from night to night.' During one performance, Spike simply walked out, leaving the rest of the cast to manage without him.

This was probably some months into the Duke of York's run of *The Bedsitting Room*. At first, Spike had enjoyed the West End. Having his name up in lights, he told his parents, was no guarantee of security. But it did mean that he had made a success in a new walk of life, confounding those who thought he was just a gag-writer.

Initially, he liked the routine of performances, the feeling that he was going to work daily at the same time and getting a weekly wage packet. But there were tensions at home, with Laura resenting her stepmother's strict ways (for example Paddy insisted on putting the girls' hair in curlers before they went to bed each night), and Spike disagreeing with Paddy's conviction that all three children should go to boarding school. They compromised, with Laura weekly-boarding at her convent, and Sean attending a Catholic private day-school, St Mary's Abbey Convent. 'I remember the name – I also remember the bills!' writes Spike.

After some months of *The Bedsitting Room*, he was 'absolutely, abysmally depressed. Yet somehow I managed to ad lib . . .' One of his improvisations, at a Saturday matinee in July 1963, made the *News of the World*, which reported that 'clowning during curtain calls, he grabbed the curtain and was hauled up nearly twenty feet from the stage and there he was stuck because the curtain jammed . . .'

He felt 'tortured', but around this time, when he was asked to write a newspaper article on how to relax, he noted that, paradoxically, he became truly relaxed when he went on stage, and felt much better when he had given a performance.

Despite the appeal of the adrenalin high, his understudy in *The Bedsitting Room* began to take over the part more and more often. Different explanations were given to the press: a slipped disc, exhaustion, migraine. This last excuse for Spike came from Paddy, who had no experience of mental illness and was deeply hurt when her husband chose to sleep in his office rather than come home after a performance. Even when he went back to the family house he wanted silence and isolation.

At this date, manic depression was hardly known about outside the world of psychiatry. Moreover the extreme and unpredictable mood swings could arouse suspicions that the sufferer was doing it deliberately, to attract attention or to avoid unwanted obligations. Indeed Joe McGrath believes there was an element of this in Spike's 'bipolar disorder', as the condition is known to psychiatrists. 'I think he could use the depressions, to dodge a confrontation or a crisis,' McGrath says.

Financial worry undoubtedly played a part in his mood swings. *The Bedsitting Room* was lucrative, but it would soon close, and Michael Foot remembers Spike envying Peter Sellers and Harry Secombe the successes they were now able to enjoy. Foot guesses that he thought it unfair that he had helped to launch their careers, and now they were speeding on without him.

Sellers had now co-starred in (to mention just his best-remembered performances) *The Ladykillers* (1955), *The Smallest Show on Earth* (1957), *The Mouse that Roared* (1959), *I'm All Right Jack* (1959), *Two Way Stretch* (1960), *The Millionairess* (1961), *Only Two Can Play* (1962), *Lolita* (1962), *Waltz of the Toreadors* (1962), *The Dock Brief* (1963), *Heavens Above* (1963), *The Wrong Arm of the Law* (1963) and *The Pink Panther* (1963). Secombe, who was now singing seriously, was in constant demand from television, and in 1963 took on the title role in a new musical, *Pickwick*, which carried him to Broadway and was often revived during the remainder of his life.

Neither of them, however, had written a novel, and when *Puckoon* came out in October 1963, Spike was able to bask in some excellent reviews. 'This is Spike Milligan's first novel, and by far the best thing he has yet done,' declared the *Observer*. '*Puckoon* . . . has a surrealist sanity, [and] is extraordinarily well written', judged the *Daily Mail*, and the *TLS*, though slightly condescending, was equally enthusiastic:

as another 'dustbin of Milligan' . . . it certainly has much to recommend it. Written in a style which suggests sometimes Samuel Beckett rewritten by Amanda Ros, sometimes Firbank yoked in unlikely collaboration with Brendan Behan . . . the book is funny, unpredictable, and sometimes salutarily disturbing; one could hardly ask for more from a novelist who knew all the rules.

True, the *Evening Standard* thought it 'a sad disappointment for Goon fans', and the *Sunday Times* suspected that the author had 'strung it together on a spare Sunday'. But the book quickly became a bestseller and has been reprinted more than thirty times.

The *TLS* review of *Puckoon* commented on its profusion of 'cheerful jokes about Negroes, Jews, Roman Catholics, homosexuals and other convenient occasions of liberal sympathy', which peppered the book 'just as if they were people like you and me instead of painful special cases to be handled with care'. When the editor of one of Spike's later books (a volume of the war memoirs) suggested that there were perhaps too many Jewish jokes in the text, Spike replied that he must be Jewish. He insisted that the Jewish jokes stayed. And he bet that the editor told Irish jokes.

*

While *The Bedsitting Room* was running in the West End, in October 1963 *The Telegoons* made their debut on BBC TV, in a series of fifteen-minute films adapted from *Goon Show* scripts by Maurice Wiltshire.

Back in 1959 Dennis Main Wilson, who had moved to television, had written to Ronnie Waldman (the BBC TV Light Entertainment supremo) suggesting that the Goons – who were then still running on radio – might be televised. He admitted that Spike's relationship with the BBC 'has a very sad history. He has done and said some very stupid things. On the other hand he *is* 10% genius, and I wonder if there would be any point in suggesting a short series of carefully tele-recorded (for self-protection) offbeat half-hours?'

In the event, the puppets got there first – though Milligan, Secombe and Sellers recorded the soundtrack of the new versions themselves, and the series was lovingly loyal to the radio originals. There were, however, two problems: first, that everyone had their own ideas of what the characters should look like; and second, while the radio scripts made even the most surrealistic happenings seem believable, this couldn't be achieved on the screen, and the films tended to look a little unexciting.

Spike thought little of *The Telegoons*, but was glad of the recording fees, and raised no objection to the making of a second series, shown during 1964. However, for the remainder of his life he refused to give approval to any other projects to bring the Goons on screen in animated or puppet form.

During 1964 he was once again trying to persuade the BBC to let him get his hands on *Housewives' Choice*. In March he tackled Anna Instone, whose department produced the programme, reminding her of her statement a long while ago that it was not BBC policy to change the existing rota of disc jockeys. He pointed out that since that time, new presenters had turned up on the programme – including Bob Monkhouse, which showed how desperate they must be. Since he was a well-behaved man with three children, who worked regularly and did nothing remarkable or peculiar would they please stop fobbing him off with excuses? If they just thought he was unsuitable, would they please say so.

Anna Instone replied that, 'as a family man', he was 'more suited to *Children's Favourites*, which he had already presented, and which they hoped to be able to invite him to do again soon. This seems not to have satisfied him in the least, and he was still firing off sporadic complaints about it five years later, when he wrote to Sir Hugh Greene, the BBC's Director General, whom he asked personally to intervene. He complained that he was a popular public figure, a musician and poet, without any anti-social attributes, but had finally extracted the wounding admission that he was not thought suitable. He could not imagine what might be the cause of being unsuitable to introduce records and read out requests from listeners.

Greene retired from the BBC a few days after getting the letter, and Frank Gillard, Managing Director, Radio, answered on his behalf on 1 April 1969:

Please don't ask for reasons. If everyone in showbiz required a written statement on why he or she was not selected for this, that or the other BBC engagement, we should quickly come to a standstill. Be assured that our affection for you is as high as ever, even if we don't see you quite in this particular disc jockey role.

This, at last, seems to have soothed Spike's somewhat paranoid anxieties on the subject. However, anyone convinced by his protest that he was the safest person imaginable to entrust with a live radio show need only dip into Barry Humphries's autobiography *My Life As Me*.

Humphries was recruited by Spike for a six-part radio series, *The Omar Khayyam Show*, which the Home Service broadcast in the winter of 1963–4. Based on a series which Spike had made for ABC in Australia, it purported to be a history of that country, but was largely a reworking of old *Goon Show* material; there were even appearances by Eccles and Minnie Bannister. Besides Spike and Humphries, the cast included Australian expatriates Bill Kerr and John Bluthal, and the music was provided by George Chisholm and his Jolly Jazzers. Charles Chilton produced. Humphries says it was 'generous' of Spike to involve him, because 'I tended to slow things down by dropping scripts and missing cues, whereas Spike's radio style was fast and furious.' But *The Omar Khayyam Show* was far less memorable than an occasion four years later, on 17 December 1967, when a producer unwisely let Humphries and Spike near a live microphone.

---

[1] In 1972 he had an exhibition at the Whitechapel Art Gallery. Pauline Scudamore writes that several of the pictures sold for about £100. Some were given to friends. Many have gone missing. In 1981 he had a watercolour hung in the Royal Academy Summer Exhibition.

Humphries recalls that they were doing a joint interview interspersed with jolly discs. To help things along, Spike had brought wine to the studio, 'and between sips and songs and comic banter, which Spike naturally dominated, we seemed to be going along swimmingly'. But it was the day on which Harold Holt, prime minister of Australia, had vanished while swimming off one of his country's more dangerous beaches; and (continues Humphries)

suddenly without warning to the veteran BBC man who was conducting our interview . . . Spike introduced the subject of [the] tragic disappearance in the form of a cod news flash.

'We're interrupting the programme, folks. Australian sources have just revealed that their Prime Minister was eaten by an opposition shark!' . . .

We all laughed – well, all except the veteran BBC interviewer. As the next record was played, two burly uniformed BBC commissionaires of the old school entered the studio, picked us up and practically frog-marched us down labyrinthine corridors and out of the building.[2]

---

[2] On 21 December 1967 Spike sent an apology (at least, it began as an apology) to the producer, David O'Clee: 'I am sorry that I mentioned Harold Holt on the broadcast. I assure you I did not come there with the intention of saying that, it just so happens with Barry Humphries being an Australian I thought I'd throw him by mentioning Harold Holt. I could have bit [sic] my tongue off when I had said it.

'What I don't understand is why you all panicked like you did. You highlighted it to such an extent by fading me out and then a national apology making front page news the next morning. I am not frightened of the BBC but I get a bit horrified at the results this organization has upon its employees . . . I know as a result of this that delightful little back-door Mafia of the BBC will see I don't do any more broadcasts. As I said, Anna Instone told me I was not suitable for *Housewives' Choice*, at last I suppose she now has a good reason.'

I do not do anything extraordinary

Give Spike a live mike and something of the sort was bound to happen. A few years later – and this time there's a recording – ABC in Australia let him sit near a newsreader; and this was the result:

[Time signal]

NEWSREADER: The news in brief. The prime minister, Mr McMahon, arrived back in Australia today after his overseas tour. He told newsmen at Sydney airport that he could not have had more valuable discussions with President Nixon, and the British prime minister Mr Heath.

SPIKE: What about Spike Milligan?

NEWSREADER: But he refused to give details of the discussions before he had spoken in the House.

SPIKE: What about Spike Milligan?

NEWSREADER: Mr McMahon also refused to comment when asked about two former ministers, Mr Gordon and Mr Kilham.

SPIKE: And Spike Milligan.

[This goes on until the newsreader finally succumbs to laughter. But he recovers, and finishes with:]

NEWSREADER: More news in one hour.

SPIKE: You'll never make it.

He got away with it there – no burly commissionaires – but when he tried something similar on Japanese television in 1980, the Tokyo broadcasters seem not to have

O'Clee replied: 'you were *not* faded out . . . The apology fifteen minutes later was a ten second non-committal, non-specific blurb designed principally to stop the telephone calls which were becoming a bloody nuisance. . . . Having got all this off my chest, may I just say that . . . I have been a tremendous admirer [of you] since the age of eleven, and I admire and respect you as one of the very few people who have ever used radio imaginatively and as a medium in itself.' He said he hoped they would work together again soon.

realised it was a joke. This time he put a false nose on the newsreader, and munched a banana. The programme's producer was instantly fired, and the Japanese press speculated that Mr Milligan had behaved like this because he was having a mental breakdown. (It was actually a repeat of what he'd done – and had been meant to do – on the *Muppet Show* a year earlier, where there'd been a sketch in which he interrupted a (puppet) newsreader verbally and physically.)

To be fair to the Japanese, he could have been having a breakdown, except that it would probably have taken the form of deep depression rather than manic high jinks. He was in the depressive depths by the end of 1963, and left the West End run of *The Bedsitting Room* at Christmas (the play closed soon afterwards).

Brian Innes, drummer with the Temperance Seven, treated this flippantly: he described Spike's habit of disappearing for 'one of his deep week-long sleeps in a nursing home at Tunbridge Wells'. But his condition in December 1963 seems to have been worse than usual, for when he went home after a couple of weeks as an in-patient he was prescribed his first course of electro-convulsive therapy (ECT), which was only tried as a treatment for depression when all else had failed.

The jazz pianist Alan Clare, who had replaced the Temperance Seven when *The Bedsitting Room* transferred to the West End, had become friends with Spike, and was making a sickroom visit to him when two men arrived in white coats with the equipment for ECT, carrying the electrodes in an old tin box. Spike remarked that they had come to electrocute him, and complained at the scruffiness of their equipment. Then, deeply depressed as he was, he began to laugh. They were using his own electricity – and charging him for the privilege. He ought to install a slot meter, and make *them* pay!

Spike writes about his life in the mid-sixties as 'the dreary years of depression', and says that during them he

began to realize that there was no cure. In 1964, I concluded that like a malformed limb, you're stuck with it. The moment I faced up to this fact I felt better. I knew *I* had to handle the illness . . . I took exercise, [and] the total concentration and exhausting qualities of squash gave me one hour a day when I didn't think of anything but that little ball.

Meanwhile his work seemed unaffected by the depressions. In the autumn of 1963 he brought out *The Little Pot Boiler*, a collection of comic verse, prose and pictures. Much of it had an ecological theme – one of the first signs of this growing preoccupation – but there were some good laughs; for example:

> *I must go down to the sea again,*
> *To the lonely sea and the sky,*
> *I left my vest and socks there,*
> *wonder if they're dry?*

He promoted *The Little Pot Boiler* at jazz and poetry evenings, where the poet Dannie Abse, encountering him for the first time, was struck by his 'impudent' manner and his 'lazy hooded eyes'. Abse also recalls his opening gag: 'I thought of beginning by reading a sonnet of Shakespeare's but then I thought why should I? He never reads any of mine.'

Though there were frequent days of depression so deep that he could only stare at the wall, and his children had to tiptoe around the house, there were occasional upswings into an exhilaration which could carry other people along with it. Perhaps the most memorable came one night when he was still in *The Bedsitting Room* at the Duke of York's. It was a warm June evening, and the audience was wonderfully in tune with the play, reports Pauline Scudamore. They went wild at the curtain calls, a standing ovation which ran on and on, so that finally the stage manager had had enough. Spike yelled for more, but the curtain remained down. He yelled again, but the stage manager was packing up and going home.

Spike, however, was not giving up. In no time at all he had formed the euphoric cast into a conga. They danced across the stage, through the backstage area, past the astonished stage door-keeper, and out into the night – reaching the front of the theatre just as the audience was emerging. There were a few moments of hilarious clapping and bowing, before Spike led them dancing on again, up the street to where the *next* theatre was disgorging its audience. More bowing and applause, and then off they went once more, following their own Pied Piper through an amazed West End.

17

The funniest thing London has seen

The Bedsitting Room left Spike temporarily rich enough to fetch his parents over from Australia, first class, so that they could spend the summer with Laura, Sean and Silé. Once Leo and Flo were installed as babysitters, Spike and Paddy headed for the Mediterranean on a cruise ship. Spike recorded that they came home refreshed, but in general he had the manic depressive's dislike of holidays: the removal of the pressure of work creates too much opportunity for intro-spection, which leads to depression. 'I myself don't gain much from going abroad for a vacation,' is how he put it. 'I don't like doing nothing. I need something to do.'

Similarly, when he was at home, he did not go in for 'hobbies'. Every spare-time task was undertaken with the same intensity and commitment as his professional work. One such project was the restoration of the Elfin Oak in Kensington Gardens, an ancient tree-trunk upon which, many years earlier, a sculptor (Ivor Innes) had carved the figures of elves and witches. These had decayed to the point of invisibility, and Spike obtained the agreement of the Ministry of Works to organise a group of people to rescue it, working on Saturdays.

He said he 'found such mental peace' when restoring the carvings; but he was soon swamped with autograph hunters, and the ministry had to install screens around the tree to give him privacy. Barry Humphries, who describes the Elfin Oak as 'an ugly tree stump' with 'sub-Arthur Rackham' decorations, and who served for a while as Spike's rather unwilling assistant in the enterprise, writes that 'Spike's keen instinct for publicity ensured that it received full media coverage.'

Spike also served on the committee of the Finchley Society, the architectural preservation group for his locality. John Betjeman sometimes attended meetings, and Spike suggested to him that all the preservation societies should join together to form one major group (a sensible scheme which came to nothing).

Small details of local scenery were always catching his eye. He noticed that on one of the north London ponds there was a lone female swan. 'I contacted Peter Scott at Slimbridge Wild Fowl sanctuary and asked him for a cob. It was delivered and released on the pond. It worked! Together, next spring, they hatched four cygnets!'

Meanwhile his success in *The Bedsitting Room* led to other offers of stage work. During 1963 he was invited to adapt and direct Alfred Jarry's absurdist classic *Ubu Roi*, but nothing came of it. However, the next year, *Oblomov*, a little known satirical Russian novel of the mid-nineteenth century, was to be staged at the Lyric, Hammersmith, and the director, Frank Dunlop, daringly offered the title role to Spike.

'I only went into *Oblomov* because I was out of work,' Spike told a newspaper a few years later. He read the novel, which is by Ivan Alexandrovich Goncharov (1812–91), and was published in 1859. The drama critic Milton Shulman described it as

a telling, satirical comment on the Slavonic character and Russian society. It concern[s] an indolent, philosophical young man who [feels] that a life of lying in bed and doing nothing [is] a more meaningful way of spending time than rushing about in pursuit of wealth, position or power. But an attack of love shakes him out of his recumbent Oblomovism. He finds that he is incapable of love, returns to his negative existence and is forever tragically unhappy for having tasted a desire for achievement and action.

Pauline Scudamore points out a significant link with Spike: Oblomov gradually subsides into what seems to be idleness; yet the descriptions of his condition suggest that it is depression. Spike, however, refused to be serious when questioned by the press about his motives for taking on the part. He told them he was looking forward to spending much of the play in bed – it would be a nice comfortable rest.

Somehow, during rehearsals in September 1964, no one noticed that Spike was failing to learn his lines. His excuse was that 'we never seemed to get round to proper rehearsal', and there was 'fresh dialogue' being added all the time. On the opening night (7 October) he was 'white with fear'. Sure enough, when he got on stage, 'I couldn't remember the script.' So he did the only thing he could think of: 'I ad-libbed into comedy.'

The first gag seems to have been accidental. One of his slippers came off, and skimmed over the stage and into the stalls. This made the audience hoot with laughter. After that, he was off.

The drama critic of *The Times* described the shaky nature of that first performance:

Mr Milligan . . . delivers ardent lines with a spasmodic shudder of the shoulders and stumbles out of reach at the first opportunity . . . [He] gets his best effects when he discards the play altogether and flashes a hand mirror round the house, and rows the revolve out of sight with an imaginary oar.

These were simple sight-gags, which sat awkwardly with the ill-remembered script. When Joan Greenwood, who was playing Olga, Oblomov's inamorata, came off-stage, she was greeted by her actor husband André Morrell, who told her bluntly that the performance had been appalling, and she must extricate herself from the production. Meanwhile Spike was trying to justify himself to a reporter from the *Daily Express*: 'There were these dry-ups and empty spaces and rather than suffer from empty spaces I filled in.' Had he intended to fool around? 'Lord, no. You can't do that to people like Joan Greenwood . . . Why not come and see us in a week? I should know the lines by then and there won't be any improvisation at all.'

However, Milton Shulman, who had been there for the *Evening Standard*, was among those who felt that Milligan was on to a good thing:

Now any resemblance between [Goncharov's novel] and the activities to be seen at the Lyric, Hammersmith . . . is not only accidental but probably miraculous. Adapted by Riccardo Aragno, the play seems to have been re-adapted by Spike Milligan . . . I suspect that there will be fresh re-adaptations every night from here on in.

Wandering about the stage like a loose-limbed, unshaven goon, Spike manages to twist each turn of the plot to fit his own nefarious, hilarious intentions. The ultimate result is equivalent to seeing the Crazy Gang as the Brothers Karamazov . . .

Spike remains his endearing, irrelevant, hysterical self. During one scene when he first realises he is in love with Olga (Joan Greenwood), he tosses off as an aside: 'I hope Milton Shulman's here.' . . .

The rest of the cast . . . seem taken aback by it all and have still not adjusted . . . For Milligan addicts, *Oblomov* can be classified as a connoisseur's treat. But for others, the send-up of this novel has to become broader and more obvious . . .

Some reviewers were lukewarm, such as Jeremy Kingston of *Punch* ('What he can be like to act with I dare not think . . . I hope the rest of the cast are equipped with tranquillisers'), and Harold Hobson of the *Sunday Times*: 'If this is improvisation, then the sooner we return to a positively slavish subservience to the author the better.' But the majority verdict was that of Eric Shorter in the *Daily Telegraph*:

Mr Milligan . . . cannot act for toffee in the dramatic sense . . . But what he can do – and does nearly all the time – is to cod-act alarmingly. The result is a bit confusing for the playgoer who wants to know what *Oblomov* is all about . . . but highly entertaining whenever Mr Milligan finds a chance to add a dash of his own bemused irreverence.

With good reviews under his belt, Spike began to ad lib even more than he had in *The Bedsitting Room*. Bernard Levin, then drama critic of the *Daily Mail*, came to watch a performance and judged it 'the funniest thing London has seen for many, many years', words that were soon being quoted by the management in press advertisements. Meanwhile Penelope Gilliatt in the *Observer* wrote of 'the rogue genius of Milligan'. (Another admirer was Peter Brook, who in his 1968 book *The Empty Space* wrote approvingly of 'Spike Milligan's theatre, in which the imagination flies like a wild bat in and out of every possible shape and style'.)

Looking back at *Oblomov*, Milligan perceived that it gave him, at last, real confidence as a performer, which he had never had during the Goon years: 'It was not my own writing and I managed to become a real clown.' After *Oblomov* had run for five weeks at Hammersmith it moved to the Comedy Theatre in the West End, where it was retitled *Son of Oblomov*.

The *News of the World*, reviewing it at the Comedy, was ecstatic: 'a hilarious evening of vintage Milligan . . . blossoming into the great and accomplished clown his devoted fans knew he would one day become'. Once again, he settled into the routine of a West End run, this time with the audience's expectations of his own performance running especially high. They were rarely disappointed; for example the film critic Philip French recalls the strange performance when the curtain went up to reveal that lying in Oblomov's bed, alongside Spike, were the film-maker Boulting Brothers, John and Roy. 'They stayed there for the entire evening, and no one ever referred to their presence,' said French, who added that he himself 'always found Milligan's stage and screen performances – as opposed to the *Goon Show* on radio – somehow rather disturbing.'

Meanwhile the rest of the *Oblomov* cast had to do their best in the face of Spike's complete unpredictability, and his determination to 'corpse' them (make them laugh). Only Joan Greenwood remained unresponsive. She never departed from the script, recalled Spike. He was totally unable to coax or surprise her out of role.

*

At Christmas 1964, nearly three months after opening in *Oblomov*, he was the speaker on the BBC Light Programme's 'God-slot', *Five to Ten* (a five-minute religious talk). Ad libbing into a tape recorder, he gave some personal history:

I had my period of life during the war when I gave up [religion]. I said 'There is no God, don't believe that war and God are synonymous.' I used to go out with women, get drunk, all the things that I wanted to do, but basically I was only putting God on one side so I could enjoy the primitive self. Well it's easier when you're older to come back to religion, but I came back to my religion through my children.

When I'd had three children – or rather my wife had them for me – they asked me questions . . . questions I couldn't answer, like how did the sun get there? Where did it come from? Well I could . . . say that it was the centre of the universe and that millions of years ago the universe exploded and shot all those molten stars into orbit. And then they'd say 'But where did *they* come from?'

And I couldn't answer them. Nobody can answer them. Nobody knows. Because science are [sic] going along a physical track to discover they don't seem to be able to compute that it's possible that God is. That you can't find God in an analytical laboratory. They're not looking for Him, so they're naturally not going to find Him . . . And they can't give me an answer to tell my children, so I'll have to make answers inasmuch as I need faith – that's the answer.

And I've suddenly realized that there just might be a God.

I'm not saying that God is perfect. I don't think He is perfect, hence the imperfections of our lives and the questions like 'Why did this child die?' I think God might be imperfect. It is possible. But that doesn't mean there's no God.

Not surprisingly, this last passage (with its very unconventional idea of God) was cut as too controversial, and the broadcast version ended as follows – tamely as far as the theological content was concerned, but with a good joke:

I've suddenly realised that there just must be a God . . .

I cannot believe that I myself am the product of unthinking matter. I cannot believe that my father was an explosion, and my mother was a vacuum.

Spike explores the idea of an imperfect deity in a poem written a little later, which describes life as 'Occupational therapy twix[t] birth and death', and suggests that the human race may be simply the plaything 'of a careless God'. In 1995 he told a journalist that he 'still attends Mass most Sundays, and [goes] to regular confession. "So why do you believe in God?" . . . "I don't. I just like Jesus."'

On Christmas Day 1964 BBC2 transmitted *Muses with Milligan*, one of a series featuring jazz and poetry, with Spike as link man. He found this job irritating, since he was expected to be funny all the time, whatever mood had been set by the poetry or the music.

The poets in this Christmas edition included Robert Graves, then about to turn seventy. A few days later Graves wrote to Spike to say how much he had enjoyed the evening. Spike, who was always liable to be awestruck in the presence of accredited intellectuals, replied that he was 'absolutely overwhelmed' by Graves treating him 'as though I was an equal'.

A rather self-conscious correspondence began, Spike realising that he must write more than ordinary letters: 'I would have to raise my game.' Later, he claimed that he and Graves had got on so well because they had a shared hatred of stupidity in other people. However, Barry Humphries suspected that Graves was already 'somewhat gaga' and didn't really know who Spike was.

'My dear Robert,' Spike wrote to Graves (who was back at his home in Majorca) in the middle of one night in March 1965, a Sunday night when there was no performance of *Son of Oblomov*. He reported that he was in bed with 'a manic depression', and was getting frightened that he might become seriously insane, like Nietzsche. He felt that life was as pointless as an electric bulb shining on a sunny day. And what about Graves? Was he dreaming on some sunny southern terrace, hoping for happiness? If he found it, he would be the first person to do so.

Looking at this letter many years later,[1] Spike recalled that he had read what he could find about insanity (including, one assumes, the life of Nietzsche, who died insane), and felt that he himself had always managed to climb out of depression without permanent mental damage. Yet he claimed that, even when the depression lifted, he had an essentially jaundiced view of life. He was *never* happy (he wrote to Graves); he could make anyone laugh except himself. He didn't know what life was for. He kept going, but there

---

[1] Milligan and Graves jointly gave the correspondence to St John's College, Oxford, of which Graves was an Honorary Fellow.

rarely seemed to be any destination in sight, other than meal times, bedtimes, Christmas, and his children's birthdays.

He told Graves of his belief that he had a special affinity with children. 'The house is quiet as a mouse,' he wrote at 'the witching hour' one night in August 1967. 'The brood are locked in their children's dreams – where adults can never venture. (I can, but then, I'm not adult.)' From this, Graves might have imagined a houseful of pre-pubertal daughters and sons. In fact Laura was almost fifteen, Sean just turning thirteen, and Silé nine. Yet Spike still kept up the pretence that the tiny letters he hid for them in the garden were written by the fairies. 'I'd wait until midnight on a pitch black night,' recalls Laura,

and then go into his room when he was in his pyjamas and say 'Oooh, Dad, I've just written to the fairies.' 'Have you, darling,' he'd say, trying hard to look pleased. 'Well, now, you go back to bed, I'm sure the fairies will find it – where did you hide it?' Twenty minutes later we'd be looking out of our window and there would be Dad, with a torch, turning over stones, sometimes in the pouring rain.

Laura describes this as the behaviour of 'a saint', but others might judge it, and his claim to be a child himself, to be whimsical in a J.M. Barrie way. Certainly there was empathy with children, but not of the sentimental sort that he liked to describe.

*

Four months after *Son of Oblomov* had arrived in the West End, on 8 April 1965, it was reported that audience members had demanded their money back after Milligan had missed two performances. He 'had a cold and was too ill to appear . . . Understudy John Collins took over.' Michael White, the show's impresario, said that the cold 'came on quite suddenly this morning'. Spike had already missed two performances earlier in the run.

Two weeks later, on 21 April, the Queen was brought to the show by Princess Margaret (with Prince Philip, Prince Charles and Princess Anne) as part of the celebrations of her thirty-ninth birthday. Peter Sellers and his new swinging sixties trophy wife Britt Ekland were in the party.

In his biography of Sellers, Peter Evans reports this ancient back-chat routine getting an airing during the performance:

MILLIGAN: Is there a Peter Sellers in the house?

SELLERS: *(in the middle of the royal party)* Yes.

MILLIGAN: Why can't a lady with a wooden leg change a pound note?

SELLERS: I don't know. Why can't a lady with a wooden leg change a pound note?

MILLIGAN: Because she's only got half a nicker.

SELLERS: I don't wish to know that.

MILLIGAN: Why does Prince Philip wear red, white and blue braces?

SELLERS: I don't know. Why does Prince Philip wear red, white and blue braces?

MILLIGAN: To keep his trousers up.

Writing in the *Daily Express* the morning after the performance, Evans reported further details of the evening: 'When Milligan came to a saucy bedroom scene, he cried out: "Philip, get that lady out of here!" Then Charles joined in lustily when Milligan invited the audience to call one of the actors "a great hairy nit".' Milligan 'also grabbed a prayer mat and did obeisance towards the [royal] visitors – "I believe in keeping in with all of 'em." At the end of the show he came forward with a sword and hinted: "If you want to knight me round the back afterwards . . . " Her Majesty declined the offer, but was definitely amused.'

When the curtain had fallen, Paddy Milligan joined Spike and they drove in his Mini to Kensington Palace, for what Princess Margaret described in her letter of invitation as 'dinner with my sister'. Spike had received the handwritten note about eight weeks earlier. 'I wanted to tell people about it, but it was that protocol thing. Paddy wanted to ring her family in the North. We had a real barney over that, because I told her not to.'

Afterwards, he described the dinner to Barry Norman of the *Mail* as 'delightfully simple, really – best whatsit of lamb. Saddle, I think, with brussels sprouts and that'. (A year later, when the euphoria had worn off, he alleged that the food 'came from Lyons', and 'all the cutlery was marked "P & O" and "British Railways"'.)

Sellers had sent him a telegram warning him to 'lay off the funny business over the dinner table'. However, 'after dinner I got up and announced: "Ladies and gentlemen, we have with us Mr Peter Sellers, the only man to have played the part of the Demon Barber of Fleet Street." . . . I remembered Sellers had played the part in the RAF, and we made him get up and go through with it – all the moustache-twirling and the asides. He kept forgetting the lines, and they loved it.'

The evening concluded with a showing of *The Running, Jumping and Standing Still Film*. (Graham Stark says the royals had acquired their own copy of it.) Joe McGrath, who was among those who had appeared in it, cast a cold eye on Spike's burgeoning friendship with royalty: 'I really resent that. I think that as a comedian you should be a figure of subversion.'

The royal party had been let off lightly at *Son of Oblomov*. Barry Cryer was there the night that Spike 'entered and walked across the stage and down some steps into the audience. "Sorry I'm late, folks," he said, "I've had this three-day cancer." He looked back at them. "And now for the world's embarrassed silence championships."' And Pauline Scudamore records an ad lib that proved disastrous.

One day as Spike was in Kensington Gardens, working on the Elfin Oak, a young man approached him and said he envied Spike's success, especially as he himself was a superb actor, who would be well known if he had had Spike's chances. Spike responded that here was his chance: he was to appear in *Son of Oblomov*. And he did, but was a total flop.

Joan Greenwood recalled that, as the young man left the stage, Spike said sourly to the audience that he must be the worst actor in the world. Greenwood found him weeping, and told Spike she would not tolerate such cruelty. But Spike remained unapologetic. He had never heard of him since, he told Scudamore, nor had anybody else. So much for being a great actor.

This is the only moment in her book when the usually sympathetic Scudamore turns sharply critical, remarking that Spike was virtually incapable of thinking that he might possibly be in the wrong. It was a character trait that undoubtedly caused storms in his second marriage. 'There were some hellish rows,' he admits in *The Family Album*. 'Paddy could have a terrible temper, as could I, and at one point there were continual rows, one after another. She even shouted at Laura, "Get out of this house!" This was too much for Laura, who resented Paddy from then on and our relationships became very strained.'

Paddy's father had his own ultra-traditional view of what was wrong. 'Spike,' he said, 'this woman wants a baby.' Spike 'promised I'd do my best'.

*

During 1965 Spike was involved with a small-scale project that exposed, very precisely, his strengths and weaknesses, and both the delights and risks in store for those who found themselves working with him.

Anthony Blond, who had published *Puckoon*, had bought some land in Islington, alongside the Regent's Canal, and invited a film-maker friend, Christopher Mason, to shoot an offbeat documentary recording the building of a new house on the site by the contractor Alistair McAlpine (who would sponsor the film in return for 'product placement'). Mason invited Spike to star. 'I'd loved *Oblomov*,' he writes,

and explained that we were free to follow his inspirations – we could invent it as we went along.

Spike said no, he couldn't work like that. There had to be a script.

So I agreed to write an outline. The story started on the canal, against the background of site-clearing, and concerned a slightly mad fisherman whose desire to land a fish leads him through a surreal sequence of events to the Zoo, where he intercepts one thrown to a seal. The actor Arthur Mullard – who would appear throughout in different guises – was the zoo-keeper who chases him, falls into the canal, and is eaten by crocodiles. Spike nearly drowns, and eventually blows himself up by throwing a lighted match at a gasometer.

I sent the script to Spike, hoping he would now feel tempted to contribute his own nonsense. He said it was perfect. Nothing must be changed.

Day 1. We stick to the script – wordless: sound-effects to be dubbed. Spike is enjoying himself. It begins to rain. He is handed an umbrella and for five minutes invents business of such comic genius that the crew, builders and onlookers are weeping with laughter. But the camera isn't prepared, so this brilliance is shot from only one angle, and from too far away.

He wouldn't repeat bits. It was impossible to edit: theatre, not film.

Day 2. Spike arrives late. Very late. He has been repainting some pixies on a tree in Hyde Park.

We'd done about a third of the film when he announced that

he was going on holiday; unforeseen and unprofessional, but we had to accept it.

He came back from holiday without his beard. This not only screwed up continuity, it changed the character from an innocent obsessive to an all-knowing, double-taking Goon.

We lived with it, but something else had changed in Spike. As the days passed, depression took hold. No one could reach him. Often, just as we were ready to shoot, he'd wander off out of sight. One of us would follow, and gently remind him that we were making a film. He went through the motions, but he was bored. He could also be nasty. One day a shot required him to walk towards camera and stop at a precise point. My young assistant (on his first film) put a mark on the pavement. Spike went berserk: 'What do you think I am, a fucking amateur?'

On rare occasions he would amaze us. Something – a chimney pot, or a TV aerial – could trigger a stream of jokes and philosophical fireworks. Then he'd revert, become morose, and reject even Arthur's attempt to get close to him.

We never had words – I was too scared to get angry, afraid that he'd abandon us with a half-made film. *Fish and Milligan* was finished and found a distributor (it surfaced at the news cinema in Victoria Station), but I was told that Spike hated it.

There are nice ideas in the film, which has a Jacques Tati–Buster Keaton flavour, but Spike's genius was essentially verbal. He wasn't a mime nor (I think) a tragic clown. And he was best with his own material.

*

He was steadily becoming more of a campaigner. When *A Book of Bits or A Bit of a Book* (which contained the same sort of mixture as *The Little Pot Boiler*) came out for Christmas 1965, it was dedicated to family planning and wildlife charities, and to President Nyerere of Tanzania 'for his enlightened attitude towards the preservation of his country's fauna'.

Much of Spike's time was taken up with writing letters to the newspapers on ecological, conservation and family planning issues. 'Spike's flair for publicity,' writes Barry Humphries, 'meant he rarely dropped out of the correspondence columns of *The Times* and the *Daily Telegraph*.'

One day the *Sun* found him displaying his oil paintings outside the Mermaid Theatre (he was an indifferent 'serious' painter, as opposed to an inspired drawer of Goons). 'The money he collected from passers-by [in a collecting box] was, he said, going to help world family planning. A surprise cause, perhaps, because Milligan is a Roman Catholic . . .' The *Daily Mail* noted that he was on the committee of the Family Planning International Campaign ('He is deeply sincere about it'), and the *News of the World* reported that, at the Mermaid, he 'sat . . . as a pavement artist shouting out to startled passers-by: "Take the Pill. Take the Pill." . . . On the Catholic attitude to birth control he was scathing. "Their arguments have got to go in the end," he said.' The *Sun* concluded its piece: 'One painting on show had nails protruding from it, and Milligan said this had been completed after a particularly hurtful attack upon himself.

'He hasn't sold anything yet. Prices may have something to do with it. Yesterday one picture was marked £20,000.'

He was clowning to the Queen again at the Royal Variety Performance in November 1965. Also on the bill were Peter Cook and Dudley Moore, then at the height of their popularity with their TV show *Not Only . . . But Also*, which had started in January. 'But Goon Spike Milligan . . . stole the top comedy spot,' judged the *Daily Sketch*. He had written a sketch about what Prince Charles could expect when he enrolled at Geelong school in Australia during 1966. 'All the pupils wore a ball and chain . . . a notice [said] "Bread Extra" . . . The scene caused roars of laughter in the Royal box.'

On 29 October the *Daily Express* reported that over two hundred people had asked for their money back when Milligan dropped out of a performance of *Son of Oblomov* because of illness; this time his part was taken over by Valentine Dyall. But the remarkable thing was that usually he kept going, week after week. His third wife Shelagh has recalled that she was with him in Australia when he was doing his one-man show: 'He was very down [with depression] for over a month and yet he went on stage every night, making the audience cry with laughter. He'd come off stage and go back to bed, stay there all night and all day and just get up to do the show again.'

He dropped out of *Son of Oblomov* again in March 1966 – 'We don't know whether Mr Milligan was just depressed or ill,' said a spokesman – and a few weeks later he walked out in mid-performance in protest at drunken heckling from some of the audience. On 5 April he began the show by giving an interview, from Oblomov's bed, to a couple of reporters (real ones), explaining why he had decided to leave the production at the end of the month. 'I'm starting to see double,' he said. 'The kids are asking at weekends, "Who's that funny-looking man?" The wife's wondering, too.' He also grumbled: 'I've made £40,000 from the show. I've put £29,000 aside for tax and it's not enough . . . Money is not real over here.' Finally he asked, 'Have you got enough, chaps?' and the reporters made an exit, with Milligan observing: 'Laurence Olivier wouldn't do this, mate.'

In *The Family Album* he writes: '*Oblomov* was still packing 'em in but I'd had enough. I'd slept with three leading ladies and I called the show off.' Graham Stark says he thinks this is rubbish – 'Joan Greenwood wouldn't have let him touch her' – and Spike was probably being more truthful when he told Robert Graves, rather pathetically: 'I am in love with every woman I see . . .'

Son of Oblomov came off at the end of April 1966. Two

weeks later: 'Doing my best has paid off. Paddy had a baby girl.' She was christened Jane Fionella. 'I did want a son but that was primitive ego at work.' He was aware that his concern about world overcrowding might seem to conflict with his own situation. He felt bad (he wrote to Robert Graves) at the way he had added four people to this overcrowded planet, but he couldn't bring himself to regret the existence of his children – they had been the very best thing in his life.

*

Four months after the birth of Jane, there was another addition to the Milligan ménage, in its way just as significant. Spike advertised for a personal assistant, and chose a young woman called Norma Farnes, who came from Yorkshire and was working in ITV. 'I told Spike I don't believe in contracts,' she recalls. 'We just shook hands and that was it. Within [the] first three months, I'd become his manager. Spike already had a manager at the time, but they had a row and Spike asked me to take on the job.' It was now, and presumably for tax reasons, that he formed a company, Spike Milligan Productions Ltd, to handle his earnings, with Norma Farnes at the helm. He told the *Sunday Express*: 'I have a company and pay myself a salary.'

Working at 9 Orme Court, where she also became Eric Sykes's assistant, Farnes soon mastered and virtually took over every practical aspect of Spike's life, ranging from paying his home telephone bill to dealing discreetly with his lady-friends (she says she had no such involvement with Spike himself, who was not her type). She received no special treatment from him, telling John Antrobus: 'He can find ways to make me wrong that I wouldn't have dreamt of in a thousand years.' But, says Antrobus, her 'dour Yorkshire humour' carried her through.

She became expert at sensing when he was about to go down with depression:

There would be warning signs. He hunches his shoulders . . . He sits down and put his hands between his knees . . . His face changes and it is not so much that he gets bags under his eyes as he gets a sort of purple discoloration down either side of his face. And he goes a dreadful ashen colour. His eyes change. It is difficult to describe but they just do.

She recalls how, when depression had struck, 'he would take himself off to his room at the top of the building and you would never hear from him. He'd be locked up there and then he would come out very quietly and thank you for everything . . . In normal life he didn't thank you for anything.' Occasionally she would go upstairs and sit with him, holding his hand: 'He needs to know that there is someone there.'

Farnes says that Paddy 'used to walk away' from Spike's depressions. 'She would go into terrible eating binges. She would come in here [Orme Court] and cry. She had a weight problem anyway . . . Spike would stay here and I would give her daily reports.' One suspects that this triangular situation added to Paddy's discomfort.

After a few years Norma felt she needed help in the office. Tanis Davies was enrolled as her assistant. Pauline Scudamore writes that the two women were masterly at the art of closing ranks to protect Spike.

Sometimes too much protection went on. In 1973 Robert Graves advised the organisers of a campaign to ban traffic on the newly repaired Albert Bridge in Chelsea to enlist Spike. They did not get past the Norma–Tanis protective wall. When Pauline Scudamore told Spike about this some years later, he was upset, and said he would certainly have lent his support.

He sometimes grumbled to Scudamore that Norma and Tanis were doing nothing on his behalf – that they were

either out at the hairdresser's or just not answering the telephone. He complained that, while they were brilliant at
doing his VAT returns, they did not find him work; he had
a big overdraft and no jobs. This was said in the 1980s,
when his television work in particular was going through
a thin time. But in 1966, the year that Norma arrived at
Orme Court, he was busier than ever.

In October that year he returned to the Mermaid for
revivals of *Treasure Island* (matinees) and *The Bedsitting
Room* (evenings). The latter transferred to the West End for
a second time, and went on a British tour.[2] The billing
outside the theatres read:

> 'Spike Milligan, of course, is an institution.' – Daily Express
> 'He lives in one.' – Spike Milligan

This wasn't just a joke: he seems to have been hospitalised at some time during this year, because a poem he
sent to Graves is dated 'Bethlehem Hospital Highgate 1966'
(a puzzle, because there is no Bethlehem Hospital in
Highgate). Another has the superscription: 'Nervous breakdown Bournemouth Feb 1967'. In *The Bedside Milligan*
(1968) he wrote:

---

[2] About two years later, Dick Lester filmed *The Bedsitting Room* for
United Artists, with Ralph Richardson as Lord Fortnum, Michael
Hordern replacing Graham Stark/Barry Humphries, and Spike repeating
his role as 'Mate'. He writes in *The Family Album* that Lester 'wanted
[the stage play] rewritten by his favourite writer, John Woods, who I
didn't think was in the same league of comedy writers that John
Antrobus and I were. There were some silly unexplainable jokes . . .
[But] the film won a peace award in Russia. I enjoyed doing it and
some bits of the original play were left in, but the stage show had
been hilarious and I was sad that the film wasn't.' Roger Wilmut
writes: 'The film got very bad reviews at the time.'

I have had five nervous breakdowns – and all the medics gave me was medicine – tablets – but no love or any attempt at involvement, in this respect I might as well have been a fish in a bowl. The mentally ill need LOVE, UNDERSTANDING – TOLERANCE, as yet unobtainable on the N.H.S. or the private world of psychiatry, but tablets, yes, and a bill for £5.5.0 a visit – if they know who you are it's £10.0.0 a visit – the increased fee has an immediate depressing effect – so you come out worse than you went in.

As yet, I have not been cured, patched up with chemicals, yes.

The year 1967 also saw him in Australia, touring to the major cities with a new project, a one-man show. 'I came here,' he told Graves, 'to make money, three months, a long slog but it's been successful.' He was also appearing in Wellington, New Zealand, 'taking the opportunity to stay with my war-time comrade, one Harry Edgington. We will consume much wine and relive those unforgettable days of World War II . . .' Then, suddenly, came a most welcome invitation: 'There must be some mistake. The BBC want me to play the part of Beachcomber on TV.' It was to be the beginning of a phase of his life in which he and British television at long last began a serious and sustained relationship.

18

What's the Q for?

The World of Beachcomber was a BBC project. Producer Duncan Wood hired Barry Took and John Junkin to adapt J.B. Morton's crazy narratives for TV – and Took found it quite tricky. Meanwhile Spike and Robert Morley were both considered for the title role. Spike was delighted when the invitation came.

On 13 November 1967 Barry Took wrote to Michael Mills, Head of Comedy at BBC Television, sending a draft of the first episode: 'Spike is obviously a great idea – if he can be contained – which in the long run may mean filming the dress [rehearsal] and editing afterwards!'

Spike queried the first *Beachcomber* script with Duncan Wood in December 1967. There seemed to be a difference of opinion whether he should or should not be playing Mr Justice Cocklecarrot – and he wanted to know the final decision as soon as possible, because he was slow at learning lines.

He didn't play Cocklecarrot (the part was taken by Clive Dunn of *Dad's Army*), but besides the linking role of Beachcomber – for which he was dressed in a tasselled cap and a smoking jacket, and was seated at a desk amid a clutter of Victorian junk – he appeared as a member of the Filthistan Trio (three utterly incompetent acrobats) and also as Dr Strabismus (Whom God Preserve, of Utrecht), a tireless inventor who, in the first programme, gave a short lecture entitled 'How to Eat Macaroni Through a Saxophone'.

Sir Michael Redgrave was engaged to read, 'perfectly seriously', excerpts from the 'Anthology of Huntingdonshire Cabmen' (an alphabetical list of absurd surnames). John Gielgud was invited to take part – the files don't reveal which character he was offered – but declined.

The World of Beachcomber began transmission on 22 January 1968, and was an immediate success. Spike was in his element, as he presided over some of the absurd characters and incidents that had helped to inspire the *Goon Show*. The series was immediately extended, a second series was commissioned, and the BBC arranged for Spike to have lunch with J.B. Morton himself, then in his mid-seventies. Spike was delighted by the experience. He reported that Morton had proved during the conversation that he still had plenty of ideas in him, and it was an awful pity that he was in retirement. (Maybe the two could have collaborated.)

The BBC invited Spike to attend *Beachcomber* script conferences, and a reporter watched as he 'sparked ideas like a Catherine wheel' – a good description of him in a productively manic mood. He was now coming to believe that his experience of depression was in some respects beneficial; he wrote to Robert Graves, who had a son suffering from it: 'Tell him, this descent into misery has a quality of giving the person a greater understanding . . .'

His own depression was still being exacerbated by insomnia; he not only found it difficult to fall asleep, but could be easily wakened by sounds in the house. Maybe it was because of this that he chose to sleep alone. 'I have always, even when married, slept in my own bedroom,' he wrote towards the end of his life. But it is hard to imagine that separate bedrooms did much good to his relationship with Paddy.

'I'm having a sticky time with my marriage,' he told Robert Graves in the spring of 1968, adding that there seemed to be no hope of improvement – it was making him deeply depressed. He had been having dinner with Peter Sellers, whose second marriage, to Britt Ekland, was now over, only Sellers was happy about it.

Just before Ekland and Sellers parted, they played host (with Milligan and Secombe) to the nineteen-year-old Prince Charles. Secombe had discovered that the heir to the throne was an enthusiast for old *Goon Shows*:

I asked his equerry, Squadron Leader David Checketts, if HRH would like to meet Spike and Peter . . . Eventually a date was fixed and Prince Charles and Checketts drove down from Cambridge together to have lunch with the three of us at Peter Sellers' house in Elstead, Surrey, where he lived in some style. [Charles] revealed an astonishing knowledge of past Goon Shows and an uncanny ability to imitate most of the characters.

This first meeting between Charles and the Goons did not get into the press. Meanwhile rumours were flying round about Spike's marriage. Dannie Abse heard that Spike and Paddy 'were not on speaking terms . . . Spike was living upstairs in his house, Paddy down below. When Spike needed a clean shirt he would send her a telegram.' But this was a familiar joke. 'Often she would not see Spike for days on end,' ran a newspaper version after Paddy's death, 'when he locked himself in his study upstairs. Then a telegram would arrive . . . : "Send up some tea. Urgently."'

In fact a 1975 interview that Paddy gave to *Woman's Realm* about living with Spike suggests that the rift between them was not so deep:

He seem[s] to do more suffering than laughing [said Paddy] . . . I'd never known that a human being could be in despair so absolute

. . . Occasionally he'll leave home and live in his office, to try and spare us the worst of it. When he does stay at home all you can give is loving and just being there. Over the years I've learned that usually you can't help at all.

Spike still had his manic upswings, when the world seemed his plaything. In February 1968 he was picked up by the police in his Mini-Cooper for driving without lights and going the wrong way up a one-way street. At the police station, where he failed a breathalyser test, he sang 'The Dustbin Song' from *A Show Called Fred*, and 'Maria, Maria, I've just met a man named Maria'. An inspector told the court next morning (where he lost his licence for a year): 'He was certainly the most entertaining prisoner I have had in twenty years.'

Between the extremes of mania and depression, there was also a Spike who was capable of sustained, concentrated hard work. 'I'm writing two books at once,' he told Graves from Australia in the early autumn of 1968, *The Magic Staircase* for children, and *It will all be over by Christmas*, a book on his life in the Army. 'As I start to fade on one I turn to the other.' He had to extend his Australian trip when his father suffered a stroke. By the time he returned to London he had written nearly 50,000 words of the army book.

*

Probably as a consequence of the success of *The World of Beachcomber*, BBC Television took the plunge and commissioned *Q5*, a series of seven thirty-minute programmes to be shown on BBC2 in March and April 1969. Spike was paid £750 for performing in each show and another fee for writing. The BBC agreed that he should have a collaborator.

Neil Shand, a journalist turned TV scriptwriter, had written later episodes of *The World of Beachcomber*, and he and Spike had hit it off. 'We'd go off to Ronnie Scott's together after recording, and sink a lot of wine,' recalls Shand.

I then moved on (during 1968) to the birth of the David Frost programmes at the new London Weekend, doing three nights a week as one of the editors. Suddenly I got a call from Spike's office, and Norma told me that the BBC had asked him to do a series; and then came the bolt from the blue: 'Spike would like you to write it with him.' Now this is someone who was a God-figure when I was in my teens – at school, and later in the news-paper office where I worked, we'd all talk about the Goons. And *he* wanted to write with *me*!

The start of the project was delayed until January 1969, when Shand could be free of his Frost commitment. Meanwhile they chose a title for the new series: *Q5*. Spike never explained this; the *Radio Times* called it 'enigmatic'. In the sixth programme a man asks, 'What's the Q for?' and receives the reply: 'Fish. It's Friday.' But it was trans-mitted on Monday evenings. Neil Shand unveils the truth: 'It was called *Q5* because they were building the *QE2*, which I think was the fourth of the *Queen* liners.[1] And one of my relatives had worked in the shipyard. So we became the fifth.'

Michael Mills wrote to Spike on 18 December 1968 in terms that show how keen the BBC was that *Q5* should be a success – and that there was some anxiety that the series was not yet written:

We have now collected together a crew of technicians, who are fully briefed on the sort of show you want to do and enthusi-astic about it. We have, for instance, a special props man at our

---

[1] It was the third.

disposal for twelve weeks, and a sound effects man who will spend two days a week (apart from the day in the studio) getting any special sound effects you want. So I hope all will be sweetness and light out there

Ian [McNaughton, the producer] tells me you have some most exciting and original ideas. All I can beg of you now is that you get as much of this material as you can down on paper and into Ian's hands as soon as possible.

Spike's requirements for visual effects equalled the complexity of the *Goon Show* sound effects:

1 portable coffin (that folds up into bag with carrying handle). Easily opened out whilst talking. Talker eventually to fall backwards into it.

1 inflatable naked plastic corpse (to fit into above). Eyes and mouth to be 'painted in' by Spike Milligan.

1 'real-looking' pistol, that when fired, 'flag' drops out which says 'BANG'.

Platform for girl to sit on (moveable – as though at White City dog racing – what was the 'rabbit' going round track, as it approaches the traps it becomes girl sitting on platform, being chased by men (instead of greyhounds).

However, Spike had already learned (from the *Fred* shows and his TV work in Australia) that television is much more resistant than radio to experiments and unconventionality. He told Pauline Scudamore that when he did experimental TV comedy it required the approval of a producer and a director who had a different sort of mind from his. Consequently he was lucky if as much as sixty per cent of the jokes reached the screen. It was very difficult to do things that were extremely unconventional. Either they were not grasping what he wanted, or they didn't dare to risk their jobs.

He was at work on the *Q5* scripts in January 1969 when he heard that his father was much worse. 'The cruel thing is,' he told Robert Graves, 'I'm writing some TV half-hours, and they're supposed to be funny. There's something very unfunny in being funny.' Leo died in February – typically supplying Spike with a good joke at the end: 'All his life he totally ignored his religion, but when he's told he's dying, suddenly! it's Good Catholic Time! "Call a Priest," he says. "No, wait, call a Bishop."'

Spike was determined that *Q5* would be as mould-breaking as the *Goon Show*. 'In writing the series,' he explains in *The Family Album*, 'I abandoned the notion that a show or even a sketch had to have a set form. This was free-form comedy. We would just end a sketch with everyone pacing towards the camera saying "What are we going to do now?" with each step. Then we were straight into the next one.'

He told the *Radio Times*, at the start of the series:

I hate the idea of just-another-show. And I don't like doing just a sketch with jokes. There has to be an idea that's funny by itself. Not easy to find – and television's a difficult medium for comedy. Your imagination gets filtered through so many people . . . There've been no great flights of fancy in TV comedy like there have with, say, the films of Ken Russell. There's never enough time, or money, or imagination.

Meanwhile Neil Shand was experiencing what he describes as quite literally the ups and downs of writing with Spike:

It was cyclical. You would go through a period when his creativity was rising, getting higher and faster, until it was spinning through the air. This would be wonderful when he was still on the way up, but virtually impossible by the time he reached the top, because by then it was going too fast – amazing things were spinning out of his mouth, but you couldn't grab them, because they were gone the next moment.

Then he started to go down again, and it would be good again until about half way down. And when it reached the bottom, he just vanished for a couple of days, locked the door of his office, and that was that. I remember knocking on the door, and almost saying those dreadful words 'Pull yourself together', and all he would say was 'Go away'.

*

The first episode of *Q5* was shown at 8.50 p.m. on Monday, 24 March 1969. The BBC destroyed many of the recordings of the series, but some videotape does survive, and the scripts are available on microfilm.

This first programme features Richard Ingrams as a television newsreader who bids good evening or appropriate alternative greetings, to viewers around the world in various time zones. He holds up a pair of smooth white-painted balls, whereupon Spike enters and lays claim to them, alleging that they dropped off while he was shaving. There is a good deal more about the balls (with plenty of sexual innuendo), and then Spike suddenly asks Ingrams if he is Jewish, to which Ingrams replies not necessarily, but he can feel an overdraft.

People keep asking each other 'Are you Jewish?' throughout *Q5*, and receive a variety of answers. Some years later, the journalist Richard Brooks went to interview Spike and was asked the same question. 'I'm a quarter Jewish,' answered Brooks. 'I thought so,' said Spike, 'you look it. Is your wife Jewish?' 'No,' answered Brooks, 'she's Catholic.' Spike seemed surprised. Looking back at the incident, Brooks sees it as straightforward, unashamed anti-Semitism, rather than any kind of joke. Neil Shand, however, regards Spike's preoccupation with Jewishness as essentially harmless: 'I'd recently been in America,' he says, 'where everyone cracked Polish jokes.'[2]

Richard Ingrams – who has himself been accused of anti-Semitism – had been editing *Private Eye* for several years by the time of *Q5*. 'Spike always took a great interest in the *Eye*,' he says.

He was always sending in letters, verses and pictures that he'd captioned with speech bubbles.

I remember when we had our first big libel case – which was the Randolph Churchill case – Spike [asked] if he couldn't be libelled. He'd always wanted to be libelled. In the next issue I wrote: 'Spike Milligan is a dirty Irish poof' – and he sued on the grounds that we'd called him IRISH!

Ingrams recalls Spike, during rehearsals for *Q5*,

shouting at the producer and making jokes about him . . . I think a lot of people at the BBC . . . thought he was out of control . . . In fact, Spike always had a clear sense of how far he could go . . . He's always been fantastically hard-working . . . a true professional. There were times when he was sitting in his dressing room with his head in his hands, but he still went out and performed.

Keith Smith, who was in the cast of *Q7*, *Q8* and *Q9*, sees Milligan as rather less of a saint: 'Spike's intolerance and impatience with people could be difficult to take sometimes.' Neil Shand says of this:

---

[2] Graham Stark supplies another example: 'The last time I met Spike, we were at a party at Jeremy Robson's, the publisher, and Jeremy's family is Jewish, and Spike looked around and said: "The place is full of Jews." I said, "Oh, Spike, come on! Don't be so fucking stupid." And I left him and went to the next room, and spent the evening with Harry Secombe instead.'

He used to say that writing the scripts with me was the best part of making the programmes – 'This is where they pay us for making each other laugh!' Which we did, a lot. But in the studio, he could be on a downer. And he used to quote his father, who said that the BBC was a bunch of Post Office engineers waiting for a pension.

Also, he got bored very quickly, and after the read-through he would tend to ignore the script and make up new versions of his own lines, which could throw the other performers, or encourage them to rewrite their lines.

Other items in the first Q5 included a party political broadcast on behalf of the Labour Party (with Spike as a candidate, desperately pleading for help) and a commercial for artificial humps, made of fibreglass and therefore washable, and designed to get the wearer an enormous amount of sympathy.

Also in the cast was Ingrams's fellow-satirist John Wells, who was the commentator on the annual Grandmother Hurling Finals at Beachy Head. Wells explains to the camera that in the preliminary rounds, more than a hundred grandmothers have been hurled out to sea. Only two of the contestants have made it back to land in the one minute allowed for this. One of the contestants tells Wells that according to the coroner his grandmother is dead, but he got a second opinion.

Spike recalls that the studio audience was not amused by the Grandmother Hurling Contest. He admitted that it was a little sadistic, but put the blame chiefly on the audience, who he said were boring people.

The second Q5 opened with Spike gazing at an electric lamp and saying that one day it would fall in love with him. Cut to Clement Freud (on film) telling us that we have just seen Spike Milligan saying that one day that lamp would fall in love with him. Cut to somebody else saying that

Clement Freud was telling us that we had been watching Spike Milligan saying that one day that lamp would fall in love with him. (It sounds terrible, but succeeds.)

Spike is then discovered apparently bicycling at high speed down a country lane with a pair of floppy false legs. An actor enters and Spike identifies him as John Bluthal, 'a former minority'. (John Bluthal is Jewish and grew up in Australia.)

A camera reveals the workings of this scene – the false legs and all – and shows us a girl tied up behind a piece of scenery. (Spike protests against this invasion of his privacy.)

An item about smoking cigarettes stunting people's growth includes the head of a tobacco firm (Spike) who is literally that – a head resting on a pair of shoes. He shouts that all the health warnings are nonsense: he smokes a hundred a day, and just look how healthy he is.

The *Observer* TV critic who reviewed the first two episodes of *Q5* was no less than George Melly: '*Q5* . . . has moments of hilarious invention . . . but I do wish that Milligan could overcome his belief that he is the personification of one of Dostoevsky's Holy Fools. He isn't, and it gets in the way.' Maurice Wiggin wrote a finely balanced critique of the first episode in the *Sunday Times*:

It was ungracious of Spike Milligan to say, in *Radio Times*, that 'there have been no great flights of fancy in TV comedy'. What about Marty Feldman? What about *Rowan and Martin's Laugh-in*? Spike's new vehicle, *Q5*, draws a little on the latter, and may fairly be compared with the former. His own flights of fancy sometimes fail to get off the ground, sometimes come down with a bump, as one expects from this strange, talented man, a great starter who has so little staying power. But he is a vital initiator. There is enough ingenuity and spontaneity in this show to keep one looking, and hoping: its best (surrealist) moments are delightful.

Spike answered Wiggin in a letter published in the *Sunday Times* on 2 April 1969:

Let me assure you that I had never seen a *Rowan & Martin's Laugh In*, until I had written this present series, *Q5*, so I cannot stand accused of taking anything from them, and I had never watched Marty [Feldman] until after I had decided what pattern the *Q5* series would take.

It's a pity that the public doesn't know the tremendous difficulties that are incurred with a show of the nature of *Q5*, which depends on high speed cutting, quick cutaways, and various depths in sound, all of which doesn't come off in the time given by the BBC to rehearse and complete such a show.

This is not an accusation against the BBC, but a fact, it's more that, if shows are to be more complicated, and quicker and more progressive, quite obviously a lot more time has got to be given if these shows are to be more successful.

In the third *Q5*, viewers were shown a bucket containing some liquid which was said to be Harry Secombe – he had melted in a Turkish bath – and John Bluthal appeared as Huw Wheldon (the Melvyn Bragg of his day), interviewing a guru, Swami Ned Teeth of 13a Tariq Alley.

Wheldon asks the Swami what is the music that he can hear – the answer being it's a mystical Indian Raga. The Swami tells him it's being played by a bunch of 'wogs' next door. Wheldon suggests that he means Commonwealth immigrants, but the Swami assures him that these are 'real wogs'.

In 1969 racism was nothing like the issue it has become since. This was also the year in which Spike appeared in the Johnny Speight-written ITV series *Curry and Chips*. Speight, who had already been criticised for the bigotry of Alf Garnet (the leading character in his series *Till Death*

Us Do Part), built *Curry and Chips* around Arthur, a white liberal-minded factory worker (played by Eric Sykes), and his Pakistani colleague Kevin O'Grady (Spike in brown make-up) who claims to be half Irish. Even though political correctness had not yet appeared on the scene, London Weekend Television was deluged with complaints, and the series was short-lived. John Spencer of the *Sun* wrote of it:

One is apparently expected to laugh AT Paddy – as when he agrees with one of his . . . workmates . . . that there are too many wogs in England. 'Oh yes!' he says. 'That is very true. I leave Pakistan because there are too many wog. I came to England and there are still too many wog.' . . . There's no doubt that it's all very funny at face value but can it be justified on moral grounds? . . . It is something to be regretted if we are fully resigned to colour prejudice. Yet this would seem to be the attitude implied by Spike Milligan who said: 'You can't solve the problem [of race relations] so you might as well laugh at it.'

*

Episode four of *Q5* takes us to the Elephant House at London Zoo. Spike, dressed as a keeper, is washing down an elephant when he hears a voice. It appears that there is somebody inside the elephant, and he wants Spike to make a phone call for him. Spike is sceptical – he can't really be in there. But when Spike tells him to walk about a bit we hear footsteps.

Spike is now convinced, but he wants to know how the fellow got in there. The man says he knows the right people, but Spike decides that he must call the police.

While the trapped man sings Cole Porter's 'I've Got You Under My Skin', Spike fetches a constable who calls another policeman, and a search warrant is produced and fed to the elephant inside a bun. (The remainder of the sketch is missing; unlike the *Goon Shows*, the BBC did not keep the scripts of Spike's TV shows assiduously, and many of the recordings have disappeared too.)

Also in episode four, we see a group of patriotic Welshmen trying to save their country by eating it; an experiment to find out who will stand up for the national anthem (shades of *Beyond the Fringe*); a Chinese vicar in a pulpit, who exhorts his congregation to sing a hymn extolling the delights of a Chinese restaurant menu; and a trunk containing the First World War, which causes the death of a customs officer when it is forced open at Heathrow.

Spike was anxious about every detail of the sketches. A note in the middle of the script for the sketch about the trunk asks for a loudspeaker to be built inside the trunk with an electric socket which can feed the sound effects into the lid. (Spike seems not to have considered that the sound effects could be added afterwards.)

The guest star of the fifth *Q5* is Eric Sykes – except that, whenever seen, he is always bound and gagged. We glimpse him in a slaughterhouse, hanging upside down as he is carried towards a bloody fate, and at the end of the programme he is roasted on a spit, while the cast wait greedily with knives and forks. Meanwhile there are more racist jokes – John Bluthal and Spike appear blacked up, like negro minstrels, with the announcement that this is the brand new BBC *Colour* Television.

Two more episodes concluded the series. Among those watching was Terry Jones, who (with Michael Palin and others) was planning a new comedy series that began transmission a few months after *Q5*, in August 1969:

I was thinking quite hard about the shape of the show, and I saw Spike Milligan's *Q5* . . . a show [where] one sketch would start and drift off into another; he made it so clear that we'd been writing in clichés, where we either did three-minute sketches with a beginning, middle and end, or we did one joke with a blackout. Terry Gilliam had done an animation for *Do Not Adjust Your Set* called Beware Of Elephants. He'd been a bit diffident about it: 'Well, it's a sort of stream-of-consciousness, one thing leads to another, it's not really about anything.' I suddenly thought, 'That's what we could do: a whole thing that's stream-of-consciousness, and Terry's animations can go in and out and link things, and the whole show would just flow like that.'

This was, of course, *Monty Python's Flying Circus*. Jones's fellow Python Michael Palin makes a slightly different point:

Terry Jones and I adored the *Q* shows, which preceded *Python*. They were filled with surrealism and invention, and [Milligan] took huge risks. He was the first writer to play with the conventions of television – having all his characters wear their costume name tags on screen, and captions to show the take-home pay of each actor . . . He played with the medium – sending up presenters or leaving gaps in the programme – just as he had on the *Goon Show*.

A third member of the *Monty Python* team, John Cleese, told David Nathan: 'Milligan is the great God of us all.'

Spike was fully aware, and proud, of *Q5*'s influence on Cleese and his friends: 'It really shook up the Pythons when they first saw it. Without *Q* there would have been no *Python*.' (The Pythons even hijacked Ian McNaughton, Spike's producer.) However, Spike tended to be a little bitter about the fact that *Monty Python* is hailed as a revolution in comedy, while *Q* is largely forgotten: 'They [the Pythons] had some wonderful performers. I didn't, I just had me, and some second bananas.' This is insulting to such skilled members of his *Q* cast as John Bluthal, and it shifts the blame away from the writing, which was certainly patchier than *Monty Python*. But Neil Shand is inclined to agree with it:

I'm afraid there's an element of truth. Sometimes I wonder what we could have achieved if we'd been six writer-performers, like the Pythons. Instead, we had a team of actors. And I remember John Bluthal having one line in a sketch, and Milligan turning to the audience, and saying: 'Do you know, he's come all the way from Australia just to say that!'

In an uncharacteristically generous moment, Spike once described *Monty Python* as 'possibly the funniest TV show in the world (I rate it the best)'. He went on: '*Monty Python* would be impossible to do in any other medium without radical changes; what I'm saying is that [it is] the only comedy really faithful to TV.' In comparison, the Q programmes weren't pure television; many of the items in them could have been adapted for radio. An unforgettable exception is the sketch from a later Q series known as 'Pakistani Daleks', in which Spike's racist humour suddenly becomes irresistible. A working-class Englishwoman is married to a Dalek with a Pakistani accent:

> *(The door to the room explodes, and through it comes a Dalek with turban on and a folded umbrella hanging from his side. Woman doesn't turn round.)*
> DALEK: Hell-o, Dar-ling, I am back.
> WOMAN: You're late tonight.
> DALEK: The Tubes were full of comm-u-ters.
> WOMAN: How did you get on, then?
> DALEK: I ex-ter-min-a-ted them . . .
> *(Dog barks. Dalek points exterminator at him. Shoots. Dog explodes.)*
> DALEK: Put him in the cur-ry.

Monty Python didn't establish itself immediately, but was sufficiently successful for a second series to begin in September 1970. Spike had to wait until 1975 before he could make *Q6*. The BBC files don't reveal why.

In March 1970, a year after *Q5*, he told the *Guardian* he was 'living off my *Beachcomber* repeats' while he devoted his time to 'green' issues. To another reporter, he said, 'Basically, I'm working for the human race.'

He opened a World Wildlife Fund exhibition at the Natural History Museum, telling the audience he didn't want his children to have to live without endangered species, with 'plastic penguins and wooden lions in the zoo'. He protested about the demolition, for a road-widening scheme, of Dickens Farm in Barnet, a Georgian farmhouse once used by Charles Dickens. He described how he had 'searched the London area for buildings worth preserving as I could see hideous concrete blocks going up everywhere'.

He claimed to have won conservation victories on visits to Dublin (where the issue was the city's canal, threatened with being filled in) and Australia (where he campaigned about the cottage that had belonged to poet Henry Kendall). He certainly helped to save Wilton's Music Hall (1843) in the East End of London, persuading the BBC to donate handsomely towards its restoration in return for an old-time evening recorded there, shown at Christmas 1970, with himself and the other performers virtually donating their services. (They included Peter Sellers, to whose film *The Magic Christian* Spike had just contributed a cameo. Joe McGrath was directing, and says that 'Spike was wonderful – he plays a traffic warden, and Peter bribes him to eat his parking tickets. They did some marvellous ad libs.')

Meanwhile Spike was deeply immersed in writing his 'book on my life in the Army', which he now intended as the first volume of a trilogy. In March 1970 he told the

Observer: 'I wrote a 40,000-word draft in Australia, but now I can't look at it. It needs working on.'

He found writing his memoirs wonderfully liberating after scripts which had to win the approval of the BBC. Joe McGrath remembers him saying:

I used to listen to those Herberts at the BBC, in their suits, telling me, 'You're over the top, Spike, pull it back.' And then I became out of favour, and started writing books, and nobody told me it was over the top, and it was published, and one year I outsold Alistair McLean! So that taught me not to listen to people who said I was over the top.

He told Pauline Scudamore that in the army memoirs he had wanted to re-create the camaraderie and the moments of sheer fun which tend to be forgotten when people recall the tragic aspects of war; also the strong friendships that had grown up. He admitted that he had 'garnished' some of the anecdotes – this is particularly true of the first volume – 'but the basic facts are . . . true'. He was able to check his memories against those of army comrades at the reunions of D Battery, and he claimed he had even looked up the weather reports for the period to confirm his memory.

November 1970 saw the screening of *The Other Spike*, John Goldschmidt's Granada documentary about his manic depression. Besides appearing as himself, Spike portrayed an unsympathetic psychiatrist, as he relived his spells in mental hospitals. The *Sun* described the programme as 'disturbing to watch, and, for Milligan admirers, upsetting'. It was also discussed, in the *Sun's* 'Point of View' column, by Liz Cowley, who was still having a discreet, low-key affair with Spike:

The Other Spike was both brilliant and honest . . . But should it have been shown? . . . I personally question whether *anyone* has the right to undress down to the heart in public . . . Perhaps by getting it out of his system in this way, Spike Milligan will have helped himself. But you have also, dear Spike, stopped those who love to laugh at you in a comfortable, uncomplicated way from ever laughing at you in quite the same way again. In future we'll feel guilty. Is this what you wanted?

George Melly reviewed it too, and recalls that he

declared [Milligan] to be a genius. But he is, like many geniuses, and especially those with problems of the mind, entirely self-obsessed. He was convinced, for instance, that they had deliberately arranged the collection of rubbish – the banging of bins and the noisy backing of lorries outside his window – in an asylum to drive him even madder. I pointed out that this was unlikely.

A few days later, I received a violent letter accusing me of trying to destroy him and asking what I had done for humanity that day (he, apparently, had been talking to an extremely depressed man and had helped to cheer him up) . . . On the other hand, the next time we met when he was on a high and he was amiability itself . . .

There can be no doubt that Spike's willingness to talk freely about his manic depression benefited other sufferers. He also liked playing Samaritan, and boasting about it. In August 1971, speaking at the launch of a Mind campaign for better treatment of the mentally ill, he said: 'People who get into states come and see me. I talk their language and I send them to psychiatrists that I know. By talking to them I have saved several people from killing themselves – I saved a chap from dying the week before last.'

This *Guardian* report was headed: 'MILLIGAN: "I SAVED SUICIDES"', while the *Sunday Mirror* opted for: 'THE LIVES I HAVE SAVED – BY SPIKE'.

A few lucky people encountered him in a benevolently

manic mood. In 1970 John Heald, nowadays chairman of
the Betjeman Society, was in charge of property damage
claims for a big insurance company. One day he learned
that Spike, who was one of the firm's clients, had sent in a
large claim following a burglary at Orme Court. Heald
decided to investigate himself – 'Milligan was a celebrity
who had given me enormous pleasure over the years' – and,
when he arrived, found himself amid rather eccentric
surroundings:

People were running from one room to another like characters
in a Feydeau farce. I could hear singing in the basement (Spike
told me later that the singer was Eric Sykes), and the attractive
telephonist was kept busy ensuring that her employer could play
squash that afternoon and then constantly having to change the
time of his arrival at the court.

Eventually he was shown in to Spike:

I was greeted with a lovely smile. All the necessary papers were
produced immediately and the claim was settled without argument. Meanwhile he wanted to know lots about me. What did I
find fascinating about insurance? What was my next job going
to be? Did I remember my dreams? Was I married and, if so,
why? And between my answers he talked about life, humour,
politics, people and many other things – a cadenza of unrehearsed
words.

He asked me if insurance people were good acrobats, and said
he would give £100 of his claim payment to charity if I did a
double somersault or stood on my head. I tried, oh how I tried!
I failed, but I made him laugh and he said my effort was worth
£90, to which I added £10 from my own pocket. A small price
for a memorable afternoon.

Equally lucky in their experience of his moods was the team

that, during late 1970, made a BBC television documentary about some of Britain's architectural follies – eccentric buildings and mad monuments – with Spike as link man, playing either the builder or some other commentator. The film and TV production designer Michael Pickwoad was a young research assistant on *Follies of the Wise*, and he describes how the programme went well – but Spike was always on thin ice:

His moonlike face gave the appearance of being stretched vertically, with eyes that darted all over the place. It was as if he were playing a part with his own vulnerability pulling the strings. This was demonstrated by his lack of co-operation during a radio interview in Edinburgh, where we were filming on Calton Hill with Spike as William Playfair, architect of the still unfinished memorial – he proceeded to slag off all the stores that he said ruined Princes Street, behaviour that offended the advertising code of the day (shops must not be named) and necessitated restarting the interview each time he did it! But generally his interest in the buildings, and maybe also the challenge of playing so many different parts, kept his depressive side at bay during the filming, and on a coach journey he might regale us at length with his love-hate of the army. Yet he was never entirely sensible about anything; you might say, with very little exaggeration, that he was completely mad but wearing a thin coat of sanity – a totally insane person living inside a precariously sane one.

*

Adolf Hitler: My Part in His Downfall was published in June 1971. Spike reported to Robert Graves that 'beyond my wildest hopes, it became a BEST SELLER!' It had sold 30,000 copies, and the publishers had to reprint almost at once. 'I can't tell you how good it feels, for a person whose education ended at 14 to be top seller.'

Ray Connolly in the *Evening Standard* judged that this first volume of the Milligan war memoirs was 'very funny indeed', a compliment which was exceeded by another reviewer, Gordon McLauchlan, in an unidentified cutting which Spike (understandably) preserved with the manuscript of the book: 'As this is one of the three or four funniest books I have ever read, I hope he comes through with the first four- or five-book trilogy in the history of literature.'

Adolf Hitler has been reprinted at frequent intervals ever since: 'Thank God! The money!' writes Spike. The second volume of the war memoirs, *'Rommel?' 'Gunner Who?'*, flowed freely as soon as he got seriously down to writing it, on yet another trip to Australia. He told Graves he had 'clocked up 60,000 words in 3 weeks – not bad for a clown'. He had realised that he would not be able to get the whole story of his war into three volumes, so he intended to be the first-ever author to write a four volume trilogy.

In another letter to Graves, he said he found the experience of re-living the war 'very nostalgic', he might even say traumatic. After spending a day immersed in the war years, it took hours to get back into the present. He almost needed the services of an exorcist.

He was still producing a regular stream of entertaining little books for adults and children. *Milligan's Ark*, which came out in November 1971 with a foreword by Prince Philip, was a little different: a collection of poems about animals by nearly a hundred celebrities, sold in aid of the Wildlife Youth Service. His concern for animals had made headlines on 30 September 1971, when he smashed a glass panel in a door at London's Hayward Gallery as a protest against the planned killing of sixty catfish by an American artist, Newton Harrison, who was exhibiting at the gallery; the fish were to have been electrocuted and then eaten by the Hayward's guests. Spike's protest apparently helped to save the fish, and he told the press: 'That makes me feel great.'

Depression was still a regular feature of his life; looking

through his diary for December 1971 he noted that 'many pages have ILL written in large letters'. He grumbled as frequently as ever that he had no paid work, despite the fact that he was writing for, and frequently guesting in, ITV's *The Marty Feldman Comedy Machine*, which began a new series in October 1971. He had also made his debut in the BBC TV children's story programme *Jackanory*, and appeared in *Oh in Colour*, a four-part series for BBC2, directed by Joe McGrath, who describes it as 'very weird, and there was a lot of improvisation'. (The title referred to the arrival of colour television.)

Also, in October 1971, John Browell, who had been the Goons' final producer, telephoned Spike's manager Norma Farnes to say that the BBC wanted to do a special radio *Goon Show* to celebrate fifty years of the BBC. 'Spike didn't want to do it,' says Norma, 'but . . . over a period of three weeks I eventually persuaded [him] to write the script.'

Part Four 1972—2002

The last
Goon of all

19

Partially sound mind

As late as 1966 the BBC had been considering a resumption of the *Goon Show*, but Spike's opinion was that Sellers was now too unreliable. The BBC's fear was that *he* was unreliable.

'I really didn't want to do it,' he says of *The Last Goon Show of All*, as the programme to mark the corporation's fiftieth anniversary was to be called, 'but the BBC had set it all up.' However, he admits that there was 'a certain euphoria about coming back after all that time'. Sellers told reporters that it was 'like a strange dream, as though we had never parted'.

The programme was to be recorded (for broadcast in October) on Sunday, 30 April 1972 in the Camden Theatre. Sellers had invited the royals – Prince Philip, Princess Anne, Princess Margaret and Lord Snowdon – and a message was sent by Prince Charles, who was serving in the Royal Navy: 'One of your most devoted fans is enraged at the knowledge that he is missing your last performance. Last night my hair fell out and my knees dropped off having turned green with envy at the thought of my father and sister attending the show.'

Producer John Browell rounded up Ray Ellington and Max Geldray (but not Wally Stott, who had had a sex change and become Angela Morley). Geldray was working for the Christian Science Publishing Society in Boston, Massachusetts; Spike and Sellers contributed to his expenses on the London trip. Wallace Greenslade had died in 1961 ('on the toilet in . . . the George',[1]

---

[1] The most popular pub with BBC drinkers.

according to Roger Lewis), and Andrew Timothy resumed the role of announcer.

As Norma Farnes recalls it, the script reached John Browell on the Monday before recording – and was 'deemed unsuitable' because Spike had decided that Secombe was to impersonate the Queen. Not until the day of recording did Sellers and Secombe persuade Spike to accept a compromise. 'Her Majesty the Queen,' says Andrew Timothy at the beginning, 'was to have opened this *Goon Show* but, owing to a nasty rumour called Grocer Heath,[2] she has declined. However, at short notice and wearing a floral creton frock, Mr Secombe has agreed to stand in for the Sovereign.'

The compromise weakened the script. 'To be honest, it was by no means a vintage show,' writes Secombe. He adds: 'It was a pity that Mike Bentine had not been invited back for this last show.' Spike himself had no great opinion of it: 'I don't . . . think it was a particularly funny script.' When a reporter asked him to summarise the plot, he replied: 'I've got a plot, it's in Golders Green Crematorium.'

Newcomers would have been puzzled by several touches of nostalgia in the script. 'Here is a preview of next winter in Jimmy Grafton's attic,' says Grytpype-Thynne, while Neddie Seagoon, contemplating a return to variety, declares: 'I can still remember that shaving routine.' The storyline is vestigial, and, when Neddie complains that they are 'having difficulty starting this *Goon Show*', Sellers (in his Willium voice) declares: 'There's no jokes in the fuel tonk [*sic*].' Actually there are one or two. 'He looks in a bad way,' says Seagoon of Moriarty. 'Has he had a medical check?' Grytpype-Thynne replies: 'Yes, thirty shillings for a new truss.'

Secombe recalls that initially both Sellers and Milligan

---

[2] Edward Heath, nicknamed 'Grocer' by *Private Eye*, was the Conservative prime minister.

'had difficulty in finding the voices of some of the characters'. But Sellers, interviewed for the *Today* programme, said it was easy to recapture Bluebottle, since he was constantly conversing with Spike in that character on the telephone.

During the recording (which was videotaped for television), Sellers can be seen clowning away for the benefit of the royal party. Spike seems rather detached. 'One good thing,' he recalls, 'was that we invited the entire family and the children came along. Laura, Sean, Silé and Jane came up on to the stage when the audience were clapping and the applause was thunderous. I think that for the first time they knew what we were all about.'

Although *The Last Goon Show of All* was not a vast success in itself, the publicity it attracted provided an excellent launch for a volume of *Goon Show* scripts, selected by Spike and published by Woburn Press. Spike had been hoping for this for years, and sales were excellent, leading to *More Goon Show Scripts* (1973) and *The Book of the Goons* (1974).[3] Prince Charles, who had become Prince of Wales, attended the publication parties and contributed a foreword to *More Goon Show Scripts*, which, says Spike, 'brought me the largest royalty earnings I had had up to that point – £18,000, folks!'

The fact that some of the scripts were now in print, along with a steadily increasing flow of LPs and cassettes of the shows, played a big part in disseminating the Goons to a new, young audience, some of whom were to become distinguished comic performers in their turn. 'When the *Goon Shows* were first made,' says comedian and actor Eddie Izzard, 'I wasn't born, and there are many other comedians who weren't born too (it's not our fault). But we have all

---

[3] This last title was published by Robson Books, newly established by Jeremy Robson, son of Spike's hypnotherapist Joe Robson.

caught the *Goon Show* bug.' Al Murray (alias the Pub Landlord) was another who bought and devoured the scripts:

My father is mad about the Goons, so they are my earliest memory of a comedy thing – other than watching *The Two Ronnies*, which you laugh at, but there's nothing rarefied about it. The Goons was this bizarre universe, and I had the scripts, and would read them, and would wonder what they actually sounded like – what would be the sound of a batter pudding being hurled?

That year, 1972, also saw the foundation of the Goon Show Preservation Society; its first newsletter came out in November. Spike describes the society as 'extremely well organised', and gave it his support.

*

A few days after the *Last Goon Show* recording, he could be seen in Oxford Street between sandwich boards, bearing hand-written information about a charity one-nighter he was giving at the Mermaid, with his wife Paddy singing, in aid of the anti-animal-testing campaign Beauty Without Cruelty. 'Tickets [are] not selling too well,' explained the *Daily Express*, so he had taken this step, 'unheard of for an entertainer of his status'.

Although the Goons' reunion helped to establish him as a comedy guru in the eyes of the younger generation, he was still convinced that he didn't have enough work and was short of money. 'Throughout the 1970s,' writes Dominic Behan, 'Spike complained whenever we spoke that he could get no work. [But] Norma Farnes . . . told me that Spike had been turning down most of the jobs he was offered . . .'

As to the jobs he accepted, they included a number of film roles, none of which made more than a fleeting impression on the public. During June 1972 he was filming at Shepperton, as the Gryphon in a screen version of Lewis Carroll's *Alice* (Sellers was the March Hare and Dudley

Moore the Dormouse). At Elstree three months later, director Norman Cohen's infuriatingly bland film of *Adolf Hitler: My Part in His Downfall* was in production, with Jim Dale ridiculously miscast as Gunner Milligan, and Spike himself making a couple of self-conscious appearances as his father, Leo. He wrote and starred in a 1972 Christmas Special, on BBC2, a miscellany of sketches called *Milligan in Winter* (one of four seasonal shows he made at this period). And during 1973, 'Dick Lester asked me to play a part in his movie *The Three Musketeers*. I played the aged husband of a young Raquel Welch! I got really good notices, especially in America. The result? Fuck all.'

Lester recalls Spike's contribution to this romp, in the role of an elderly innkeeper with a young and beautiful wife: 'When I introduced [Raquel Welch] to the man who was going to be her husband, Raquel had what could only be described as an old fashioned look on her face – it was a bit of a shock for her!' Spike told an Australian radio interviewer that, in the bedroom scene, 'I was much too old to do her any damage!' He was now fifty-five, but looks ten years older in the film, as much through body language as make-up.

Lester added an anecdote which shows how the *Goon Show* had spread Spike's reputation among at least some Americans:

He was going to be tortured and interrogated by Charlton Heston [playing Cardinal Richelieu]. He was very nervous about it, saying, 'What am I doing, playing a scene with Charlton Heston – it's such an honour, I can't do it.' I told him he had to – and when Charlton came on to the set, he said: 'I am so much in awe of this – it's so much a privilege to play a scene with Spike Milligan.'

Spike also filmed *The Great McGonagall* in 1973. He played the title role himself, with Joe McGrath directing, and the two of them collaborated on the script. Spike had decided that it should be shot (over three weeks) entirely in his beloved Wilton's Music Hall, partly so that money would be generated for the still ongoing restoration of the elderly building. The cast also included Valentine Dyall, John Bluthal and Victor Spinetti, with Peter Sellers making two brief appearances as Queen Victoria.

Asked by a reporter why he had chosen to portray McGonagall, author of some of the most ludicrous poetry ever written, Spike declared: 'He was a poetic genius, like me . . . I've been a fan [of him] ever since 1956 when Peter Sellers gave me a book of his poetry to read . . . Peter and I persuaded some people to put up money [for the film], and we've chipped in [with] some ourselves.' The reporter prophesied that it would be a smash hit: 'There are gems like Peter Sellers playing Queen Victoria on his knees, four fake Kenneth McKellars wrapped up in one kilt, and Milligan and Sellers singing a duet of McGonagall's words set to Noël Coward's music!' Spike's final words to the reporter were 'Keep clear of transparent kilts.'

Like other directors, Joe McGrath found that Spike could be entirely different people on different days:

There were two ways you could go with him, if you were directing and he was writing and performing. He could go with you, and trust you, and if things went wrong he'd say 'Never mind, we'll sort this out.' Or he might fight and argue, and say 'This isn't what I want', and have a headache, and the shooting would stop. Or he might go the other way – his eyes would become heavy and close, you could see the blood drain from the face, and he'd become haggard – have no energy, and just sit gazing into space, and it would be impossible to get him to go on. He just had to be helped to the car.

The Great McGonagall has some inspired moments, such as Queen Victoria playing Erroll Garner-style jazz on the harmonium, and McGonagall attempting to recite on the music-hall stage but being removed at high speed by the stage manager's giant hook. Milligan conveys real affection for the poor Scottish poet who tries to break into high society – perhaps seeing McGonagall's failure as a warning to himself. 'McGrath has confirmed that the film . . . is in large measure a Milligan self-portrait,' write Matthew Coniam and Richard Larcombe, in a perceptive essay on the film, 'a reflection of a deep and sincere empathy with an eccentric creative talent who pursued his personal vision in the face of both apathy and antipathy.'

The failure of the film to get proper distribution was a major blow to Spike. According to Coniam and Larcombe, 'he genuinely believed that [the film] would establish him in cinema as *Oblomov* had on stage, and . . . was angry and saddened [by its failure], and convinced to the last that its day would come.'

Another 1973 film project gave him a taste of the fickleness of the industry. He recalls how he

received a phone call from Kyrenia, Cyprus, from a worried producer. He was making a film called *Ghost in the Noonday Sun* starring Peter Sellers and Tony Francisco. Peter didn't like the script and wanted me to come and rewrite it . . . It was absolute crap, really just a remake of *Treasure Island*. I flew to Kyrenia . . . All I wrote was destroyed. It was a complete nightmare . . .

He was back at the Mermaid at Christmas 1973 in time for another revival of *Treasure Island*, which had now evolved into a musical. According to the press, this created difficulties for Spike: 'He cannot sing and dance at the same time . . . "In fact," he says, "I cannot do any two things at the same time. I cannot even open a door and talk at the same time. If someone says 'Spike!' as I'm approaching a door, I walk straight into it."'

Meanwhile he was experiencing much greater success in books than in films. That same year saw the publication of *Badjelly the Witch*, in which the publishers, M. & J. Hobbs, reproduced the calligraphic handwriting of Spike's fair-copy manuscript throughout. 'I wrote it longhand in a very good, painstaking, calligraphic style to encourage youngsters to learn how to write. The book did very well . . .'

John Antrobus was among those who enjoyed the 'loops and twirls' of Spike's calligraphy: 'He loved the very act of writing and would not be hurried.'

Badjelly is an ordinary fairy story in conception, but spiced with people showing their bottoms, which always gets a laugh from children. One teacher wrote in the *Guardian*: 'It's been slaying every class I've read it to.'

It was also in 1973 that he wrote *'Rommel?' 'Gunner Who?'*, the second volume of his war memoirs. When the book was published the following year, the title page stated that it was 'edited by Jack Hobbs'.

Eight years younger than Spike, Hobbs was a Yorkshireman whose small publishing company specialised in humour. He was also a jazz pianist, and had served in the war – two good qualifications for becoming (after publishing *Badjelly*) Spike's editor for the war memoirs.

Spike described him as 'Jack Hobbs, friend, pianist and fellow manic depressive'. The publisher Alan Brooke, then at Michael Joseph, says Hobbs was 'a very necessary person, who would jolly Spike along and spend a lot of time with him, which would probably have been quite difficult for an in-house editor to manage'. Joe McGrath recalls:

Jack could play the piano, so he could sit in the office and play and sing,[4] and so could Spike. And Jack would laugh at what Spike was saying, and make notes, and make suggestions – and

---

[4] There was a piano in Spike's room at 9 Orme Court.

he could do short-hand, so he was very quick at getting it all down. Jack was also a very good editor, and Spike accepted that.

Spike's recall of the events of his war was greatly enhanced by the D Battery reunions, which he attended regularly, and helped to organise. The one at Bexhill in April 1973 included a surprise:

Waiting for me was Eamonn Andrews and 'Spike Milligan, tonight, *This is Your Life*.' I was nonplussed, flabbergasted . . . All my family was there, including my mother all the way from Australia with [his brother] Desmond and [Desmond's wife] Nadia. Peter Sellers came dressed as a German soldier and denied all knowledge of me . . . Harry Secombe overwhelmed me with praise and ended with a raspberry to which I replied tenfold.

Harry Edgington, pianist in the D Battery band, contributed to *This Is Your Life* from his home in New Zealand. 'We are closer than ever,' Spike writes of him in *'Rommel?' 'Gunner Who?'*. 'Our correspondence is prodigious, his letters fill 3 Boxfiles, likewise recorded tapes, in which he sends his latest compositions, asking my opinions.'

*

In the summer of 1973, Paddy Milligan discovered a small lump in one of her breasts. She was first of all told it was benign; then this diagnosis was reversed, and she underwent a mastectomy. Pauline Scudamore writes that Spike was 'shattered' by his wife's cancer; but a letter he wrote to Robert Graves on 19 February 1974, about ten weeks after Paddy's return from hospital, gives a different impression: 'I've not long left the dinner table at the Trattoo restaurant [in Kensington] with a dark, beauteous lady, who played the piano delightfully and retrospectively.' He told Graves he had to have an affair in progress, or he felt incomplete – fortunately, there always seemed to be one going on. Each seemed completely sincere when it began, but in time they all melted away like the snow.

One of his collections of serious poems, *Open Heart University* (1979), is full of references to affairs and girlfriends; it was published the year after Paddy's death, so there was no need for secrecy. Rather oddly, given this subject matter, most of the illustrations in *Open Heart University* are by his daughter Laura.

One day in July 1974, when Paddy had been back from hospital for half a year, a 'temp' from an agency came to 9 Orme Court to work with Spike, who was on a high and was dictating letters at top speed. She was twenty-eight-year-old Shelagh Sinclair, dark-haired and plump and laughing a lot. Spike asked her why she was temping. She said she was a full-time production assistant at the BBC, but she was temping during her holidays to make some badly needed money. Spike said he was having dinner that evening with his son Sean – who was now twenty – and would she like to join them?

Shelagh Sinclair was from the Wirral. Her father was a lieutenant colonel in the Royal Artillery, and she had been fleetingly an actress before joining the BBC. When she was in her teens, her parents had taken her to see *Son of Oblomov*, sitting in one of the theatre's boxes, and Spike had drawn attention to her during the performance. More recently, when he was making *Q5* at Television Centre, he had spotted her in a corridor and given her the eye, so that (as she recalls) 'I dived into the nearest Ladies. Spike came after me and banged on the door.'

Her first thought on being told she would be working for Spike Milligan was 'Oh God, that loony.' She quickly changed her mind. The first letter he dictated to her was to Robert Graves, the second to the Pope. Many people would indeed have judged him a loony, but Shelagh was captivated.

Spike recalls his own first impressions of Shelagh, after many years of marriage to her: 'She was a nice, jolly woman and I took her out to dinner and things went on from there.' On another occasion he says, rather unflatteringly, of her: 'I never thought I'd fall in love with a girl who wasn't a glamour puss . . . But I did. I have.'

Shelagh said she was never conscious of the age gap of nearly thirty years between them. 'The only thing I'm aware of with Spike is my constant struggle to keep up with him! And of course there's his incredible presence. He fills a room – and he opens my eyes.' They had a certain amount in common, Shelagh being of largely Irish blood, and a Catholic.

She says that, after their July 1974 meal, 'I worked for him from time to time after that and saw him for dinner occasionally.' She had experienced his manic letter-writing on her first day at Orme Court; he would fire off epistolary protests on a wide range of topics[5] to *The Times* and the *Daily Telegraph*, and Norma Farnes recalls that one year he decided to hand-draw five hundred Christmas cards.

Some of the causes he took up were highly deserving of his attention. Pauline Scudamore describes his correspondence with an incontinent girl incarcerated in a long-stay hospital, who with his encouragement eventually became continent and independent. *The Spike Milligan Letters* (1977) show him attempting to rescue quite a number of 'life's sad cases', as he called them. He would correspond with fellow depressives, for example giving this advice to one young man: '(1) I suggest you accept the fact that you are ill and you might have to live with it, and (2) You will go up and down emotionally but it will not kill you.' And to another sufferer:

---

[5] Including animal rights. He wrote abusively to scientists who experimented with animals, and said of them: 'These sort of humans are the rightful material for the bomb. Why protect them? Tell me that.'

My mother is 78 now, she gets up at 6.30 in the morning . . . she cleans the house . . . washes all the sheets by hand, looks after the garden and makes jam preserves, and really I don't know of a happier person. I myself when depressed work as hard as I can and as well as I can, and but for that I think I would go mad . . . So . . . work is almost Godlike.

On the other hand he would devote the same amount of energy to what many people might regard as doomed, time-wasting causes. For example in 1969 he wrote to the then prime minister, Harold Wilson, complaining that one of his shirts had been ruined by a burst ballpoint pen, and that the manufacturers and the Citizens' Advice Bureau had failed to respond to his complaint. 'Please help,' he asked Wilson, who of course didn't.

*

From the *Sun*, 14 May 1974:

BOY SHOT IN SPIKE'S BACK GARDEN

A sixteen-year-old boy was recovering last night after having been shot in Spike Milligan's back garden. The boy's parents are asking . . . for an assault summons . . . 'Two boys aged 15 and 16,' . . . said police . . . 'were allegedly trespassing in Mr Milligan's garden and the 15-year-old was shot in the shoulder. He was taken to hospital where a pellet was removed.'

From the *Daily Mail*, same date: 'Comedian Spike Milligan may be accused of assault . . . Detectives are understood to have interviewed 56-year-old Mr Milligan following the incident.'

From the *Daily Telegraph*, 15 May 1974:

Spike Milligan, 56, was charged last night with assault occasioning actual bodily harm . . . He is to appear at Highgate magistrates court on May 30 . . . He was charged that on May 12, at Holden Road, he did unlawfully assault Peter Francis Bell . . .

Yesterday morning the actor's wife Paddy, 39, fought back tears at Hornsey coroner's court during an inquest on Alban Stapleton, 64, a sales representative, who died after her car hit him near her home in Holden Road on Dec. 17.

PC Russell Boyd . . . said Mrs Milligan told him: 'I came round the corner and went into a skid. I tried to control it and it went completely out of control and hit the old man down on the pavement.'

Mrs Milligan was not called to give evidence and . . . the coroner, recording a verdict of 'accidental death', informed his jury that notice of intended prosecution had been served on her.[6]

From the *Sun*, same date: 'Mr Stapleton . . . died in hospital two weeks later.'

From the *Evening Standard*, 30 May 1974:

Milligan pleaded guilty to causing actual bodily harm . . . But after hearing of the two-year reign of vandalism at the bottom of the ex-Goon's garden in Holden Road . . . the magistrate decided that Milligan had been under 'very extreme provocation' . . . [The] Chairman of the Bench . . . gave Milligan a 12-month conditional discharge with the stern warning that 'Society would not condone the use of loaded weapons against others.'

In a statement read out to the court, the comedian described the destruction which led him to stalk youths with his air-gun. He said: 'For the past two years I have been plagued with vandalism . . . My fence . . . is continually being ripped down. They have tried to set fire to my daughter's Wendy hut and have smashed all the furniture in there. I have also built a studio in my garden and this has also been smashed and attempts made to break into

---

[6] My researches have failed to discover whether she was in fact prosecuted.

it. They excreted on the steps and in my daughter's Wendy hut. All these previous incidents have been reported . . . and I decided, as all lawful methods had failed, to try and trap them myself . . .

'I am not a violent person . . . but I think you will agree that under the circumstances I was acting under extreme provocation . . .

'Things have got so bad we are going to move house.' . . .

Bidding goodbye to the reporters, he told them: 'The magistrate didn't know the full truth. In fact I am a trainee murderer for the IRA. I'm off to rifle practice now. Seriously, though, I am very happy with the magistrate's decision and I am sending him my autograph.'

This report in the *Standard* carried a photo of Spike using his right hand as a pistol. One of the papers refers to him as 'Gunner Milligan'.

From the *Daily Telegraph*, three weeks later:

Spike Milligan . . . has been sacked from two of the animal welfare organisations which he supports following remarks he made after a recent court case in which he was conditionally discharged for firing his airgun at a youth . . . Mr Milligan's explanation for having an airgun was that he would 'shoot up the arse' any cat that raided the bird nesting boxes in his garden. The threat has split the many societies which have enjoyed Mr Milligan's patronage. Some took it seriously, while others assumed it was a bit of 'goonery'.

He attempted to justify his remark about shooting cats (which he had made on Radio 4's *The World at One*) in a letter dated 18 June 1974 to Animals' Vigilantes:

It is very interesting that nobody seems at all concerned about the boy I shot, everybody said 'good, you should have shot him' but shoot a cat and the world is up in arms . . . I have two cats of my own, both of whom I love and they love me . . . [But] when I see a well fed sleek cat about to kill fledglings or raid the nests and I am unable to get there physically to stop their death I would take the action of shooting at the cat with an air pellet. This does no more than sting the cat . . . To date I have never shot a cat as I have managed to shoo them away . . .

He remained unrepentant of the shooting and the threat, and a few months later he was in the press again for his behaviour at the launch party for *'Rommel?' 'Gunner Who?'*, at the offices of the publisher Michael Joseph. 'Mr Milligan was signing copies,' reported the *Daily Mail* (8 October 1974).

Suddenly he whipped round and autographed a picture by Michael Ayrton hanging over the mantelpiece. He struck out the artist's signature, wrote 'A fake' over the top and 'S. Milligan 1919' in the opposite corner. Managing Director Mr Edmund Fisher who owns the painting said: 'Good grief! That's a valuable picture. It's worth nearly a thousand pounds.'

Mr Fisher tried to laugh the matter off by telling Mr Milligan: 'I shall have to deduct the money from your royalties – or put up the price of the book to fifteen guineas.' But an unrepentant Mr Milligan said: 'Nonsense. I've vastly increased the value of the painting.' And went home.

Alan Brooke, who was on the staff of Michael Joseph, recalls that Michael Ayrton (who had praised the Goons on *The Critics* years earlier) came into the office to look at the damage. 'He was appalled to see his own painting disfigured, and we sent it off to be restored, which cost about a hundred pounds. I think there was some debate in the company as to whether Spike should be sent the bill.' But he wasn't.

Similar behaviour was recorded in the press some years

later, when he was lashed to fury by one of his obsessive hatreds, piped music in lifts: 'The ex-Goon got into a lift fitted with speakers playing music from the studio at Radio Hallam, Sheffield – and ripped the wires off the wall. Then Spike . . . coolly autographed the damage.' He did the same thing before one of his television appearances in 1991: 'I ripped the Tannoy off the dressing-room wall while I was waiting to go on the Jonathan Ross show. It kept squawking on and on with messages for people I had never heard of.'

On one of his contracts with Michael Joseph, alongside his signature, Spike has written: 'Being of partially sound mind.'

*

The year of the shooting – 1974 – was also when he gave the first British performance of his one-man stage show (which wasn't strictly one-man, since it included musicians), an enterprise which augmented his income and offered him a new artistic challenge: 'I wanted to show that I could be a stand-up comedian.'

At first, the stand-up technique seemed to be beyond him. 'He reads everything from a script – songs, stories, asides, even I imagine his tee-hees,' wrote John Barber in his *Daily Telegraph* review of the show, which had opened at the Adelphi in the West End on 17 June 1974 (only a couple of weeks after his court appearance for the shooting), under the title *For One Week Only*. 'But it all sounds spontaneous,' continued Barber,

and he twists his head askew with delight whenever jokes go particularly well.

A lot of these are about the war . . . He does Rommel for us, and Hitler . . . as well as every sort of Army three-stripe and one-pip and haughty brigadier ('Silence when you're speaking to an officer!'). Getting his own back on all that mob is a big part of the Milligan stock-in-trade.

One feels for his two companions on stage. The pianist called Alan [Clare] has to have his piano oiled during a serious ballad . . . A young singer with a guitar, Jeremy Taylor, does well . . . Suddenly Spike is back . . . embarrassing us with some dead-serious poems about dolls and kiddies . . . But here, all the same, is a twinkling, avuncular, marvellous droll, and certainly one of the quickest wits alive.

He soon learned the script – and managed to make it sound ad libbed – and the Adelphi format continued to be used by him, with variations, for at least the next ten years. A fifteen-year-old member of the Goon Show Preservation Society, David Lancaster, reviewed the show in the society's newsletter when it reached Leeds (where it was called *For Three Nights Only*) during 1975:

The Grand Theatre, Leeds, is a large Victorian building . . . The audience shuffle in their seats as they look down on the stage cluttered with bits of paper, hats and dummies. A stage hand comes in with a guitar case and two mugs of beer. The lights are lowered, the curtain at the back is raised to show the theatre's seventy-feet-long loading bay. Two men in denims and overalls are working there. They stop, look aghast, remove their overalls and come forward. Spike Milligan and Jeremy Taylor have arrived . . .

Spike [was] in top form . . . dashing about the stage, making silly noises when gags failed . . . reading from *Adolf Hitler* and *Rommel*, uttering abuse to the people in the boxes at the side of the stage . . .

Jeremy Taylor is by no means a stooge. His witty, satirical songs are tuneful and well sung . . .

Spike also did a Henry Crun impersonation [and] a talk between himself and Eccles . . . The show closed with Spike playing his trumpet . . .

Sometimes he finished with his parody of 'I Left My Heart in San Francisco' ('I left my teeth on Table Mountain, / High on a hill they smile at me . . .').

A visit to his mother in Australia in the summer of 1974 was spent working on his next book of war memoirs – *Monty, His Part In My Victory* – and when he returned to England in September it was to a new address. His account (in *The Family Album*) of the sale of 127 Holden Road and the purchase of Monkenhurst, a Victorian mansion in The Crescent, Hadley Common, on the northern edge of London, makes no mention of the shooting incident as a motive for moving, but alleged that a property developer offered him Monkenhurst (too big and too far out for most people's taste) as a straight swap for the Finchley house.

Monkenhurst, which towers in rather sinister fashion above its neighbours, was also going cheap because the developer had cannibalised most of its garden as plots for new homes. Spike thought the house 'sumptuous', with its stained-glass windows and Adam fireplace. Moreover, by buying some extra land, he 'saved' two nineteenth-century trees, a copper beech and a weeping ash, 'and this made me feel good'. It cost him a further £12,000, the sum he was offered seven years later to perform in South Africa. He accepted, 'making sure that my contract stated that I appear for "multi racial audiences"', and was surprised to find himself blacklisted for supporting apartheid.

A journalist made Monkenhurst sound like Toad Hall:

. . . his turreted mansion home in the gentrified commuter belt . . . the drawing-room . . . vast, high ceilinged . . . seems a last bastion of elegance . . . Valuable oils and etchings grace the walls. A grand piano stands regally at one end, and a blazing fire radiates heat from an Adam-style marble fireplace at the other.

The new owner liked people to appreciate that he was no vulgar parvenu:

I keep up very good standards in my home. We have manners, we're civilised, we do things properly. We have a Sunday tea, and friends round – boring Sunday English tea, with no television or radio; we sit and talk! We go out to dinner occasionally; we put on evening dress, and I put a rose in my jacket, so we have some kind of style. It's not snobbery, it's the fun of dressing up like when you were a child.

His life at Monkenhurst largely excluded Paddy, and took place in his own bedroom (he was still sleeping alone):

I . . . put up . . . shelves and started to collect books, mostly autobiographies, biographies and books on war. The walls were hung with my children's paintings. I had an intercom which connected to every room, a telephone, a radio and a TV set. I have always been a telly addict and it was luxury for me to be able to lie in bed and watch TV.

Joe McGrath recalls that the number of Spike's bedroom telephone – a direct line, independent from the main house phone – was a highly guarded secret: 'I was very privileged in having it. Whenever he moved house, he'd give me the new one.'

He installed double-glazing in his bedroom to blanket out the sounds of the external world. It failed, and he tried an extra layer, which failed too. He said he would have liked more land and more privacy, some insulation from the noise of neighbours' whirring mowers. Yet he alleged to the *Sunday Mirror* (22 December 1974) that he and Paddy wanted to adopt a baby. 'My youngest child is eight now . . . Unless we have another child that marvellous noise of children round the house – that laughing sound – will disappear from our house for ever. I couldn't bear that.'

*

Early in 1975, the BBC at last repeated some *Goon Shows* – a mere ten, but as Spike put it in a letter to Goon Show Preservation Society secretary Mike Coveney:[7] 'It is, as you call it, a "break through".' The corporation also commissioned *Q6* for television, six years after *Q5*. Six half-hour programmes, again co-written with Neil Shand, were shown in November and December 1975; Ian McNaughton produced once more, and the cast included Cardew Robinson, Peter Jones and John Bluthal.

Among the *Q6* sketches were a spoof of David Attenborough's natural history programmes – Spike as Attenborough, investigating a tribe called the Cock-a-nees (Cockneys); also Spike sitting alongside real TV newsreader Corbet Woodall and commenting on items in the bulletin (much as he had done for real in Australia); and a TV programme called *Where Does It Hurt?*, in which contestants vie with each other to get the Painometer to register the highest score (the winner has himself squashed flat by a concrete box). There was also a silent film about the first Irish rocket to the moon (the crew are 'Astr O'Nauts', and the rocket is a garden shed with dynamite packed beneath it), and – at last – the sketch involving the girl substituting for the electric hare at a dogtrack. It's the 100-metres Sex Maniacs' Dash.

Q6 was reviewed anonymously in the *Goon Show Preservation Society Newsletter*:

The series left a lot of people, including Goon Show nuts, a little bewildered . . . It certainly had flashes of brilliance . . . but when

---

[7] Not to be confused with the drama critic of the same name.

we had a chase round Television Centre *déjà vu* set in – had not Michael Bentine been through all this in his *Square World* series? Could not Mike Yarwood [have] made a better job of sending up David Attenborough?

Another series, *Q7*, was recorded in August 1977 and started on BBC2 after Christmas. 'There is a fair amount,' wrote the Goon Show Preservation Society reviewer,

that will shock the average viewer (yes even today), including Spike's use of the female bosom and male genitalia for visual gags . . . Several members have written in saying they found this aspect of *Q7* rather sick . . .

In several programmes we have detected him trying to bolster a sagging script by ad lib lunacy, usually succeeding, but also failing as in the Charlie Chan sketch . . . The actual writing and format seem uncomfortably near the Monty Python style . . .

Neil Shand and Spike also collaborated, during 1975, on *The Melting Pot*. The idea may have come from the fact that, in November and December 1969, Spike had appeared in Johnny Speight's six-part (one series) sitcom *Curry and Chips*, taking the role of 'Paki' Kevin O'Grady, a Pakistani who claims to be Irish.

The Melting Pot features the misadventures of two illegal immigrants who have come from Pakistan to Brixton via Amsterdam, where the father (played by Spike) has acquired the name 'Mr Rembrandt' and the son (John Bird) is 'Mr Van Gogh'. They find a home (of sorts) in a lodging house run by an Irish Republican coalman and his voluptuous daughter Nefertiti, 'where their fellow inmates [runs the blurb to the published scripts] are of all shades of complexion and outrageous opinion'.

The series was commissioned by the BBC and partly made, with the appropriately named Roger Race producing. Spike's first choice for the John Bird part was Peter Sellers, but of course he was not available.

Neil Shand says:

We wrote a series called *The Melting Pot*, for the BBC, and I still think it was wonderful. However, the Runnymede Trust, I think it was – an organisation concerned with racism – had seen this, and had written to the BBC. And I said, 'There's nothing to defend, it's all okay, and anyway we're just pre-filming.' So we made six episodes. And they never went out.

In fact the first episode went out, as a one-off Comedy Playhouse, on BBC1 on 11 June 1975; the entire series was scheduled for transmission in October and November of the following year, but was quietly dropped at the last minute. Spike was more puzzled than angered by this, though political correctness was now arriving in Britain:

SPIKE: I realise I can never say the word 'nigger' without them taking offence, but that's their problem – what's wrong with it?

INTERVIEWER: Except that 'nigger' is a term of abuse – it's a defamatory word, is it not?

SPIKE: Yes. But if I'd reacted every time I was called a silly bastard in the army, I'd have had a fight a day – you just don't take it that way. You just accept it. I'm sorry that you can't call people 'niggers' any more. Or 'wogs' – it's a funny term, a very amusing term. I should be able to call people 'niggers' because I'm not a racialist.

In 1977 he wrote to *Private Eye* objecting to the building of a mosque in Regent's Park. Receiving a letter from two readers accusing him of racism, he replied:

I am all for each race surviving . . . but what I object to is the destruction of the environment by architecture which has no harmony with the surroundings. I think a Mosque in the middle of London looks bloody awful . . . Obviously you would like a Zulu Resting Camp in Hyde Park, so I hope one day they will build one there . . .

In a one-off show he made for Channel 4 in December 1985, *The Last Laugh Before TV-am*, he included a sketch with himself in a public library ordering Agatha Christie's *Ten Little Niggers*. 'The mere mention of the taboo word "nigger",' wrote Herbert Kretzmer in the *Daily Mail*, 'was enough to tilt the entire library over on its side, like an ocean liner going down in a hurricane . . . The scene was pure distilled Milligan, a joke bolstered by a sense of scorn at the enduring lunacies of man.'

*

Paddy Milligan was given a medical all-clear in 1977; but soon afterwards it was discovered that the cancer, far from being eliminated, had spread to her spine and upper neck. Spike did not want her to know this, but she apparently discovered the truth, and (as he recalls) 'went to see a naturopath who had "cured his own cancer". Amongst other things, he said we must remove all vapour-producing medicines in the house – Vick's etc.' Her general practitioner tried to persuade her to undergo normal anti-cancer treatment, but she refused, and became more and more ill. (She also refused to take any drugs that she believed had been tested on animals.)

Spike and Paddy's daughter Jane was now eleven. Spike kept her in the dark about her mother's cancer till the very end. 'The day before it happened,' writes Spike, 'I said, "Darling, Mummy's dying." She said, "No, she'll be better by Christmas." I said, "No, darling." She said, "But I'm only eleven." Oh God, the pain.'

Paddy died on 8 February 1978, aged forty-three. Buckingham Palace sent a message of condolence. Spike later told the *News of the World* that, as the end approached, he had persuaded 'a doctor I knew' to speed Paddy out of her pain with 'a fatal dose of morphine'. He added: 'I believe in euthanasia.'

20

In the psychiatrist's chair

After Paddy's death, the family was looked after by 'Nanna', Mrs Jean Reid, an Ayrshire nanny and mother's help who had been with them since Jane was a baby. Nanna described Paddy as having been utterly loyal to Spike; she had never heard her say a word of criticism of him, even though he was hard enough to live with.

In November 1978, nine months after Paddy's death, Spike told 'William Hickey' of the *Daily Express* that he was 'in love again'. 'Spike's new sweetheart is Irish-born Shelagh Sinclair, 34. The couple are inseparable, and Shelagh has already endeared herself to Milligan's four children. [He says:] "They keep asking me when I am going to pop the question . . . "'

Meanwhile, in April and May BBC2 had transmitted *Q8* (six episodes). Once again an anonymous Goon Show Preservation Society critic was less than wholly enthusiastic:

Some of it has glimpses of the old genius from the earlier days . . . [such as] the running joke . . . of the Chelsea pensioner with the long arms; but some of it seems a little thin. He seems to be drawing on ideas from . . . about 1972, for example in the 'Idiot of the Year' sketch . . . I don't feel that the series has reflected Spike at his best.

Although very little of the *Q* programmes is available on video (just a few sketches in BBC compilation tapes of Spike's life and work), one screen performance he gave during 1978 does remain accessible. John Cleese tells the story:

When we were filming *Monty Python's Life of Brian* in Tunisia in 1978, we discovered that Spike was there on holiday [revisiting the Second World War battlefields for his war memoirs] and asked him to appear in the movie . . . He came along, was very friendly and very cheerful, and shot the scene in the morning. Then in the afternoon, after he had had lunch with us, and we went out to shoot the rest of the scene, he had gone. So we had to improvise. Still . . . his unplanned appearance in that film was our homage to him.

Michael Palin doesn't recall Spike disappearing: 'He was brilliant as the man who finds Brian's shoe and gets trampled on . . . though I can remember him being slightly testy about the number of takes . . .'

Many of his TV appearances were now as an interviewee in chat shows. 'Television interviews are so boring and predictable,' declared the newsletter of the Goon Show Preservation Society, 'that Spike is always able to let in a breath of fresh air.' However, the same writer described him as 'completely uninterviewable', and Michael Parkinson, on whose shows he often appeared, writes: 'People assumed he was God's gift to talk shows, but he wasn't. He could veer from being absolutely obnoxious to being wonderful, depending on the mood you found him in.'

The interviewer might begin with 'You're looking very well, Spike,' and get the response: 'Rubbish, I've been dead for years, and nobody's brave enough to tell me.' Spike himself said of his repartee: 'What happens is that you have a few drinks and get very worked up. It depends upon how much you can inflate your ego until you think yourself brilliant. Or you are so frightened that you can't help but try and do funny things all the time to hide your fear.'

Yet he could be co-operative. Libby Purves, presenter of Radio 4's *Midweek*, recalls an edition in which Spike was being interviewed by an inexperienced guest interviewer – she thinks it was a young Ian Hislop – who nervously upset his glass of water over his notes.

They were in soluble felt pen, and before his horrified eyes his questions began to blur into illegibility. Spike, never an easy interviewee, looked at him with an ever-widening, shark-like glee, as if to say 'Got you!' with Grytpype-Thynne menace. But then he gave a most lamb-like, gentle, generous, co-operative interview designed to make the interviewer feel good. I think he was in far better control of his moods and whims and misbehaviours than he ever let on.

Q9, which proved to be the final Q series, was broadcast in June and July 1980. It included jokes about the country's new Conservative prime minister, elected just over a year earlier.

John Bluthal asks who is the woman with the big boobs, and Spike replies that the biggest boobs are made by Mrs Thatcher. In Spike's one-man show during the years of the Margaret Thatcher government, whenever a joke failed to go down well with the audience, he would beat a life-size Thatcher dummy ferociously with a heavy stick.

Q9 also included a brief guest appearance by Peter Cook, who is seen standing outside Claridges, wearing full evening dress but behaving like a busker and singing the 'Goodbye' song he wrote with Dudley Moore. Spike appears, looking like a tramp, and manages to steal coins from Cook's collecting mug using a horseshoe magnet. Strikingly, Cook tells him he used to love him in the early Goon days when Michael Bentine was still in the show.

The TV critic of the *Daily Star* wrote: 'Trying to find the humour . . . in Q9 is for me rather like looking for an oasis in the desert . . . Bizarre sketches can be hilarious . . . But Milligan's attempts leave me cold.' Yet Barry Took judged Spike in Q9 'worth watching for [his] occasional moments of brilliance'.

On 26 May 1980, while Q9 was in mid-series, Peter Sellers sent a telegram:

DEAR SPIKE I AM DESPERATE TO HAVE SOME REAL FUN AGAIN WITH YOU AND HARRY. PLEASE CAN WE GET TOGETHER AND WRITE SOME MORE GOON SHOWS? WE COULD PLACE THEM ANYWHERE I DONT WANT ANY MONEY I WILL WORK JUST FOR THE SHEER JOY OF BEING WITH YOU BOTH AGAIN AS WE WERE. LOVE PETER.

Spike knew better than to take such proposals too seriously (they were a mood that passed), but he and Secombe made a date with Sellers, who flew to London – and collapsed in his room at the Dorchester on 22 July from a massive heart attack. He died in hospital two days later, aged fifty-four.

At a gathering of the Goon Show Preservation Society two months later, Spike was talking about his 'guilt' at bringing Sellers to England. But he gave a comic account of the funeral:

---

[1] Cook had admired Milligan from schooldays, when he sent the BBC a radio script that was virtually a *Goon Show*. They passed it to Milligan, who was so impressed that he gave Cook lunch in London. In 1962 Cook and the other members of *Beyond the Fringe* had collaborated with the Goons on the LP *Bridge Over the River Wye*, and Cook and Dudley Moore played a pair of policemen in the film of *The Bedsitting Room*.

Terribly sombre event . . . until the vicar announced the ceremony would close with a favourite tune of Peter's, specified in
his will. We were expecting *Land of Hope and Glory* when
suddenly out came the swinging strains of Glenn Miller's *In the
Mood*. It was very emotional – Graham Stark next to me burst
into tears. I was in fits, though – Peter hated the damn tune!

In a TV interview immediately after Sellers's death, he
talked caustically about Sellers's habit of making generous
gifts and then suddenly withdrawing them; he specifically
remembered Alan Clare being given an electronic organ,
which Sellers soon had removed and given to Princess
Margaret instead. By the end of the 1980s, Spike was even
joking about Sellers being dead: 'Peter Sellers – he's no longer
with us, in fact he's no longer with anybody!'

Spike's lack of nostalgia for working with Sellers was
demonstrated in April 1981 when he put his own set of 232
Goon Show scripts up for sale at Christie's. The BBC claimed
ownership, but Spike ignored this, and the scripts were sold
for £14,000 to Elton John, who put on a Bluebottle voice
to explain how much he loved the Goons.

Prince Charles was to marry on 29 July 1981, and the
Daily Mail reported that Spike would be among the guests
– but he had seriously considered declining the invitation:

Spike, a fervent conservationist, wrote to the Prince asking him
to give up hunting. He received a non-committal reply and said
he would have to think very hard about whether to go to St Paul's
. . . : 'I have been asked by conservationists not to go, and it put
me in an awkward position. I thought deeply about it and, in the
end, decided that I have been invited as a friend and it would be
pretty nasty of me to turn him down.' . . . He added . . . : 'I am
going to the wedding as soon as I get the suit out of hock. I saw
Secombe's suit and I think I will share it with him.'

On the way to the service in St Paul's Cathedral, his chauffeur-driven limousine was held up in traffic. 'The ex-Goon,' reported the *Sun*, 'in a grey morning suit, leaped out [and] had the crowds roaring. Then they mobbed him – and . . . Spike dashed back to his car. At the cathedral, he desperately searched for his invitation . . .' (But he found it.)

Early in 1982, as he approached his sixty-fourth birthday, he let the press reveal his own engagement: 'His fiancée . . . Shelagh Sinclair, 37 . . . has been the ex-Goon's close companion for the past four years. Spike has bought her a ring, but they have not yet fixed a date for the wedding.'

Three months later, he took part in a conversation with Anthony Clare on Radio 4's *In the Psychiatrist's Chair*.

*

'He was reasonably well at the time,' writes Professor Clare, 'although he had been quite seriously depressed not long before.' He told Clare: 'I'm getting better at controlling it now.'

The broadcaster Gerald Priestland, who suffered from depression, wrote this memorable description of it:

Others may think you are fortunate, but *you* know it is all an empty fraud, and that one day the hollow balloon will burst, you will be found out and your crime exposed. What crime? You don't know; you only know you are guilty; and you can hear them coming down the corridor to get you.

Spike's depressions were not like this. Pauline Scudamore witnessed the onset of one, in 1982. His one-man show was about to tour England, beginning in London in November, and when the first night approached, Spike began to display depressive symptoms. He cancelled appointments and interviews and took to his room at Orme Court, revelling in self-regarding melancholy. He was in there for five days, sometimes telephoning Norma Farnes, who was downstairs, to dictate angry letters on animal rights or piped music in public places. He also spent one night tape-recording a message to Harry Edgington in New Zealand, with whom he had now fallen out. Now and then he would dope himself for a few hours with sleeping pills.

When Spike and Anthony Clare met in a radio studio a few months before this, Spike talked about his experience of depression:

SPIKE: It's a gift and a curse at the same time. You get the pain much worse than anybody else, but you see a sunrise much more beautiful than anybody else.

CLARE: Would you forgo the one for the other?

SPIKE: No. Having reached the age of sixty-five, I realise that this bath of fire I went through has made me a much more tolerant human being, with a vast spectrum of under-standing and tolerance for people . . .

CLARE: But *are* you a tolerant man?

SPIKE: Not of idiots and fools . . .

CLARE: I'd say there might be some evidence that you're quite an impatient man . . . Now when you get depressed . . . do you feel guilty about [being intolerant]?

SPIKE: No. I realise that I'm the victim of a condition, and I just lock myself in my room and stay away for a couple of days.

CLARE: I mean, do you ever feel you're hard on other people? [*A long silence*]

SPIKE: Please, God, let me tell the truth. [*Pause*] No, I don't think so, Tony. I might demand the truth of them, but I'm not actually hard on people . . . I'm not an excep-tionally difficult person.

CLARE: You're not?

SPIKE: Not really, no, I don't think so. If they find me diffi-

cult, they must be an awful pain in the arse to themselves
. . . I set my sights on some kind of humanity . . . on the
utopian scale, and to think that I was reduced to being
just another appalling person – I'd think, what kind of
message am I trying to preach, when I myself am commit-
ting the very crimes that I'm trying to tell people I don't
want committed? . . .

CLARE: If you were to pinpoint something about yourself
that you dislike, what would it be?

SPIKE: Um . . . I can't think of anything particularly at the
moment . . . Being ungenerous to people who can't match
me mentally: I suppose I dismiss them too easily.

If Clare felt that Spike's depressions were not like other
people's – that they were chiefly a manifestation of anger
rather than sadness, and were more like a schizophrenic's
episodes of paranoid delusion than the low period in the
cycle of manic depression – he said nothing about it, either
in the radio programme or what he wrote on Spike. 'I could
find no single cause for his illness,' he reported. 'I know
there was a family history of depression.'

However, in the radio interview he did ask one delicate
question:

CLARE: Some people might say, listening to you, that you
describe (at times) a manipulative ability – that is, you
turn on and off your moods to get things around you
changed, or you have some control over it?

SPIKE: [*apparently misunderstanding or not taking in the question*] Yes . . . Early days, I had no control over it, but
[it's] like getting used to a hump on your back.

*

'Although he fires with a scatter gun and not all of his gags
quite connect, there is . . . a running strand of manic thought

tying together random themes.' This could be Anthony Clare discussing Spike's humour. In fact it is an *Evening Standard* critic reviewing *There's a Lot of It About*, as the BBC had chosen to call what was in effect *Q10* – a six-part series by Spike and Neil Shand which began on BBC2 in mid-September 1982. 'What, you may ask,' wrote this critic, Ray Connolly, 'is funny about Spike with his face blacked and lips whitened dressed in a woman's long fur coat and hat, standing outside Harrods claiming to be "Al Jolson, News at Ten"? I'm not sure I know the answer, but I laughed.'

However, one viewer who wrote to the press thought that *There's a Lot of It About* was objectionably racist:

When inspiration fails him . . . Mr Milligan clowns about as a Sikh or laces the programme with references to the Irish or Chinese. His final dig at the Jews – a Mrs Rita Goldberg of Golders Green playing Tchaikovsky on a cash register while wearing a large plastic nose . . . – was in the worst possible taste.

The BBC did not commission another series. Spike's comment was: 'I don't believe anybody at the BBC wants me back at all – they think of me much as they think of cancer of the balls!'

In January 1983, a few months after the screening of *There's a Lot of It About*, Shelagh gave an interview to the *People*, in which she said she had 'no idea' when she and Spike would marry; it might be never. But she admitted she had moved in to Monkenhurst: 'I love making Spike's vegetarian meals but I am aware I can stand on people's toes . . . "Nanny" . . . has been with the family for fourteen years . . . I haven't any right to change anything.' He had been a fish-eating vegetarian since the 1960s, though he made an exception for venison from culled herds.

In fact Spike and Shelagh were married soon after this interview, in July 1983, at a Catholic church in Barnet.

According to the *Daily Mail* (thirteen years later): 'Spike made it quite clear [to Shelagh] that . . . having babies . . . was not on the agenda – he did not want more children.'

In the November following the marriage, Spike featured in the *Sunday Times*' 'A Life in the Day', indicating that his demands on Shelagh were much the same as those on June thirty years earlier:

I have a bit of a sleep problem – I need eight hours a day . . . If I'm doing a nightly show in the theatre, I might not wake till eleven or midday . . . Once I'm awake I give Shelagh a buzz on the internal phone: 'Hullo, hullo, good morning. Any chance of some breakfast?' If I'm lucky she brings me up my usual: mushrooms on toast, honey, Earl Grey tea . . .

Shelagh has a cup of coffee and stays with me for about half an hour, during which we chat about the day ahead. It's also the time I like to organize things that need to be repaired or replaced. I'm a great believer in house maintenance and a stitch in time. I'm terribly organized, with files, systems and methods, and everything has to be in its place.

In 1987 Shelagh described Spike as 'one of the sanest men she knows – "but impatient"'.

He said in 'A Life in the Day' that he did twenty press-ups, twenty sit-ups and twenty minutes on an exercise bike each day, 'and, if possible, a game of squash'. Neil Shand used to play squash with him at a club in Notting Hill Gate, and says that even on the court he behaved like a performer: 'We'd be patting the ball around in quite a relaxed fashion, but then two or three spectators might appear on the gallery above us – and Spike would change, he'd become this demonic opponent, tearing up and down the court. And then they'd go away, and he'd calm down again.'

A rare glimpse of the effect on his children of his shifting moods was obtained during Spike and Shelagh's absence in

Australia shortly before their marriage, when a *Daily Mail* reporter inveigled her way into Monkenhurst for an interview with the Milligan daughters. She noted: 'Silé works as a secretary in a photographic printing company in North London . . . Laura is one of a small team selling tiles. Sean runs his own decorating business . . . Only Jane . . . wants to be in show business and is working as the dresser to the star in the West End play *Steaming*.'

Twenty-five-year-old Silé, flagrantly ignoring her father's NO SMOKING signs, discussed the embarrassment of having a parent who was manic as well as depressive:

'It shocks us too when we see him clowning around at the royal wedding or sticking bananas in the ears of Chinese interviewers – but you get used to it.' On the other hand she and her sisters reduced themselves to helpless giggles as they recalled the occasion when a local restaurant concluded their father's birthday dinner with a superb specially-made birthday cake, topped with cream. 'The waiters stood proudly around waiting for him to cut it. Nothing happened for a few seconds and, as often happens with Dad, we all got the feeling he was about to do something crazy. Suddenly he just flopped face-forward right into the middle of it! It was amazing. He wasn't drunk or anything. It was just his idea of a joke.'

Spike and Shelagh's honeymoon was spent in South Africa. He told the press: 'With the aid of Prince Philip, we are saving a rain forest near Durban and I'll be visiting an elephant which I bought as part of a preservation scheme some years ago. She's called Mrs Thatcher.' This was the controversial trip which he used to fund the saving of the two trees at Monkenhurst. He told Dominic Behan: 'I outraged my hosts because I insisted on taking the black stage hands with me wherever I went to eat or drink.'

A few months later, in February 1984, Prince Charles

made the first of several visits to Monkenhurst for dinner. Spike later told the press that, on one evening, Charles had brought along his copy of McGonagall and read aloud from it. 'Really,' Spike remarked, 'I don't think the English people know what they have got on their hands. He would much rather be a clown and a joker, I think, than being the next king.'

He alleged that Charles was 'always offering to wash up', and he showed John Antrobus 'a teacup washed up by Prince Charles when he was here. It's still badly stained round the bottom and he's coming back to finish the job when he's got time.'

In return, Spike and Shelagh were invited to dine and sleep at Highgrove, Charles's country house. 'They were a normal family,' Spike recalls of Charles and Diana after her death, '[with] dogs running about and children . . . William and Harry came down in their pyjamas and [Charles] said, "Look, Spike, would you like to sing *The Ying-Tong Song* to them?" and I had to sing this bloody song.'

According to another account, Spike started to sing it but then had a memory lapse, and Charles took over. 'He sang a scat version [writes Spike] which left me helpless with laughter. Diana turned to me and said, "I don't know what's come over him."'

At times, Spike's relationship with the Prince was almost like a love affair. Spike claimed that he had replied to Charles's wedding invitation back in 1981 with a telegram reading: 'THANKS FOR THE INVITATION BUT ITS NOT GOOD ENOUGH I WANT TO MARRY YOU.' And on 2 October 1985 there was a night-time tryst between the Prince and the Goon. Charles had agreed to meet Spike under one of the Victorian lamps that Spike had already helped to save from modernisation on Constitution Hill, outside Buckingham Palace, so that they could agree on an appropriate type of light bulb. His note to the Prince read: 'Dear

Von Charles, I will meet you under the lamp-post. Signed, Lili Marlene.'

Spike arrived first, grumbling in a Bluebottle voice about the Prince being late, and when Charles eventually emerged from an engagement in the palace, Spike told him that the orange bulbs then in use made the place look like a fairground. Charles said he would suggest to the Department of the Environment that they be toned down to match with the gas-lights at the palace front.

Charles also intervened personally over the vexed matter of Spike being refused British citizenship, which would flare up periodically over the years; a cynic might say that it reappeared whenever Spike wanted some publicity. But not even a letter from HRH to the Foreign Office did the trick. 'All he has to do is to sign the oath of allegiance,' replied the officials.

Charles passed on the message: 'Please, Spike, take the oath. It's not as bad as you think. After all, I had to take it myself.' But Spike still refused, on the grounds that his war service had demonstrated his loyalty to the monarch; and when the Foreign Office reminded him that he was entitled to an Indian passport he responded: 'I shall have to call myself Patel Milligan, open a corner shop and get mugged by the National Front.' Some years later he told the interviewer Lynn Barber he did not want to take the oath 'along with a lot of Pakistanis and Jamaicans'.

In December 1987 he gave an interview to *Blitz* magazine in which he rubbished Prince Philip as 'fucking lucky to marry the Queen. He had fucking nothing when he met her. His arse was hanging out of his trousers.' The *Sun* reported the warning of 'Palace insiders' that 'Charles won't take kindly to these outrageous remarks about his father'. But all was apparently forgiven, since Charles was guest of honour at the 1988 D Battery reunion at Bexhill. On a previous occasion he had sent the Battery a telegram:

'Remember, if it had not been for Milligan the war would have ended two years earlier.'

*

Spike's Australian summer trips continued, and in 1984 he took his one-man show to Perth, where it was recorded for a commercial video. The tape has some wonderful moments, such as the notion that the show has to be 'started' like a car, with cranking noises and much use of the choke (this had first turned up in a Q programme); and there are some splendid ad libs which demonstrate his quicksilver wit, like the one addressed to a noisy woman latecomer: 'I thought I told you to stay in the car and bark like a dog if anyone came near.'

However, much of the material is tired and over-familiar – there is a dreary repeat-performance of the journey down to Bexhill which opens *Adolf Hitler* – and some is in dubious taste: a whole raft of racist jokes (including Jewish and Pakistani), and a lengthy physical assault on a lifesize inflatable dummy of the Australian Labour prime minister Bob Hawke (replacing Maggie Thatcher), which puzzled and rather shocked the audience.

Back in England for the winter, Spike was able to satisfy a long-held ambition, to appear in a pantomime – as the nice robber (to Bill Pertwee's nasty one) in *Babes in the Wood* at Chichester. The experience was good enough for him to sign up for another panto at Richmond the following Christmas. But this time the writer-director, Jimmy Perry of *Dad's Army*, wanted Spike to stick to the script. Spike became depressed, and took it out on the stage staff.

'Spike has answered every question I have put to him,' writes Pauline Scudamore in *Spike Milligan: a biography*, which was published during 1985. He had given her unlimited access to his family, friends and papers, and he declined to read the manuscript (let alone censoring anything).

Mrs Scudamore, who had first met him through Robert Graves, told her readers she had never been a Goon fan: 'It was the non-Goon Milligan that first attracted me.' Indeed her book, though well researched, sometimes seemed to be about a man who had never said or done anything funny in his life. 'It did show several layers of me but it didn't go very deep,' said Spike himself when he finally read it after publication. 'I think it over-stressed mental illness. You'd have thought that I was a lunatic . . . There was a bit too much about that, I thought.'

Not surprisingly, such a portrait of Spike did nothing to encourage TV chiefs to commission new scripts from him. In April 1986, at the launch of a Granada documentary about his life, he claimed that the BBC now treated him as 'the leper of the light entertainment industry'; it was four years since they had commissioned his last series. He said he had also been spurned by Channel 4; he made a pilot for them, 'and they never even phoned me back about it. I bet you that I never have my own show again.' He added: 'I remember everyone who has ever made me unhappy and would gladly take a shotgun to them.'

The BBC responded after Spike had repeated these remarks in August 1986. Typically, the Corporation denied that they no longer wanted him to create comedy shows, but confirmed that there were 'no plans for him to do another series'. Consequently Spike had to resort to extreme measures to keep in the limelight; like the occasion when he was thrown out of Harrods after trying to stuff twenty-eight pounds of spaghetti down the mouth of the food hall manager. 'I told him it might give him some idea of how a goose feels being force-fed maize to make *pâté de fois gras*. Everyone looked stunned and their faces fell.'

He was obliged to take work from people who had once been his junior colleagues. Neil Shand persuaded TV talk shows to book him, and in 1986 John Antrobus wrote a six-part radio series in *Goon Show* style called *The Milligan Papers*, with Spike leading a cast that included John Bluthal. 'They are only using me now . . . because the writer John Antrobus asked for me,' he told journalist Andrew Duncan.

'He was sitting comfortably in the den of his home in Barnet, where he lives with his third wife Shelagh,' wrote Duncan,

sipping a rather decent Meursault provided by Bill Wyman who had come to dinner with a stunning teenage girl. 'I realize why he goes for them so young – they are guaranteed AIDS-free,' said Milligan . . .

He is meticulously fussy to the point of obsession. There are 'No Smoking' signs throughout the house, and a notice on the large front door says, 'This door can be closed without slamming it. Try it, and see how clever you are.' . . .

His books are in alphabetical order in their separate categories. 'If you're organized, life is so much easier. People think I'm a lunatic who goes screaming around the house, naked all day, drinking whisky. But I think I'm a very normal person.

'I'm an ongoing failure . . . I thought I had the same comic ability as Peter Sellers, because I used to match him in the *Goon Shows*, but the cards fell right for him when he went into films and never came right for me . . .

'I wasn't happy with the *Goon Shows*, but I suppose they made people laugh.' . . .

He is tired of the tormented genius tag . . . though he still goes into depressions which last from a day to a week. 'The moods come on very suddenly, and I try to exploit them to my advantage. I find that I can write serious poetry, which I can't do when I'm normal . . . It gives you a new spectrum of emotions that you didn't realize you had . . .'

He looks years younger than his age [68], with a relaxed, gentle face. 'I exercise every day and used to play squash until I ran out of partners – my wife gave up smoking, became overweight, and now can't run the court, and all my friends dropped by the wayside because they don't have the same determination to keep fit. I want to stay alive for my children, to give them love, protection, confidence and continuity. I owe them my life.' . . .

The conversation returned again to the BBC. He isn't bitter so much as surprised that he has not been offered more work . . . 'Some of my Q shows on television were superbly funny and progressive. Monty Python copied idea after idea . . . I wish they'd give me the chance to go on experimenting because I only turn on and become funny when I do a show . . . But they have cut me off completely, probably because I'm into extra-terrestrial comedy – not the new-wave stuff which seems full of immature sexual innuendo and where you say, 'Good morning everybody, and fuck the lot of you.'

Or as he put it elsewhere, 'Alternative comedy? . . . Pick your nose, hang your willy out and tell a joke.'

Dominic Behan's biography of him (sketchy but with good quotes from Spike himself) came out during 1988. 'I have attempted to place Milligan in the context of [his] Irishness,' declared Behan, who didn't interview anyone but Spike: 'I couldn't find any of Spike's enemies, and his friends had said all they had to say a long time ago.'

Behan described Spike's second novel, *The Looney*, published in 1987, as 'the history of an Irish Oblomov'. Mick Looney, a Kilburn labourer, believes he is descended from the kings of Ireland, and sets out for his ancestral village of Drool in the hope of proving it. The book (says Spike in a prefatory note) uses 'some characters and sketches from my ill-fated BBC series *The Melting Pot*'. It is both more accomplished and less enjoyable than *Puckoon*: Spike has learned the novelist's craft, but one misses the rough edges and strange narrative twists of the earlier book.

'What prompted him, after more than forty books, to return to the novel . . . ?' asked an interviewer.

'The money,' he said instantly. 'I was running out of TV series. Younger people come along and the media put you out to grass. There's nothing like an overdraft to get you banging away again.' On the other hand, around the same time he said: 'Fortunately I have enough money not to worry any more and I just take my time writing books I want to write.'

His editor at Michael Joseph, who were still bringing out the war memoirs volume by volume, was now Sally Holloway. 'It was quite peculiar,' she says,

putting a twenty-six-year-old in charge of a man like that. I used to go and see him at his home – I can't remember him ever coming to the office. Also some of the publicity girls were a bit scared of him, so I used to ferry him around quite a lot, taking him to bookshops for signings.

I didn't feel I knew the man at all, really. When you're editing a book with an author, you often have a very close relationship, because you're getting into their ego, talking to them in quite a personal way. With him it wasn't like that at all. Firstly, there was Norma, who was Cerberus at the gates. Then there was Jack Hobbs, who co-authored a lot of the books with him (and, with his wife, had some deal by which they got named as Spike's co-publishers). I never knew who the Hobbses were, or how their involvement had begun, or what the balance was in the collaboration, but Jack certainly did a lot of the day-to-day running around for Spike. And then there was Spike, who only spoke to you when he chose. You didn't phone him – you waited for him to phone you.

I was a bit scared of him, because you never knew how he was going to react. And you never edited his manuscripts in the conventional sense at all – you just accepted whatever he sent you, dotting a few i's and crossing a few t's. You couldn't have a dialogue with him.

Did he make a pass at Holloway, or at anyone else in the publisher's? 'No, I don't think so. He said he liked me because I looked Irish – that I was a colleen. But that was as far as it went.'

She recalls that, as well as Spike's bouts of depression when 'the phone would be taken off the hook', he had dreadful insomnia, and was using some heavy knock-out pills he had persuaded a doctor to prescribe, so that he would be incommunicado all morning. 'I lie in bed till twelve,' he told a reporter; 'my wife brings me eggs and bacon at one' (despite being a vegetarian). Holloway comments: 'What a long-suffering woman Shelagh must have been!'

Yet Holloway's respect for Spike himself steadily increased:

I think he was more of a pro than people give him credit for. He was enormously popular at bookshops – there'd be people queuing around the block. I would pick him up from his home, and he'd be really grumpy and snappy to me and the chauffeur on the drive into central London. He'd also have issued instructions to the bookshop: they had to turn off their muzak (if they had it) and their air-conditioning, and provide him with a plate of digestive biscuits, which is all he would eat in the middle of the day, because that was his contribution to world starvation!

But when we actually arrived, and he walked through the swing doors, he would just click into good humour. It was great, because he really enjoyed talking to ordinary people. In particular, if some old codger turned up with a copy of Spike's war memoirs, and started reminiscing about the war, Spike would talk to him for ages. His relationship with ordinary people was miles better, in fact, than with so-called professionals.

I used to notice that the customers who wanted their books signed by him were about ninety per cent male, and the few women who turned up in the queue were only there to get them signed for their husbands or whatever. Actually the awful thing is, I myself don't find a lot of his stuff very funny. And to my taste it's quite crude, a lot of it. But I think the war memoirs do have a lot of integrity. And with the other books, everyone let him get away with it. There was no quality control. Norma was very good at sorting out his life, but she didn't criticize his work, the way some agents do.

Asked how the collaboration with Jack Hobbs worked, Holloway says she had no idea. 'He used to turn up at the office unannounced, and you couldn't get rid of him. But he was quite a good buffer between us and Spike. He was perpetually being fired by Spike, and then the next day the collaboration was back on again.'

Holloway recalls that Spike never consulted her or anyone at Michael Joseph about what to write next. Manuscripts just turned up; *The Looney* (which the firm had certainly wanted) was followed by a collection of poems called *The Mirror Running*, which they didn't want. 'But it sold well,' recalls Holloway. 'Everything did.'

It was quite impossible to guess what he would come up with next. 'I'm writing a book called *William McGonagall Meets George Gershwin and The Who*, and another book I'm writing, called *The Magic House*, is for children,' he told the Goon Show Preservation Society in October 1987.

During the run-up to the 1987 general election he proposed himself as a candidate to the Green Party, to stand opposite the Tory MP for his constituency of Barnet – who was none other than Margaret Thatcher. 'Two chaps came down to see me and I told them I'd like to stand,' he recalls. 'I gave £100 towards party funds, they went off and I heard nothing more.' In fact his attitude to Thatcher was partly admiration: 'I think she's very strong, very dominating, very honest.'

He celebrated his seventieth birthday in April 1988. Richard Ingrams, interviewing him for the *Independent*, wrote: 'He looks as if he is about 50.'

Another interviewer found him in 'a rented oasthouse in Sussex where the tranquillity is deafening'. He explained: 'It's just a temporary home while Shelagh and I look for a house in this area.'

Sally Holloway had been greatly taken by Monkenhurst: 'On the outside it was a gothic mansion with turrets – there ought to have been bats! However, it was a very calm, beautiful place inside.' But the Milligans were now leaving Barnet.

He liked people to believe that it was the increasing noise of London which had driven him out; though when he told the press that the specific trouble had been noisy neighbours, the family who had lived next to him in Holden Road claimed that he had made his fair share of noise himself. 'I used to see him playing his trumpet in the garden,' said Mrs Elena Gane. 'He was one of the noisiest people in the street.'

The true motive for the move seems to have been financial. 'As you get older you earn less money,' he observed in one interview, 'and I couldn't afford to keep the house on in London. So I put it up for sale, and they said, "We've got this Japanese bloke to buy it, you don't mind him buying the place?" I said, "It's OK, I'll wire it up to explode on the anniversary of Pearl Harbour."' [2]

Elsewhere he said that the Japanese man had 'offered me a million pounds for it, and I thought, "Milligan, this is your only chance to ever be a millionaire." Of course he sold it for even more and it's been turned into flats.'

The Milligans spent a year looking for what Spike was

----

[2] Neil Shand asks: 'Why are Japanese jokes acceptable when all the rest are labelled racist?'

determined would be a dream home by the sea. At last, in the autumn of 1988, he paid £300,000 for a big six-bedroom house called Carpenters, in the village of Udimore near Rye in East Sussex. Spike was delighted with the superb view over the English Channel, and there were large gardens, a swimming pool and a tennis court. But he had failed to take in the material with which the 1960s Georgian-style house was built: 'I bought it because I thought stone would last longer, then found it was really a kind of cement.' Shelagh was said to have hated it on sight, and reporters were soon describing it as 'hideous'. Spike's response was to put a plaque by the front door saying 'THE BLIND ARCHITECT'.

'Only HE could live in a place called Dumbwoman Lane. Only HE could live in a house which resembles a nuclear bunker,' commented one journalist. And Spike was failing to find it peaceful: 'It's not quiet at night. There's some kind of noise that goes on and on. To wipe it out I turn up the "black" sound on my radio – the hissing which sounds to me like rainfall.' But on a clear night he still enjoyed 'the twinkling lights of Boulogne'. He told a reporter: 'We should have burnt the house down and bought the view.'

Nearly a year after moving into Carpenters, he agreed to meet the Irish singer-songwriter Van Morrison for *Q* magazine. The encounter, at Carpenters, was written up by journalist Paul du Noyer:

Across and around the sunlit lawn of an English country garden, there romps a spry old gent of 71 years, dressed for the occasion in a floppy black hat. He also sports, we note with some curiosity, a large, pink, penis-shaped false nose, affixed to his face with elastic . . .

The meeting had been Van's idea. A most reluctant customer when it comes to promoting himself and his music through the media, Morrison had made it known he'd find an interview to be a more congenial experience if it was conducted by a fellow artist. He suggested Spike Milligan. Ever since he tuned in to the Goons on the wireless, back in Belfast childhood, Van has revered the other man's work – an aspect of Morrison's passions that few might expect, given the brooding, spiritual intensity that seems to inform so much of his singing. Indeed, the two men have met before (backstage at one of Spike's shows, at the Gaiety Theatre in Dublin), while Milligan himself has been impressed by Van's music, especially his collaborations with the Chieftains.

And so the arrangements were arranged, and Morrison has made the two-and-a-half-hour car trip down to Milligan's home in this secluded corner of Sussex . . .

SM: Did you hear about the Tipperary hurling team? They had to leave at half-time to catch their train home. So the other side went on scoring and won the game! Marvellous! Only in Ireland . . .

VM: How long have you lived down here?

SM: Only a year . . . If you're ever stuck for lyrics, I won a song lyric contest once. I'm an environmentalist, I'm a romantic. I'm not trying to make money out of you, I've got enough money. I like experimenting. If you've got a strange song, that nobody can put words to, throw it at me. I don't want any money for it, I'll just do it for kicks . . . I love writing books. I do odd gigs on television, interviews and chat, and all these shows like *Guess My Arsehole*, and *Whose Legs Are These?* – all that shit. They're grim, aren't they? Of course when I go on I clown it up and fuck up the show and they never ask me again.

The following summer, Spike's mother died in Australia, only three years off her hundredth birthday. He had seen her a short while earlier, and had then flown back to appear on the 1990 Edinburgh Festival Fringe, reading his poetry and his war memoirs, and taking questions from the audience, in an evening called *Visiting District Milligan*. His daughter Jane was his stage manager: 'She can't even switch on a light,' he joked to the press.

Channel 4 had arranged an interview with him in Edinburgh, and he gave Fiona Murch, the station's arts correspondent, a hard time. Why had he come to the festival this year? 'That's a leading question, like – why are you alive? I came to do a show. That a good enough answer? I thought it was a better answer than the question actually. Do you change your knickers frequently?' In other interviews he slagged off present-day TV comedy: *Blackadder* was the most tedious thing he had seen since the war, and of today's comedy stars he said he admired Rory Bremner, 'but no one else'.

Harry Hill, the doctor turned stand-up comic, met him in a TV studio during the 1990s. Hill wanted to tell Spike how much his work had inspired him. 'I introduced myself, but he just snapped at me and told me to go away. I think a lot less of him now.' Told of this, Spike remained unrepentant. 'Harry who? I've never heard of this man and if I met him again I'd be just as rude. I don't care who he is.'

His Edinburgh show was a sell-out before it opened. 'He should be listed as a national institution,' wrote one of the critics. 'Yes, like Wormwood Scrubs,' responded Spike. 'If I get too famous they'll pull me down and build a branch of Sainsbury's.'

Returning from the Fringe, he was interviewed for the *Sunday Correspondent* by Lynn Barber, who when she arrived at Carpenters was shocked by his appearance: 'He is 72 . . . and suddenly looks it . . . His voice is dusty and far off. I wonder if he is seriously ill . . . His wife, Shelagh, says that on a scale of one to ten, today rates as "just about a five, maybe".' Barber gathered that 'nowadays the down periods outnumber the ups', and she soon realised that 'his downs are repellent, full of pessimism, vindictiveness and violent misanthropy . . . This is the tiresome thing about him: his desire to tell other people what they're doing wrong, to put them down, while simultaneously playing holier-than-thou.' For example, 'he tells the photographer he may only shoot six frames of film because film uses silver and he doesn't want to waste the Earth's resources.'

He readily agreed with Barber that he was unforgiving, and she concluded with one or two positive points: 'There are things that are so nice about him. He is not puffed up. He is almost heartbreakingly honest . . .'

He had become the patron of the Manic Depressive Fellowship, the first celebrity to stand up and identify himself as a sufferer; he claimed that it made him 'the world's number one manic depressive'. He agreed to collaborate with Anthony Clare on a book called *Depression and How to Survive It*, on the model of the John Cleese-Robin Skynner collaboration *Families and How to Survive Them* (1983). But that wasn't how it worked out.

'In November 1990,' writes Clare,

I talked to Spike in the penthouse room of the Gresham Hotel in Dublin . . . He was in the grip of a depressive swing which had started some time before. He looked wretched . . . and appeared as flat as an exhausted battery . . . 'I have got so low that I have asked to be hospitalised . . . 'I have had thoughts of suicide . . . I get depressed that I am old . . .'

In fact it seems he had already been given a spell in hospital. 'Comedian Spike Milligan has been admitted to a psychiatric hospital,' reported the *Daily Mail* on 24 October 1990.

The 72-year-old former Goon sought help after mental problems caused the postponement of several television appearances.

He is being treated at the £185-a-night Godden Green Clinic in the Kent village of Seal, near Sevenoaks.

Yesterday his close friend and former colleague Michael Bentine spoke of his sorrow at the news and suggested Milligan's depression may have been the result of the death of his mother . . .'

Spike's mum died about three months ago. She was a major influence on his life.'

A day later, the *Mail* added that Spike

has been having electric shock treatment . . . He can go out during the day but returns in the evenings. Yesterday he joked with fans as he signed copies of his book *It Ends With Magic* at a London shop. He said: 'I think the reason for the electric shock treatment is because the shares are down [there had been a stock market slump]. It doesn't make any difference, though, because I'm still a loony.'

The joking tone of these remarks suggests that he was not in a bad way. However, when Anthony Clare met him again later in November, he noted that Spike's depression

was now so crippling that he had been forced to withdraw from the forthcoming pantomime [*Cinderella*, with Spike as Baron Hardup] in Tunbridge Wells. He had never had to do this before and it was clearly causing him guilt and anguish. He worried whether it marked the beginning of the end of his career as a performer.

He told Clare that he had had a rift with his brother Desmond. Later, he said that during this depression he planned suicide:

I worked it out with military precision . . . I'd take 100 tablets of the hypnotic tranquilliser drug Tuinal. [But] I thought, God, look at the sorrow I'm about to inflict upon my wife and my children and my friends . . . I could see them standing by my grave . . . tears streaming down my children's faces . . . And at the back of my mind was the thought that I'm a Catholic and that suicide is a mortal sin.

He said he wasn't totally without hope. He placed little faith in medication, telling Clare: 'It is a little like jacking a car. The psychiatrist can jack up the car but he can't change the tyre.' But 'knowing that with time it [depression] has passed before helps'; and he managed to keep writing: 'I wrote my last book [*Peace Work*, the seventh and final volume of his war memoirs] in my semi-depressed state. I think I hang on.'

His marriage was a support: 'Shelagh helps.' But 'I have reached an age when I am not sexual any more . . . It has just stopped . . . Sex has gone completely.' This depressed him still further.

Anthony Clare pressed on with the project, but began to realise 'how demanding he can be of other people . . . At times it made me wonder whether he liked people at all.'

Their very first recorded interview for the book started badly. Spike became irritated when Clare revealed he had seven children:

This revelation provoked a tirade about over-population, global contamination, environmental pollution, despoliation of the planet. His views – uncomfortably reasonable in many ways, indeed quite conventional by today's standards, were expressed with extraordinary vehemence, an almost personal hostility which was extremely disconcerting.

Spike said to an *Observer* reporter around the same time (the spring of 1991): 'Don't tell me your daughter was planned. It was just a shag.' His words to Clare were: 'How can you bring so many children into a world that is grossly overcrowded, polluted, packed like sardines? How can you be so irresponsible?' Clare responded that Ireland didn't have a population problem, but Spike refused to listen: 'Everything you are saying is death to the planet.'

His racism, too, began to manifest itself in their conversations. 'He became particularly incensed,' writes Clare,

about people who approve of multiracialism . . . [and] upset about the fact that Desmond's son, Michael . . . is married to a Chinese girl . . . 'The races as we know them will disappear . . . What will happen to our songs, the stories, the music?' I protested that he himself was the product of an Irish-English union, but he would have none of it. 'I am not an ethnic mess,' he replied, by which he appeared to mean someone like Trevor McDonald, the ITN newsreader – 'The man is African but he has a Scottish name.'

He had said the same to Lynn Barber: 'Take poor Trevor McDonald. He speaks with an Etonian accent; he's jet-black and he's got a Scottish name. That's making a *fool* of a person.'

Clare also got him to admit (as he had on *In the Psychiatrist's Chair*) that his depressions never undermined his faith in himself: 'Yes. Even when depressed I do have the satisfaction of feeling that I am right, that all the philosophies I have put together are right. Being depressed does not affect me . . . I retain my beliefs.'

During later conversations for the depression book, Clare 'was struck by the number of people who had been close but had fallen into disfavour . . . Spike remarked to me, "My father said to me before he died, 'Spike, people are made of shit, yes, every little tiny bit.'"' Clare concluded that Spike believed that 'despite his best efforts, people, all people, will let him down, cannot be trusted, are profoundly and unforgivably flawed'. When Clare tentatively suggested that Spike himself 'might not be the easiest person in the world to live with', Spike seemed to be 'genuinely baffled'.

Clare dealt with another disturbing aspect:

In the *In the Psychiatrist's Chair* interview in 1982 I asked Spike whether he had ever been violent. 'I wanted to be violent [he admitted] but somehow I felt inhibited . . . I felt like killing people [but] I thought that would be the last straw if I turned violent . . .

Clare was apparently not aware of the gun threat to Graham Stark, nor of the air-gun incident. He completed the book on depression as best he could in the circumstances, explaining to readers:

During the time it took to write this book, Spike Milligan suffered a severe attack of depression, one of the worst of his entire life. For over a year he remained . . . a shadow of his normal self. This episode proved particularly resistant to . . . hospitalisation, drugs, ECT, reassurance, counselling. Then, about one month before Christmas 1991, the depression lifted as suddenly and as inexplicably as it had originally struck, and the old, humorous, outgoing, enthusiastic and sociable Spike returned.

This un-depressed Spike came back just in time to face one of the biggest personal crises of his life.

21

Just one of those things

On Sunday, 19 January 1992, the front page of the *People* carried a banner headline:

SPIKE'S SECRET SON

Madcap comic Spike Milligan has a secret son he has never met – born after an eight-year affair.

The boy, now 15, was the result of a romance between Spike and artist Margaret Maughan.

Over the years, the ex-Goon has helped support son James, who bears a striking resemblance to him.

At first Spike, 73 – who has four other children – did not want to talk about the boy. But last night he admitted: 'It's all true. James is my secret son and I'm not ashamed of it.'

On an inside page, the *People* reported that James had watched Spike on TV proudly telling the world how much he loved his four children, and had asked: 'Why doesn't he ever talk about me?' This had prompted Margaret Maughan to write to Milligan, asking him to see the boy. 'After my letter,' she said, 'he phoned and reluctantly agreed to meet James.'

Now, she had 'decided to speak out – for the sake of her child. "I've no hard feelings towards Spike," she explained. "But I'm tired of waiting. The most important thing for James is public recognition. He is very proud to be Spike's son, but he's sick of telling lies about who his dad is."'

Margaret told the *People* she had first met Milligan backstage at the Theatre Royal, Newcastle, in 1967 when she was twenty-six.

She was making puppets and hoped to get Spike's backing for a children's TV show. 'It was obvious Spike liked women,' Margaret recalled. 'I was dressed in purple fishnet tights and purple dress and I relieved the boredom for him. He laughingly said: "You should come up to Glasgow with me tomorrow" but then added: "I didn't mean that. I've got a wife and four kids."' . . .

Margaret went on: 'We were both creative people and had an instant rapport.' They first made love in Spike's London office after a night on the town. But Margaret had no illusions about her relationship . . . 'He had commitments and I fitted in with them,' she said. They met either in London or in hotels when Spike was working outside the capital. 'On average we saw each other at least once a month and it carried on like this for years.'

By the time Margaret realised she was pregnant in 1975, the affair was cooling. 'He was horrified when I told him and said his family would be devastated if they found out. I knew he had a lot to lose. That's why I accepted what he did – he just disappeared. Two months later I got a postcard from him saying he was in Australia with his mum.'

James was born at a Newcastle hospital on 12 June 1976 – and a friend informed Spike. Said Margaret: 'He sent a huge bunch of flowers with a card saying something like "You naughty girl". It was hardly the kind of support I was looking for.

'But then he sent me £100 in cash. When I sent it back, he pleaded with me to put it into an account for James. He was very generous and carried on sending money – normally about £50.'

Later Spike . . . asked for James to be given the middle name Turlough after his Irish ancestors. He also sent James a christening present of a silver mug.

When James was just two, Spike was shattered by Paddy's death . . . 'I thought that with her death he might want to see James [said Margaret], but he didn't. Then he met his current wife Shelagh and everything went out the window.

'My mum rang Spike's agent, Norma, when James was five and said: "Children don't live on thin air, you know." It was then that he arranged a standing order of £30 a week, later increased to £50. When he was eight, he also paid for him to go to a private school.

'The cash kept coming until 1990, when Spike said the £50 a week would be reduced back to £30 . . .'

The *People* had rung Spike's doorbell in hopes of an interview, but 'an unshaven Spike, bleary-eyed and dressed in pyjamas, said: "I don't want to get involved if you don't mind." And asked if he wanted to meet James, he said: "I don't think I could." But he added: "I have been very supportive to him."'

The same day, however, he let the *News of the World* into the house for an 'exclusive interview', in which he declared he did want to see James:

'It's something I've got to do before I die,' he said, his voice shaking with emotion . . . 'Maybe the timing of this story is fate's way of telling me the time is right.' . . .

He was close to tears as he recalled how lover Margaret Maughan, now 46, fell pregnant and refused to have an abortion . . .

Spike decided to speak out after the child's mother tried to hawk her story to another newspaper for tens of thousands of pounds.

He spoke of the affair having happened during 'an unhappy period in my marriage [to Paddy]. How naïve I was . . . because, to this day, I don't know whether [Margaret] was on the Pill. The pregnancy was a mistake and it was Margaret's decision to have the child.'

*

Anthony Clare was still at work on the depression book when the story broke, and Spike talked to him about Margaret and James. He claimed he 'wasn't upset' that the boy's existence had been revealed.

The journalists tried to make me deny it . . . I told them I maintained his schooling and education, etc., gave an allowance. It was just one of those things. But they wanted me to deny it . . . It wouldn't make a good story otherwise. One chap came all the way out here [to Sussex] and said, 'Don't you deny it?' I said, 'No.' He went away flabbergasted.

CLARE: But why had you denied it [sic] for so long?

SPIKE: I don't really know. I worried about people who didn't know. I am glad that my mother and father weren't alive when it came out . . . I had my own wife and children at the time – I wanted to spare them and me the publicity. I didn't meet him [James] because I just didn't believe I could cope with it.

CLARE: His mother honoured the secret for sixteen years. Why do you think she broke it now?

SPIKE: She went to the newspapers. For some money, I suppose. Good luck to her.

CLARE: Did you have any inkling that she was going to do this?

SPIKE: None at all. Although it's silly. You can't be father to two separate families. You can't have two wives. One has to go by the board. I helped her as much as I could. I stayed in touch. Now here I am talking about over-population! I haven't a ghost of a chance in the witness box!

A week after the original story, the *People* printed some of Spike's letters to Margaret. 'You have had a baby,' he had written to her two weeks after James's birth in 1976,

I am the father. I should come and see you, but I'm not like any other person in the street, everybody recognises me. I'm well known, so if anything scandalous occurred in my life . . . it would make great newspaper copy . . . It would destroy me, my wife would sue for a divorce. I would be separated from my children . . .

I never knew you were in a state of conception. I was under the impression that you took the pill and so never took any precautions. So the whole thing came as a shock to me, whereas it made you happy. For me it was and still is like sitting on a volcano.

Meanwhile the *News of the World* printed this comment:

There must be many of us who've never thought of Spike Milligan as a sex symbol. He's the clown who has brought us years of pleasure. But yesterday Spike spoke candidly about the son he has kept secret. Now he wants to meet the lad. Good luck Spike – that livewire teenager might even cure your manic depression!

A few weeks later, on 1 March 1992, the *People* reported that James and his father had at last met:

Last Monday [James] travelled from his home . . . with his mum to an hotel close to the star's £400,000 home in Rye . . . On Tuesday afternoon, after nervously greeting each other in the street outside the hotel, Spike and his wife Shelagh spent more than an hour having tea with James and Margaret, 50.

The next day Spike . . . proudly picked up the teenager from the hotel to take him home for the afternoon. There he treated the happy youngster . . . to cream cakes. And as James left, Spike and his wife invited him to stay in the Easter holidays.

Afterwards Spike . . . told Margaret: 'I'm so excited, I feel high. I want to see James as much as possible.' . . . That evening he found time to have dinner with James at the hotel.

'When he got out of the car, all I could think of was that I had seen him on TV,' said James . . . He admitted: 'I was a bit shocked at how old he appears.'

James's visits to the Milligans continued. 'He always brings a friend,' said Spike in December 1993. 'They sit around not saying very much. I think they may be shy. I give them money to go to the disco in Rye.' In March 1996 the *Sunday Express* alleged that Spike's daughter Jane resented James (now twenty) being 'admitted to the family', because she realised that he had been conceived 'while her mother was fighting cancer'. Shelagh, on the other hand, 'had taken it all in her stride'.

Anthony Clare recorded that Spike had soon begun to joke about the conception of James: 'It was Châteauneuf du Pape that did it. I'm going to sue the company!'

*

The broadsheet press tactfully ignored the whole episode, and in the 1992 Birthday Honours he was awarded the CBE – honorary, because he was a citizen of Ireland. Around the same time, with the war memoirs finished, he started the 'According to' series of books, in which famous classics were converted into a string of gags. *The Bible According to Spike Milligan* (1993) was the first, followed by his versions of *Lady Chatterley's Lover* (1994, with a second part in 1996), *Wuthering Heights* (1994), *Black Beauty* (1996), *Frankenstein* (1997), *Robin Hood* (1998), *The Hound of the Baskervilles* (1998) and *Treasure Island* (2000). He maintained this relentless pace despite undergoing a triple heart bypass operation in August 1993, at the age of seventy-five.

As to the quality of the writing, Angela Huth observed of the *Lady Chatterley* spoof: 'Milligan's humour is certainly not for everyone . . . jokes coming so fast and often thin have a soporific effect. But no one could be immune to the charm of the footnotes, witty asides in which Milligan quibbles with Lawrence.' On the other hand Matthew Jarron of the Goon Show Preservation Society wrote at the end of the series: 'Were they really that bad? Well, yes and no. You have to admit that they started well . . . [But] Spike seemed to churn them out faster than Ernie Wise wrote plays,[1] and in my opinion only *Frankenstein* was a real winner.'

A few months after Spike's heart operation, the *News of the World* printed a photo which they claimed showed that he was physically a broken man – but it turned out to be a photo of someone else, and after the Milligans had issued a writ the paper had to print an apology.

It got its own back on Sunday, 13 February 1994:

SECRET LOVE-CHILD NO. 2 FOR GOONS STAR SPIKE MILLIGAN

Comic Spike Milligan has a second secret love-child, the *News of the World* can reveal.

The former Goon fathered Romany Watt in 1973 during a three-year fling with a journalist – but he has never met her.

At the time Spike, [now] 75, was married to his second wife AND having a relationship with Margaret Maughan . . . Spike, now re-married, confessed: 'It's true and very depressing. I've never met my daughter – and I don't want to.'

Spike split from the mother Roberta Watt before Romany was born on 2 August 1973 at West Hill Hospital in Dartford, Kent. Tragically, Roberta died in January 1981 aged 36 after a gall-stone operation.

Romany was adopted by her grandparents Burt and Josephine Watt in Nelson, British Columbia, where she is still a student. Spike had bought Roberta a house near Dartford to be held in trust until Romany became an adult. In return, Roberta agreed

---

[1] A *Private Eye* cartoon in 1984 had a bookshop with a sign in the window: 'Spike Milligan will be here to write his latest book at three o'clock.'

to retain custody of Romany and support her financially. The deal ended Spike's responsibility towards them.

Spike is recovering . . . after major heart surgery. He said: 'I've seen pictures of Romany and supported her financially, but to be honest that was only to keep her mother quiet. I'd rather just forget this, if you don't mind.'

Asked by a reporter (in 1998) if she had known about Spike's two illegitimate children before the exposé in the press, Shelagh Milligan answered: 'Of course I knew about James. But I didn't know about Romany.'

*

On 4 December 1994 Spike made headlines at the British Comedy Awards, which was being televised live. Jonathan Ross called him up for a lifetime achievement award, and Spike had tears in his eyes as he acknowledged the ovation and declared: 'I am not going to thank anybody – because I did it all myself!' Ross then tried to read out a tribute from the Prince of Wales: 'I must confess that I have been a lifelong fan of the *Goon Show* participants, and particularly Spike Milligan—' At which point Spike interrupted with: 'Oh, the little grovelling bastard.'

Maureen Lipman, who was there, recalls: 'There was a moment of incredibly pregnant silence, followed by roll upon roll of wild laughter.' ITV, who were showing the awards, received complaints, but Spike, far from apologising to Prince Charles, sent him a fax saying: 'I suppose a knighthood is out of the question now?'

According to one magazine a few weeks later, 'Charles has written back: "If you keep grovelling a bit, you might get one."' Shelagh Milligan's version is: 'Try a little judicious grovelling.'

In April 1996, more than a year after the event, Shelagh told a reporter she was convinced that Charles had forgiven the insult, but there had been no more invitations to Highgrove. However, two years later, at the time of Spike's eightieth birthday, Shelagh said that they had been invited to the palace and Highgrove.

Spike himself said of his remark, a month after making it:

I didn't know the award was going to happen. Something came over me. [Elsewhere he said he had drunk two bottles of wine.] It was impromptu and I was desperate to say something. I will be banished from England to a lonely island off the Scillies where I will be chained to a ram and dressed in rags.

That he was entirely unrepentant became clear when he collected the Oldie of the Year award in April 1995 – it was reported that he told 'a rude joke involving Prince Charles and a sperm bank'.

*

From *Black Beauty* onwards, the 'According to . . .' series was taken over by Virgin Books, and Rod Green, a quietly spoken Scot in his mid-thirties, became Spike's editor. Green says, defensively, of the series: 'There was still a lot of classic Milligan humour in there, definitely some laugh-out-loud moments.'

They became friends when travelling together in the back of a car to book signings. These journeys usually turned into competitive joke sessions. 'He loved laughing,' says Green. 'You could *see* him laugh, but you couldn't *hear* anything – he just used to shake.'

At the book signings, 'women would come up and ask for books to be signed "To John", and he would look up and say, "Ah, your boyfriend. Is he good at it?" And the poor girl would go bright red, and the whole queue would be sniggering – mainly because it wasn't happening to them.'

In 1999 Rod Green secretly arranged for Spike to be given a lifetime achievement award at the British Book Awards, reflecting the fact that he'd written more than sixty books and had sold millions of copies. It was a complete surprise to him, and (as with the comedy award) moved him to tears. Another recipient at the ceremony was a young woman doctor who had written about her work with the Air Ambulance. 'She's very attractive,' says Green, 'and she came round to introduce herself to Spike, in a beautiful ball-gown, and said she'd been a fan of his since she'd read *Silly Verse for Kids* as a little girl. And Spike said: "You have magnificent boobs." And then he turned to me and said: "You can get away with that when you're eighty-one."'

*

The awards and tributes in his late years also included a second appearance (in February 1995) on *This Is Your Life*. 'Missing from the BBC1 show,' reported *Today* magazine,

was 18-year-old James Maughan-Milligan [as James had now decided to call himself]. Student James . . . said: 'Spike rang to warn me that the show would be on. He assured me if it was up to him I would have been there.' . . . A show spokesman said: 'We talked to Spike's agent and his family and it was thought better not to bring James and them together because they hadn't met.'

Spike had also changed his mind about Romany. 'At 77 there is one great ambition he still hopes to achieve,' reported the *Sunday Express* on 10 September 1995.

Three thousand miles away in Canada there is a 19-year-old girl he has never met. Her name is Romany. She is his daughter.

'Her mother was a Canadian journalist I was friendly with,' says Spike. 'It was a sort of trap really. She wanted a child and thought I should do it. I bought her a house near the racetrack at Brands Hatch but we didn't stay in touch. Sadly she died after a gallstone operation in 1981 and Romany was taken back to Canada by her grandparents. I had a lovely letter from her recently and I have written back to ask if she would like to fly over and meet me.'

The next month the *Daily Mail* reported that Margaret Maughan 'is about to be evicted from her rented house in Hexham . . . while Milligan shares a luxury £400,000 house in Rye'. Margaret had sold the *Mail* a fuller version of her story (heavily written up by a reporter).

In March 1997 James revealed that it was he rather than his mother who first broke silence about Spike being his father. James told an *Express* reporter that, becoming angry with Spike's failure to acknowledge him publicly, 'I started telling my best friend . . . then another friend'. Consequently 'reporters began hanging around'.

*

Naturally I wished to meet Margaret and James, who by 2002 had left university and was working in London. I found Margaret in the telephone directory, and a date was fixed when she would be down from Northumbria to visit James.

We met outside Broadcasting House, and as they approached me along the pavement I found myself looking at the young Spike. Margaret (who speaks in a soft Northumbrian accent) later remarked to me that James's body language keeps reminding her of his father. Fortunately he hasn't inherited the manic depression.

That day, we had lunch, and they both talked freely – but not into my tape recorder; they wouldn't let me interview them for the book until financial terms had been agreed. This, and the drawing up of a formal contract – at the insistence of James rather than his mother – took some weeks, and it was nearly Christmas when we got together again, in a borrowed flat near the BBC, and I switched on.

Why, I asked Margaret, had she picked on Spike in 1967 as someone who might help with the TV puppet project?

MARGARET: I was an avid *Goon Show* listener – I had lots of female friends at art school who loved it, and my nickname was Min, not necessarily because of Spike's Min; it could have been from Minnehaha [in *Hiawatha*], because I used to wear skirts with fringes on them. I'm still called Min by my college friends – and Spike thought this was very funny.

My father was in the Merchant Navy, and then he met my mother and ran a farm for a number of years; he was a quiet, gentle Northumbrian man. I was born in 1941; the farm eventually had to be sold, and after that he managed farms for various aristocrats around Northumberland, so we were quite nomadic – we lived in about fourteen different houses, and I went to a lot of schools, and had a very colourful life.

I went to art college, first in Carlisle, then Newcastle, then Goldsmiths. I then worked in London for two years, not far from where Spike used to live before the war, at Hither Green School for Boys – a shock to the system, I can tell you! Then I teamed up with some college friends, one of whom was a film-maker, and we were working on Irish legends, making puppets, and it was my job to find somebody who could help us. And that's how I met Spike – I'd read a lot about him, and knew he was impressed with Irish things.

The play that had come to Newcastle was *The Bedsitting Room*, and it was brilliant. My whole family went – we had a box – and I just sat and watched Spike; there was something about him. (He was wearing a tramp's outfit, and had a shoulder-bag that looked like a Daz washing-powder packet.) I used to tease him afterwards, and say his name should be Magnetic Milligan, because people were drawn towards him, and he had a tremendous rapport with his audience – a very warm human being, at that time.

I waited patiently outside the theatre with my puppet portfolios, and eventually got in to see him. At that time I was going through a very Celtic period, and I'd hennaed my hair, and had made a dress out of a lovely printed fabric – purples and blues – and I had purple fishnet tights on. I must have looked absolutely too much!

He was very helpful; he said he was interested in our ideas, and would do all he could to help. And he did – he approached various people in the BBC, who weren't interested, and he tried Irish TV, but there was no interest. I think he was disappointed, but it didn't matter, because that was the beginning of our friendship.

CARPENTER: His first thing was to say jokingly that you should come on tour with him – but he had a wife and kids?

MARGARET: I think he just liked to flirt with people – he just liked people. I think he thought I was interesting, and there was the Irish thing.

CARPENTER: The next time you met was in London?

MARGARET: Yes, he invited me to meet Bernard Miles, because he was playing Ben Gunn at the Mermaid, with Barry Humphries as Long John Silver. He'd done his make-up all himself. And when the treasure chest was opened, he'd arranged for it to be full of chocolate money, which he threw into the audience.

CARPENTER: When did it become a relationship?

MARGARET: Certainly not then. It was just a friendship for about a year and a half. He loved Paddy – he loved her very much. I met her once: Paddy, Spike, Jane and Jane's nanny came to visit my studio at St Katharine's Dock [near the Tower of London]. This was prior to my appearing on TV with Spike, in *One Pair of Eyes*, when he was filmed visiting it. They all just came and looked round. It was quite unnerving for me.[2]

CARPENTER: I get the impression that the marriage to Paddy was quite stormy from the beginning.

MARGARET: Well, I wouldn't know about that. But he was certainly very unhappy. (*Pause*) Always with Spike, work came first, people came second.

CARPENTER: (*to James*) Did you feel that about him, when you made your visits to him – that work came first?

JAMES: Not at all, not at all in the latter part. I think he'd figured it out, figured his depression out. He'd figured life out, I think. That's how he seemed when I met him, perfectly content. A lot calmer.

CARPENTER: (*to Margaret*) Given that you'd got a friendship with him that was flourishing, what was it that turned it into an affair?

MARGARET: I'd moved back from London to Northumbria, and I had a flat at Seahouses, and he came to see me, and he was very sad, very unhappy. And I comforted him, because I really wanted to help him. And it just happened. And once you get involved sexually with someone, it's very difficult to undo that and go back to friendship.

CARPENTER: What was it that made him so unhappy on that occasion – do you remember?

MARGARET: No. He wouldn't discuss it.

CARPENTER: That's interesting. Liz Cowley, who like you had a friendship with him that turned into an affair, said he was someone who kept his life in compartments, and

---

[2] In the 1973 documentary about Spike in the *One Pair of Eyes* series on BBC2, he is seen visiting Margaret's studio to discuss designs; Paddy and Jane appear in different scenes.

didn't open doors to other ones when he was with her. Was that your impression too?

MARGARET: Oh, well, I think most people have things they won't discuss with their spouses or best friends.

CARPENTER: Yes, but she meant more than that. They didn't discuss their marriages with each other, for example.

MARGARET: I find that very odd. Spike was always, with me, very honest, and there was nothing hidden – I had no illusions at all.

CARPENTER: Liz used occasionally to encounter him when he was in a deep depression, and wouldn't talk to her – did you ever experience that?

MARGARET: Well, when he was very depressed he just used to lock himself away in his room.

CARPENTER: But did you ever arrive to see him when he'd done that?

MARGARET: There was once when I was very worried about him, and I took some food, in a box, and rang the door-bell, and he came to the door, and it was as though his spirit had gone. And he didn't want to be handed food. He used to say that when he was depressed, he was at the mercy of every fool, so it was easier to be on his own, locked away.

CARPENTER: I believe he wasn't a classic depressive, because when he was low, he regarded other people as fools, rather than directing the blame at himself.

MARGARET: I would question that. He certainly didn't blame other people to me.

CARPENTER: (*to James*) When was the last time you visited him before he died?

JAMES: October [2001]. I went down from London for a day visit.

CARPENTER: What sort of state was he in, physically?

JAMES: He seemed the same as he'd always seemed when I visited – just an old man. Very high spirits, settled, content, sitting in his chair. Shelagh said he was ill, a lot worse, on dialysis, but he seemed okay, happy to see me.

CARPENTER: (*to Margaret*) You're quoted as saying you came to feel marginalised by him – just before James was conceived.

MARGARET: I've always been on the outside.

CARPENTER: One of the newspaper articles about you quotes you as saying 'Being a mistress badly affected my self-esteem', and you say you conceived a baby by him as revenge for his trying to hush up his relationship with you.

MARGARET: I've always been on the outside; I've never really been included in any major happening with Spike's family. I've always been hidden – 'that artist'.

CARPENTER: But you wanted to have a baby by him?

MARGARET: Yes.

CARPENTER: Why?

MARGARET: I don't know why. I think it was because I loved him so much. I sacrificed my life, really, for Spike. There's lots of people that I met that I could have married. But the damage was done. In fact to this very day, Spike was the love of my life. It just felt that, if [the pregnancy] was to happen, I would be very pleased.

CARPENTER: Do you think his feelings for you were as strong as yours for him?

MARGARET: No, no, I don't think so. I think he did love me, in his way. But if he had really loved me, when Paddy died and I had James, that would have been the time when he could have come north and said, 'How about – ', you know, maybe not marriage, but could we live together?

CARPENTER: But this *Mail* piece presents you as having a baby for revenge. That isn't true?

MARGARET: No, no, not at all. When you really love somebody, there's a part of you that becomes unrealistic. I am a bit of a dreamer, and very much a creative person, and

I had the idea of having a child by someone I really loved, as a conclusion to a love affair, which was very selfish of me. And my mother was horrified that I'd had an affair with a man who was married; she couldn't care less about the fame thing.

CARPENTER: You saw having the baby as the conclusion to the affair?

MARGARET: Subconsciously I must have done.

CARPENTER: But not consciously?

MARGARET: No. (*Pause*) Spike liked people. And he told me that Shelagh, at that stage in his life, was full of fun. He felt at that time in his life that he wanted fun. And the prospect of family life with another child [James] didn't appeal to him at all.

CARPENTER: He was a large child himself.

MARGARET: That's what I liked about him.

CARPENTER: Did you consider saying to Spike that you wanted to have a baby by him?

MARGARET: No.

CARPENTER: Why not?

MARGARET: Because I felt if it happened, that was fate. It was just a deep relationship that ended up in pregnancy.

CARPENTER: Did you tell him that you were pregnant?

MARGARET: No, I didn't. He was in Australia. (*Pause*) I think Paddy wasn't well from when Jane was born. I think, reading between the lines, there was no sex again after that, because he did say to me, 'I might as well not be married.' And this is when we were friends, before we became lovers.

CARPENTER: James was born, and you told him then?

MARGARET: Well, I told him before James was actually born, when I was five months pregnant. And I had hoped to see him, but he was in Australia. I had sent a letter to Orme Court, and it was forwarded to Australia.

CARPENTER: You didn't feel he was running away from the

situation?

MARGARET: No, no. His mother was ill, and he had gone to be with her.

CARPENTER: Because that was implied by the journalists. Anyway, James was born, and Spike started making financial contributions?

MARGARET: Not straight away. I thought I could manage on my own – I'm a bit like that. He did send money, for the baby, and he sent a lovely christening mug, which he had designed himself, and it had James's initials on it.

CARPENTER: Oh yes – James's second name, Turlough.

JAMES: I hated it as a child, but now I like it.

CARPENTER: How do you pronounce it?

JAMES: Turloch.

MARGARET: No, it's Turlow. (*They argue about this.*)

CARPENTER: But eventually your mother rang Norma and said, 'Margaret can't bring up the baby on the smell of a herring?'

MARGARET: No, she didn't ring Norma, she rang Spike.

JAMES: If Mum can get by herself independently, she'll try, to the very last.

MARGARET: I gave up teaching, and set up a little business doing silk screen printing and doing kaftans, and things like that, in a place near Seahouses. Spike loved it up there; he'd come and visit me if he was working in Edinburgh or Newcastle.

CARPENTER: But your mother rang Spike?

MARGARET: Yes, without my permission. And a standing order was set up.

CARPENTER: When did Spike start paying the standing order to you?

MARGARET: That was when James started school.

CARPENTER: Did he start out at a private school?

MARGARET: No, no. At a local primary school.

CARPENTER: Why the changeover to private school?

MARGARET: My mother had been privately educated, and she felt it would be beneficial for James to go to private school. He was a quiet, withdrawn little boy, and school was turning out to be tough. So we sent him to a local private day school.

CARPENTER: (*to James*) When did you begin to become aware of who your father was?

JAMES: I have been aware the whole time, but it's just never been an issue for me. What you don't have, you don't miss, and I wasn't concerned with his life or the rest of his family – I think maybe surprisingly so; people don't comprehend that I didn't give a monkey's about half-sisters, half-brothers or anything. I just have no interest in it.

CARPENTER: It's been suggested that the secret got out because you talked to your friends about who your father was.

MARGARET: Well, my mother had died, and James was fifteen –

JAMES: Can I tell it?

MARGARET: Yes, you tell it.

JAMES: No, that's not the case. I didn't tell anyone until one day at school there was a reporter hanging round – that's the first I was aware of it – and then that set me off a little bit, and that's the first time I told anyone else. I told the person who was my best friend at the time.

MARGARET: I had a dilemma, because somebody in Spike's office had telephoned the newspaper, and the newspaper people were going to print a story that was not true, and I decided that we would turn it to our advantage.

CARPENTER: You say your mother had died – but what had that got to do with it?

MARGARET: Well, we were feeling very vulnerable. Everything seemed to happen at once. In fact while my mother was still alive, there were rumblings going on. I was trying to arrange a meeting with Spike, because James wanted to meet him.

JAMES: I didn't, that's wrong.

MARGARET: You didn't want to meet him? Oh. Well maybe we thought you *should* meet him. Poor James, being manipulated!

JAMES: That's what everyone says, 'Poor James.' I've had more love from Mother here – enough for two lots of families.

MARGARET: You had a very devoted grandmother as well. But we had been trying to arrange a meeting, and whoever it was in the office – I haven't found out to this day. Suddenly, telephone calls, people coming to the door.

CARPENTER: And you decided you might as well capitalise on it?

MARGARET: Yes, yes, I did.

CARPENTER: And you negotiated with one of the newspapers financially?

JAMES: Well, it was going to happen anyway.

CARPENTER: Which paper? The *People*?

MARGARET: Yes – and there were a lot of them who tried to get it prior to that.

CARPENTER: And the Sunday after the first article, they printed letters from Spike to you, which you had obviously let them have?

MARGARET: I was tricked into that. They were asking, 'Is there anything that you've got from him?' I regret that now. I respect Spike and it was not a very nice thing to do, really.

CARPENTER: James, what about that first visit, when you went to Rye? It had all been very much set up by the press, and I don't imagine you were really desperate to meet Spike at all?

JAMES: No – and I didn't speak much during it. I keep things very much to myself unless somebody opens me up, and that never happened with Spike. We were probably waiting for each other!

CARPENTER: Did he really ring you to apologise for the fact that you wouldn't be in *This Is Your Life?*

JAMES: Yes.

MARGARET: He spoke to me, and he was very upset about it.

CARPENTER: You felt that his official family didn't really want to know you?

JAMES: I think they felt it was someone else asking for his attention – just another person to have to share the great Spike with.

CARPENTER: We haven't talked about Romany [the illegitimate daughter] at all.

MARGARET: (*to James*) We don't know anything about Romany, do we?

CARPENTER: She was at the funeral, but you didn't meet her?

MARGARET: That's right – we didn't meet anybody.

JAMES: I had an idea which one she was, but I couldn't be definite. Hey, do you think he's got any more kids? There's probably one or two in Australia.

MARGARET: An Aussie cousin, there's a thought!

(*Laughter all round. The recording ends.*)

22

I told you I was ill

Spike finally met Romany (then aged nineteen) in March 1996, shortly before his seventy-eighth birthday. 'It's been wonderful to see her,' he told the press, and an unidentified 'close friend' said he was experiencing 'a sense of sins forgiven'. However, Shelagh seemed to be somewhat tense on the issue. When the *Daily Mail* spoke to her after Romany's visit, and suggested that Romany and James had been conceived when her own relationship with Spike was beginning to blossom, she replied: 'I am not going to discuss those children. I promised the family that I won't. It's painful. There's been enough said and written on the subject.'

It's doubtful how much difference the reconciliation with Romany really made to Spike. When a reporter asked him in October 1996, 'Mr Milligan, how many children *do* you have?' he replied: 'Three.' The reporter blamed this (probably unfairly) on the lithium he was now taking, observing: 'His brain seems to slip in and out of focus. "I don't want to find out what would happen if I stopped taking the tablets. I am frightened that I would go back to those awful grim days of depression."'

When New Labour came to power in 1997 he resumed his old campaign against over-population just as if his own hands were entirely clean on the issue. He wrote to Tony Blair urging the introduction of a ban on new babies for five years: 'Over-population is a serious issue. The human race will soon have to get used to twelve in a room.'

Shelagh told a reporter in the spring of 1996 that he had been 'evened out' for the past five years on daily doses of lithium, a usually highly effective damper on manic-depressive mood swings. 'He always says that lithium had stabilised him,' recalls Spike's books editor Rod Green, 'and now he quite liked living in a stable.'

The drug did seem to lower his level of mental electricity. Shelagh complained: 'You don't talk to me any more', to which Spike responded: 'I don't seem to have that much to say any more.' Nevertheless he was still capable of causing trouble. In the autumn of 1996 he went to Paris to meet Marie Antoinette Pontani, the adorable 'Toni' of the war memoirs (she still called him 'Terry'). 'Why I didn't marry her, I'll never know. I do regret that,' Spike told a reporter on his return – in front of Shelagh. And even more surprisingly, he announced that he wanted to find his first wife, June.

He asked his daughter Silé, who was apparently in touch with her mother, to act as a go-between so that he could apologise for his behaviour more than thirty-five years earlier. Shelagh first heard about this not from Spike, but from a reporter: 'Did he really say that? . . . Well, they both know where to find each other,' she remarked tartly.

Just as he was living his private life totally in public now, so he was making no secret of his disappointment that the BBC regarded him as a geriatric has-been. 'I'm an outsider,' he told one interviewer. 'I used to send scripts to the television people, but they'd send them back with "Unfunny" written on them . . . I guess I've gone out of fashion.' He added that he had recently written a script, for Eric Sykes and himself to star in, about two old comedians who could no longer find work. And he mused: 'I could have done that "One Leg in the Grave".'

In fact he was still occasionally booked as an actor. He played the ancient wizard Arnold of Todi in a Radio 4 adaptation of John Masefield's *The Box of Delights*. But when he wrote to John Cleese, asking for a part in the film *Fierce*

Creatures, all he got was a curt letter from a secretary saying all roles were filled. He was avenged when he and Secombe attended the launch of the BBC's plans to repeat *The Last Goon Show of All* on Radio 2 on 5 October 1997, the twenty-fifth anniversary of its original broadcast (some cut material was to be restored). 'The two surviving Goons proved they had lost none of their touch,' declared a reporter. 'Milligan, close to his 80th birthday, looked frail but retained his mischievous twinkle. When told that his friend John Cleese was unable to make the event, he retorted: "John Cleese is a miserable bastard. He is never able to make it."'

Norma Farnes – assisted by Chris Smith of the Goon Show Preservation Society – had now put together a history of the programme, called *The Goons: The Story*, and Spike ended his contribution to it with his usual grumble: 'Despite all the continued adulation the BBC are ignoring the *Goon Shows* on radio and my *Q* series on television, so to the BBC, you are a lot of bastards, and here endeth the chapter.' Meanwhile, on 14 October 1997, he gave a solo performance, *An Evening with Spike Milligan*, at St David's Hall, Cardiff, which proved he could still do it; the show was practically sold out, and got excellent reviews.

The irony was that the BBC, while refusing to take on any newly written work by him, granted him revered iconic status when it came to celebrating his past achievements. His eightieth birthday was marked, on Saturday, 18 April 1998 (two days after the actual event), by a 'Spike Night' on BBC2 in which Terry Wogan introduced homages from other comedians. There was also a documentary on him, an interview with him, and a version of his one-man show; but far from being gratified he described the evening as 'way over the top', and complained that 'Spike Night' had been 'demoted' to 'bloody BBC2. Aren't I good enough for BBC1?'

The top brass at the BBC also invited him to a celebratory lunch – but got a righteous reprimand from Spike: 'My contribution to world hunger is not to eat lunch. I've told them at the BBC to go and take a running jump. They'll be having lunch without me.' And the eightieth birthday documentary had caused trouble at home. 'I said for this television thing . . . that the love of my life was Toni Pontani, and Shelagh heard this . . . I said to her "That was fifty years ago." . . . But she didn't like [it].' Pressed for a comment on the Toni business, Shelagh said: 'Spike is not a grown-up. He's a naughty little boy sometimes . . . a romantic, a total romantic. He has to be in love.'

Spike told *Hello!* magazine that he feared Sean (now forty-three) would not be at the family celebrations of his birthday: 'He's in India at the moment . . . I haven't seen him for years . . .' Meanwhile *Hello!* let Spike give a very upbeat account of his own health: 'Every evening I get on the exercise bike and do half an hour's pedalling, about ten miles. I do sit-ups, press-ups, knee-bends. I never give a thought to how old I am. I wake up each morning and say, "Ah! Still alive. Good – I'll get up."'

He had said for some while that he wanted to mark his eightieth birthday with his first-ever parachute jump, and to everyone's horror it turned out that he was serious. Fortunately no doctor would sign the papers.

By the eightieth birthday he had stopped taking lithium, claiming that it had slowed him down. Undoubtedly much of the slowness was simply old age. Sabine Durrant, interviewing him for the *Guardian*, drew a very different picture from the exercise freak interviewed by *Hello!*:

The man I met was frail, he walked, head bent, at a slippered shuffle . . . His mouth doesn't always seem to obey the directions from his brain and . . . it is not altogether easy to understand what he says . . . When we met, he'd been in bed for three days with a bad back. 'I was on the exercise bike [and] did it too much . . .'

Just before Christmas 1998 he managed to give a performance of his one-man show at the London Palladium. Clive Davis wrote in *The Times* that it was almost 'a conventional poetry reading', and that he was 'too frail' to make much of the question-and-answer session at the end. 'What did he think death would be like? Much like now, he replied with a weary grin.'

The accolades continued to come in. On 1998's National Poetry Day (October) it was announced that 'On the Ning Nang Nong / Where the Cows go Bong!' had been voted the nation's favourite comic poem, in a BBC poll. And he was still occasionally working as an actor. In April 1999 he was on location with the BBC television adaptation of Mervyn Peake's *Gormenghast*, in which he had been cast as the aged headmaster Deadyawn. The producer, Estelle Daniel, gave this account of working with him:

Spike Milligan, most senior member of the cast, arrives to play the Headmaster. Much has gone before him in terms of advice about his needs and desires. We are reliably told he may not be able to tolerate much in the way of make-up and would probably most appreciate being left in peace in his dressing room.

After arrival and a friendly exchange, we tactfully leave him to rest in his dressing room. He puts his head round the door of the make-up room some while later, asking indignantly why he hasn't been done yet. Surely he must have white death make-up! Once on set he tells me he has read the Trilogy three times at different points in his life and is delighted to be part of the film. Whenever I attempt to add something to an anecdote he says, 'Don't jump on my jokes!' . . .

We set up for the scene and Spike eagerly asks Andy [Wilson] for some direction. Andy tells him rather ruefully that his function in the scene is to sleep throughout. Distinguished snoring on the first take . . .

The cast for the *Gormenghast* school scenes included Stephen Fry, who says it was the only time he worked with Spike – though they met on a few other occasions: 'You never knew whether he was going to fall into your arms or tell you to bugger off. He did have an endearing habit (not) of rushing up and flicking the cigarette out of my mouth with the cry of "There! Saved your life."'

Four months after *Gormenghast*, Spike was Paul Merton's guest on the BBC2 chat show with the Orwellian title *Room 101*. Invited to consign people or things he hated to oblivion, he did so with an anger that many found shocking. 'The inventor of Muzak committed suicide,' he gleefully told presenter Paul Merton, 'and I sent his wife a congratulatory telegram.'[1] His wishes for the bumptious media celebrity Chris Evans were 'leprosy' and 'an early death'. The *Guardian* reviewer commented that this only just managed to be funny. But he could still come up with quality jokes. Richard Ingrams recalls:

In later years he became a regular attender of the *Oldie* literary lunches at Simpson's. I was sitting next to him . . . when he suddenly asked, 'Why are they serving bread-and-butter?' 'Because it's Lent, Spike,' I replied. 'When do we have to give it back?' he said, without a second's hesitation.

Sometimes he would sit in silence looking rather glum, and it was during one of these silences that Barry Cryer tried to cheer him up, whispering, 'You realise, Spike, there are a lot of paedophiles here at this lunch.' Spike looked at him sorrowfully. 'Why do you hate us?' he asked.

---

[1] His hatred of Muzak could lead to some splendidly Milliganesque situations. 'In phoning Qantas,' he recalls, 'I was put on to "hold music". When I finally got through to the man, I said: "Just a minute", I then sang him a whole chorus of *Hey Jude*, which seemed to baffle him entirely.'

By the autumn of 1999, Harry Secombe was recovering from a stroke and confined to a wheelchair, 'so I can't get out easily or read very well,' Secombe told the *Guardian*. 'Spike . . . came to tea recently, but complained at the time it took to get to my home.' Spike had grumbled to Anthony Clare (around 1991):

Secombe seems totally enclosed in his Welshness. He never comes out. When you phone up there's always a Welsh voice on the phone . . . very clannish. He must be a sanctimonious bastard. He does that TV God slot and he never goes to church, never says a prayer . . . He was always easy to know – a bit insecure, I suppose.

Secombe, presumably unaware of all these quibbles, reported delightedly, in November 1999, that Spike had sent him a fax which said: 'I hope you go before me because I don't want you singing at my funeral.'

A few months later, Spike was in front of a TV camera to read his children's book *Badjelly the Witch* for an animated film made by Ragdoll Productions, the company behind the Teletubbies. Anne Wood, Creative Director of Ragdoll, says:

I thought he was the Edward Lear of our time. We'd been talking about it for years, and eventually Norma Farnes rang me up and said, 'If you don't do it soon, he's going to die.'

I was a little nervous, because he came doddering up the path, and he obviously hadn't read the script. But he loved doing the sound-recording, and soon started changing things – improvising away – so we rapidly had to absorb those changes into what we were going to film in vision! We shot him reading the story, and drawing, and we made an animation out of that – bringing his own pictures to life on the page, in black and white.

He had a good day, and actually thanked me when he left, which was very unusual! Norma said, 'That doesn't happen very often.'

Around this time, Rod Green left Virgin Books, and lost touch with Spike. 'I last saw him in the spring of 2000, just before I left Virgin. During the six or seven years I knew him, I'd seen his health deteriorate, but the last time I saw him he was actually looking better, walking better, and feeling more lively. Then he had a bad illness, renal failure, and I think he went very swiftly downhill from then. But I'm glad to say the last time I saw him, he was still sparky, still laughing – and still being rude!'

*

Robin Littlefield, an American girl whom Spike's son Sean had met in India and with whom he was having a relationship, first met Spike at the restaurant meal to celebrate his eighty-second birthday, in April 2000, and says that the encounter was a mostly negative experience: 'He was basically very distant with everyone. I found it very hard to have a conversation with him. I thought he wasn't terribly interested in anything, or anybody, including himself.'

Sean and his half-sister Jane had told Robin that when they were growing up, Spike was a wonderful father, 'and I've seen family photos and videos to prove it,' says Robin, 'and there's the children's poetry. But I think when they got older, he didn't know how to relate to them. The children were damaged by this. But then I would see Sean with Spike, and it was obvious that Spike loved him so much.'

Did the children really feel uncomfortable about their father? 'Not Jane. She's the one who should feel most bitter, because of Spike's extra-marital affairs while her mother Paddy was dying. But Jane's always been totally devoted to him.'

In September 2000, Sean and Robin went to America:

We arrived in Boston, and there was a message from Silé saying that Spike had gone into hospital. And no one knew whether he was going to live, and Sean was on the phone to him, and there was this panic going on. But when we got back in November or so, he was out of hospital and at home.

He was also working again, albeit merely for a stills photographer. 'Playboy Peter Stringfellow and legendary comedian Spike Milligan are the latest stars to lend their faces to a UK press and poster campaign for Aer Lingus,' reported the *Guardian* at the end of September 2000.

The ads will promote the frequency of Aer Lingus flights and the company's membership of the Oneworld airline alliance. One ad features a photograph of Stringfellow alongside copy that reads 'Being unfaithful has its benefits'. This refers to the airline's frequent flyer scheme. The second spot features Milligan with his eyes closed, while the copy reads 'The late Spike Milligan?'. This will be followed three days later by a second ad featuring an animated Milligan and the line 'The late Spike Milligan? Not likely.'

The photos of Spike – displayed on London Underground platforms – were magnificent. And while they were on display, the *Guardian* marked National Poetry Day 2000 by publishing the league table of sales of poetry books by living poets. Spike came ninth, well behind Ted Hughes (the top of the league, with sales comfortably in six figures), but beating Andrew Motion, the Poet Laureate.

Then, in the New Year's Honours, announced on 30 December 2000: 'Hon KBE: Terence Alan "Spike" Milligan, services to entertainment.' Evidently he had grovelled enough.

When Shelagh told him he had been given a knighthood,

he simply said, 'Help!' But she told the press he was 'deeply pleased'. The knighthood was conferred by Prince Charles at St James's Palace on 1 March 2001. Press reports stated that Spike was now 'recovering from severe kidney failure', and he looks very feeble and frail in photographs of the occasion.

Harry Secombe – who had been knighted some while earlier – died the following month, at the age of seventy-nine. Spike forgot his niggling criticisms of his fellow Goon, and told the press: 'I grieve for an unbelievable friend.' Michael Bentine had died in 1996, so Spike was now the one remaining Goon. Reviewing one of his TV appearances, Gary Bushell of the *Sun* wrote: 'I wish someone would do a deal with God and let Spike Milligan live forever.' Spike's response was: 'I wouldn't stop him.'

New projects still interested him. When it was announced that Richard Attenborough was to star in a film of *Puckoon* (in the role of the author-narrator), Spike told the press that seeing his novel on screen 'may be the last dream he ever has as he is now 82 and not in the best of health'. His message to the director was: 'No hold-ups. I may pop off at any time!'[2]

He was too frail to attend a recording of a very early (untitled) *Goon Show* script, broadcast by Radio 2 on 29 May 2001, as part of an evening to mark the fiftieth anniversary of the first edition of *Crazy People*. Andrew Secombe (Harry's son), Jeffrey Holland and Jon Glover took the principal roles, with announcements by Christopher Timothy (Andrew's son, and a well-known actor), and music from Lance Ellington (Ray's son) and harmonica player Harry Pitch. The evening, presented by Eddie Izzard, also included an informal epilogue by Prince Charles, reminiscing off the cuff: 'Of course I can still sing *The Ying-Tong Song* – I'm not going to do it now!'

[2] The film was released a year after his death.

In August, users of the BBC website were invited to choose the Funniest Man of the Millennium. Spike was voted top, with John Cleese and Billy Connolly in second and third places. The blurb to the paperback of Spike's novel *The Murphy* (another story of the *Puckoon/The Looney* type), which was published during 2001, rightly declared that he was now 'regarded by many as the father of modern comedy'.

In December, the *Daily Express* reported that

ill health . . . is making him a virtual recluse . . . Ailing Spike, who has survived a heart by-pass operation and kidney failure, has hardly been seen in public since picking up his honorary knighthood . . . in March . . . He was . . . unable to see [his daughter] Jane make her West End debut starring in *Return to the Forbidden Planet* at London's Savoy Theatre last week. 'Dad is a bit frail,' explained his concerned daughter . . .

*

Robin Littlefield described what she saw of Spike and Shelagh around this time:

Shelagh did love Spike – one night we had a conversation about love, and she said he was the love of her life. And I really did feel this was true. But Spike would have been a very difficult person to live with. You'd have to be very happy and secure in yourself to be with him, because he would never give you anything emotionally, and I think that over time, that would make you become bitter.

What I saw was a woman who probably did initially love him, wanted to please him, but became over time sort of damaged, so that there were probably two sides going on – loving him, but being very hurt.

I saw Spike in hospital, one of the times when he was thought to be dying. He looked radiant, like an angel or a child; all the hardness and lines on his face were gone. His short-term memory seemed to have packed up, so that he'd ask the same questions – where was Sean, when would he be leaving this place? I think he was scared of dying, but on the other hand he didn't understand how ill he was.

Towards the end, they had nurses for him at home.

*

The end came in the early hours of Wednesday, 27 February 2002:

Spike Milligan dies at 83 . . . at his Sussex home, his agent announced today. [He] was surrounded by his family when he died of kidney failure early this morning . . . Norma Farnes, his agent and manager, said: 'For 35 years he has been the dynamo in my life and he was my dearest friend. I will miss him terribly.' . . . Jenny Abramsky, BBC director of radio, said: 'He was a genius . . . He was unmatched anywhere.'

Asked what he felt about death, he had often said: 'I don't mind dying. I just don't want to be there when it happens.' On a TV programme called 'The Obituary Show' he had remarked: 'I'd like to be buried in a washing machine, just to puzzle archaeologists – "This chap seems to have been *washed* to death."' And what would his epitaph be? 'I TOLD YOU I WAS ILL.'

According to *The Times*, he had not believed in an afterlife: '"I don't believe in Heaven and Hell," he once said. "When you snuff it you just go."' The *Guardian*, however, alleged that 'Milligan was in two minds about the existence of heaven. Once he said: "I'd like to go there. But if Jeffrey Archer is there I want to go to Lewisham."'

The funeral was on 8 March at St Anthony's Catholic Church in Rye. All six children were there, including James and Romany. Peter Sellers's son Michael (who had for a while been Sean Milligan's partner in a decorating business) read passages from Spike's favourite poems. Prince Charles sent a wreath of roses with the message: 'For dear Spike – In grateful and affectionate memory.'

James and his mother Margaret sat at the back of the church, and afterwards James complained in the *Daily Mail* that the rest of the family (except Jane) had made him feel left out, and that he had difficulty in finding out where the burial was taking place. It was in nearby Winchelsea, where the coffin – draped in the Irish flag – was lowered into the ground to the sound of a lone piper.[3]

The memorial service was held in London on 24 June. It included Jane Milligan singing a song by Spike and Alan Clare, and among the readers were Stephen Fry and Eddie Izzard, both of whom went in for some slightly uncertain clowning. No one seemed aware that St Martin-in-the-Fields, where the service was taking place, had been blown up by the Goons in *The Starlings*. However, there was a real *frisson* when Harry Secombe's son David reminded the congregation of Spike's message to his father – 'I hope you go before me because I don't want you singing at my funeral' – and went on: 'However, we have found Harry's recording of "Guide me, O thou great Redeemer".' And that fine Welsh tenor rang out through St Martin's before we all joined in.

*

Prince Charles apparently couldn't make it to the memorial

---

[3] A year after Spike's death the *Mail on Sunday* (16 February 2003) reported that his children were in dispute with Shelagh over his will. This reportedly left only the royalty income to the children and the residue, including the house, to Shelagh. The children were allegedly trying to have this current will made invalid and an earlier one reinstated which left them a share of the house as well. Shelagh responded that she would inherit little more than the house because Spike's nursing fees had used up much of the capital.

service, which seemed a little odd (surely a mutually convenient date could have been found); and when one of Spike's
showbiz friends had dinner at Highgrove a few weeks later,
and kindly asked Charles on my behalf whether he would
let me interview him for this book, the answer was no.

'Basically he's pretty ambivalent about Spike to say the
least,' wrote my distinguished go-between.

He'd have liked to have been able to come to the memorial, but
as far as talking or saying anything about him goes, he won't go
much beyond the known facts of how much he enjoyed the Goons
as a child. Spike the man was different. It genuinely upset him
when Spike was rude about him or to him in public – all right,
it was a joke calling him a cringing little creep, but actually rather
wounding and difficult to respond to. Also the hunting and so
on, painting HRH as someone who doesn't care about animals
or the countryside. Impossible to respond to. So, in the end, Spike
was as frustrating for him as he was for many people. So he begs
to be excused from talking about him.

One's first reaction is that Prince Charles's attitude is
ridiculous – he must have known how much Spike valued
his friendship, and that the rudeness was how Spike treated
everyone. Unfortunately the words 'Spike was as frustrating
for him *as he was for many people*' ring all too true. As
John Antrobus puts it: 'The reason Spike has remained so
popular and beloved by the public is because they don't
know him!!!!' And Alan Clare: 'Spike is two people, number
one is the greatest guy you'll ever wish to meet, and number
two, I avoid like the plague.'

Certainly a lot of the difficult side of his character can
be attributed to his manic depression. Strikingly, when talking
to Anthony Clare for the book on depression, he rejected
the stereotype of it's-all-been-worth-it-for-my-art:

I cannot reassure myself that it has all been worthwhile . . . I do not hold with this romantic view of depression . . . that it is the downside of my achievements . . . I would have willingly forgone my fame and achievements to have been rid of it. What is more, I have known . . . many sufferers from manic depression who have had . . . no creative talent whatsoever – what do you say to them about the value of suffering this miserable disorder?

But he probably said this when depressed.

Norma Farnes wrote, towards the end of his life: 'If you ask Spike how he would like to be remembered, he'll always say "as a clown".' But elsewhere she has said: 'I don't think Spike is a funny man, a funny writer – yes, but . . . I know the man, and there's a lot more to Spike than him just being funny.' Spike himself told a meeting of the Goon Show Preservation Society: 'I'm such an un-funny person normally; I'm not a funny person at all – desperately serious all the time. But there was this obsession to write something, because I wanted the human race to look like idiots.'

Which brings us up smack, once again, against his misanthropic anger, a characteristic that seems to have no connection with his vast talent not merely to amuse, but to reduce us all (or at least those of us who find him funny) to helpless and enduring laughter. And, as I warned you at the beginning of the book, his *Goon Show* scripts seem to me easily his greatest achievement as a humorist. So, as a ghostly Andrew Timothy or Wallace Greenslade reads the closing announcements, and Max Geldray prepares to play us out with 'Crazy Rhythm', I'll leave the last word to Sir Neddie Seagoon, as he recalls the hilarious happiness of those Sunday recording sessions at the Camden: 'It was a time for hysteria and brandy, for soaring upward on the thermal currents of Milligan's imagination, a time for wishing every day of the week to be a Sunday.'

Bibliography

The abbreviations are those used in the Source Notes.

ABC archives: Video and audio recordings supplied by the Australian Broadcasting Commission

AH: Spike Milligan, *Adolf Hitler: My Part in His Downfall*, Penguin Books, 1972 (first published by Michael Joseph in 1971)

Antrobus: John Antrobus, *Surviving Spike Milligan*, Robson Books, 2002

Barber: Lynn Barber, 'The Unforgiving Goon', *Sunday Correspondent*, 1 September 1990

Bentine: Michael Bentine, *The Long Banana Skin*, Wolfe Publishing, 1975

BM: *The Bedside Milligan, or, read your way to insomnia*, Margaret and Jack Hobbs, 1969

BOG: *The Book of the Goons,* incorporating a new selection of Spike Milligan's *Goon Show* scripts . . . , Robson Books, 1974

Bradbury & McGrath: David Bradbury and Joe McGrath, *Now* That's *Funny! Conversations with Comedy Writers*, Methuen, 1998

BSR: Spike Milligan and John Antrobus, *The Bedsitting Room*, Tandem, 1972

Bullets: Spike Milligan, *Where Have All the Bullets Gone?*, Penguin Books, 1986 (first published by M. & J. Hobbs and Michael Joseph in 1985)

Celebration: Spike Milligan: A Celebration, compiled by Roger Sawyer, Virgin Books, 1996

Companion: Roger Wilmut and Jimmy Grafton, *The Goon Show Companion*, Robson Books, 1976

Coniam & Larcombe: Matthew Coniam and Richard Larcombe, 'The Great McGonagall': Spike Milligan's Lost Masterpiece', typescript lent by Joe McGrath

Cowley: Elizabeth Cowley, *A Tender Contempt*, Book Guild, 1998

Cowley interview: Interview with Elizabeth Cowley, London, 11.10.02

DB: Dominic Behan, *Milligan: the Life and Times of Spike Milligan*, Methuen, 1988

Depression: Spike Milligan and Anthony Clare, *Depression and How to Survive It*, Arrow, 1994

Draper: Alfred Draper with John Austin and Harry Edgington, *The Story of the Goons*, Everest Books, 1976

DRDS: Pauline Scudamore (ed.), *Dear Robert, Dear Spike: the Graves–Milligan Correspondence*, Alan Sutton, 1991

Duncan: Andrew Duncan, 'A Most Successful Ongoing Failure', January 1987, original source not known, reprinted in *GSPSN*, July 1987

Dustbin: Spike Milligan, *A Dustbin of Milligan*, Dennis Dobson, 1961

FA: Spike Milligan, *The Family Album: an illustrated autobiography*, Virgin Publishing, 1999

Games: Alexander Games (ed.), *The Essential Spike Milligan*, Fourth Estate, 2002

Goodbye Soldier: Spike Milligan, *Goodbye Soldier*, Penguin Books, 1987 (first published by Michael Joseph in 1986)

Goon Show Special: Goon Show Special, BBC Radio 2, 29.5.01

Green: Interview with Rod Green, London, 18.12.02

GS . . . WAC: Goon Show scripts on microfilm at the BBC Written Archives Centre, identified by the title (where there is one) and date of first transmission

GSPS: Archive of the Goon Show Preservation Society

GSPSN: The Goon Show Preservation Society Newsletter

GSS: The Goon Show Scripts, written and selected by Spike Milligan, Woburn Press, 1972

Harris: 'The clown with a talent to abuse', SM interviewed by Martyn Harris, reprinted in *GSPSN*, April 1995

Humphries: Barry Humphries, *My Life As Me*, Michael Joseph, 2002

Innes: Brian Innes, *A Long Way from Pasadena*, Montgalliard, 2001

Letters: Norma Farnes (ed.), *The Spike Milligan Letters*, M. & J. Hobbs in association with Michael Joseph, 1977

Lewis: Roger Lewis, *The Life and Death of Peter Sellers*, Arrow Books edition, 1995

Littlefield: Interview with Robin Littlefield, telephone, 22.12.02

Magic: Spike Milligan, *It Ends with Magic . . . : A Milligan Family Story*, Michael Joseph, 1990

McGrath: Interview with Joseph McGrath, London, 9.10.02

MGSS: *More Goon Show Scripts*, written and selected by Spike Milligan, Woburn Press, 1973

Monty: Spike Milligan, *Monty: His Part in My Victory*, Penguin Books, 1978 (first published by Michael Joseph in 1976)

More Letters: Norma Farnes (ed.), *More Spike Milligan Letters*, Penguin Books, 1985 (first published by M. & J. Hobbs and Michael Joseph in 1984)

Mussolini: Spike Milligan, *Mussolini: His Part in My Downfall*, Penguin Books, 1980 (first published by Michael Joseph in 1978)

Nathan: David Nathan, *The Laughtermakers*, Peter Owen, 1971

'Obituary Show': 'The Obituary Show', Channel 4, 10.12.91

O'Hagan: Interview with SM by Sean O'Hagan, *Observer*, 3.12.95

PS: Pauline Scudamore, *Spike Milligan: a biography*, Granada, 1985 [Page references are to the first edition. The book was reissued by Sutton Publishing in 2003, re-titled *Spike: a biography*, re-paginated, with new illustrations and a Postscript.]

Psych. Chair: In the Psychiatrist's Chair, SM interviewed by Anthony Clare, BBC Radio 4, June 1982

Puckoon: Spike Milligan, *Puckoon,* Penguin Books, 1965 (first published by Anthony Blond in 1963)

PW: Spike Milligan, *Peace Work*, Penguin Books, 1992 (first published by Michael Joseph in 1991)

'Relative Values': Interview with SM and his daughter Laura, *Sunday Times* magazine, 9.10.88

RGW: Spike Milligan, *'Rommel?' 'Gunner Who?'*, Penguin Books, 1976 (first published by Michael Joseph in 1974)

Room 101: Room 101, SM interviewed by Paul Merton, repeated on BBC2, 5.10.02

Sally Holloway: Interview with Sally Holloway, Oxfordshire, 26.9.02

Scunthorpe: Spike Milligan, *Scunthorpe Revisited,* Michael Joseph, 1989

SDS: Small Dreams of a Scorpion, poems by Spike Milligan, M. & J. Hobbs in association with Michael Joseph, 1972

Secombe, *AR*: Harry Secombe, *Arias and Raspberries*, Robson Books, 1989

Secombe, *SC*: Harry Secombe, *Strawberries and Cheam*, Robson Books, 1996

Shand: Interview with Neil Shand, telephone, 6.1.03

Simpson & Galton: Interview with Alan Simpson and Ray Galton, Hampton Court, 22.7.02

SJP: Spike Milligan papers at St John's College, Oxford

SMATB: Spike Milligan at the Beeb (SM reminiscing about his life and career, taken from a number of radio programmes). Two audio cassettes first released in 1998 in the BBC Radio Collection, ISBN 0563 38834X

Spiked!: Spiked! The comic genius of Spike Milligan, 1995 video cassette of television documentary, Telstar TVE 6014

Stark: Interview with Graham Stark, London, 9.1.03

TGTS: Norma Farnes (ed.), *The Goons: The Story,* Virgin Publishing, 1997

Ventham: Maxine Ventham (ed.), *Spike Milligan: His Part in Our Lives*, Robson Books, 2002

Vertue: Interview with Beryl Vertue, telephone, 8.1.03

VM: 'Interview with Van Morrison, performed by Spike Milligan, written down by Paul Du Noyer', Q *Magazine*, August 1989

WAC: Scripts and correspondence held at the BBC Written Archives Centre, Caversham Park, Reading

Wood: Interview with Anne Wood, telephone, 3.12.02

Source Notes

Quotations are identified by the first words. When two or more quotations from the same source follow each other with little intervening narrative I have used only the first quotation for identification. Abbreviations refer to the Bibliography.

1: The Rangoon Show

'May I shake', Ventham 114

'The *Goon Show*', *People*, 5.5.91

'I'm Irish', *Evening Standard*, 22.12.99

'I'm an Irishman', *The Tingle Factor*, BBC Radio 4, 11.7.89

'really much more English', 'Obituary Show'

'I was born', *Scunthorpe* 16ff

'my father', Ventham 111

'we were descended', *Sunday Express*, 6.12.92

'My father was like', *GSPSN*, January 1988

'Very Irish working-class', VM

'They were starved', ABC archives

'He lied about', DB 4

'Jazes Christ, Leo', DB 25

'He was so incensed', VM

'My old man', DB 7

'India was possibly', *SMATB*

(Footnote) 'based on all these', DB 33

'over-protective', Nathan 45

'I hope somebody', ABC archives

'Nuns are notoriously', *FA* 55

'So I went on', *Evening Standard*, 3.6.71

'I've been a clown', Nathan 45

'I didn't think', *PW* 32

'He [Leo] used to dress up', DB 50

'indulging his cowboy', *FA* 46, 61, 53, 66, 56, 58

'I sort of got lost', DB 44

'We were second class', *FA* 71

'England . . . had weather', DB 60

'It was the first time', *Spiked!*

'must have spent', *FA* 73

'the end of our vacation', DB 60

'He had no idea', *FA* 81

'I couldn't bear', DB 64

2: Catford days, Harlem nights

'Spike . . . is still', Ventham 185f

'Norbury, SW16', Kingsley Amis, *Memoirs*, Hutchinson, 1991, 16

'burglary and car theft', www.knowhere.co.uk

'Back in London', *Magic* 21

'the landlady was', *FA* 84, 85f

'She knew that Dad', DB 69

'He has a very', *FA* 90, 87

'I was a clerk', *FA* 87

'Oh, what did class', *PW* 32

'Around this time', *FA* 87

'I was in love', DB 76

'It was in', *FA* 87

'I just did it', *PW* 17

'I was earning', *FA* 88

'I've listened to music', VM

'I wanted an instrument', *FA* 89

'one hundred randy', *FA* 89

'I was at the back', DB 73

'It was four', *FA* 90, 92

'Eddie Lang', *PW* 17

'a bunch of spotty', *AH* 20

'I was blowing', VM

'started [such] an unending', *Depression* 105

'I'm a lapsed', O'Hagan

'It was soul-destroying', *FA* 93, 95; DB 74

'I'll never forget', DB 74

'Have pity', *FA* 94

'Mum was a great one', *Spiked!*

'One day an envelope', *AH* 19

3: Gunnery or . . . Goonery

'Joined the Regt.', PS 66

'an unreliable history', *Mussolini* 5

'Well, this makes him', ibid.

'The sergeant-major', DB 94, 92, 75

'Spike used to', *Spiked!*

'during an interval', *DRDS* 72

'We'd say that', DB 93

'we were enjoying', *Spiked!*

'very much in the vein', DB 92f, 90, 93, 95f

'6/10 [illegible] Guitar', WAC

'the Goons in', *AH* 77

'a hairy, hulking', Fred M. Grandinetti, *Popeye: an Illustrated History*, McFarland & Co Inc, 1994, 5

'There was a creature', Nathan 49

'Gunnery, or', *Mussolini* 112

'The door flew', *AH* 97

4: WHOOSH-BANG!

'Poor bastard', *AH* 133
'We brought the roof', DB 103
'I don't understand', *Monty* 29
'You couldn't believe', DB 109
'Did you miss', *Monty* 101
'It was as though', PS 99
'sunny Salerno', *Mussolini* 7, 97, 185
'The last thing', *Observer*, 15.3.70

5: Khaki limbo

'frigging around', *Bullets* 7, 38
'At times', *Psych. Chair*
'I couldn't speak', *Ventham* 13
'It was billed', *Bullets* 59
'Most musicians', *Celebration* 37
'someone from Mars', *Bullets* 201

6: Screaming, chattering and farting

'a little myopic', *Bullets* 201
'was the life', Secombe, *AR* 15f, 52, 78, 98, 118–22

'an entire', *PW* 36
'I didn't know', Secombe, *AR* 123
'a screaming duet', *Bullets* 202, 213, 215
'She was so', *Goodbye Soldier* 4, 59f

7: Grafton's

'He was the', *PW* 20
'The business was', Secombe, *AR* 142
'Poor thing', Bentine 152
'like a dynamo', *PW* 21
'My sides ached', Secombe, *AR* 141
'the youngest Intelligence', Bentine 86, 102, 149
'a whiff of the establishment', Secombe, *AR* 192
'The whole lot', Bentine 150
'This was the nearest', *PW* 38f, 26, 87
'Well-known comedians', *Companion* 13
'Heard *ITMA*', *Mussolini* 256
'*ITMA* which', *Goodbye Soldier* 186
'And she says', *GSPSN*, July 1988
'*Men at Work* was', *PW* 59
'I'm a long-time', BBC press handout, January 1968 (WAC)
'Spike used to', *TGTS* 168

'It was Spike', Simpson & Galton

'I passed an audition', Secombe, AR 145, 163, 150

'Demobbed at the same', Bentine 161

'In 1946', Companion 16, 26, 31

'he was a shrewd', PW 66

'I'd sit in Jimmy', O'Hagan

'I was writing', PW 59f

'the youthful', Bentine 161

8: I live in an attic

'was "spraunced" up', PW 60

'Peter wanted', FA 124f

'I have no personality', Lewis xviif, 34

'Of the four', Secombe, AR 188

'Peter was annoyed', Companion 30, 28

'at Huddersfield', Lewis 4n, 47, 51, 69, 76, 89, 57, 94, 100, 133, 163f

'an experimental', Humphrey Carpenter, The Envy of the World, Weidenfeld & Nicolson, 1996, 89

'He could perform', Barber

'Four young men', Draper 25

'King Of Goons', Secombe, AR 187

'it seemed to me', Companion 33

'a sort of Addams', Lewis 195

'Who are you?', Companion 32–4

'I didn't think', Lewis 195

'I hope you', FA 116

'imitations of wallpaper', PW 193f

'DESCRIPTION', WAC

'I had no confidence', PW 60, 197

'Normally a comic', FA 117f

'although really', Ventham 27f

'a relative', Lewis 179n

'quintessential "idiot" voice', Secombe, SC 19

'represent[s] the permanency', Nathan 48

'When they get', Guardian, 28.2.02

'Eccles, I have', Companion 27

'Eccles was really', DB 162

'Well, Spike', PW 226

'He was using', DB 134

'His mind was', Companion 26

'we all christened', Secombe, AR 190

'Spike's highs', Companion 25, 31

'hilarious', FA 126

'Arnold and Mrs Fringe', Lewis 213

'Pe-eggy – Pe-eggy', PW 192

'Always changing', Lewis 61

'Parp! Parp!', 'Tiddleywinks', GS 10.3.58, WAC

'Heavens', 'The Last Smoking Seagoon', *GS* 28.1.60, WAC

'Spike was still', *Companion* 34

'grotesque knockabout', PS 147

'scholarly and intelligently', Bentine 162

'a terrific chap', Carpenter, op. cit., 89

9: Crazy People

'This implicit', *Companion* 35

'the Milligan scripts', WAC

'Larry Stephens was', *TGTS* 172, 53f, 116

'Larry was the', *GSPSN*, November 1978

'Stephens's plots', *Companion* 114

'[Spike] has to be', Ventham 70f

'Mike would', *Companion* 39, 37

'Not many people', *FA* 127

'Do you know', *TGTS* 45

(Footnote) 'a little girl', *TGTS* 45

'We regret', Games 16

'They consisted of', *Companion* 37

'This was all right', *BOG* 9, 56

'any situation', *Companion* 37, 76

'I started writing', *Scunthorpe* 18

'This is the BBC', Games 3f, 7, 10f

'Gad, it's hot', *GS* 30.11.54, WAC

'I can see', Games 14

'The Goons got', *News Chronicle*, 31.5.51

'It was written', *Crazy People*, 11.6.51, WAC

'One collapsible', *Crazy People*, 18.6.51, WAC

'Control calling', *Crazy People*, 25.6.51, WAC

'Eccles!', *Crazy People*, 16.7.51, WAC

'I used to', Nathan 49

'My first port', Secombe, *AR* 206f

'We'd start', Lewis 197f

'mystified more', Secombe, *AR* 201

'The audience', *FA* 127f

10: Exit Pureheart

'Round this time', *FA* 128

'THE GOON SHOW', *Radio Times*, 22.1.52

'one puzzled planner', *Companion* 37

'How beautiful', *Crazy People*, 20.9.51, WAC

'that sheet-metal', McGrath; Bradbury & McGrath 17

'a solicitor', DB 149

'Why are you carrying', 'Her', GS 18.3.52, WAC

'The present state', *Sunday Times*, 2.3.52

'I think that the Goons', WAC

'turned into a sort', *Radio Times*, 7.11.52

'Peter Eton was', DB 148

'I was nearly', *TGTS* 120

'I honestly do', WAC

'I knew, intuitively', Bentine 186f

'a permanent', Lewis 199f

'He was full', DB 134

'I don't think', *Independent*, 17.4.90

'He [Bentine] wasn't', DB 150

'He was one', PS 154

'I went to', Bradbury & McGrath 17

'since Spike had', Ventham 43

'The *Goon Show*', WAC

'that wonderful', *Goodbye Soldier* 117

'big money', DB 135

'Sound effects', *FA* 136

'Dear Mr Milligan', WAC

'I had to write', Lewis 181

'Anyone who was', Simpson & Galton

'I was seen', *FA* 129f

'The madness', *TGTS* 116

11: Life's work

'Milligan walked straight', *Sun*, 14.11.70; *News of the World*, 8.11.70

'As I got out', *FA* 130

'No one seemed', *MGSS* 13

'they put me', *FA* 130f

'In the end', Draper 61

'I found I was', *TGTS* 116

'By February', *FA* 131

'Spike used to', Lewis 213f

'two so-called', WAC

'didn't have the sane', *GSPSN*, July 1988

'The monsoons broke', GS 28.4.53, WAC

'and step on it', GS 28.4.53, WAC

'HARRY *(as Wynford*', GS 3.6.55, WAC

'We created some', *TGTS* 58

'GRAMS: ORGAN STARTS', *GSS* 150

'Greenslade would be', WAC

'Greenslade . . . was an', *GSPSN*, October 1987

'Stop the show', *Sun-Herald* (Sydney, Australia), 8.8.82

'a young idiot', *Companion* 50

'Thank you', GS 4.12.53, WAC

'Bluebottle was a character', *SMATB*

'I am only', Lewis 55f

'Now uniformed doorman', DB 143

'Informs all visitors', GSS

'All the Goon', Lewis 211n

'The Goons gave', TGTS 120

'Major Denis Bloodnok', MGSS 151

'The Goons were', TGTS 120

'For years we'd', Lewis 212

'It's been quite', 'The Whistling Spy Enigma', GS 28.9.54, WAC

'Open your wallet', 'Dishonoured', GS 14.12.54, WAC

'a surreal response', Lewis 202

'Essentially, it is', Books & Art, December 1957

'Myself and Sellers', O'Hagan

'Peter [Sellers] could', FA 128f

'It was a time', Ventham 151, 153, 156, 83

'The Goon Show was less', BOG 10

(Footnote) 'Milligan had propounded', Companion 94

'the satire of', ibid. 99, 65

'he is a traditionalist', Ventham 75

'it is the only', WAC

'radio, where the pictures', TGTS 118

'the great mind medium', Nathan 50

'I didn't see', 'The Spanish Suitcase', GS 7.12.54, WAC

'very finely balanced', WAC

'St Martin's will', The Starlings (on Goon Show microfilm), 31.8.54, WAC

'The Starlings was', WAC

'Peter imitated', BOG 10

'the wittiest', WAC

'hundreds of letters', Radio Times, 4.2.55

12: Fun Factory

'I thought he', TGTS 164, 169

'I can remember', Simpson & Galton

'I didn't really', Vertue

'Hancock eventually', Simpson & Galton

'I was starving', Celebration 86

'We had about', Simpson & Galton

'By that time', Vertue

'We would come', Simpson & Galton

'Larry was a', Vertue

'I worked a long', FA 130

'quite an uncomplicated', Vertue

'I really had', TGTS 171, 169f

'more consistently high', Companion 55

'the Goon Show . . . began', The Critics, 23.1.55, WAC

'Mr T. Milligan', WAC

'Since the party', WAC

'I was to do', Secombe, SC 13

'When the door', Draper 37

'the steaming hell', Companion 83, 85

'Yes, frequently', Simpson & Galton

'She was a lovely', 'Relative Values'

'I couldn't go', FA 133

'Enter Milligan', WAC

'The agent', WAC

'With the pop', VM

13: So certain of roars of laughter

'absolute total disaster', Celebration 80

'this satirical saga', Evening Standard, 25.2.56

'we played out-of-work', Graham Stark, Remembering Peter Sellers, Chivers Press, 1991, 49

'In terms of', Guardian, 8.12.99

'I wasn't aware', McGrath

'one camera suddenly', Stark, op. cit., 49

'A man plays', Evening Standard, 3.5.56

'When you're feeling', FA 134

'For reasons best', WAC

'there was the danger', Companion 62

'The remark about', WAC

'The BBC doesn't', Reuters story, 5.5.58, WAC

'his now rather', WAC

'Remember that day', 'The Sinking of Westminster Pier', GS 15.2.55, WAC

'I couldn't believe', TGTS 59

'It has always', MGSS 10

'on his transistor', Sun, 22.6.77

'My father was', Epilogue to Goon Show Special, BBC Radio 2, 29.5.01

'dragged away protesting', Sunday Dispatch, 2.3.58

'I was grossly', WAC

'People used to', TGTS 101

'Yes, among the', Simpson & Galton

'On a typical', Secombe, SC 9

'Outside the Camden', Lewis 219

'We never saw', TGTS 101

'Peter [might have]', Lewis 217, 220

'Thanks for your', WAC

'For three days', Sunday Graphic, 22.12.57

'The typewriter clicking', Antrobus 111, 62f, 21, 37f

'eight Tryptizol', Scunthorpe 47, 119, 111f

'He has changed', Sunday Graphic, 22.12.57

'The point is', *Books & Art*, December 1957

14: Gone for ever

'Will you explain', WAC
'He cocked it up', *TGTS* 59
'Mr Milligan would', WAC
'Spike's moments', Simpson & Galton
'Larry Stephens', WAC
'In his Kensington', *Daily Mail*, 5.3.58
'the Great Barrier Reef', ABC archives
'Woy it is', *Dustbin* 66
'She came home', *FA* 138
'It's a fabulous', *News Chronicle*, 1.10.58
'At first', *Companion* 67
'I get bored', DB 142, 144
'doubtful', WAC
'Larry Stephens . . . died in', Bradbury & McGrath 15
'Larry Stephens died conveniently', *GSPSN*, July 1988
'I don't know', *Companion* 71
'I said to Peter', *Spiked!*; *Daily Express*, 13.2.60
'There was a wanker', *Spiked!*
'I think I grew', 'Relative Values'
'Children', *Independent*, 17.4.90

'I think I have stayed', *Psych. Chair*
'My earliest recollections', *Spiked!*
'I remember', *Observer*, 15.3.70
'a token', *FA* 139
'some heavy', *Sunday Express*, 31.3.96
'We, the undersigned', *Companion* 71
'I was allowed', *FA* 140
'old Milligan's a bit', 'The Last Smoking Seagoon', *GS* 28.1.60, WAC
'we would like', WAC
'macabre and doom-laden', Nathan 52, 55
'a glimmer of hope', WAC
'"GOONS" HAVE GONE', *Daily Herald*, 1.11.60
'I gave you', WAC
'I don't think', *FA* 136, 152
'most of those', *TGTS* 59

15: The unfunniest person in the world

'When the Goons', Nathan 50
'no new names', WAC
'Thank you for', WAC
'So fair is she', *Dustbin* 23
'All the time', McGrath
'seducing famous men', Cowley 99, 105

'I learnt later', *Daily Telegraph*, 16.1.98

'Physically I thought', Cowley interview; *Daily Telegraph*, 16.1.98

'There was a woman', *Express*, 4.10.98

'I have quite', McGrath

'Dear Jack', WAC

'I had the detective', *FA* 142

'Ray and I', Simpson & Galton

'I wanted to', Vertue

'No matter what', *Letters* 10

'way ahead of', Ventham 158

'I made that', *GSPSN*, October 1988

'And so', *Spiked!*

'Hollywood has discovered', *Daily Express*, 22.4.60

'I'd very much', *Evening Standard*, 3.6.71

'desperately unfunny', *FA* 145, 147

'How dare he!', *Dustbin* 37, 31

'Spymill', Cowley 102

'There is little', *TLS* 1.12.61

'to prove to', DB 34

'become a real', *SMATB*

'It was wonderful', *FA* 187

'a much longer', DB 36

'nearly drove me', *FA* 156

'Did you write', *Puckoon* 9

'I must be', DB 36

'born in India', *Puckoon* 88, 76–8

'the divorce was', *FA* 144

'fully realizing', ibid.

'The man my', *Observer*, 3.3.91

'When my first', *Psych. Chair*

'We lived in', 'Relative Values'

'They seemed to', *FA* 147

'It nearly drove', *Daily Mail*, 8.11.61

'Don't call me', *Daily Express*, 28.4.62

'Paddy was different', Simpson & Galton

'I've been trying', *Daily Mail*, 1.3.60

'the new Private', WAC

'convulsed', *Radio Times*, 31.8.61

'I told him', *Sunday Express*, 24.3.68

'Spike Milligan, crouched', *Evening Standard*, 14.12.61

'The most original', *Punch*, 20.12.61

'the best Ben', *BSR* 8

'Spike stole the', Ventham 95f

'with the door', *BSR* 7

'Mr Milligan and', *Observer*, 18.2.62

'a long talk', WAC

16: I do not do anything extraordinary

'We became firm', Ventham 62

'As Paddy and', *FA* 148

'On the way', *News of the World*, 29.4.62

'become a Hindu', DB 3

'Paddy nearly drove', *FA* 154

'With his best', *Spiked!*

'Occasionally the jokes', *Evening Standard*, 1.2.63

'started as a', *Plays and Players*, March 1963

'It is both', Gerald Frow, *The Mermaid Theatre: the First Ten Years*, Mermaid Theatre, 1969, 61

'brilliantly funny', Antrobus 81–4

'He was very naughty', Stark

'I wanted to', *Depression* 30

'You mean you', Humphries 176f

'absolutely magnificent', DB 167

'A telegram arrived', Humphries 177f

'I remember the', *FA* 148

'absolutely, abysmally depressed', *Depression* 29

'clowning during curtain', *News of the World*, 7.7.63

'tortured', *Depression* 29

'I think he', McGrath

'This is Spike', *Observer*, 13.10.63

'Puckoon . . . has a', PS 207

'as another "dustbin"', *TLS*, 18.10.63

'a sad disappointment', PS 206

'strung it together', *Sunday Times*, 13.10.63

'has a very sad', WAC

'Many moons ago', WAC

'generous', Humphries 181f

'The news in brief', ABC archives

'one of his deep', Innes 250

'the dreary years', *Scunthorpe* 112

'I must go down', *The Little Pot Boiler*, Dennis Dobson, 1963, 51

'impudent', Ventham 98

17: The funniest thing London has seen

'I myself don't', *DRDS* 32

'an ugly tree', Ventham 96

'I contacted Peter', *FA* 160

'I only went', *Sunday Express*, 24.3.68

'a telling, satirical', *Evening Standard*, 8.10.64

'we never seemed', Nathan 57

'I couldn't remember', *FA* 163

'Mr Milligan . . . delivers', *The Times*, 8.10.64

'There were these', *Daily Express*, 9.10.64

'Now any resemblance', *Evening Standard*, 8.10.64

'What he can', *Punch*, 14.10.64

'If this is', *Sunday Times*, 11.10.64

'Mr Milligan . . . cannot', *Daily Telegraph*, 8.10.64

'the funniest thing', advertisement in *Evening Standard*, 1.11.64

'the rogue genius', *Observer*, 11.10.64

'Spike Milligan's theatre', quoted by Coniam & Larcombe

'It was not', Nathan 49

'a hilarious evening', *News of the World*, 6.12.64

'They stayed there', telephone, 21.12.02

'I had my period', WAC

'I've suddenly realised', BBC Sound Archive, tape T28866

'Occupational therapy', *DRDS* 43

'still attends Mass', Harris

'absolutely overwhelmed', *DRDS* 5, vi

'somewhat gaga', Humphries 180

'My dear Robert', *DRDS* 10, 66

'I'd wait until', *DRDS* 33

'had a cold', *Daily Mail*, 8.4.65

'Is there a', Peter Evans, *Peter Sellers: the Mask Behind the Mask*, Severn House, revised edition, 1981, 185f

'When Milligan came', *Daily Express*, 22.4.65

'I wanted to', *Daily Sketch*, 23.4.65

'delightfully simple, really', *Daily Mail*, 23.4.65

'came from Lyons', *Daily Mail*, 6.4.66

'lay off the', *Daily Sketch*, 23.4.65

'I really resent', McGrath

'entered and walked', Ventham 116

'There were some', *FA* 172

'I'd loved *Oblomov*', to the author, 28.12.02

'Spike's flair for', Humphries 180

'The money he', *Sun*, 11.8.65

'He is deeply', *Daily Mail*, 17.2.64

'sat . . . as a pavement', *News of the World*, 15.8.65

'But Goon Spike', *Daily Sketch*, 9.11.65

'He was very', *People*, 3.1.83

'We don't know', *Sun*, 9.3.66

'I'm starting to', *Daily Mail*, 8.4.66

'*Oblomov* was still', *FA* 174

'Joan Greenwood wouldn't', Stark

'I am in love', *DRDS* 18

'Doing my best', *FA* 174f

'I did want', *DRDS* 41f

'I told Spike', *Celebration* 7

Source Notes

'I have a company', *Sunday Express*, 24.3.68
'He can find', Antrobus 148
'There would be', *Depression* 193–6
'I have had', Games 115
'I came here', *DRDS* 71
'There must be', *FA* 185

18: What's the Q for?

'Spike is obviously', WAC
'sparked ideas like', *Sunday Express*, 24.3.68
'Tell him, this', *DRDS* 77
'I have always', *FA* 208
'I'm having a', *DRDS* 80
'I asked his', Secombe, *SC* 15f
'were not on', Ventham 99
'Often she would', *Daily Mail*, 9.2.78
'he seem[s] to do', PS 242
'He was certainly', *Sun*, 28.2.68
'I'm writing two', *DRDS* 85
'We'd go off', Shand
'We have now', WAC
'The cruel thing', *DRDS* 96
'All his life', *Mussolini* 190
'In writing the series', *FA* 204
'I hate the', *Radio Times*, 20.3.69
'It was cyclical', Shand
'Good evening, or', *Q5*, episode 1, WAC

'I'm a quarter', telephone, 20.12.02
'I'd recently been', Shand
'Spike always took', *Celebration* 117
'Spike's intolerance and', Ventham 79
'He used to', Shand
'Helpppppppppp!', *Q5*, episode 1, WAC
'It was a bit', Nathan 59; *GSPSN*, October 1988
'One day that', *Q5*, episode 2, WAC
'Q5 . . . has moments', *Observer*, 6.4.69
'It was ungracious', *Sunday Times*, 30.3.69
'Guru, for the less', *Q5*, episode 3, WAC
'One is apparently', *Sun*, 21.11.69
'Excuse me', *Q5*, episode 4, WAC
'And now for', *Q5*, episode 5, WAC
'I was thinking', *Observer*, 3.10.99
'Terry Jones and', Ventham 157
'Milligan is the', DB 158
'It really shook', *FA* 204
'They [the Pythons]', 'Obituary Show'
'I'm afraid there's', Shand
'possibly the funniest', Spike Milligan, *Indefinite*

Articles, M. & J. Hobbs, 1981, 130f

'(*The door to the room*', Games 255

'living off my', *Guardian*, 17.3.70

'Basically, I'm working', *Evening Standard*, 3.6.71

'plastic penguins and', *Daily Telegraph*, 14.8.69

'searched the London', *Daily Mail*, 10.10.69

'Spike was wonderful', McGrath

'I wrote a 40,000-word', *Observer*, 15.3.70

'I used to', McGrath

'garnished', *AH* Preface

'disturbing to watch', *Sun*, 14.11.70

'*The Other Spike* was', *Sun*, 18.11.70

'declared [Milligan] to be', Ventham 102

'People who get', *Guardian*, 2.8.71

'Milligan was a', to the author, 20.11.02

'His moonlike face', to the author, 3.1.03

'beyond my wildest', *DRDS* 112

'very funny indeed', *Evening Standard*, 3.6.71

'Thank God!', *FA* 203

'clocked up 60,000', *DRDS* 116, 121

'That makes me', *Daily Mail*, 1.10.71

'many pages have', *FA* 206

'very weird, and', McGrath

'Spike didn't want', *TGTS* 2

19: Partially sound mind

'I really didn't', *TGTS* 61

'like a strange', *The Times*, 1.5.72

'One of your', *TGTS* 139

'on the toilet', Lewis 221

'deemed unsuitable', *TGTS* 184, 143

'To be honest', Secombe, *SC* 17

'I don't . . . think', *TGTS* 61

'I've got a', *The Times*, 1.5.72

'Here is a preview', *TGTS* 147, 151, 145, 149

'had difficulty in', Secombe, *SC* 15

'One good thing', *TGTS* 61

'brought me the', *FA* 213

'When the *Goon Shows*', *Goon Show Special*

'extremely well organised', *FA* 195

'Tickets [are]', *Daily Express*, 5.5.72

'Throughout the 1970s', DB 159

'Dick Lester asked', *FA* 211

'When I introduced', *Celebration* 81

'I was much', ABC archives

'he was going', *Celebration* 81

'He was a poetic', *Daily Express*, 9.8.73

'There were two', McGrath

'McGrath has confirmed', Coniam & Larcombe

'received a phone', *FA* 214

'He cannot sing', *Daily Mirror*, 12.12.73

'I wrote it', *FA* 217f

'loops and twirls', Antrobus 69

'It's been slaying', *Guardian*, 28.6.73

'Jack Hobbs, friend', Spike Milligan and Jack Hobbs, *William McGonagall Meets George Gershwin*, Michael Joseph, 1988, 5

'a very necessary', telephone, 9.10.02

'Jack could play', McGrath

'Waiting for me', *FA* 209

'We are closer', *RGW* 157

'shattered', PS 261

'I've not long', *DRDS* 122

'I dived into', *Express*, 16.4.98

'Oh God, that loony', *Daily Mail*, 13.4.96

'She was a nice', *Daily Mail*, 18.12.93

'I never thought', *Daily Express*, 20.9.82

'The only thing', unidentified cutting, GSPS archive

'I worked for', *People*, 3.1.83

'(1) I suggest', *Letters* 106, 112, 146

'It is very interesting', *Letters* 60f

'He was appalled', telephone, 9.10.02

'The ex-Goon got', *Sun*, 15.11.82

'I ripped the', *People*, 5.5.91

'I wanted to', *GSPSN*, October 1988

'He reads everything', *Daily Telegraph*, 18.6.74

'The Grand Theatre', *GSPSN*, n.d. (1975)

'sumptuous', *FA* 219

'and this made', *DRDS* 130f

'making sure that', *The Times*, 6.8.83

'his turreted mansion', unidentified cutting, GSPS archive

'I keep up', *Psych. Chair*

'I . . . put up', *FA* 208

'I was very', McGrath

'It is, as you', *GSPSN*, March 1975

'The series left', *GSPSN*, April–May 1976

'There is a fair', *GSPSN*, February 1978

'We wrote a', *Spiked!*

'I realise I', ibid.

'I am all', *More Letters* 189

'The mere mention', *Daily Mail*, 3.12.85

'went to see', *FA* 221f

'a doctor I knew', *News of the World*, 12.9.82

20: In the psychiatrist's chair

'in love again', *Daily Express*, 6.11.78

'Some of it', *GSPSN*, October 1979

'When we were', Ventham 152, 157

'Television interviews are', *GSPSN*, October 1979

'People assumed he', Ventham 141, 75

'What happens is', Nathan 59

'They were in', e-mail, 21.8.02

'Who's that bird', *Q9*, episode 6, WAC

'Trying to find', *Daily Star*, 23.7.80

'worth watching for', unidentified cutting, GSPS archive

'DEAR SPIKE', *More Letters* 118

'Terribly sombre event', unidentified cutting, GSPS archive

'Peter Sellers – he's', *The Tingle Factor*, BBC Radio 4, 11.7.89

'Spike, a fervent', *Daily Mail*, 20.7.81

'The ex-Goon', *Sun*, 30.7.81

'His fiancée . . . Shelagh', *Daily Mirror*, 2.3.82

'He was reasonably', *Depression* 14

'Others may think', quoted in John Baxter, *A Pound of Paper*, Doubleday, 2002, 195

'It's a gift', *Psych. Chair*

'I could find', Ventham 184

'Some people might', *Psych. Chair*

'Although he fires', *Evening Standard*, 28.9.82

'When inspiration fails', unidentified cutting, GSPS archive

'I don't believe', *GSPSN*, October 1988

'no idea', *People*, 3.1.83

'Spike made it', *Daily Mail*, 13.4.96

'I have a bit', *Sunday Times Magazine*, 13.11.83

'one of the sanest', Duncan

'We'd be patting', Shand

'Silé works as', *Daily Mail*, 11.5.83

'With the aid', *Daily Mirror*, 25.8.83

'I outraged my', DB 161

'Really, I don't', *Yorkshire Post*, 7.10.85

'always offering to', *Daily Star*, 20.5.86

'a teacup washed', Antrobus 139

'They were a', *Daily Mail*, 13.4.96; *GSPSN*, October 1998

'He sang a', *The Times*, 31.10.98

'THANKS FOR THE', *More Letters* 107

'Dear Von Charles', *Daily Telegraph*, 3.10.85

'Please, Spike, take', *Daily Star*, 7.2.86

'I shall have', *Daily Star*, 25.11.86

'along with a', Barber

'fucking lucky to', *People*, 13.12.87

'Palace insiders', *Sun*, 8.12.87

'Remember, if it', *Sunday Express*, 17.4.88

'I thought I', videotape, *Spike Milligan: Return of a Legend*, VVL VFC 12628

'It did show', *GSPSN*, January 1989

'the leper of', *Daily Express*, 8.4.86

'and they never', *Sun*, 8.4.86

'no plans for', *GSPSN*, August 1986

'I told him', *Guardian* online, 27.2.02

'They are only', Duncan

'Alternative comedy?', *GSPSN*, October 1988

'the history of', DB 154

'What prompted him', *GSPSN*, January 1988

'Fortunately I have', *GSPSN*, January 1989

'It was quite', Sally Holloway

'I lie in', *GSPSN*, January 1989

'What a long-suffering', Sally Holloway

'I'm writing a', *GSPSN*, January 1989

'Two chaps came', *Evening News*, 6.3.87

'He looks as', *Independent*, 15.4.88

'a rented oasthouse', *GSPSN*, January and July 1988

'On the outside', Sally Holloway

'I used to', *Daily Star*, 9.5.92

'As you get', VM

'offered me a', Harris

'Only HE could', *GSPSN*, April 1997

'It's not quiet', *Sunday Express*, 6.12.92

'the twinkling lights', *Room 101*

'We should have', *Sunday Express*, 10.9.95

'Across and around', VM

'She can't even', *GSPSN*, October 1990

'That's a leading', *The List*, 17–23.8.90

'but no one else', *Sunday Express*, 10.9.95

'I introduced myself', *Evening Standard*, 18.11.97

'He should be', *GSPSN*,
  October 1990
'Yes, like Wormwood',
  Antrobus 102
'He is 72', Barber
'the world's number', *Daily
  Mail*, 18.12.93
'In November 1990',
  Depression 15
'was now so', *Depression* 17
'I worked it', *Sunday Express*,
  6.12.92
'It is a little', *Depression* 18f
'Don't tell me', *Observer*,
  3.3.91
'How can you', *Depression*
  117f, 20
'Take poor Trevor', Barber
'Yes. Even when', *Depression*
  119, 21f, 30, 6

21: Just one of those things

'wasn't upset', *Depression* 113f
'There must be', *News of the
  World*, 19.1.92
'He always brings', *Daily
  Mail*, 18.12.93
'while her mother', *Sunday
  Express*, 31.3.96
'It was Châteauneuf',
  Depression 115
'Milligan's humour is', *GSPSN*,
  July 1994, May 2001
'Of course I', *Express*,
  16.4.98

'I am not going', *Daily
  Telegraph*, 5.12.94
'There was a moment',
  Ventham 198
'I suppose a', *Guardian*
  online, 27.2.02
'Charles has written', *Today*,
  25.1.95
'Try a little', *Express*, 16.4.98
'I didn't know', *GSPSN*,
  January 1995, April 1995
'There was still', Green
'Missing from the', *Today*,
  20.2.95
'is about to', *Daily Mail*,
  25.10.95
'I started telling', *Express*,
  5.3.97

22: I told you I was ill

'It's been wonderful',
  Observer, 24.3.96
'close friend', *Sunday Express*,
  31.3.96
'I am not', *Daily Mail*,
  13.4.96
'Mr Milligan, how', *Daily
  Telegraph*, 10.10.96
'Over-population is', *GSPSN*,
  January 1998
'evened out', *Daily Mail*, 13.4.96
'He always said', Green
'You don't talk', O'Hagan
'Why I didn't', *Daily
  Telegraph*, 10.10.96

'Did he really', *Daily Mail*, 13.4.96

'I'm an outsider', O'Hagan

'I could have', Harris

'The two surviving', *GSPSN*, January 1998

'Despite all the', *TGTS* 61

'way over the top', *Hello!* magazine, 18.4.98

'demoted', *Guardian*, 11.4.98

'My contribution to', *Hello!* magazine, 18.4.98

'I said for this', *Guardian*, 11.4.98

'Spike is not', *Express*, 16.4.98

'He's in India', *Hello!* magazine, 18.4.98

'The man I', *Guardian*, 11.4.98

'a conventional poetry', *The Times*, 22.12.98

'Spike Milligan, most', Estelle Daniel, *The Art of Gormenghast: The Making of a Television Fantasy*, HarperCollins Entertainment, 2000, quoted on BBC website

'You never knew', e-mail, 16.7.02

'The inventor of', *Room 101*

'In later years', Ventham 205

'so I can't get', *Guardian*, 3.9.99

'Secombe seems totally', *Depression* 28

'I hope you go', *Observer*, 7.11.99

'I thought he', Wood

'I last saw', Green

'He was basically', Littlefield

'Playboy Peter Stringfellow', *Guardian*, 28.9.00

'Help!', *Mirror*, 30.12.00

'recovering from severe', *Express*, 2.3.01

'I grieve for', *Guardian*, 12.4.01

'I wish someone', *TGTS* 7

'may be the last', *Guardian*, 12.6.01

'ill health . . . is', *Daily Express*, 17.12.01

'Shelagh did love', Littlefield

'Spike Milligan dies', *Guardian* online, 27.2.02

'I don't mind', Ventham 186

'I'd like to be', 'Obituary Show'

'I TOLD YOU I WAS ILL', O'Hagan

'I don't believe', *The Times*, 9.3.02

'Milligan was in', *Guardian* online, 27.2.02

'For dear Spike', *Sun*, 9.3.02

'The reason Spike', Ventham 71

'Spike is two', *Letters* 10

'I cannot reassure', *Depression* 41

'If you ask', *Celebration* 7

'I don't think', *Letters* 9

'I'm such an', *GSPSN*, January 1988

'It was a time', *GSS* 190

Acknowledgements

My thanks to:

Emma Kingsley, for suggesting that I write the book; Shelagh Milligan, for writing me a friendly letter – even if, after that, there was silence; Norma Farnes, for giving those crucial permissions (see below) – and I look forward to Norma's own book on Spike; and Ray Galton and Alan Simpson, for agreeing to be the first people I interviewed, and talking so entertainingly about him.

They were followed by others who had much to say or write: John Antrobus, Alan Brooke, Elizabeth Cowley, David Freeman, Philip French, Stephen Fry, Rod Green, John Heald, Sally Holloway, Richard Ingrams, Brian Innes, Roger Lewis, Robin Littlefield, Christopher Mason, Joe McGrath, Margaret Maughan, James Maughan-Milligan, Michael Pickwoad, Libby Purves, Pauline Scudamore, Neil Shand, Graham Stark, Beryl Vertue and Anne Wood.

Meanwhile, at the BBC Written Archives Centre, Jeff Walden excelled even his own previous record as the world's fastest and most knowledgeable researcher, as (with the blessing of Jacquie Kavanagh, head of the WAC) he made it possible for me to study the whole of Spike's BBC career. Over in Australia, Anna Burns of ABC played a similar role with regard to Milligan in Oz.

Early on, I made contact with the Goon Show Preservation Society, whose archivist Steve Arnold quickly became a friend as well as a tireless helper. Another GSPS stalwart, Tina Hammond, kindly let me have one of the society's precious allocation of tickets for Spike's memorial service.

My psychiatrist cousin-in-law Sara Forman read the first draft of the book, and corrected some misconceptions about manic depression. The film expert Alan Frank found me some rare Spike movies.

Then there were the individuals who contributed all kinds of backstage help: Roderick Balkham, Rebecca Bean, Julian Birkett, Christopher Cook, Russell Davies, Mike Diprose, John Dugdale, Alex Games, Caroline Gascoigne, Vanessa Green, Penelope Gresford, Alec and Susan Hamilton, John Kaufman, Christopher Lloyd, Ned Sherrin, Alyn Shipton, Hilary Stafford-Clark and Simon Winder.

My agent Felicity Bryan worked at top speed to find the right publisher, almost the moment that Spike died, and I was fortunate enough to land up initially with an old friend, Roland Philipps at Hodder & Stoughton. Roland then moved to Albemarle Street to look after the newly Hodder-owned John Murray, and his successor as publishing director and my editor turned out to be Rowena Webb, who is now a friend too. Other Hodder credits: thanks to Jacqui Lewis (editorial) and Juliet Brightmore (pictures), while Morag Lyall was a sensitive and helpful copy-editor.

Now to the copyright credits. My thanks to the following, for permission to quote material as stated:

Norma Farnes and Spike Milligan Productions Ltd, for quotations from unpublished scripts and letters by Milligan. The BBC, for material drawn from internal memoranda. Andrew Duncan, for the use of an interview. Roger Lewis, for quotes from his book *The Life and Death of Peter Sellers*. Methuen Publishing Ltd, for material from Dominic Behan, *Milligan*. Penguin Books Ltd, for quotes from the seven volumes of Spike's war memoirs. Random House Group, for quotes from *Depression and How to Survive It*. Robson Books, for quotes from John Antrobus, *Surviving Spike Milligan*; Harry Secombe, *Strawberries and Cheam* and *Arias and Raspberries*; Maxine Ventham (editor), *Spike Milligan:*

His Part in Our Lives; and Roger Wilmut and Jimmy Grafton, *The Goon Show Companion*. Virgin Books Ltd for quotes from Milligan's *The Family Album*, from *The Goons: the Story*, and from *A Children's Treasury of Milligan*. Finally, to the syndication departments of all those newspapers who licensed quotations.

All efforts have been made to trace the copyrights of passages quoted and photographs reproduced in the book. Any aggrieved person is encouraged to contact the publisher so that amends may be made.

End of grovel department. Finally let me consign to a Goonish fate the author of a previous book on Spike who refused to let me quote from some unique interviews with him in it, on the grounds that I should write my own book and not draw on anyone else's (!) . . . and the person who bred a foul virus that killed off my computer the day after I'd finished the first draft. (But I had a back-up – ha ha ha!) To them, I wish this:

FX: WHOOSH – SPLOSH – BATTER PUDDING HITTING THEM
BOTH: Ooooooooooooooooooooooooohohohohohohohoho-hohohohoho . . .
ORCHESTRA: SIGNATURE TUNE.
(Applause)
MAX & ORCHESTRA: 'CRAZY RHYTHM' PLAYOUT.

Index

'SM' indicates Spike Milligan

56th Heavy Regiment Royal
  Artillery 32
  D Battery 33, 35, 36, 37, 40, 41,
    42, 44, 45, 46, 51, 53–4, 55,
    56–7, 59, 61, 282, 299, 327
ABC television 187, 194, 228, 240,
  241
Abramsky, Jenny 376
Abse, Dannie 243, 267
Adelphi Theatre, London 306, 307
Admiral Owen Inn, Sandwich, Kent
  65
*Adolf Hitler: My Part in His
  Downfall* (film) 6, 295
Aeolian Hall, New Bond Street,
  London 112, 119, 144
Aer Lingus 373
Afragola camp, near Naples, Italy
  60
Ahmadnagar, India: SM born in 5
Albert Bridge, Chelsea, London 262
Alberts, the 172, 193, 220
Aldermaston Marches 148, 213
Alexandra Palace, London 82
Algiers 48–9, 53
Alice (film) 294–5
Allen, 'Poppa' 79
Allen's bar, Windmill Street, London
  79
Amalfi, Italy 62, 71
Amalfi Rest Camp 56

Ambrose 67
Amis, Kingsley 18
Andrews, Eamonn 205, 299
Angers, Avril 109n
Angry Young Men 147
Animals' Vigilantes 304
Ann Lenner Trio 99
Anne, HRH The Princess Royal
  254, 291
Announcer *see* Greenslade, Wallace;
  Timothy, Andrew
Antrobus, John 25n, 110–11, 148,
  158, 180–83, 186, 210, 222, 223,
  261, 263n, 298, 326, 378
  The Bedsitting Room (with SM)
    222, 229–30, 231–2
  The Milligan Papers 330
Aragno, Riccardo 248
Archer, Jeffrey 376
Aristophanes 149
Army Welfare Services Wardrobe 99
Arnhem, Battle of 78, 87
Arnolds, Sergeant 60
Askey, Arthur 83
Associated London Scripts (ALS)
  156–9, 181, 185, 209, 222, 223
Associated Press photo library 23,
  65
Associated Rediffusion 169, 170,
  172
Atkins, Robert 80

Attenborough, Sir David 310, 311

Attenborough, Sir Richard, Baron 374

Attlee, Clement 65

Australian *TV Times* 229

Ayrton, Michael 153–4, 305

Babes in the Wood 328

Baiano, Italy 61

Band Wagon (radio programme) 83

Banerjee (SM and Sellers) 151

Bannister, Miss Minnie (SM) 239
  geriatric 18
  saxophone-playing 37
  and *Bumblethorpe* 109n
  first appearance 124
  better imagined than seen 130
  the voice 131n
  oyster sexer 142–3
  endless staircases in her bungalow 150
  SM's car named after her 162

Barbary Coast show 74

Barber, John 306–7

Barber, Lynn 327, 338–9, 342

Bari 73

Barker, Eric 109n

Barnet, Greater London 323, 334, 335

BBC1 353, 367

BBC2 251, 295, 315, 323, 357n, 367, 370

BBC (British Broadcasting Corporation)
  SM auditions at the Maida Vale studios (1941) 43
  watches the *Goon Show* for 'smut' 56
  Bill Hall Trio broadcasts 82
  radio comedy performers 82–3
  faith in the Goons 141, 142
  SM paid show by show 173
  SM's complaining letters 185–6

BBC Contracts Department 199

BBC Dance Orchestra 113, 127

BBC European Service 107

BBC General Overseas Service (later World Service) 151, 174

BBC Home Service 96n, 112, 117, 120n, 143, 152, 153, 188, 206

BBC Light Entertainment Department 177, 185, 199, 224, 237

BBC Light Programme 96, 117, 127, 205, 250

BBC Radio 2 367, 374

BBC Radio 4 61, 147, 195, 304, 317, 320, 366

BBC Regional Home Services 120

BBC Television 100, 166, 268

BBC Television Centre 311

BBC Third Programme 96

BBC Transcription Service 151

BBC Variety Department 98, 107, 112, 140, 175, 177

BBC Written Archives 109n, 114n

Beachcomber (J.B. Morton) 39, 84–5, 114, 264, 265, 266

Beatles 211, 227

Beauty Without Cruelty 294

Bedsitting Room, The (film) 263n, 318n

Behan, Dominic 7, 18n, 101, 189, 228, 294, 331

Belgaum, India 10

Bell, Peter Francis 303

Bennett, Lance-Bombardier Reg 62

Bentin, Adam 80

Bentine (Bentin), Michael xi, 89, 292, 317
  Secombe meets 79
  background 80
  wartime experiences 80
  captivated by SM 80
  artificially manic personality 88
  Third Division 96

Sellers' Castle 98
on Pat Dixon 105
ideas for *Goon Show* scripts 111
leaves the show 128–9, 141
sparring match between him and
   Sellers 129
jealousy between him and SM
   over ideas 129–30
visual style 130
SM's comments 130–31
Square World series 311
on SM's depression 339–40
death (1996) 131, 374
The Long Banana Skin 90
Bentley, Dick 83n
Bergen, Edgar 101
Bertorelli's Italian restaurant,
   Shepherd's Bush, London 181
Betjeman, John 5, 246
Betjeman Society 284
Beveridge, Mrs (housekeeper) 226
Bexhill-on-Sea, East Sussex 31–47,
   299, 328
Beyond the Fringe (satirical review)
   146, 147, 153, 213, 278, 318n
Bill Hall Trio 66–7, 71–2, 73, 81–2,
   88, 99
Bird, John 311
Birthday Honours 349
Bizerte docks, Tunisia 54
Black, Stanley 113, 127
Blackadder television series 338
Blackfriars, London 27
Blackpool 81
Blackshirts 25n, 233
Blagden, Judge 216
Blair, Tony 365
Blitz magazine 327
Blond, Anthony 257
Bloodnok, Major Denis (Sellers) 52,
   56, 98, 124–5, 165, 175, 196
creation of 10n, 81, 85
better imagined than seen 130

in 'bad taste' 145
catchphrase 149n
Blue Lagoon club, London 81
Bluebottle (Sellers) 17–18, 52, 93,
   110, 174, 293, 319, 327
Splutmuscle an early version of
   115
voice of 144
catchphrase 149n
immortality 150
and Finchley 165
Bluthal, John 239, 275, 276, 278,
   279, 280, 296, 310, 317, 330
Bologna 73
Books & Art 146
Bosch, Hieronymus 153
Boulting, John 250
Boulting, Roy 250
Bournemouth 263
Box of Delights, The (Radio 4)
   366
Boyd, PC Russell 303
Braden, Bernard 109, 156
Braine, John 147
Bremner, Rory 338
Brettell, Tommy 26
Bridge on the River Wye, The (LP)
   227, 318n
Brien, Alan 231
British Book Awards 353
British Comedy Awards 351
British Empire 14
British Raj 9, 10
British Union of Fascists 25
Broadcasting House, Portland Place,
   London 198, 233, 343, 354
Brook, General Sir Alan (later Lord
   Alanbrooke) 35
Brook, Peter: *The Empty Space* 249
Brook Street, London 209, 210
Brooke, Alan 298, 305
Brooks, Richard 272
Brough, Peter 155

Browell, John 178, 188, 189, 190, 287, 291, 292
Brown, Harry 114
Brown, Jacques 99, 111–12
Brown, Janet 98
Brown, Mike 121n
Brownhill Road School, Catford, London 15
Buckingham Palace, London 314, 326, 352
Budden, Lieutenant Cecil 41
Bumblethorpe radio series 109n
Buñuel, Luis 171
Burma 10, 11, 14, 15, 38, 109
Burnside family 5
Bushell, Gary 374
Butler Education Act (1944) 22
Butterworth, Peter 98
Bygraves, Max 78

Cable Street riot, East End, London (1936) 25
Calcutta 94
Calton Hill, Edinburgh 285
Cambridge University Tiddlywinks Club 176–7
Camden Theatre, north London 177, 178, 198, 291, 379
Camp X, Algiers 48, 50
Capri 73, 74
Carpenters, Udimore, near Rye, East Sussex 336, 338, 348, 354
Carr, Carole 113n
Carroll, Lewis 116, 150, 213, 294
Carthage 52
Case of the Mukkinese Battle Horn (film) 172–3
Caserta, near Naples 59, 63
Catford, south-east London 15, 18, 20, 26, 27, 33, 46
Catford Labour Exchange, London 30

Central Pool of Artists (CPA), Vomero, near Naples 66–73
Chan, Charlie 311
Channel 4 329, 338
Channel Nine 170, 313
Chaplin, Charlie 7, 102
Charles, HRH The Prince of Wales 3, 176, 254, 259, 267, 291, 293, 319, 325–8, 351–2, 374–5, 377
Checketts, Squadron Leader David 267
Chevreau, Cécile 113n
Chichester, West Sussex 328
Chieftains 337
Children's Favourites radio programme 205, 225, 238
Chilton, Charles 184, 223–4, 239
Chisholm, George 3, 128, 239
Chislehurst Laundry, Kent 24–5
Christian Science Publishing Society, Boston, Massachusetts 291
Christie, Agatha: *Ten Little Niggers* 313
Christie's auctioneers 319
Churchill, Randolph 273
Churchill, Sir Winston 65, 153, 175
Cinderella 340
Citizens' Advice Bureau 302
Clare, Alan 243, 307, 319, 377, 378
Clare, Anthony 17, 61, 195, 216–17, 233, 320–22, 323, 339–43, 349
    Depression and How to Survive It 339, 341, 343, 347, 378
Clark, Major Tony 63
Cleese, John 147, 148, 279, 315–16, 375
    Families and How to Survive Them (with Robin Skynner) 339
    Fierce Creatures 366–7
Clubbers 45

Index

Cobblers, William 'Mate' (Sellers) 143, 144, 230, 292

Coconut Grove club, London 81

Coe, Peter 221

Colleano, Bonar 109n

Collins, John 253

Combined Services Entertainment 73, 82

Comedy Theatre, London 249

Coniam, Matthew 297

Connolly, Bill 375

Connolly, Ray 285, 323

Connor, Kenneth 109n, 170, 189

Constable, John 34

Constitution Hill, London 326

Cook, Mary 99

Cook, Peter 138n, 153, 227, 233, 259, 317–18

Cooper, Tommy 78

Coronation of Queen Elizabeth II (1953) 140, 141

Cortez, Leon 109n

Counsell, John 41

Courtney, Mr (of Bexhill-on-Sea) 38

Coveney, Mike 310

Coventry Hippodrome 164–5

Coward, Noël 296

Cowley, Liz 5, 206–8, 282, 357–8
  A Tender Contempt 206–7

CPA *see* Central Pool of Artists

'Cranley, Betty' 65

Crazy Gang 107, 248

Crazy People see under Goon Show

Critics, The (arts review programme) 153, 163

Crosby, Bing 23, 25

Croydon Empire, Surrey 101

Crun, Henry (Sellers) 93, 98, 307
  geriatric 18
  first appearance 124
  better imagined than seen 130
  catchphrase 149n

Cryer, Barry 4, 255, 370

Cumberland House, Kensington High Street, London 159

Curran, Sir Charles 182n

Curry and Chips (ITV series) 276–7, 311

D Battery *see under* 56th Heavy Regiment Royal Artillery

D-Day 107

Daily Express 38, 85, 211, 219, 224, 248, 254, 260, 263, 294, 315, 375

Daily Herald 200

Daily Mail 137, 190, 197, 219, 220, 236, 249, 255, 259, 302, 313, 319, 325, 339–40, 354, 359, 365, 377

Daily Sketch 259

Daily Star 318

Daily Telegraph 216, 249, 259, 301, 302–3, 304, 306

Dale, Jim 295

Dale, Stanley 'Scruffy' 156, 157, 159

Dalí, Salvador 171

Danger – Men at Work radio comedy show 84, 99

Daniel, Estelle 369

Dartford, Kent 350

Davidson, Jim 184, 199, 224

Davies, Tanis 262–3

Davis, Clive 369

De La Warr Pavilion, Bexhill-on-Sea 36, 47

de Manio, Jack 206

Department of the Environment 327

Diana, HRH Princess 326

Dick Barton 115

Dickens, Charles 281

Dickens Farm, Barnet, Greater London 281

Dimmock, Peter 141

Dixon, Pat 96, 105–6, 111, 114, 150, 166, 173, 174–5, 179n, 184

Do Not Adjust Your Set 279
Dobson, Dennis 194, 196, 213
Does the Team Think? radio panel
  game 205
Dominion Monarch, SS 74
Donat, Robert 93, 94
Donegal 6
Dostoevsky, Fyodor 275
Douggan, Gunner 53
Douglas, James *see* Grafton, Jimmy
Down Among the Z-Men (film) 130
Draper, Alfred 138
  The Story of the Goons 97,
  164
Dublin 81, 214, 281
Duke of York's Theatre, London
  231, 234, 244
Dumont, Margaret 84
Duncan, Andrew 330–31
Duncan, Jack 223
Dunford, Lily 25–6
Dunkirk evacuation 34, 35
Dunlop, Frank 246
Dunn, Clive 265
Durban, South Africa 325
Durbin, Deanna 69
Durrant, Sabine 368
Dyall, Valentine 109n, 137, 170,
  188, 220, 260, 296
Dye, Bob 'Dipper' 45

Eccles, Mad Dan 'The Famous'
  (SM) 17–18, 98, 110, 117, 174,
  196, 239, 307
  SM's drawings 44
  source of the voice 101
  the real SM 101
  first appearances of 118–19
  becomes a well-developed char-
    acter 125
  catchphrase 149n
Eddser, Arthur 39
Eddy, Nelson 70, 72

Edgington, Harry 34–7, 39, 41, 43,
  46, 48, 51–3, 55, 65, 264, 299,
  321
Edgwarebury Club, London 122
Edinburgh 361
Edinburgh Festival 211
Edinburgh Festival Fringe 337–8
Educating Archie 155
Edwards, 'Professor' Jimmy 78, 79,
  83n
Ekland, Britt 254, 267
El-Alamein, second Battle of 50
Elfin Oak, Kensington Gardens,
  London 245–6, 256, 257
Elizabeth II, Queen 146, 147, 153,
  228, 254, 259, 292, 327
Ellington, Lance 374
Ellington, Ray (Henry Brown) 113,
  114, 117, 127, 151, 167, 178,
  291, 374
Elsread, Surrey 267
Elstree Studios 295
Eltham recruiting centre, south
  London 30
Emery, Dick 78, 103, 137,
  172
Establishment Club, London
  234
Eton, Peter 109n, 110, 113, 128,
  131, 134, 137, 140, 143, 145,
  146n, 148–9, 151–2, 154, 166,
  173, 188, 219
Eton, Squirrel 219
Evans, Chris 370
Evans, Peter 254
Evening News 97
Evening Standard 170, 171, 231,
  236, 248, 285, 303–4, 323
Evening with Spike Milligan, An
  one-man show 367

Fabrizi, Mario 192
Fagg, Harold 27

Index

Family Planning International
  Campaign 259
Farnes, Norma xii, 113, 210,
  261–3, 287, 292, 294, 301, 321,
  332, 334, 346, 361, 371, 372,
  379
  The Goons: The Story (with Chris
    Smith) 367
Feldman, Marty 275, 276
Ferguson, Mrs (housekeeper) 218
Fields, W.C. 84
Fierce Creatures (film) 366–7
56th Heavy Regiment Royal
  Artillery 32
  D Battery 33, 35, 36, 37, 40, 41,
    42, 44, 45, 46, 51, 53–4, 61,
    62, 282, 299, 328
Fildes, Alf 36, 38, 43, 48, 55, 56
Finchley, London 165
Finchley Society 246
Finnegan's Wake pub, Victoria,
  London 87
First Army 48
First World War 7, 8, 10, 25, 54
Fisher, Edmund 305
Five to Ten radio religious talk
  250–51
Flanagan, Bud 107n
Flaubert, Gustave 40
Florence 73
Florida club, Carnaby Street,
  London 81
Follies of the Wise television docu-
  mentary 285
Foot, Michael 148, 199, 235
For One Week Only one-man show
  306–7
For Three Nights Only one-man
  show 307
Foreign Office 228, 327
Fosters agency 77
Francisco, Tony 297
Frank Weir Orchestra 105

Freeman, Dave 186
French, Philip 250
Freud, Clement 274–5
Front Row (BBC Radio 4) 147
Frost, Sir David 269
Fry, Stephen 370, 377

Gabriel Street, Honor Oak Park,
  London (No.22) 18–19
Gaiety Theatre, Dublin 337
Galley Hill, East Sussex 35
Galton, Ray 85, 101, 134, 156–61,
  177, 209
Games, Alexander, ed.: *The
  Essential Spike Milligan* 114n
Gandhi, Mahatma M.K. 38, 225
Gane, Elena 335
Gang Shows (Ralph Reader) 94
Geelong school, Australia 259
Geldray, Max (Max van Gelder)
  113, 114, 127, 136–7, 167, 177,
  189, 291, 379
George pub, London 291
George V, King 27, 28
George VI, King 123
George Chisholm and his Jolly
  Jazzers 240
Ghost in the Noonday Sun (film) 297
Gibbons, Carroll 99
Gibbs, Lily 25
Gielgud, Sir John 266
Gillard, Frank 238
Gilliam, Terry 279
Gilliatt, Penelope 249
Glasgow 81
Glover, Jon 374
Godden Green Clinic, Seal, Kent
  339
Goldschmidt, John 138, 282
Goldsmith, Lieutenant Anthony
  40–41, 52
Goldsmiths College, London 24, 355
Goon Show 83

first series (*Crazy People*) 29,
108–9, 149n, 155, 177
first show 114–17
fiftieth anniversary 374–5
second series 109–14, 123–7
third series 127, 131–2, 134–5,
140
'The Ascent of Mount Everest'
140–41
Coronation special 141
fourth series 142, 143, 144
'The Giant Bombardon' 129
fifth series 143, 162
'The Affair of the Lone Banana'
162
'China Story' 163
'The Dreaded Batter Pudding
Hurler of Bexhill-on-Sea' 162
'The Mystery of the Marie
Celeste (Solved)' 163
'Nineteen Eighty-five' 163
'The Sinking of Westminster
Pier 55, 142–3
'The Whistling Spy Enigma'
162
sixth series 166
'The Great Tuscan Salami
Scandal' 167
'The Mighty Wurlitzer' 142
seventh series 173–5, 179
'The Mysterious Punch-up-the
Conker' 110
eighth series 180, 184–5
'African Incident' 113n
'The Evils of Bushey Spon' 185
'The Thing on the Mountain'
185
ninth series 188–90, 198
'The Scarlet Capsule' 189
'The Seagoon Memoirs' 188–9
'The Tay Bridge Disaster' 189
'Who is Pink Oboe?' 189
tenth series 190, 198, 199

'A Christmas Carol' 198
'The Last Smoking Seagoon'
105, 199
'The Tale of Men's Shirts' 198
origin of the term 44–5, 64
precursors 46, 48, 84
as SM's 'life's work' 4
Beachcomber's influence 39, 84–5
mixing the absurd with a pun 98
pilots 98–9, 105–6, 108
SM commissioned to write a
series 108
sound effects 119, 125, 133, 134,
142–3, 155, 179, 270
the routine 120, 177–8
ratings 120–21, 124
Secombe's song 124, 127
audience reports 131–2
magnetic tape used for recording
142
editing becomes possible 142
Eton's comments 148–9
catchphrases 149n
overseas audiences 151
classlessness 154
fan mail 161
censorship 174–5, 184
continued popularity 175–6, 198
SM wants to be rid of the show
183, 190–91
SM highly paid for 185
last programme broadcast on 28
January 1960 199
SM writes six more scripts (never
performed) 200
BBC repeats 310
SM's scripts sold to Elton John
319
recording of an earlier script
(2001) 374
The Last Goon Show of All 287,
291–4, 367
Goon Show Preservative Society

Newsletter 121n, 150, 310–11, 316

Goon Show Preservation Society 110, 146n, 190, 191, 294, 307, 310, 311, 315, 318, 334, 350, 367, 379

Goonland (film) 44

Gordon, Leon: *White Cargo* 64

Gordonstoun school 176

Gormenghast television adaptation 369–70

Grafton Arms, Victoria, London (King's Arms; now Finnegan's Wake) 87, 88, 95, 96, 103–4, 108, 119

Grafton, James 103

Grafton, Jimmy 107, 140, 292
  army record 87
  Variety bandbox 87
  Secombe's scriptwriter/manager 87, 103
  SM's patron 88, 99, 102–3
  first impressions of SM 88
  on Sellers 91–2
  pilot Goons script with SM (*Sellers' Castle*) 97–8
  on Eccles 101
  writes *Hip Hip Hoo Roy* 102
  on SM's manic depression 104, 105
  edits the Goon series 108, 109, 110, 142
  on Bentine's contribution 111
  on the shape of early *Goon Shows* 113
  writes screenplays for Goon films 130n

Grafton, Sally 103

Grafton family 87, 104

Granada television 282, 329

Grand Theatre, Leeds 307

Graves, Robert 252, 253, 262, 266

Great McGonagall, The (film) 295–7

Green, Rod 352–3, 366, 372

Green Party 334

Greene, Sir Hugh 238, 239

Greenslade, Wallace 143, 177, 178–9, 199, 291, 379

Greenwood, Charlotte 113n

Greenwood, Joan 247–8, 250, 256, 260

Gresham Hotel, Dublin 339

Griffin, Reg 35–6

Grosvenor pub, London 120

Grytpype-Thynne, Hon. Hercules (Sellers) 18, 55, 143, 145, 149n, 200, 292

Guardian 101, 231, 283, 298, 368, 370, 373, 376

Guinness, Sir Alec 227

Hackney Empire, London 82, 90, 96n

Haggard, Rider
  King Solomon's Mines 50
  She 125

Hailsham, East Sussex 41

Hall, Bill 66, 70, 71, 73, 77, 99

Hall, Nina 22, 25, 26

Hancock, Tony 108, 109, 157–60

Hancock's Half Hour radio programme 128

Handley, Tommy 83, 94

Happy Go Lucky 156

Hard Day's Night, A (film) 211

Harlem Club Band 29

Harrison, Newton 286

Harrods department store, London 329

Harry, Prince 326

Hawke, Bob 328

Hayward, Ruxton 144

Hayward Gallery, London 286

Heald, John 284–5

Heath, Sir Edward 292

Heath, Neville 81

Hebrides 94
Hello! magazine 368
Hendon, Greater London 162
Heston, Charlton 295
Hewitt, Tod 13–14
'Hickey, William' 315
Hicks, Mrs (lodger) 77
Highgate magistrates court, London 302–3
Highgrove House, Gloucestershire 326, 352, 378
Highview, Highgate, London (Flat 4) 126
Hill, Benny 78
Hill, Harry 338
Hillary, Sir Edmund 140
Hillyard, Pat 173, 200, 201
Hip Hip Hoo Roy radio show 102–3
Hislop, Ian 317
Hither Green School for Boys, London 355
Hitler, Adolf 25n, 39, 65, 134, 306
Hobbs, Jack 298–9, 332, 334
Hobson, Harold 231, 248–9
Hoffnung, Gerard 194
Holden Road, Finchley, London (No.127) 165, 216, 303, 308, 335
Holland, Jeffrey 374
Holloway, Sally 332–4, 335
Holloway, Stanley 69
Holt, Harold 240
Hope-Wallace, Philip 231
Hordern, Michael 263n
Horne, Kenneth 95
Hornsey coroner's court, London 303
Hot Club de France 67, 71
Housewives' Choice radio programme 205, 238–9, 241n
Howerd, Frankie 78, 86, 158, 159, 180

Hudd, Roy 101
Hughes, Spike 37
Hughes, Ted 373
Humphries, Barry 222, 232, 233–4, 239–40, 245–6, 252, 259, 263n, 356
   My Life As Me 239, 240–41
Hungary, Soviet invasion of (1956) 174
Huth, Angela 349–50
Hyderabad, India 10

Idiot Weekly Price 2d., The television series 169–70, 171
Idiot Weekly Price 2d., The television series (Australian version) 187, 194, 196, 229
Ilfracombe, Devon 93
In the Psychiatrist's Chair (BBC Radio 4 programme) 61, 195, 216–17, 320–22, 342, 343
Independent 335
India
   Leo first posted to (1911) 8
   Leo marries Florence in 8
   Leo posted to Ahmadnagar (1917) 8
   SM born in (1918) 5, 8
   SM's love of India 9
   Leo often separated from the family 11
   number of British troops cut 15
   Milligan family returns to England (1933) 15–16
   compared to London 18–19
   SM claims to have glimpsed Gandhi 38
Ingrams, Richard 11, 222, 223, 272, 273, 274, 335, 370
Innes, Ivor 245
Instone, Anna 238, 240n
Invasion Quartet (film) 211, 212, 219, 225

Index

Ionesco, Eugene 150
Irish potato famine 6
Irish TV 356
Ischia 73
ITMA (*It's That Man Again*) radio
   show 64, 83–4, 94, 154
ITV 169, 171, 261,287, 351
Izzard, Eddie 293–4, 374, 377

Jackanory (children's story
   programme) 287
Jacob, Sir Ian 185
James, Clive 32
Japanese television 241–2
Jarron, Matthew 350
Jarry, Alfred: *Ubu Roi* 246
Jaye, Bobby 188
jazz 26, 27, 55
Jenkins, Major 54, 55, 57, 59, 61
John, Elton 319
Johnson, Teddy 100–101
Jones, Peter 310
Jones, Spike 37, 72
Jones, Terry 278
Joyce, James 213
Junior Crazy Gang, The 107
Junkin, John 265

Kafka, Franz 149, 153
Karno, Fred 7
Katz, Dick 114, 178
Kaye, Danny 102
Keaton, Buster 170, 194, 258
Kendall, Henry 281
Kenny, Sean 221
Kensington Palace, London 255
Kent, Princess Marina of Greece,
   Duchess of 177
Keown, Eric 221
Kerr, Bill 79, 103, 220, 239
Kettlebank family 5
Kidgell, Doug 36, 38, 43, 48, 52–3
Kingston, Jeremy 248

Kingsway House, London 21, 42
Kirkee, near Poona, India 10
Kneale, Nigel: *Quatermass and the
   Pit* 189
Knockabout Kids 7
Kretzmer, Herbert 224–6, 313
Kubrick, Stanley 232
Kyrenia, Cyprus 297

Labour Party 25, 65
Lacey, Bruce 193
Ladykillers, The (film) 167
Ladywell Baths, Lewisham, London
   23
Ladywell Recreation Track,
   Lewisham, London 30
Lalkaka (SM and Sellers) 151
Lancaster, David 307
Lang, Eddie 26
Larcombe, Richard 297
Larkin, Philip 27
Last Goon Show of All, The 287,
   291–4
Last Laugh Before TV-AM, THE
   show 313
Laura (film) 132
Lauro, Italy 56
Lawrence, Ted 32–3
Leacock, Stephen 85
   *Arcadian Adventures with the
      Idle Rich* 85
   *Moonbeams from the Larger
      Lunacy* 85–6
Lear, Edward 150, 196, 213, 371
Leathwell Road, Deptford (No.3)
   77
Lennon, John 213
Lester, Richard 150
   Idiot Weekly shows 169, 170
   *The Running, Jumping and
      Standing Still Film* 191, 193,
      211
   A Hard Day's Night 211

The Bedsitting Room 263n
The Three Musketeers 295
Levin, Bernard 249
Lewis, Patti 170
Lewis, Roger 90–91, 94, 98, 104, 129, 144, 145–6, 291–2
Lewis, Steve 64
Lewisham Hippodrome, London 23
Lewisham Hospital, London 30, 31
Linden Gardens, Notting Hill, London (No.13) 77, 81
Lindsay, Margaret 113
Ling, Peter 109n
Lipman, Maureen 351
Listen, My Children radio show 96n
Little Jim (SM): catchphrase 149n
Littlefield, Robin 372, 373, 375–6
Liverpool docks 46
Lloyd, John Selwyn (Baron Selwyn-Lloyd) 213
Lodge, David 193
London
  noisy, cold and grey 18–19
  raids on 39–40
London Palladium 88, 107, 369
London Weekend Television 269, 277
London Zoo 182, 210
Loss, Joe 105
Luftwaffe 39
Lupino, G.B. 220
Lynn, Robert 212
Lyric, Hammersmith, London 246, 248

M. & J. Hobbs 298
McAlpine, Alistair 257
MacDonald, Jeanette 70, 72
MacDonald, Ramsay 15
McDonald, Trevor 342
McGrath, Joe 130, 171
  and *A Show Called Fred* 171

and *The Running, Jumping and Standing Still Film* 191, 193, 194
on Liz Cowley 208
and SM's depressions 235
and SM's friendship with royalty 255
The Magic Christian 281
Oh in Colour 287
The Great McGonagall 295, 296, 297
on Jack Hobbs 298–9
McKem, Leo 192, 193
McLauchlan, Gordon 286
McLean, Alistair 282
Macmillan, Harold, 1st Earl of Stockton 153, 174, 213
McMillan, Margaret 113
McNaughton, Ian 270, 279–80, 310
Maddaloni, Italy (O2E) 63–5
Magic Christian, The (film) 282
Magnificent Seven Deadly Sins, The (film) 233
Mahler, Gustav 24
Mail on Sunday 377n
Manic Depressive Fellowship 339
Mankowitz, Wolf 25n, 170, 171
Margaret, HRH Princess 254, 255, 291, 319
Marks, Alfred 79, 98, 103, 109n
Marlowe Theatre Canterbury 222, 223, 231
Martin, George 227
Marty Feldman Comedy Machine, The (ITV programme) 287
Marx, Groucho 84, 153, 170
Marx Brothers 27, 40, 84, 114, 116, 128, 149
Mary, Queen 127n
Masefield, John: *The Box of Delights* 366
Mason, Christopher 257–8
Matthews, A.E. 185

Index

Maughan, Margaret 344–8, 350, 354–64, 377

Maughan-Milligan, James Turlough (SM's son) 344–9, 353, 354, 355, 357–64, 365

Maze Road, Kew, Surrey (No. 14) 197, 216

Melly, George 275, 283

Melody Maker 26, 43

Melting Pot, The (BBC television series) 17, 311–12, 331

Mendoza, Mrs ('Belle Ray'; Sellers' grandmother) 92, 126

Men's Performing Show, The (ITV show) 220

Mermaid Theatre, City of London 221, 222, 225–6, 229–32, 259, 263, 294, 297, 356

Merton, Paul 370

Mesopotamia 8

Messiter, Ian 111

MGM (Metro-Goldwyn-Mayer) 200, 211, 218, 225

Michael Joseph (publishers) 298, 305, 306, 332, 334

Midweek (Radio 4 programme) 317

Miles, Bernard 109n, 221–2, 356

Mill Wood, near Bexhill-on-Sea, East Sussex 44, 45

Miller, Glenn 319

Miller, Jonathan 102, 138n, 227

Milligan, Desmond Patrick (SM's brother) 48
  birth 11
  skilled artist 21
  in the 'Ox and Bucks' infantry regiment 65
  and Beachcomber 85
  emigrates to Australia 122
  flies in for *This Is Your Life* 299
  rift with SM 340
  his son married to a Chinese girl 342

Milligan, Florence (née Kettleband; SM's mother) 82, 124
  meets and marries Leo in India 8
  Gwen Gorden and Leo Gann act 8, 10
  on S's early contact with the stage 8n
  shipwrecked on journey from India to London 9
  relationship with SM 11, 29–30, 65
  and the home at Gabriel Street 18
  a domestic tyrant 20, 29–30, 33
  Catholicism 27, 42
  emigrates to Australia 122, 133
  sent 'The Yin Tong Song' 167–8
  SM visits in Australia 187, 229, 308, 337, 361
  spends the summer in England 245
  SM's *This Is Your Life* 299
  death 337, 340

Milligan, Jane Fionella (SM's daughter) 261, 293, 313, 315, 325, 338, 349, 356–7, 372, 375, 377

Milligan, June (née Marlow; SM's first wife) 179, 189
  meets SM 122
  marries SM 123, 227
  goes to Australia 123
  pregnancy 126
  ill after the birth of Laura 132–3
  and SM's breakdown 137, 138
  Beryl Vertue on 162
  Simpson on 165
  Laura on 166
  SM detaches himself from her 166, 217n
  in Australia 186–8
  leaves home, taking the children 196, 197

the new man in her life 197, 198, 216
divorce case 208, 216
SM said he wanted to find her (1996) 366
Milligan, Laura (SM's daughter) 293
  birth (1952) 132–3
  distracts SM from his writing 155
  childhood 165, 194, 217–18, 253
  on her mother 166
  education 228, 234
  cries at SM's marriage to Paddy 229
  relationship with Paddy 234, 256
  illustrations to Open Heart University 300
  employment 325
Milligan, Leo (SM's father) 4, 82, 124, 214, 274, 342
  birth (1890) 7
  'lunacy' 5
  military career 6, 7, 8, 11, 15
  semi-professional actor 6, 7–8, 20
  appears on Australian TV 6n
  'Leo Gann' stage name 7–8
  first posted to India (1911) 8
  meets and marries Florence 8
  Gwen Gorden and Leo Gann act 8, 10
  war service 8
  posted to Ahmadnagar (1917) 8
  promoted to quartermaster sergeant 8
  shipwrecked on journey from India to London 9
  often separated from the family 11
  cowboy obsession 13
  vacation in England (1931–2) 14
  appearance 15
  returns to England (1933) 15
  unemployed 20

at Associated Press 23, 65
defends SM in court 29
rejoins the army as an officer 42
and SM's transfer request 42
emigrates to Australia 122, 133
SM visits in Australia 187, 229
spends the summer in England 245
has a stroke 268
death 271
SM appears as his father in Adolf Hitler 295
Milligan, Michael (SM's great-grandfather) 6
Milligan, Nadia (Desmond's wife) 299
Milligan Papers, The 330
Milligan, Patricia (Paddy; née Ridgeway; SM's second wife) 0
  meets SM 212
  introduced to SM's children 218
  singing career 212, 219, 220, 294
  marries SM 227–8
  appears in the Australian Idiot Weekly 229
  and SM's behaviour during The Bedsitting Room 232
  relationship with Laura 234, 256
  Mediterranean cruise 245
  at Kensington Palace 255
  birth of Jane 261
  response to SM's depressions 262
  failing marriage 267–8
  mastectomy 299
  details of SM's affairs published after her death 300
  car accident 303
  and Monkenhurst 309
  dying of cancer 313, 372
  death 314, 315, 345, 359
  and Margaret Maughan 356–7, 359, 360
Milligan, Sean (SM's son) 293, 300

birth 162
childhood 165, 194, 195, 372
and his parents' quarrels 187
education 234
employment 325, 377
in India 368, 372
relationship with Robin 372
Milligan, Shelagh (née Sinclair; SM's
    third wife) 260, 330, 333, 338,
    341
    works as SM's secretary 300
    appearance 300, 301
    endears herself to SM's children
        315
    engaged to SM 320
    moves into Monkenhurst 323
    marries SM 324
    and Carpenters 336
    and Margaret Maughan 345
    and SM's illegitimate children
        348, 349, 351, 359, 365
    and SM's insult of Prince Charles
        351–2
    and SM's medication 365–6
    and 'Toni' Pontani 366, 368
    and June Milligan 366
    and SM's knighthood 373–4
    love for SM 375
    SM's will 377n
Milligan, Silé (SM's daughter) 185,
    195, 198, 293, 325, 366, 373
Milligan, Spike (Terence Alan
    Milligan)
    birth (16 April, 1918 in
        Ahmadnagar, India) 8
    early contact with the stage 8n
    love of India 9
    shipwrecked on journey from
        India to London 9
    life in India 10
    relationship with his mother 11,
        29–30, 65
    father often absent 11

education 11–15, 21, 22, 207
    potential careers 13–14
    joins a cadet troop 14
    discovers musical talent 14
    vacation in England (1931–2)
        14–15
    appearance 15, 207, 258, 338,
        349, 368, 375–6
    leaves his birthplace forever
        (1933) 15–16
    fails to become an RAF pilot 21,
        42–3
    day-jobs in London 21–5, 27–8,
        30, 33
    first girlfriend (Nina Hall) 22, 25
    in dance bands 23, 27–8, 29
    learns the bass 23–4
    joins the Young Communist
        League 25
    trumpet-playing 26, 29, 30, 35–6,
        41, 50, 52, 62, 63, 101, 180,
        335
    Catholicism 27, 42, 53, 55, 56,
        74, 197, 225, 251, 259, 341
    steals to pay for a new trumpet
        28–9
    in the war see Second World War
    meets Secombe 68
    demobbed (April 1946) 73
    meets Bentine 80
    first visit to Ireland 81–2
    in the Grafton Arms 88
    meets Sellers 90
    pilot Goons script with Grafton
        (Sellers' Castle) 97–8
    co-writes Hip Hip Hoo Roy
        102–3
    tours American army and air
        bases in East Anglia 105
    commissioned to write the first
        Goon series 108
    co-writes Bumblethorpe 109n
    meets June Marlow 122

his parents and Desmond
  emigrate to Australia 122
marries June 123, 227
birth of Laura 133
financial worries 133, 205, 226
breakdown 135, 136–40
Aldermaston Marches 148
revives and revitalises the music-
  hall joke 149
forms Associated London Scripts
  156–9
working method 160, 161, 180
telegrams 159–60, 161, 267
relationship with his children
  162, 165, 166, 194–5, 196,
  228–9, 253, 261, 372
Coventry incident 164–5
and *Idiot Weekly* shows 169,
  170
Fred shows awarded Best TV
  Show of the Year 172
chronic insomnia 173, 266, 333
tiddlywink battle 176–7
complaining letters to the BBC
  185–6
in Australia 186–8, 194, 196,
  228–9, 308, 337, 361
Jill leaves him, taking the children
  196–7
suicidal 197, 240–41
blamed for the demise of the
  Goon Show 200–201
divorce case 208, 216
cast in MGM films 211–12
granted custody of his children
  216–18
marries Paddy 227–8
citizenship issue 228, 327
gun incident 232–3, 343
The Telegoons 237–8
ECT 243, 343
Mediterranean cruise 245
Elfin oak project 245–6

Spike Milligan Productions Ltd
  261
tours Australia with one-man
  show (1967) 264
The World of Beachcomber 264,
  265–6
failing second marriage 267–8
start of *Q5* 272
in *Curry and Chips* 277
The Last Goon Show of All 291–3
attends D Battery reunions 299
and Paddy's illness 299
shooting incident (1974) 40,
  302–5, 308, 343
move to Monkenhurst 308–9
on Paddy's death 314
at Prince Charles' wedding
  319–20
marries Shelagh (1983) 323
relationship with Prince Charles
  326–8, 351–2
illegitimate children (James and
  Romany) 344–51, 353–64
CBE award 349
triple heart bypass operation 349,
  350, 351, 375
awards 352, 353
eightieth birthday 367–8
renal failure 359, 372, 374, 375
knighthood 373–4, 375
voted the Funniest Man of the
  Millennium 375
death (27 February 2002) 376
Guardian obituary 101
funeral 376–7
will 377
memorial service 377–8
personality
  anti-Semitism 173, 233, 272–3,
    323
  capacity for hate 225, 370
  conservationism 40, 245–6,
    256, 257, 326

family planning issue 258, 259, 261, 341–2, 365
Irishness 4–5, 6, 331
love of music 26
manic depression 4, 8, 12, 40, 61, 64, 88, 104, 105, 136, 139, 161, 164–5, 179, 183, 189, 217, 235, 242–5, 258, 260–64, 266, 267, 268, 283–4, 287, 320–22, 325, 333, 338, 339–40, 348, 354, 358, 365–6, 378–9
pacifism 40
paranoia 135, 138–9
pro-animal rights 40, 225, 258, 286–7, 294, 301n, 304–5, 321, 329
racism issue 151, 173, 276–7, 278, 280–81, 312–13, 323, 328, 342
response to criticism 12, 186
romanticism 21, 22
unable to think he could be wrong 256
unforgiving 338
vegetarianism 40, 323, 333
writings
Adolf Hitler: My Part in His Downfall 6, 18n, 30, 32, 35, 42, 46, 286, 307, 328
Badjelly the Witch 298, 371
The Bedside Milligan 263–4
The Bedsitting Room (with Antrobus) 222–3, 226, 229–37, 242–6, 249, 263, 355–6
The Bible According to Spike Milligan 349
Black Baggage 64
Black Beauty According to Spike Milligan 349, 352
'Bloodnok's Rock'n'Roll Call' 167
A Book of Bits or A Bit of a Book 258

The Book of the Goons 293
'Catford 1933' 19
A Dustbin of Milligan 206, 213, 225
The Family Album 4, 10, 19, 25n, 197, 198, 201, 229, 256, 260, 263n, 271, 308
Frankenstein According to Spike Milligan 349, 350
Goon Show scripts 293
The Hound of the Baskervilles According to Spike Milligan 349
'I'm Walking Backwards for Christmas' 167
'In the Land of the Bumbley Boo' 196
It Ends with Magic 18–19, 340
It will all be over by Christmas 268
Lady Chatterley's Lover According to Spike Milligan 349–50
The Little Pot Boiler 243–4, 258
The Looney 331–2, 334
The Magic Staircase 268
Men-in-Gitis 64
Milli-News (comic newspaper) 48
Milligan's Ark 286
The Mirror Running 334
Monty, His Part In My Victory 308
More Goon Show Scripts 293
The Murphy 375
Mussolini: His Part in My Downfall 57
'On the Ning Nang Nong/Where the Cows go Bong!' 196, 369
Open Heart University 300
Peace Work 104, 341
Puckoon 7, 214–16, 219, 226, 236–7, 257, 331, 374
Robin Hood According to Spike Milligan 349

'Rommel?' 'Gunner Who?' 286, 298–9, 305, 307

Silly Verse for Kids 194–6, 212, 353

The Spike Milligan Letters 301–2

Treasure Island According to Spike Milligan 349

William McGonagall: The Truth at Last (with Jack Hobbs) 326

Wuthering Heights According to Spike Milligan 349

'The Ying Tong Song' 167, 176, 326, 375

Milligan, Willie (SM's uncle) 7

Milligan in Winter seasonal show 295

Milligan Preserved (LP) 225, 227

Mills, Michael 265, 269–70

Milne, A.A. 196

Mind 283

Ministry of Works 245

Mitchell, Warren 212

Monkenhurst, The Crescent, Hadley Common, Barnet 308–9, 323, 325, 326, 330, 335–6

Monkhouse, Bob 108, 238

Mons, battle of 7

Monsanto 218

Monte Cassino, Italy 56, 81

Montgomery, Field Marshal Bernard 38, 147

Monty Python and the Holy Grail (film) 173

Monty Python's Flying Circus 148, 279–80, 281

Monty Python's Life of Brian 316

Moore, Dudley 259, 294–5, 318n

More Goon Show Scripts 189

Moreton, Robert 98, 109n

Moriarty, Count (SM) 55, 145

Morley, Angela (previously Wally Stott) 291

Morley, Robert 265

Morrell, André 247–8

Morrison, Van 6, 336–7

Morton, J.B. see Beachcomber

Mosley, Oswald 25n, 233

Moss Empires theatres 164

Motion, Andrew 373

Much-Binding-in-the-Marsh radio sitcom 148

Muir, Frank 79, 83n, 96, 105–6

Mulgrew, Johnny 67, 71, 72, 73, 77, 81

Mullard, Arthur 212, 257, 258

Muppet Show 242

Murch, Fiona 338

Murdoch, Richard 83

Murray, A1 294

Musclewhite, Gunner 57

Muses with Milligan (television programme) 251–2

Musicians' Union 167

Naples 60

Nathan, David: The Laughtermakers 200

Nation, Terry 158

National Poetry Day 369, 373

Natural History Museum, South Kensington, London 281

NBC 175

New Era Rhythm Boys 23

New Labour 365

New Ritz Revels 26, 27

Newcastle-upon-Tyne 152, 344, 345, 355, 361

Newman, Pat 175, 185

Newquay Road, Catford (No.15) 18

News Chronicle 111, 114, 116, 175, 188

News of the World 136, 227–8, 234–5, 249, 259, 314, 346, 348, 350

Nichols, Joy 83n

Nietzsche, Friedrich 252

Norbury, south-east London 18
Norden, Dennis 79, 83n, 96
Norman, Barry 255
Normandy 107, 114
Nottingham 105
Nuffield Services Club, London 99, 100, 102, 109
Nyerere, President Julius 258

Oakes, Philip 146, 183
'Obituary Show, The' television programme 376
Oblomov (Goncharov) 246–50, 297
O'Brien, Miss (nanny) 218
Observer 197, 222, 249, 275, 282, 341
O'Clee, David 241n
Oh in Colour television series 287
O'Hagan, Sean 4–5
Old Town Hall, Bexhill-on-Sea 36
Oldie literary lunches 370
Omar Khayyam Show, The (radio series) 239
One Pair of Eyes series 357
Oneworld airline alliance 373
Open University 182n
Orkneys 94
Orme Court, Bayswater Road, London (No.9) 209, 210, 224, 261, 262, 263, 284, 298n, 300, 301, 320, 360
Orwell, George 38
1984 163
Osborne, John 147
Other Spike, The (television documentary) 136, 282–3
Otranto, SS 46
Over the Page show 67, 71–3
Oxford English Dictionary 44
Oxfordshire and Buckinghamshire Light Infantry 65

Palin, Michael 148, 211, 278, 316

Panama club, London 81
Parkinson, Michael 316
Parry, Harry 43
Peake, Mervyn: *Gormenghast* 369
Pearl Harbour 335
People 323, 344, 346, 347, 348, 363
Percival, Lance 212
Perelman, S.J. 153
Perry, Jimmy 328
Perth, Australia 328
Pertwee, Bill 328
Peterborough 95
Pevensey Beach, East Sussex 35
Philip, HRH The Duke of Edinburgh 176, 254, 286, 291, 325, 327
Phillips, Sergeant Phil 63
Pickwoad, Michael 285
Pink Panther films 172
Pitch, Harry 374
Playfair, William 285
Plays and Players 231
Pogson, E.O. 127–8
Pompeii, Italy 54
Pontani, Marie Antoinette ('Toni') 74, 82, 122, 366, 368
Poona, India 5, 10–14
Popeye newspaper strip (Segar) 44–5, 112
Portici officers' rest camp, Italy 62–3
Postman's Knock (film) 211–12, 224, 225
Potter, Stephen 163
Powell, Ellis 113n
Powell, Sandy 69
Priestland, Gerald 320
Private Eye 165, 213, 222, 223, 273, 292n, 312, 350n
Prosser, Lance Bombadier Len 63, 64
Prowse, Keith (ticket agency and music shop) 27–8

Puckoon (film) 374
Punch magazine 221, 248
Pureheart, Captain Osric (Bentine)
115, 124, 125, 130, 131
Purves, Libby 317

Q magazine 336
Q series 268–81, 315, 328, 331,
367
Q5 268–79, 281, 310
Q6 281, 310–11
Q7 273, 311
Q8 273, 315
Q9 273, 317–18
Qantas 370n
Queen's Music Hall, Poplar 7
Race, Roger 311
Radio Hallam, Sheffield 306
Radio Luxembourg 37
Radio Newsreel programme 206
Radio Rhythm Club (BBC
programme) 43
Radio Times xi, 102, 111, 113,
121, 127, 154, 220, 269, 271,
275
Ragdoll Productions 371
Rangoon, Burma 10, 14, 15
Rattigan, Terence 40
Raven (RAF newspaper) 102
Ray, Ted 95
Ray Ellington Quartet 113
Ray's a Laugh radio show 95
Reader, Ralph 94
Reason Why, The audienceless show
153n
Redgrave, Sir Michael 266
Reed, Driver 48
Regent Street Polytechnic, London
198
Regent's Park Mosque, London
312–13
Regent's Park open-air theatre,
London 80

Reid, Jean ('Nanna') 315
Return to the Forbidden Planet
(film) 375
Reveille forces' newspaper 207
Richardson, Ralph 263n
Richmond, Surrey 197, 208, 328
Riseldine Road, London (No.4)
18n
Ritz Brothers 128
Robert Stigwood Group 210
Robinson, Cardew 310
Robson, Jeremy 273n, 293n
Robson, Dr Joseph 173, 293,
Robson Books 293n
Roche 183
Rome 72, 73–4
Rommel, Erwin 50, 52, 306
Ronald, Tom 184
Ronnie Scott's jazz club, London
269
Room 101 chat show 370
Ross, Jonathan 306, 351
Rowan and Martin's Laugh-in 275,
276
Rowlands, Colonel Stanley 81
Roy, Derek 86, 87, 102, 103,
156
Royal Academy Summer Exhibition
239n
Royal Air Force (RAF) 21, 40,
42–3, 78, 80, 94, 255
Entertainment Division 94
Royal Artillery 6, 36, 69, 180,
300
Training Depot show 70
Royal Court Theatre, London
223
Royal Navy 291
Royal Variety Performance 259
*Running, Jumping and Standing
Still Film, The* 191–4, 211, 255
Runnymede Trust 312
Rushton, William 223

Index

Russell, Ken 271
Rye, Kent 349, 354, 363

St Anthony's Catholic Church, Rye
   376
St David's Hall, Cardiff 367
St James's Palace, London 374
St Katharine's Dock, London
   357
St Luke's hospital, Woodside
   Avenue, Highgate 137, 140
St Martin-in-the-Fields church,
   London 152–3, 377
St Mary's Abbey Convent 234
St Paul's Cathedral, London 319,
   320
St Paul's school, Rangoon, Burma
   14
Salerno, Italy 54
San Francisco Film Festival 211
Sanders, George 132, 143
Savoy Theatre, London 375
Schoenberg, Arnold 24
Scott, Sir Peter 246
Scott, Ronnie 64
Scudamore, Pauline xi, 6, 18n, 25,
   29, 37, 101, 111, 151, 164, 165,
   228–9, 239n, 244, 247, 256, 262,
   299, 301, 320
   Spike Milligan: a biography
      328–9
Seagoon, Neddie (Secombe) 17–18,
   83, 116, 124, 292
   fooled by Grytpype-Thynne and
      Moriarty 55
   'my Capatain' 115
   attempts the land speed record
      142
   in the final programme 199
Seahouses, Northumberland 357,
   361
Secombe, Andrew 374
Secombe, David 377

Secombe, Fred 68
Secombe, Sir Harry Donald 88, 89,
   101, 130, 273n
   birth 68
   early influences 68–9
   singing 69, 236, 371, 377
   education 69
   in the war 69–71
   army shows 69, 70
   raspberry blowing 70, 71, 72,
      299
   in CPA 71
   SM's first impressions 68
   in the *Over the Page* show 67,
      71, 72–3
   personality xi, 72
   demobbed 73–4
   at the Windmill Theatre 77–81
   tour of Germany 82
   Variety Bandbox 86
   Listen, My Children 96n
   Third Division 96
   becomes the *Goon Show* straight
      man 124
   Coventry Hippodrome episode
      164
   in hysterics at Sellers/SM ad
      libbing 174
   tiddlywink battle 176–7
   on the Camden recording sessions
      177–8, 379
   signs contract for another *Goon
      Show* 201
   subsequent successes 235
   the Telegoons 237
   in *The Last Goon Show of All*
      292
   ill-health 371
   SM's comments 371
   knighted 374
   death (2001) 374
Second World War
   SM called up 30

Bexhill-on-Sea (1940–43) 31,
  32–46
SM discovers books and the
  English countryside 34
'Spike' nickname 37
SM leads the D battery band
  37–9
goons in 44–5
SM established as the Battery
  clown 45–6
SM shipped out to Algiers 46, 48
Camp X 49
Tunis 50–52
SM's promotion 51, 59, 63
Stand Easy variety show 53
SM's sand-fly fever 54
direct hit on the Battery's guns
  56–7
SM injured in the leg 57, 58
end of SM's career as an active
  soldier 58
rehabilitation 59–62
SM creates shows at O2E 64–5
SM plays on VE Night 65
SM in the CPA 66–73
Over the Page show 67, 71–3
SM returns to the UK 74
Edwards' bravery in 78
Wilson's experience 107
and the Goon Show 145–6
SM revisits battlefields (1978)
  316
Segar, E.C. 44–5
Sellars, Bill (Peter's father) 92, 93,
  104
Sellers, Anne (née Howe; Peter's
  first wife) 122, 126
Sellers' Castle 97–8
Sellers, Lynne (née Frederick; Peter's
  fourth wife) 144
Sellers, Michael 376–7
Sellers, Peg (Peter's mother) 92, 93,
  104–5

Sellers, Peter (Richard Henry
  Sellars) 227, 312
a spoilt only child 91
education 92–3
Jewishness 92, 93
has to caricature Jews in the
  Goon Show 93, 151
dominated by his mother 93
adept at voices xi, 93–4
in the RAF 94–5, 255
at Kensington Palace 255
infiltrates officers' messes 10n, 94
at the Windmill 95
SM meets 90
joins the group 89, 95
appearance 89, 90, 94, 105
personality 90–92
Third Division 96, 105
SM visits 104–5
obsession with cars 105, 178
and SM's insomnia 134–5
SM decides to kill him 135, 136–7
acts SM's parts in his absence 137
lack of sympathy for SM's
  emotional state 139
Coventry Hippodrome 164
Idiot Weekly shows 169, 170
Pink Panther films 172
tiddlywink battle 176–7
tension between him and SM 178,
  182, 190
only misses one programme in the
  entire run 189
signs contract for another Goon
  Show 201
subsequent successes 235–6, 330
The Telegoons 237
and Son of Oblomov 254
failed second marriage 267
The Magic Christian 281–2
in The Last Goon Show of All
  292–3
in Alice 294

in *The Great MacGonagall* 296
Ghost in the Noonday Sun script 297
at SM's *This Is Your Life* 299
death (1980) 318
funeral 319
The Best of Sellers (LP) 227
  'Balham, Gateway to the South' sketch 18, 96
Shakespeare, William 244
Shand, Neil 268, 269, 271–3, 280, 310, 311, 312, 323, 324, 329, 335n
Shearing, George 43
Shepperton Film Studios 294
Sherwood, Tony 79, 88
Shorter, Eric 249
Show Called Fred, A television series 170–71, 268, 270
Shulman, Milton 221, 231, 246–7, 248
Sicily 53
Simpson, Alan 85, 101, 134, 156–61, 177, 185, 209, 220
Skynner, Robin 339
Sligo 7
Slimbridge Wildfowl & Wetlands Trust, Gloucestershire 246
Slogett, Dennis 32, 33
Smith, Chris 367
Smith, Keith 273
Snagge, John 128, 141, 143, 152, 153, 177
Snowdon, Lord 291
Son of Fred television series 171–2
Son of Oblomov 249, 252–7, 260, 270, 300
South Africa 308, 325–6
Speer, Roy 98, 175, 179, 184
Speight, Johnny 158, 182, 276, 311
Spencer, John 277
Spiers & Ponds 28–9
Spike and the Boys 37–8

Spike Jones and his City Slickers 37
Spike Milligan Offers A Series of Unrelated Incidents at Current Market Value (television programme) 220–21
Spike Milligan Productions Ltd 261
Spike Milligan Show, The 229
'Spike Night' (BBC2) 367
Spinetti, Victor 296
Splutmuscle, Ernie (Sellers) 115
Stainless Stephen 69
Stalin, Joseph 45, 147
Stand Easy military variety show 53
Standing, Michael 126, 127, 140
Stapleton, Alban 303
Stargazers 113, 124
Stark, Audrey 232
Stark, Graham 25n, 103, 109n, 137, 141, 169–70, 171, 177, 189, 192, 193, 220, 230–33, 255, 260, 263n, 273n, 319, 343
Starlings, The audienceless show 152–3, 377
'Stars in Battledress' 111
Stephens, Diana 190
Stephens, Larry
  war service 109
  and the first Goon series 108–9
  co-writes *Bumblethorpe* 109n
  and the second Goon series 109–10
  SM on 110
  not on speaking terms with SM 140
  drops out of the show 142
  Galton and Simpson on 160–61
  white gloves 161
  and *The Case of the Mukkinese Battlehorn* 172
  and the seventh series 179
  high blood pressure 179–80
  and the eighth series 185
  and the ninth series 186, 189

death 190
Sterling, Joseph 172
Stigwood, Robert 209
Stones' Engineering, Deptford 21–2, 23
Stoppard, Tom 141
Story, Jack Trevor 212
Stott, Wally (later Angela Morley) 127, 178, 185, 291
Stringfellow, Peter 373
Suez crisis (1956) 174
Summerson, John 163
Sun 136, 259, 277, 283, 302, 303, 320, 327, 374
Sunday Correspondent 338
Sunday Dispatch 177
Sunday Express 261, 349, 353
Sunday Graphic 179, 183
Sunday Mirror 284, 309
Sunday Telegraph 231
Sunday Times 126, 231, 236, 248, 275–6, 324
Swansea 68
Swansea Art School 68
Swift, Jonathan: *Gulliver's Travels* 149
Sydney 187, 194, 233
Sykes, Eric 78, 179, 284, 366
  Leacock's influence on SM 85
  on Larry Stephens 109
  the only co-writer SM treated as an equal 111
  SM shares his office 155
  war service 155
  Educating Archie 155
  co-writes most of the fifth series 162–3
  edits *Idiot Weekly* shows 169, 170
  SM and his children spend Christmas with 198
  owns freehold of Orme Court building 209

Norma Farnes works for 261
  in *Curry and Chips* 277
  in *Q5* 278
Sylvester, Victor 149n
Symons, Julian 171

Take It From Here radio show 83, 96, 148, 156
Tanfield, Paul 190, 197
Tati, Jacques 258
Taylor, Jeremy 307
Taylor, John Russell 231
Telegoons, The 237–8
Teletubbies 371
Temperance Seven 231, 242, 243
Tenzing Norgay, Sherpa 140
Thatcher, Margaret, later Baroness 317, 328, 334–5
Theatre Royal, Newcastle 344
There's a Lot of It About series 323
Third Division radio series 95–6, 105
This Is Your Life (television programme) 299, 353, 364
Thomas, J.P. 111, 114, 116–17
Three Musketeers, The (film) 294
Three Stooges 138
Thurgar, Alf (SM's uncle) 18
Thurgar, Kath (née Milligan; SM's aunt) 18
Tilbury, Essex 18
Till Death Us Do Part (television series) 276–7
Times, The 247, 258, 301, 369, 376
Timothy, Andrew ('Tim') 98, 99, 99, 113, 120, 125, 128, 143, 292, 374, 379
Timothy, Christopher 374
TLS (*Times Literary Supplement*) 213, 236–7
Today magazine 353
Today radio programme 206, 293
Tomorrow's Audience 222, 223

Tonight television programme 206

Took, Barry 265, 318

Torre del Greco, Italy 60

Townley, Dr William 163–4

Train, Jack 83–4, 109n, 189

Trans Antarctic Expedition (1956) 174

Trattoo restaurant, Kensington, London 299

Travers, Bill 212

Treasure Island 221–2, 225, 263, 297

Tunbridge Wells, Kent 340

Tunis 50, 52, 53

Tunisia 316

TV Times 169, 171

Two Ronnies, The (television series) 294

Tynan, Kenneth 222–3, 231

Union Jack Club, Waterloo, London 18

Union Jack forces' paper 71–3

United Artists 263n

United Dairies 152

Uxbridge Road, Shepherd's Bush, London (No.130) 155, 156, 158, 159

Valentine, Dickie 109

Van Damm, Vivian 78, 79

Variety Bandbox (radio programme) 86, 87

Variety Parade (BBC Television) 166

Vaughan, Norman 79

Venice 74

Ventura, Ray 114

Vertue, Beryl 157, 158–9, 161–2, 182, 185, 201, 205, 209–10

Victoria Palace, London 107n

Victoria Pavilion, Ilfracombe 93

Virgin Books 352, 372

Visiting District Milligan one-man show 337

Vomero, near Naples 66

Walden, Jeff 109n

Waldini and His Gypsy Band 93, 94

Waldman, Ronnie 237

Waller, Fats 14

Watt, Burt 350

Watt, Josephine 350

Watt, Roberta 350–51, 353–4

Watt, Romany (SM's daughter) 350–51, 353, 354, 364, 365, 376

Webb, Lizbeth 113n

Welch, Raquel 295

Wellington, New Zealand 264

Wells, John 274

West Hill Hospital, Dartford, Kent 350

Wheldon, Huw 276

Where Does It Hurt? television programme 310

White, Michael 253–4

Whitechapel Art Gallery, London 239n

Whitfield, June 83n

Wiggin, Maurice 126, 275–6

Wildlife Youth Service 286

William, Prince 326

Wilmut, Roger 82–3, 96n, 110, 114, 142, 143, 149, 163, 174, 188, 263n

The Goon Show Companion (with contribution by Jimmy Grafton) 92, 110n, 130n

Wilson, Andy 369

Wilson, Dennis Main 95, 107–8, 111

the Goons' first producer 107, 119, 128

war service 107

and SM's room-smashing 233, 343

Wilson, Harold (later Baron Wilson of Rievaulx) 302

Wilton's Music Hall, East End of London 281, 296
Wiltshire, Maurice 185, 186, 189, 237
Winchelsea, East Sussex 377
Windmill Theatre, London 74, 77–81, 95
Windsor Repertory Company, Berkshire 41
Windust, Mrs 18
Wisdom, Norman 78
Wise, Ernie 350
Woburn Press 293
Wogan, Terry 367
Woman's Realm 267
Wood, Anne 371–2
Wood, Duncan 265
Woodall, Corbet 310
Woods, Gunner 50

Woods, John 263n
Woolwich & Greenwich Day Continuation School, London 21
Woolwich Arsenal, London 29, 50, 65
Workers' Playtime radio show 95
World at One, The (Radio 4 programme) 304
World of Beachcomber, The 264, 265–6, 268, 269, 281
World Wildlife Fund 281
Worsley, T.C. 163
Woy Woy, Australia 187, 214, 229
Wyman, Bill 330
Yarwood, Mike 311
Young Communist League 25

Zurich 82

Photographic Acknowledgements

© BBC: 1, 10.
© Granada Television: 7.
© Hulton Archive/Getty Images: 9.
© Mirror Syndication International: 8, 12, 13, 14, 15.
© News International Syndication: 4, 5, 11.
© Popperfoto: 2.
© Rex Features: 3, 6.

Every reasonable effort has been made to contact the copyright holders, and if there are any errors or omissions, Hodder & Stoughton will be pleased to insert the appropriate acknowledgement in any subsequent printing of this publication.